The Epic Poem
Prophesied
by
Michel de Nostredame
(a.k.a. Nostradamus)

The Prophecies in a Revised Order

The Epic Poem
Prophesied
by
Michel de Nostredame
(a.k.a. Nostradamus)

The Prophecies in a Revised Order

Translated, Edited, and Ordered

By

Robert Tippett

Copyright © 2011

All rights reserved. Produced in the United States of America. No part of this publication may be reproduced, or transmitted, in any form or by any means electronic, mechanical, photocopying, recording, or otherwise, without the prior written permission of the author.

ISBN 978-0-9801166-5-6

Published by Katrina Pearls, LLC

Table of Contents

Introduction 1

The Preamble 7

1. An Important General Overview
The ONLY Way to See the Future Is … 9
For Protecting the Body, Soul and Spirit 10
The Changing Role of Religion 12
Foretelling Holy War Coming 13
Some Call It Armageddon 15
The Following Angers and Persecutions 16

2. Pre-History
The Set-up – The Advent of the Common Man . . .18

3. The Ultimate Rise of Common Man
Led By Inhuman Tyrants 25
    Adolph Hitler 26
    Francisco Franco 28
    Joseph Stalin 29

4. The Lessons Learned of Secrecy and Denial
Stealing Land for A New Israel Requires Strong
Allies .32
    Munich Olympics, 1972 34
    Shah of Iran 35
    Ayatolla Khomeini 36
    Saddam Hussein 36
    Moammar Gaddafi 38
The World Becomes Aware of Islam and Fatwa . . .40

5. Diametrically Opposite Sects & Religions & Reigns
The Final Corruption of a "Christian" Reign 40
    The Murder of Lady Diana Spencer

    The Final Corruption of a "Christian"
        Religion 48
            The Murder of Pope John Paul I
    The Final Corruption of a "Christian" Sect 54
        The Assassinations of John and Robert Kennedy

6. The State of the World before the Dominoes Fall
    We Are the Champions of the World 58

7. Closing the Century of Gold
    Pre-existing Conditions 63
        Saddam Hussein Still in Power
    The Burning Bush Plots Revenge. 64
    The Tyrant without a Land Waits for His
        Moment 68

8. The Day the Earth Stood Still
    Prelude to the 21st Century 71
    September 11, 2001 72

9. United We Stand
    A Declaration of War Against Ghosts 78
    The Revenge in Afghanistan. 79
    Wanted Dead or Alive 80

10. Divided We Stand Alone
    The Worst Laid Plans of Eagles and Lions 86
    War Against Iraq 89
    Wave Goodbye to Saddam 91

11. Not Turning the Other Cheek
    Unification Church and the Moon People 96

12. Expanding Terrorism
    Homeland Insecurity. 104

13. Mediterranean Woes
    Eroding the Edges. 113

14. The Power of Nature
    And Great Earthquakes Shall be in
        Diverse Places. 124
    Great Signs Shall There be from Heaven. 127
    Another Major Quake Soon Follows 135

15. Fanning the Flames of War
    Eastern European Unrest 140
        Balkans 140
        Reunified Germany. 142

16. Fearing Ones Neighbors
    Western Europe Acts Defensive 144
        Italy. 144
        Greece. 148

17. A Return to French Glory
    By the Process of Elimination 151

18. Another Infamous Day in American History
    Like Shooting Fish in a Barrell. 171

19. No More Spanish Armada
    Spain is Invaded 181

20. Meanwhile in Central Europe
    187

21. Christianity's Defender Attacked
    Italy is Invaded. 196

22. Spearheads to Submission
    The Italian Campaign 209

23. A World at War Again
   France is Invaded 223
24. The Unholiness of War
   Rome is Attacked 234
25. France Tries Not to Surrender
   The French Campaign 246
26. Paris Burning
   The Fall of Paris 270
27. A Greater Holocaust
   Italy is Punished 278
28. A Flase Pope
   The End of the Papacy 291
29. Converting Christians to Islam
   France is Punished 308
30. Moors Coming Home
   Spain is Converted 314
31. The Onset of War in the West, Outside of Europe
   The Effects on England 317
32. War into the Far West
   The Effects on the United States of America . . . 331
33. War into the Near East
   The Inevitable War with Israel 340
34. War Along the Fringes of Europe
   . The State of Greece. 347

Changes In Northern Europe 372

35. The Effects of War on the World
Changed Views of Christianity and Religion . . . 354
World Economy 357
Plight on Nature 358

36. Unity for A Counter-Offensive
The Hibernating Bear Awakes 361
All For One and One For All 362
Another Invasion to Liberate France 364
Islamic Persecution of the Gold Standard . . . 369
The Russian Naval Assault on the Gibraltar
Blockade 371

37. When the Going Gets Tough Use A Nuke
The Big Mistake 372

38. The Flip Side of Persecution is More Persecution
The Tide Has Turned 379

39. Post-War Punishments and Lost Lessons
American Justice 388
The Lost Continents 391
And If That Wasn't Enough 392
The Return of Christ 396

The Epic Poem Prophecied by Nostradamus

Introduction

For ten years now, I have been trying to make the world aware that there is more to *The Prophecies* of Nostradamus than meets the eye. All the while, I have been personally growing, both in my awareness of the depth of meaning the verses and letters hold and in my learning abilities to do the peripheral matters that make mass awareness possible (publishing – print and electronic). This book is one that has long been in the back of my mind as necessary. This book is one that I have held back on making public because I did not foresee any public interest. At this point, it has become a matter of, "Ready or not, here it comes."

It is my firm belief that Nostradamus wrote every quatrain contained in this book at one time. By that I mean he did not spend years between writing the poems contained within *The Prophecies*, as the published record would have one think. Instead, he wrote all 948 quatrains (one can actually be called a quintrain) over a short period of time (relatively speaking), and he wrote them in a logical order that made them string together and tell one very long tale, of epic proportions. He then dissected this complete work into its basic elements, and rejoined them in a random order.

Once someone has a product to sell, which for packaging purposes is unassembled, the individual parts are then containerized in plastic bags, rather than tossed haphazardly into one box holding everything. The bolts, washers, and nuts are in one sealed bag, with the wood screws, lock-washers, and little assembly tools in another. These are meshed in with the larger pieces, which are themselves in parts, laid flat so as to stay immovable in transit. None of this ordering has anything to do with what the finished product will look like, after all the pieces have been taken out of the containers and placed together in their proper places.

This is why *The Prophecies* has "*Centuries*." Each section bearing that word in the title is nothing more than a sealed plastic bag announcing that it contains 100 quatrains (give or take one or more). This is because the word "*centurie*" is a French version of the Latin word "*centuria*," meaning a group of one hundred. To leave Nostradamus' work in its ten sealed bags (albeit clear bags, so the contents can be observed) and claim that a work of art is misguided, if not insane. The parts are designed to be reconstructed into the right order. However, there is some excuse for that project having ever been completed, if ever begun before now.

Instructions that clearly state "Assembly Required" are nowhere to be found. This is not to say they are nowhere to be found at all. The instructions that tell readers of *The Prophecies* the essence of directives are stated in the letters that accompany the verses. By not saying, "These quatrains are randomly placed to show the order I saw them, while staring into a bowl of dark water," the letters are saying, "These quatrains need to be put together to make sense of these letters." Think of this as if you just opened a flat box advertising a TV stand is enclosed, only to find a bunch of parts that look alike and a set of instructions written in Japanese characters and scripts (which you do not know how to read). The result is you sell the TV stand at a yard sale in a year or two, after you go out and buy one already put together.

This is what most people have done with Nostradamus' most famous work. They act as if they know what it is, but because they do not know how to put it all together so it speaks for itself, they leave it as is and pretend it is best not disturbing the "rudimentary" condition it came in.

There is even some excuse for leaving *The Prophecies* alone. That excuse comes from the title, which means what it says. Each of the 948 quatrains is indeed a "*Prophecy*," with a capital "P." As such, looking through the clear plastic bag holding a group of 100 true "*Prophecies*" can allow one to see a true stand-alone "*Prophecy*."

This is like seeing a piece in a TV stand box that is clearly a leg, and then proclaiming, "Look everyone, a leg!" The truth is so obvious even a fool can see it; but a leg not being a leg (doing all that a leg is designed to do) means it is losing some of its truth-value. In epic tales told in poetic style (what *Les Propheties* actually is), one can read the leg-in-a-TV-stand-box metaphor as saying; "A leg out of context is not a whole leg." Thus, a quatrain read out of context keeps one from realizing the whole meaning intended by one quatrain.

Since I have been able to understand *The Prophecies*, going back to my very first days of enlightenment (when I was far from a thorough understanding), I have seen the most core requirement for understanding being the realization that the parts are in the wrong order. It is like a huge word puzzle that has to be pieced together to know what the whole story says. In my beginning, I could piece only a small portion of the whole together; but that was enough for me to see just how amazing this puzzle is. The whole does not need to be put together, but putting some of it together so that stories appear is elevating. It is so uplifting that I believe everyone should experience the joy of knowing only God could have made

Introduction

a creation as deep as *The Prophecies*.

My personal experiences have ignited my soul. It is more than reading words and stories, as any book in a book store can provide that entertainment; but seeing how intricately one quatrain reaches and connects to so many other quatrains, on so many levels, proves that God is present in our world. It became apparent to me that God chose Nostradamus to write *The Prophecies* and mask it as an amazing puzzle for a reason. That reason was so that believes in God would be able to experience the power of God working within them, through a willingness to test my claims for truth, in turn allowing their own understandings to blossom.

That is why I have finally made this attempt to show the new order of *The Prophecies*, with all of the plastic bags (divisions into *Centuries*) thrown away. It is to make it possible for others to experience the whole-truth value God intended. It is a whole-truth value that expands one's awareness to other works of true Prophecy, such as those contained within the *Holy Bible*. God speaks through all Prophets, using the same divine language from which *The Prophecies* has been written. Learn to read that language and one has learned to speak in holy tongues.

Part of my hesitation towards producing this work has been my beliefs (about the divinity of *The Prophecies*) have sent me towards writing other works that have been designed to lead others to act on their pre-existing levels of belief in God and Christ (or even God and Allah, or just God). This is because the ultimate story told by *The Prophecies* is one of a devastating self-destruction mankind will bring upon itself, due to the propensity of faithlessness in the world. Repeatedly, I have attempted to tell people of the values brought out by understanding Nostradamus, only to hear people voice rejection. People of faith do not think is necessary to test Nostradamus as a test of their faith in God and Christ. Because they have positioned themselves so strongly as believers, I have urged them to act on their pre-existing faith to change the world away from its current path towards destruction.

Another part of my hesitation has been my lack of deep meditative reflection on the most difficult of the quatrains to understand, due to their being so far into the future I have no touch with that reality. In other words, while I have been able to see the whole story (through the letters and a major, yet partial, reconstruction of the quatrains), I have not been able to connect well enough to see an in-depth link between all 948 quatrains, so that a "set in stone" order can be established.

I explain this lack of focus as being unnecessary, should anyone listen to what I have been saying over the past decade, and make the governmental changes that would postpone the immediate future, and buy humanity more time to work out long-term controls. Why does one need to know what the end will be like, if one wants to listen to divine advice and stop moving towards an end with no rewards?

I also have felt how corrupt this world we live is has become, such that to tell it what is prophesied to come is like making the prophecy come true faster. The theme of *The Prophecies* is how "inhuman tyrants" will gain control over the masses, and then lead the world to ruin in hopes they will profit. What Adolph Hitler did along these lines will pale in comparison to what is still to come. Therefore, I have wanted individuals to hear what I have to offer first, before making it known to those who are the causes of this misdirection.

I have kept images in my mind's eye of groups working together to solve the various puzzle pieces that do not yet have a clear fit in this future that awaits. In that process, more and more people would experience the spirit of a divine presence, leading more and more people to turn back to God, and away from their idol worship (political figures and the "rich and famous"). I still hold on to that image, but I feel it is too late for such groups to benefit the world, or to slow the world's rapid degeneration.

To have a 948-poem story told, when each one of the individual Prophecies are written in an enigmatic style requiring a new language system be learned first, before any one of them can be fully understood, means some assistance and guidance is necessary. To that end, I have written the book *The Systems of Nostradamus*, which is an in-depth breakdown of the syntactical elements of this new language. For anyone who reads that tutorial, this book will provide order, translation, and suggestive notes that will help one find meaning in what was actually written by Nostradamus. My opinion is based on my own awareness, but I could care less if belief in Robert Tippett grows. Belief in God and Christ is the goal, and that can only grow through one's own actions to elevate belief to the point of receiving the Holy Spirit.

In this book, I have written chapter headings that break up the quatrains into groups, which are smaller than one hundred. These headings offer my insights, and along with my section headings they combine to present some of my views of judgment on what has been prophesied to come. Some of these views are filled with parody, while others make somber statements of the sadness that will come, after no changes have been made.

Anyone able to read on a collegiate level should be able to see what the theme of *The Prophecies* is, simply by reading the Table of Contents.

Introduction

One does not need to be a believer in Nostradamus as a true prophet of God to get that from this book. However, if one wants to be able to read the verses of this epic poem, one will need one key ingredient that I cannot provide. That is God allowing His "good angels" to sit with you and whisper hints and thoughts that will allow one to find conclusions on one's own. Those who are true believers will trust these insights of intuition and act on them. Those who are pretenders trying to take advantage of a holy work will leave scratching their heads, being unable to see what anything means. The only advice I can offer that will enhance one's success rate in this endeavor is to pray for guidance, with sincerity in one's heart.

I pray that everyone who tries to understand Nostradamus and *The Prophecies*, be it through this book or by other means, be rewarded with a dawning that it is indeed holy. As a holy document, it has been sealed from all hands with evil intentions. *The Prophecies*, like the mythical sword Excalibur, has remained locked in the stone that is a random presentation. That keeps its meaning unknown, while publicly on display for all to attempt to use it as they would, lusting for power through material gains. So far, all who have tried to gain from *The Prophecies* have failed. Only the one designated by God to unlock *The Prophecies* will be able to do so, and only for the benefit of others.

I believe with my whole heart that I have been filled with the Holy Spirit and made capable of understanding that which others have failed to discern. I claim no special powers of intelligence, and I have no abilities that would explain how I understand *The Prophecies*, other than through divine inspiration. Still, as one who does possess a brain, with the ability to remember what I have experienced, I am able to take that which I have been led to learn on my own, and test that knowledge through the powers of logic and reason.

I produce this book for others to test with the disclaimer that while I have been led to sort quatrains into this particular order, based on some time having been spent contemplating each quatrain, minimally while translating it (multiple times), and for some through more in-depth analysis, I do not claim this order is perfection and incapable of being challenged. I offer it as the first attempt to present *The Prophecies* of Nostradamus as a completely assembled work of literary magnificence, demonstrating *The Epic Poem Prophesied by Michel de Nostredame (a.k.a. Nostradamus)*.

Robert Tippett
December 15, 2011

The Epic Poem Prophesied by Nostradamus

The Epic Poem
Prophesied
by
Michel de Nostredame
(a.k.a. Nostradamus)

The Prophecies in a Revised Order

The Preamble

Covenant chant against foolish literary criticism.	*Legis cantio contra ineptos criticos.*
Those whom accused one of treachery delegating authority to these lines of writing anticipated assessment,	*Quos legent hosce versus mature censunto,*
Uninitiated the people, & inexperienced not should lay hands on:	*Profanum vulgus, & inscium ne attrestato:*
All which: Astrologer Simpleton, Rude at a distance are,	*Omnseque: Astrologi Blenni, Barbari procul sunto,*
Who in different ways it will be exploited, this in due form, consecrated to be.	*Qui aliter facit, is ritè, sacer esto.*

Note: Latin: The word *osce* = *a bird from whose note an augury was taken (i.e.: crow, raven)*. The word *Blenni* = *Blockhead, Dolt, Idiot*. Originally listed as quatrain 100 in Centurie VI. The 1568 Lyon edition does not number this quatrain, although it follows the quatrain numbered "ICIX" (Roman number for "99"). The heading acts as a fifth line, as a quatrain follows it. The heading is in what could be described as "regular font" or the same font as the other quatrains, although appearing to be a slightly larger typeset (perhaps representative of a standard being 12, with the

The Epic Poem Prophesied by Nostradamus

heading being 14). The text of the quatrain is, however, written in italic font, which is the same as the type for the letters of preface and explanation to Henri II. This is an indication, along with every word being in Latin, not French, that this "quatrain" is not one of the regular quatrains, even though it appears at the end of Centurie VI.

Chapter 1

An Important General Overview

The ONLY Way to See the Future Is …

BEING placed from darkness inward study meditation,	*ESTANT assis de nuict secret estude,*
Alone settled (or thrust back) upon the seat of brass,	*Seul repousé sus la selle d'aerain,*
Blazed sparingly issuing out of solitude,	*Flambe exigue sortant de solitude,*
Made to utter that which not is to believe frivolous.	*Faict proferer qui n'est à croire vain.*

Note: Latin: *aeraus* = made of copper/bronze; *exigue* = sparingly, scantily. Originally this was listed as the first quatrain of The Prophecies, as quatrain number 1 in Centurie I. As was the style in the first publications, the fisrt word of the first quatrain in each Centurie was written in all-caps or most caps. The word *selle*, in line two, can also translate as "*a saddle*"; however that makes no sense in a private place of study. Still, the word *estude* can mean a private closet, where "*a stool*" would be placed for use as a toilet (which was the case before indoor plumbing, especially indoors at night). The mythology of the oracle of Delphi was set into a saddle, suspended by a tripod of bronze, before she would be held over the vapors coming from a crevice in the rock and sent into an ecstatic state of prophecy. The word *repousé* is in question, as the translation is as "*reposé.*"

Will rise high before the virtue more in opportune,	*Montera hault sur le bien plus à dextre,*
Will abide appointed upon the stone square:	*Demourra assis sur la pierre quarree:*
In the presence of the midday set in there opening for light,	*Vers le midy posé à sa fenestre,*
Staff crooked in hand, mouth closed.	*Baston tortu en main, bouche serree.*

Note: *Latin: fenestra = opportunity, opening for light.* Originally listed as quatrain number 75 in Centurie V. In Latin, the word *dextre* means "*skillfully.*" The word pierre is personified as Peter, thus as Peter square, or stone squared, it becomes like a cornerstone, which Jesus was to the Church of Christ. Peter was the rock, or the foundation stone to that church. The word main can mean, "a quire of paper". A quire is 24-25 sheets of paper, 1/20th of a ream. It also was "a collection of leaves of parchment or paper folded one within the other in a manuscript or book.

There small staff in hand placed in the middle of BRANCHES,	La verge en main mise au milieu de BRANCHES,
From the wave he cast a mold & the fringe & the foundation.	De l'onde il moulle & le limbe & le pied.
One fearfulness & voice is shivering by reason of them handles,	Un peur & voix fremissent par les manches,
Splendor coming from God. The divine near sits down.	Splendeur divine. Le divin près s'assied.

Note: French: *Branch* also means *lineage, petigree*. Latin: *limbus = border, edge*. Originally listed as quatrain number 2 in Centurie I. The word *vergé* (accented – past tense) makes the main theme statement also say: "*There streaked with long, rod-like rays thereof hand placed ...*" The Latin word *limbus* means, "*a border, hem, fringe.*" The word *fremissent* is the present subjunctive of the verb *fremir* (*to shiver, shake, tremble*), but the subjunctive (not used in English) means that the word "that" is implied to precede the form used; and this also implies some doubt of the action actually occurring. This means that the "*One*" that would be experiencing "*fearfulness*" more importantly (the use of ampersand). Voice is not actually vocalized, due to the "*shivering.*"

The divine word will minister to the substance (or matter),	Le divin verbe donnra à la substance,
Contained within the limits of firmament earth, now hidden with the feat mystical (or sacred):	Comprins ciel terre, or occult au faict mystique:
Body, soul, spirit having all ability (or power),	Corps, ame, esprit aiant toute puissance,
So much beneath his feet, like at the throne celestial (or divine).	Tant sous ses pieds, comme au siege celique.

Note : Latin: *verbum = a word, verb*. Originally listed as quatrain number 2 in Centurie III.

For Protecting the Body, Soul and Spirit

Substance of exalted ones without end to the eye visible ones:	Corps sublimes sans fin à l'oeil visibles:
To make cloudy will be coming by reason of their judgments:	Obnubiler viendront par ses raisons:
Body, forehead comprehended, reason principal & invisible ones,	Corps, front comprins, sens chief & invisibles,
Qualifying them made holy ones prayers.	Diminuant les sacrées oraisons.

Chapter 1 - An Important General Overview

Note: Originally listed as quatrain number 25 in Centurie IV. The word *Corps* can also mean, "whole bulk of" and *sublimes* can also mean, "raised (past-tense)" and "honorable." The use of "Substance of" connects this quatrain (IV – 25) to the last quatrain (III – 02), where the main theme statement there stated "The divine word will minister to the substance".

The body without soul more not to be at sacrifice,	*Le corps sans ame plus n'estre en sacrifice,*
Day from there death set at birth:	*Jour de la mort mis en nativité:*
The spirit divine will make the soul happy,	*L'esprit divin fera l'ame felice,*
Seeing the word in its everlastingness.	*Voiant le verbe en son eternité.*

Note: Originally listed as quatrain number 13 in Centurie II. The 1555 Albi edition lists this quatrain as number 12, with different punctuation. It should be noted that God is The Word, as stated in the Bible. God is everlasting and immortal. Line two also implies birth comes from Heaven and God, with the day of death known at birth.

There shining bright with virgin joyous,	*La splendeur claire à pucelle joyeuse,*
Not will yield a radiant luster more, long time will be without salt,	*Ne luyra plus, long temps sera sans sel,*
With merchants, pimps wolves hateful,	*Avec marchans, ruffiens loups odieuse,*
Total pell mell pattern universal.	*Tous pelé meslé monstre universel.*

Note: Originially listed as quatrain number 98 in Centurie X. The city of Rome's historic fable about Romulus being raised by wolves makes Rome the city that becomes hateful to the Vatican.

Him opportunity present with that it things past,	*Le temps present avecque le passé,*
Will be judged for great Jovialist,	*Sera jugé par grand Jovialiste,*
The world past due he will be wearied,	*Le monde tard luy sera lassé,*
And unfaithful by the clergy jurist.	*Et desloial par le clergé juriste.*

Note: Originially listed as quatrain number 73 in Centurie X. A *Jovialist* must be seen as rooted in the word *Jove*, another form of the name Jupiter. Jupiter was the supreme god for the Romans (Zeus for the Greeks) and thus the supreme judge of mankind. In astrology the symbolism of Jupiter, as the ruler of the 9th house, has the planet ruling all forms of justice. Line two combines this concept with the word *great*, making it become a judgement of those humans acting *great* and a major act of Judgment.

The Epic Poem Prophesied by Nostradamus

In places & time flesh in the fish will minister calling,	Es lieux & temps chair au poisson donrra lieu,
There law enjoyed in common will be made to the contrary:	La loy commune sera faicte au contraire:
Aged will hold strong then removed from the center,	Vieulx tiendra fort puis osté du milieu,
Them allways commonly friends placed luck fallen.	Le παντα κιονα φιλων mis sort arriere.

Note: Line four's Greek letters spell: *Panta koina filwn*. Originally listed as quatrain number 32 in Centurie IV. Line four says, "Pànta choina philon", in the 1557 Utrecht edition. The 1555 Albi edition shows this written in Greek letters, spelled best as Panta koina filwn. This combination is attributed to being from an ancient adage, "Friends hold all things in common," known to Nostradamus by the Renaissance humanist Erasmus, and his book Adagia. It is important to notice that line four ends with a saying in Greek, which was the predominant language of the New Testament. Still, the saying is attributed to the Greek philosopher Plato, who was one of the Old School Philosophers of Nostradamus' day. The future will have the Bible give way to New Philosophers.

The Changing Role of Religion

The land hidden impaired by Quicksilver,	Le sol caché eclipse par Mercure,
Risen will be thrust into that considering it heaven inferior:	Ne sera mis que pour le ciel second:
To Vulcan Hermes will be forged sustenance,	De Vulcan Hermes sera faite pasture,
Sun will be seen observing perfect shining & light yellow.	Sol sera veu pur rutilant & blond.

Note: Originally listed as quatrain number 29 in Centurie IV. In this section it become important to understand the symbolic nature of *Sun, Mercury-Hermes* and *Vulcan*. The *Sun* stands for the Son of God, Jesus Christ and thus Christianity. This is due to the light cast for all humanity to see the way, away from darkness. Also note both lower case and upper case spellings of *sol*. In Old French the word *sol* could also translate as "foundation," making line one also say that *The foundation hidden*. The planet (and god) *Mercury* stands for communication, and as such, the Word of God. The god *Hermes* is the Greek name for *Mercury*, but rather than the speed of the god *Mercury*, as the messenger of God, *Hermes* stands more for the healing abilities of medicine. The Roman god *Vulcan* was a hidden force, from within, which stoked the fires from which he forged wonderful creations. This is then symbolic of the fire, or Spirit, within us all.

Chapter 1 - An Important General Overview

Where everything virtuous is, all benefit Gold & silver	Ou tout bon est, tout bien Soleil & lune,
East overflowing one's subvercion themselves drawing near:	Est abondant sa ruine s'approche:
From the sky they before hand to play upon your destiny,	Du ciel s'auance varier ta fortune,
In the same trade in sort there seventh rock.	En mesme estat que la septiesme roche.

Note: Originally listed as quatrain number 32 in Centurie V. Just as the *Soleil* stands for Christianity, the *lune* stands for *Islam*, the religion of nations that display the crescent *moon* on their flags. The word *roche* can also mean a rocky crag or hill, meaning line four can be referencing Rome, where seven hills are part of its makeup.

There law of the Sun, & Venus those at odds with,	La loy du Sol, & Venus contendens,
Accomodating the opinion of prophecy:	Appropriant l'esprit de prophetie:
Not the one, not the other neither will be understanding ones,	Ne l'un, ne lautre ne seront entendens,
On land will keep there rule of the great Messiah.	Par sol tiendra la loy du grand Messie.

Note: Originally listed as quatrain number 53 in Centurie V. The planet *Venus* stands for love and beauty, but has some connections to Islam, as some Islamic nation flags have the crescent moon along with a star. This star represents the planet *Venus*. However, the French word *Venus* can be seen as an important (capitalization) form of *venu*, with the *s* then written as "ones," making it become the plural form. *Venu* is the past participle of *venir*, meaning "arrived." Then, the "Arrived ones" are the "debated ones." Still, if seen as *contendent-s*, it can be the present participle of *contend*, making it represent the *ones contending* with the *Sun*.

Foretelling Holy War Coming

The reign & law under Venus elevated (or promoted),	Le regne & loy soubz Venus eslevé,
Saturn will have above Jupiter rule:	Saturne aura sus Jupiter empire:
There law & government by the Sun lifted,	La loy & regne par le Soleil levé,
By reason of Sullen ones will suffer the bad.	Par Saturnins endurera le pire.

Note: Originally listed as quatrain number 24 in Centurie V. The planet *Jupiter* stands for the

The Epic Poem Prophesied by Nostradamus

supreme god (God) in one sense; but, it is most symbolic of the Judgement of God. The planet *Saturn*, stands for the father principle, thus God as our Father; but, this Father is more the one of the Old Testament, who teaches us lessons and carries out justice through discipline and punishment. One who is then a *Saturnin* is one who sees submitting punishment in the name of God as one's purpose and role on earth. They thus see God as the Punisher, more than the one who loves and is justly forgiving.

Then that Venus to the land will be veiled,	*Lors que Venus du sol sera couvert,*
Beneath the glory will be character secret:	*Souz l'esplendeur sera forme occulte:*
Mercury in the fire them will hold detected,	*Mercure au feu les aura descouvert,*
By rumbling of war will be reduced to the affront.	*Par bruit bellique sera mis à l'insulte.*

Note: Originally listed as quatrain number 28 in Centurie IV.

Jupiter joined more Venus that to the Moon,	*Jupiter joint plus Venus qu'à la Lune,*
Passing above with fullness white:	*Apparoissant de plenitude blanche:*
Came ones hidden beneath the whiteness god of the Sea,	*Venus cachée soubz la blancheur Neptune,*
From Mars blasted by the large lineage.	*De Mars frappée par la granée branche.*

Note: Originally listed as quatrain number 33 in Centurie IV. In Latin the lower case *venus* can mean: loveliness, charm, love, a loved one. Neptune was known as the god of the sea, since the planet named Neptune was not discovered until the 19th Century. The statement in line three will be fully explained in a future chapter, as an Islamic surprise naval attack, from beneath.

In the wedge of the night will arrive to bring to pass,	*Dedans le coing de luna viendra rendre,*
Where will be seized & set on country foreign,	*Ou sera prins & mys en terre estrange,*
Them fruits not changed ones will be to great slaughter,	*Les fruitz immeurs seront à grand esclandre,*
Great blamed, to the one mighty reputation.	*Grand vitupere, à l'un grande louange.*

Chapter 1 - An Important General Overview

Note: Originally listed as quatrain number 65 in Centurie IX. The word *coing* can mean: coin, wedge, corner, angle, and quince. The word *luna* (lower case) is Latin, meaning: the moon, night, month, crescent shaped ornament. The word *render* means: to render, pay back, restore; to yield; to vomit. The word *immured* means: confined within, as if within the walls of a prison. Line three reminds one of Abu Ghraib.

Weary that one will see great people extremely grieved,	*Las qu'on verra grand peuple tormenté,*
And there Law religious in total ruin:	*Et la Loy saincte en totale ruine:*
By other ones laws whole Christian-dom,	*Par autres loix toute Chrestienté,*
When from gold, to silver obtained rare mined.	*Quand d'or, d'argent trouve nouvelle mine.*

Note: Originally listed as quatrain number 53 in Centurie I.

Some Call It Armageddon

There Moon in the plain of night above him high mountain,	*La Lune au plain de nuict sus le hault mont,*
A new wisdom from one single brain the vow:	*Le nouveau sophe d'un seul cerveau la veu:*
By his pupils to be everlasting summon,	*Par ses disciples estre immortel semond,*
Eye at the midday, in one's hands, body with the fire.	*Yeux au mydi, en seins mains, corps au feu.*

Note: French: *semondre* = to bid, invite, summon, warn Originally listed as quatrain number 31 in Centurie IV. This quatrain is about Osama bin Laden. It is interpreted in my book *The $25-Million Answer*.

More eleven times Moon Sun not will desire,	*Plus unze fois Luna Sol ne vouldra,*
All enlarged ones & declined one of means:	*Tous augmentés & baissés de degré:*
As well as lowest part of placed that scarce gold one will sew on,	*Et si bas mis que peu or on coudra,*
That following famine pestilence detected it inward.	*Qu'apres faim peste descouvert le secret.*

Note: Originally listed as quatrain number 30 in Centurie IV. Line one in the earliest editions shows Roman numerals and astrological glyphs (for Sun and Moon). The word *fois* is best translated to

The Epic Poem Prophesied by Nostradamus

mean "time"; however, it is also acceptable meaning "turn". This would indicate months, as each month there is a full moon and each month the sun moves into a different sign. The number 11 means eleven months without a lunar or solar eclipse. Still, as the period indicates an abbreviation of the number 11, it could mean the 11th. That would act as an indicator of the *11th* hour, as found in Matthew 20:1-15. The alchemical metal for the Sun was gold.

In defense of the plenty of the armed scattered abroad,	Pour l'abondance de larme respanduë,
With the high at bottom of through a depth of in the more secret,	Du hault en bas par le bas au plus hault,
Mightily great loyalty for sport life cast away,	Trop grande foy par jeu vie perduë,
Of thirst to die by abundant defection.	De soif mourir par abondant default.

Note: Originally listed as quatrain number 100 in Centurie VIII. In line one the word *larme* is singular, meaning a translation to the word "tear" does not work well.

The Following Angers and Persecutions

It impartial to injury with death the one will arrive to bring	Le juste à tort à mort l'on viendra mettre
In the face of the world, & from the medium extinguished:	Publiquement, & du milieu estaint:
Surely great infection in this rank will happen to rise from,	Si grande peste en ce lieu viendra naistre,
That them judging ones to escape will be compulsion.	Que les jugeans fuyr seront contraint.

Note: Originally listed as quatrain number 11 in Centurie IX. The 1568 Lyon edition spells "fouyr" in line four, rather than the generally accepted "fuyr" of the other editions. In Old French, the word fouïr meant, "to dig, delve, mine, make holes in the ground." This should play a role in better understanding.

Fretting continual, dry making of the virtuous groom,	Ronge long, sec faisant bon valet,
At the last not will enjoy what his permission,	A la parfin n'aura que son congie,
Stinging poison & letters to the neck	Poignant poyson & lettres au collet
Will be laid hold on freed of danger.	Sera saisi eschappé en dangie.

Note: Originally listed as quatrain number 82 in Centurie VIII. In line two, à la parfin is a French idiom that says, "at length, in the end, at last, when all is done, when all comes to all."

Chapter 1 - An Important General Overview

Most editions after 1568 convert congie to congé. This appears to be a valid representation, as an alternate spelling is show to be cong'e, with the same meanings as congé.

There finish the wolf, the lion, bull & the ass,	*La fin le loup, le lyon, beuf & lasne,*
Cowardly lady will be with mastiffs,	*Timide dama seront avec mastins,*
Had pleased not expensive to them the kind open basket,	*Plus ne chera à eux la doulce manne,*
More wariness & overseer of the rude fellows.	*Plus vigilance & custode aux mastins.*

Note: Originally listed as quatrain number 99 in Centurie X. Note: The 1568 edition shows dama in line two, making it possible to be the future tense of damer. The verb damer meant, "to queen", as in a game of chess, where a pawn reaches the opponent's baseline. In the game of "draughts" (maybe like Checkers), damer meant to "double a man, or make a king." In modern French, the verb damer means, "to ram or pack down," as "to best" in competition. That option must be considered, even though other editions convert dama to dame.

From the more learned ones above them performed ones ones divine ones	*Des plus letrés dessus les faits celestes*
Being by reason of princes ignorant ones blamed ones:	*Seront par princes ignorants reprouvés:*
Chastised ones from Edict, chased ones, like wicked ones,	*Punis d'Edit, chassés, comme scelestes,*
And put to death there where being found ones.	*Et mis à mort la ou seront trouvés.*

Note: French: *lettré* = lettered, learned. Latin: *editio* = a statement, *scelestus* = guilty, wicked. Originally listed as quatrain number 18 in Centurie IV.

Twenty years from the reign of the Moon transported ones,	*Vingt ans du regne de la Lune passés,*
September millennium year ones aother will enjoy its government:	*Sept mil ans autre tiendra sa monarchie:*
At what time the Sun will undertake its days ensnared ones,	*Quand le Soleil prendra ses jours lassés,*
In that time to fulfill & feature my prophecy.	*Lors accomplir & mine ma prophetie.*

Note: Originally listed as quatrain number 48 in Centurie I.

Chapter 2

Pre-History

The Set-up – The Advent of the Common Man

There land & the air will be freezing so great water,	La terre & l'air gelleront si grand eau,
In that season which one will grow upon Thursday to respect,	Lors qu'on viendra pour jeudy venerer,
Those who will be a very long time risen had been so proper,	Ce qui sera jamais ne feut si beau,
Of the four parts it will be growing to respect very much.	Des quatre pars le viendront honorer.

Note: Latin: *veneror = to ask reverently, to revere, respect, worship*. Originally listed as quatrain number 71 in Centurie X. This is a perfect outline of the discovery of America (the New World), the original Thanksgiving and the attraction to European Protestants seeking religious freedoms. The 1568 Lyon edition spells words differently than later editions, and the 1566 Lyon edition. For instance, gelleront is spelled with one "l", and pars is shown as parts. The word jeudy is not capitalized in French, but carries the same meaning as an English Thursday. The word feut is shown in other editions as fut.

At the borders to CHANGE to transform it power feeble ones,	Aux fins de VAR changer le pempotans,
Near to the seaside them three proper men to rise.	Pres du rivage les trois beaux enfans naistre.
Destruction to the populous by reason of time capable ones	Ruine au peuple par aage competans
Dominion in the country to convert more to oversee to grow.	Regne au pays changer plus voir croistre.

Note: Latin: *vario = to vary, change, alter.* Greek (N.T.): *pempo = to send (persons or things).* French: *tan = furie, madness.* Latin: *competo = to come together, to meet.* Originally listed as quatrain number 97 in Centurie VIII. The word *pempo* is clean Greek, as written in the New Testament books of the Bible. The word translates a "to send," specifically in reference to general persons and things. If the word is seen as a form of *p-impotent-s*, then this would translate as "for power-wanting ones." This would be the ones causing the *madness*. This is the foundation of the United States, from 13 original colonies to the world's greatest power. The word VAR is clearly in all-caps in the 1566 and 1568 editions, although the 1568 edition lists le, instead of les before pempotams (a plural word typically requiring a plural article). The singular le also appears in the 1698 Lyon edition. The word pempotans is manufactured, and not a word of any language. With the p separated, becoming a prefix abbreviation, it then falls under the allowed definitions for the letter P as an abbreviation. P is accepted to represent both momentum (in physics) and power. The word empotan is then transformed to match the real word important, which was the Medieval French for "importance." Seeing Pempotams as representing the powerfully important ones, Kings, Church and Sects.

Him great empire will be by reason of England,	Le grand empire sera par Angleterre,
He to send fury of the years more to three estimates,	Le pempotan des ans plus de trois cens,
Mighty ones troops to pass on sea & land,	Grandes copies passer par mer & terre,
Them Lusitanian ones not in will be for contented ones.	Les Lusitains n'en seront par contens.

Note: Latin: *Lusitania* = Roman name for Portugal. Originally listed as quatrain number 100 in Centurie X. The word *pempo* is Greek and used several times in the New Testament, meaning, "to send." From Old French, the word *tan* is said to mean, "*fury*, enragedness, frenzy and madness." The word *cens* was a clean word in Old French, meaning, "assist rent." It can also be seen as Latin, a form of *censio*. The name *Lusitain* is possibly a reference to a person from the Roman province named *Lusitanie*, which was most of Portugal south of the Douro River and part of Spain. The people there were the source of the name, as they were called the *Lusitani*, making possible a simple anagram.

The Royal absolute rule will be forced against its will from to seize,	Le Royal sceptre sera contrainct de prendre,
This that its predecessors adopting urged:	Ce que ses predecesseurs avoient engaigé:
Moreover by the signet ring one will act bad to get intelligence,	Puis par l'aneau on fera mal entendre,
In that time that one will come him government house to destroy.	Lors qu'on viendra le palays saccager.

Note: French: *Imperfect plural of avoir* = *avaient*, and the infinitive *engaigner* = *to incite, provoke*. Originally listed as quatrain number 23 in Centurie VII. In line two the word *engaigé* may well be from the word that since lost the "I," or *engagé*, meaning "engaged." This is not too far from matching the *provoked* meaning. Line three sounds Masonic.

The Epic Poem Prophesied by Nostradamus

Hundreds time will decay it tyrant barbarous,	Cent fois mourra le tyran inhumain,
Set in his place scholarly & gentle,	Mys à son lieu scavant & debonnaire,
All the counsel of citizens will be beneath his public authority,	Tout le senat sera dessoubs sa main,
Offended will be for malicious silent theme.	Fasché sera par malin themetaire.

Note: Originally listed as quatrain number 90 in Centurie X. In 1676, a *hundred* years before the American Revolution, an uprising called the Bacon Rebellion occurred. The events of this *time* mirror the attitude of Americans to resist the declarations of *inhumane tyrants*, keeping the land free of them, by a carefully worded Constitution.

In Time enters this lamented Turban,	Dans Fois entrez cejulée Turban,
Also will domineer least developed Saturn,	Et regnera moins evolu Saturne,
King You-urbane white Byzantium opinion banishment:	Roy Turban blanc Bisance coeur ban:
Sun, Mars, Mercury near there the urn.	Sol, Mars, Mercure pres la hurne.

Note: French: *T'urban* = *You urban*; *evolve* = *advanced, broad-minded*; *Byzance* = *of Byzantine style*. Originally listed as quatrain number 73 in Centurie IX. In Latin the word *cerula* means, "a little piece of wax." In Italian *cerulee* means "earwax." In Old French the word *ceruelle* meant "the brain," particularly the part holding memory. The first line's use of *Turban* can become *Tourb(e)-an*, meaning, "Trouble-year." Still yet, the root can be the Latin word "turbo," the source of the French word "turbine," becoming a "spinning year," or when from the Greek *turbe*, "year of turmoil." Line three's *King Turban* is foretelling of the coming of the Ottoman Empire, with the Christian focus of the Byzantine Empire *banned*. During the *time* of Nostradamus the Ottoman Empire was just beginning to peak at its highest degree of power and influence, stretching as far as Morocco and the Atlantic coast of North Africa (1553). The word *hurne* loses the *h*, becoming *urne*. When following the astronomical orbs stated, *together after the urn* means: *together near the sign Capricorn*, since the sign of *the urn* is Aquarius, and the sign after that is Capricorn. Capricorn is also ruled by *Saturn*, the main word in line two.

In the year five estimate eight before more & less,	En l'an cinq cens octante plus & moins,
One will look for a century very alienated:	On attendra le siecle bien estrange:
Into the twelve months September hundreds, & three heavens upon testimonies,	En l'an sept cens, & trois cieulx en tesmoings,

Chapter 2 - Pre-History

That many governments one to five will be causing change.	*Que plusieurs regnes un à cinq feront change.*

Note: Latin: *censeo* = to estimate; French: *cens* > cents; *ciel* (plural: *cieux*) = heaven. Originally listed as quatrain 2 in Centurie VI. The rule of "years" means that a string of number words do not combine to make a set year. Line one appears to say, "In the year five hundred(s) eighty." The word *cens*, in such a case as this, should not be read as "*cents*."

More Mace-bearer than king in England	*Plus Marcelin que roy en Angleterre*
Rank no reputation not have of violence will have the sovereignty:	*Lieu obscur nay par force aura l'Empire:*
Unworthy without faith, besides law will bleed region,	*Lasche sans foy, sans loy saignera terre,*
His time itself draws near to so close that I upon sigh.	*Son temps s'approche si pres que j'en suspire.*

Note: Originally listed as quatrain number 76 in Centurie VIII. As a simple anagram, *Macelin* can become *Macilen*, from the Latin word, *macilentus*, meaning, "lean, thin, meager." However, it is a word manufactured to denote the official Sergeant at Arms bearer for the English Parliament, who carried a ceremonial *silver mace*. Oliver Cromwell is said to have raised this mace in Parliament, saying the House of Commons mace was, "A fool's bauble". Thus, Oliver Cromwell was more of a leader of Parliament's House of Commons, than a king.

One new sect of Philosophers,	*Une nouvelle secte de Philosophes,*
Neglecting dead, gold, reputation ones & wealth ones:	*Mesprisant mort, or, honneurs & richesses:*
To the mountains German ones not being bordering upon ones,	*Des monts Germains ne seront limitrophes,*
From them to pursue will be possessing thing to lean on & print ones.	*A les ensuivre auront appuy & presses.*

Note: Originally listed as quatrain number 67 in Centurie III. The word *importuned* means: to beset with insistent and repeated requests; entreat pressingly. This is a perfect match for the money lenders of Geneva, who pressures young king Louis XVI for repayment of debt loans, while protecting a new breed of philosophy and religious reformation.

The Epic Poem Prophesied by Nostradamus

Those whom will be supporting in realm because to have a good acquaintance of,	*Ceulx qui estoient en regne pour scavoir,*
To the Kingly transformation will be becoming impoverished ones:	*Au Royal change deviendront apouvris:*
Some exiled ones without stay, gold not to have,	*Uns exilés sans appuy, or n'avoir,*
Skilled ones & court decrees not being with stately ones seized.	*Lettrés & lettres ne seront à grans pris.*

Note: Originally listed as quatrain number 8 in Centurie VI. The word *deviendront* comes from the root word, "*devenir,*" which means: to wax, to grow, to become. Therefore, a substitute word for "waxing" would be "increasing." The translation of "impoverished" becomes the intended translation, where "impoverished" leads into line two, which then points out a change from *Royal* rule,. This will greatly increase an impoverished state for the common people.

So many of years them wars in France will be suffering,	*Tant d'ans les guerres en Gaule dureront,*
Opened there a race with the Moral-the-one monarch:	*Oultre la course du Castulon monarque:*
Victory uncertain three great ones will be crowning,	*Victoire incerte trois grands couronneront,*
Eagle, cock, crescent moon, lion, sun in sign.	*Aigle, coq, lune, lyon, soleil en marque.*

Note: Latin: *castus* = chaste, pure, clean / *Castu-l'on* = *The Pure One* . Originally listed as quatrain number 31 in Centurie I. This quatrain becomes an excellent forecaster of the order of importance, as "the greats," beginning with the *Eagle* (USA), followed by (lower case words) *cock* (France), *lune* (Islamists). These become the "three great ones" of line three. The *lion* represents Great Britain, but after its collapse and reformation under a new royal kingdom; and, *sun in sign* means the sign of the *lion*, or Leo. The proper name *Castulon* also appears in quatrain I – 93. In both cases it represents Jesus Christ, as well as Jerusalem and Israel. As such, it can be read as *C'astre-l'on*, meaning This starred the one.

The excess good time mainly to goodness majestic:	*Le trop bon temps trop de bonté royale:*
Heavy burden & defeated ones prepared hasty laziness,	*Fais & deffais prompt subit negligence,*
Swift will have confidence in falseness to spouse loyal,	*Legier croira faux d'espouse loyale,*
Him put to death through her well-being.	*Luy mis à mort par benevolence.*

Chapter 2 - Pre-History

Note: Originally listed as quatrain number 43 in Centurie X. The overthrow of Louis XVI and Marie Antoinnette in 1789, which would lead to the rule of the common man. This is focused on the excesses of Louis XIV, the Sun King, who spent to make lavish palaces. While he was doing this, he spent money on wars (funded the American Revolution), placing a heavy burden on the national treasury. He borrowed money hastily. Louis XVI would face the swiftness of France's debt collectors. His spouse, Marie Antoinette, through her suggestion for the peasants to eat cake (to her, she was wishing them well, with a more enjoyable food delight). Young Louis placed his confidence in those who plotted his overthrow, from within.

Long in coming arrived the fulfillment of a judgment effected,	*Tard arrivé l'execution faicte,*
A rumor against, learned ones to the course laying hold on ones:	*Le vent contraire, lettres au chemin prinses:*
The calling of the people ones. 14th. wave faction:	*Les conjures. xiiij. dune secte:*
Through Rousseau twelve them attempted ones.	*Par le Rosseau senez les entreprinses.*

Note: Originally listed as quatrain number 7 in Centurie I. The period mark after *conjures* makes it an abbreviation, most probably of "conjurature" or "conjuration," meaning *conspirator* or "conspiracy." Rousseau was a philosopher (*sect*) who wrote the important book *The Social Contract*, published in 1762. He was a philosopher born in Geneva. His philosophy is said to have inspired the French Revolution. The Roman numeral xiiij would be the way kings were numbered, such that that could mean Louis XIV. Louis XIV died in 1715, while Rousseau was born in 1713. Louis XVI became king in 1774, with 1778 being his last year before the revolution in 1789, his 15th year.

A government civil of angelic engendering,	*Le regne humain d'angelique geniture,*
Will forge its realm agreement union to uphold,	*Fera son regne paix union tenir,*
To restrain from liberty contention half from one's shutting up free speech,	*Captive guerre demy de sa closture,*
Continual opportunity there peace them will work to defend.	*Long temps la paix leur fera maintenir.*

Note: Originally listed as quatrain number 42 in Centurie X. This is the original focus and purpose for the Declaration of Independence and the Revolutionary War, for the United States of America.

The Epic Poem Prophesied by Nostradamus

Past hope for recovery obtained, conveyed away from even as long age,	*Perdu trouvé, caché de si long siecle,*
Will be shepherd to some degree God honored:	*Sera pasteur demi Dieu honore:*
Before that there Crescent-shaped concluded its great time,	*Ains que la Lune acheve son grand siecle,*
By reason of different ones prayers will be discredited.	*Par autres veutx sera deshonoré.*

Note: Originally listed as quatrain number 25 in Centurie I.

Of them main branch to the courageous body	*Par le rameau du vaillant personaige,*
From France last, through it priest made unproductive:	*De France infime, par le pere infelice:*
Dignities, wealth ones trouble into its decrepit time,	*Honneurs, richesses travail en son viel aage,*
For to have believed the assembly of subject simple.	*Pour avoir creu le conseil d'homme nice.*

Note: Latin: *infimus [sup. of inferus]* = lowest. Originally listed as quatrain number 14 in Centurie III. This is telling of the overthrow of the French royal branch, to be replaced by strength of a few common leaders, whose power will be gained by ignorant followers. The "National Assembly" of 1789, which was called the "Commoners", is the assembly of subject simple.

Chapter 3

The Ultimate Rise of Common Man

Led By Inhuman Tyrants

Within there Sardinia one noble King will come.	*Dans la Sardaigne un noble Roy viendra.*
Who born will occupy that three years the realm,	*Qui ne tiendra que trois ans le royaume,*
Many gluers with him will co-unite,	*Plusieurs colleurs avec soy conjoindra,*
He himself following care slumbering martyr disgrace.	*Luy mesme apres soin sommeil marrit scorne.*

Note: Originally listed as quatrain number 88 in Centurie VIII. This is about the first *King* of Italy, Victor Emmanuel II, between 1861 and 1878, when Italy was unified as the Kingdom of Italy. The line of Kings will end in disgrace, at the advent of Mussolini, and the subsequent Republic. The House of Savoy was in Sardinia. Line two's statement of has to be read as "born will occupy that three," meaning Victor Emmanuel III, from 1900 – 1946.

To the lake Leman (Geneva) them orations made unto the people will be bringing to a loathing,	*Du lac Leman les sermons fascheront,*
From the courts will be reduced ones through the weeks:	*Des jours seront reduictz par les sepmaines:*
After month, then year, moreover all will be languishing,	*Puis mois, puis an, puis tous deffailliront,*
The rulers will be giving judgments against their ones laws empty ones.	*Les magistratz damneront leurs loix vaines.*

Note: Originally listed as quatrain number 47 in Centurie I. The combination lac Leman is accepted to be Lake Geneva, although the lower case lac is simply descriptive of a lake being near the city named Geneva. A powerless League of Nations to keep tyrants in check.

The Epic Poem Prophesied by Nostradamus

Adolph Hitler

One Emperor will be born nearby from Italy,	Un Empereur naistra pres d'Italie,
That which has the Empire will be transferred to another with good reason very acceptable:	Qui a l'Empire sera vendu bien cher:
Will be declaring with whose folk he himself reunited,	Diront avecques quels gens il se ralie,
Who one will find least sovereign then to shut up.	Qu'on trouvera moins prince que boucher.

Note: French: *rallie* = *rallied, reunited*. Originally listed as quatrain number 60 in Centurie I. The word *boucher* does translate as *butcher*, but also means *slaughter-man* and has a verb meaning: to stop. Line three makes this identify Adolph Hitler (and not Napoleon) because of his alliances and temporary treaties.

From lineage Trojan will be born courage Germanic	De sang Troyen naistra coeur Germanique
That it will grow into so might army of men:	Qui deviendra en si haulte puissance:
Out of will pursue people alien Arab-like,	Hors chassera gent estrange Arabique,
Altering the congregation of Christians in old preeminence.	Tournant l'eglise en pristine preeminence.

Note: Originally listed as quatrain number 74 in Centurie V. This matches the rise of Hitler to power and the build up of the German army, with the abuse of the Catholic Church. Line three applies to the alliance of Germany with the Arab states, because of the "Jewish problem" facing Germany and a need for oil.

In Germany will be growing repugnant ones factions,	En Germanie naistront diverses sectes,
Themselves drawing near unto forcible from the prosperous paganism,	S'approchant fort de l'heureux paganisme,
A mind captive & young ones taken in ones,	Le cœur captif & petites receptes,
Will be forging a coming back with to requite them just tithe.	Feront retour à payer le vray disme.

Note: Originally listed as quatrain number 76 in Centurie III. The word *disme* also means "tenth," such that *tithe*s are 1/10th of a believer's income. This quatrain could relate to the actions Hitler

Chapter 3 - The Ultimate Rise of Common Man

took, against the religions of Germany, forcing the Cardinal to sign papers agreeing to make the Roman Catholic Church the official (and only allowed) Church of the German state.

From the more deep with the West to Europe,	*Du plus profond de l'Occident d'Europe,*
Of unfortunate ones people one fasting child will be produced by:	*De pauvres gens un jeune enfant naistra:*
Who by its common language of nations will seduce mighty multitude of people,	*Qui par sa langue seduira grande troupe,*
One's public voice in the rule to East more will rise in height.	*Sont bruit au regne d'Orient plus croistra.*

Note: Originally listed as quatrain number 35 in Centurie III. Line four requires one recognize Japan having a flag depicting the "rising" sun.

One leader to there great Germany	*Un capitaine de la grand Germanie*
Himself will come to restore by reason of private hatred relief	*Se viendra rendre par simulé secours*
With the Pope to the head men second from the land along the Danube,	*Au Roy des roys ayde de Pannonie,*
That his rebellion will act with race great running.	*Que sa revolte fera de sang grand cours.*

Note: Latin: *simultas = rivalry, hatred*. French: *simulté = grudge, private hatred*. Originally listed as quatrain number 90 in Centurie IX. The word *Pannonie* is representing the ancient land of Pannonia. This land included: Austria, Croatia, Hungary, Serbia, Slovenia, Slovakia, Bosnia & Hergezovina. Basically, it is Hungary and the former Yugoslavia. Line four sounds like the Jesse Owens Munich Olympics. He was a member of the Negro race, running a race for the great nation of the USA.

From the great Prophet them decrees will be put on ones,	*Du grand Prophete les lettres seront prinses,*
Together the public authorities with the tyrant will be waxing:	*Entre les mains du tyrant deviendront:*
To fetch over its king being near attempted ones,	*Frauder son roy seront les entreprinses,*
More his violent takings quite swiftly he will be troubling.	*Mais ses rapines bien tost le troubleront.*

Note: Originally listed as quatrain number 36 in Centurie II. French, including Old French, used *tyran* as the word meaning "tyrant." This means that the word tyrant very possibly is intended

The Epic Poem Prophesied by Nostradamus

to convey tyrant, while actually representing the present participle of the verb "tirer" (to draw, drag, pull, trail, tug, etc.), as "drawing, dragging, stretching, exacting from, portraying, or making towards." The Latin word meaning tyrant is tyrannus, with French only having –ing endings involving –ant.

Unknown envy with the great Pope supported,	*Ignare envie au grand Roy supportée,*
Will hold purpose to defend them written ones:	*Tiendra propos deffendre les escriptz:*
His woman not wife by one other tempted,	*Sa femme non femme par un autre tentée,*
More copy of writing two neither able bodied bred proclamations.	*Plus double deux ne fort ne criz.*

Note: Latin: *ignarus* = ignorant, unknown. Originally listed as quatrain number 57 in Centurie IV. Seems a good fit for the Hitler - Cardinal of Germany (later to be pope) relationship that made Roman Catholicism the Church of State for Nazi Germany. Line two would then be the Word of the Bible. Line three would be Eva Braum. If King refers to a true King, and not a Pope, this could also fit Louis XVI, who was courted by the rebellious rebels of America, in a war for independence from their King. The statement, envy with the great, shows a subversive element seeking the King's support, which would later bring down the King. The writings would then be the Declaration of Independence and the new Constitution of the Republic for France. At that time, neither nation was strong enough to defend their proclamations.

Francisco Franco

The one of the more great ones will refuse to deal with the Spanish ones,	*L'un des plus grands fuira aux Hespaignes,*
That upon long shorelines after will come to bleed:	*Qu'en longue plaie apres viendra saigner:*
Passing troops through them high mountain ones	*Passant copies par les hautes montaignes*
Devastating all & then in peace to rule.	*Devastant tout & puis en paix regner.*

Note: Originally listed as quatrain number 54 in Centurie III.

Chapter 3 - The Ultimate Rise of Common Man

Within them Spanish people will grow King very-wealthy,	Dans les Espagnes viendra Roy tres-puissant,
By sea & land subjugating now south,	Par mer & terre subjugant or midy,
From pain will forge, abased him half-moon,	De mal fera, rabaissant le croissant,
To humble those winged ones with those of the Friday.	Baisser les aisles à ceux du vendredy.

Note: Originally listed as quatrain number 95 in Centurie X. The word *aisle* (also *aile*) means "wing," but can also mean the brim of a hat.

Joseph Stalin

To the Fortress themselves will embrace there Feudal Noble,	A la Ferté se prendra la Vidame,
Nicolas reputed red that had produced there life,	Nicol tenu rouge qu'avoit produit la vie,
A great Legislated will be brought forth that will make claim,	La grand Loyse naistra que fera clame,
Giving Burgundy with Britons by reason of envy.	Donnant Bourgongne à Bretons par envie.

Note: Latin: *teneo* = *to hold, keep, grasp*. Originally listed as quatrain number 59 in Centurie IX. Many French cities with a fortress are named La Ferté – (name of the city). The word *Vidame* means the one in charge of an abby *(French Feudal Law)*, as one of a class of temporal officers who originally represented the bishops, but later erected their offices into fiefs, and became feudal nobles. The name Nicholas is spelled Nicolas in French, and Nicolau in Català. The name Bourgongne is spelled Bourgonha in Occitan, and Bourgonya in Català, making Bourgongne a combination spelling. This last line means that Russians, under Czar Nicolas, was allied with Great Britain during WWI; and, upon the Czar's return to Saint Petersburg (having lost huge numbers of soldiers), Russia surrendered and ceased warfare.

With the great to This-heremon place of assembly,	Au grand de Cheramon agora,
Being ones marked with the cross by rank all fastened ones,	Seront croisez par ranc tous attachez,
The tenacious Fortified-towns, & mandrake,	Le pertinax Oppi, & mandragora,
Re-trough-one of October the third will be cowardly ones.	Raugon d'Octobre le tiers seront laschez.

Note: Greek: *agora* = *Greek city*, *name* = *marketplace*. Latin: *pertinax* = *tenatious* / Italian: *oppi (plural of oppio)* = *Opium*. French: *Ravigoré -on* = *recovered one*. If *R'aug-on* = *Again*

The Epic Poem Prophesied by Nostradamus

augur one. Originally listed as quatrain number 62 in Centurie IX. The word *Raugon* is translated as *ravigoré*, which means "recovered, restored vigor, and cheered up again.. This quatrain has significant differences in different editions. The above presentation is from the 1568 Lyon edition. The name Heremon is Irish, the 7th son of a Spanish King, who is said to be the blood from which all kings from Scotland (from the 7th Century) and England (since Henry 2) are descended. The name Agora also means the place of assembly in any Greek city. Mandrake is a deadly poison, but is used for pain. It produces hallucinations. The word Raugon can be broken into R(e)'auge-on, meaning Re-trough-one, or Again augur one. A trough is typically what farm animals are fed in, but it also is a V-shaped mason's plaster holder and a gulley. Oppi is plural for Oppio, which is Italian for Opium. Line three gives a feel for the advisor to Tsarina Alexandra, Grigori Rasputin.

By reason of living & dead transformed government of Hungary,	*Par vie & mort changé regne d'Ongrie,*
There decree will be more harsh than hire for service:	*La loy sera plus aspre que service:*
Their great city of howling ones complained ones & shouted,	*Leur grand cité d'urlements plaincts & crie,*
Castor & Pollux enemies within the free.	*Castor & Pollux ennemis dans la lyce.*

Note: Latin: *castor* = beaver; *polluo* = to defile, pollute, dishonor. Originally listed as quatrain number 90 in Centurie II. Both *Ongrie* and *urlements* are properly spelled with an "H" at the beginning (although valid without in Old French), which shows the system of symmetry again. *Castor & Pollux* are, of course, the two brightest stars of the Gemini constellation, which were named from Greek mythology and the two twins – one immortal and one mortal. They were heroes of the Golden Fleece quest, on the Argos (among other tales). The use of *Castor & Pollux* needs to be seen as the two divisions that had become one Germany, after the Soviets took Eastern Europe after World War II.

With the court being half-ones them two great ones presidents,	*Du jour seront demis les deux grandz maistres,*
Their great to have power themselves will oversee amplified:	*Leur grand pouvoir se verra augmenté:*
There country new will be at its most glorious ones pedigree ones,	*La terre neufve sera en ses haults estres,*
To the blood-thirsty a number reported.	*Au sanguinaire le nombre racompté.*

Note: Originally listed as quatrain number 89 in Centurie II. In line three the combination of *land new* cannot be overlooked as a reference to the New Land of America, while also the *new laand new law* would create (Israel). In Old French the word *estre* also meant *to be*, meaning line three's *secret ones* would be the *to be ones* as well. Still, the word *haults* can simply mean *high ones*, meaning America wanted to have the highest number of nuclear arms (a secret endeavor), thus becoming the *to be ones* of the arms race.

Chapter 3 - The Ultimate Rise of Common Man

This which weapon flame not has understanding to execute,	*Ce que fer flamme n'a sceu parachever,*
There pleasing speech at the assembly of counsel will come to act:	*La doulce langue au conseil viendra faire:*
For peace, dreamed, the king will make to sweat again.	*Par repos, songe, le roy fera resver.*
More the enemy on light, lineage military.	*Plus l'ennemi en feu, sang militaire.*

Note: French: *n'a-sceu = not has knowledge, understanding, acquaintance of.* Originally listed as quatrain number 97 in Centurie I. The word *doulce* leads to the word *doux*, which also means: sweet, delicious, soft, smooth and gentle. The word *resver* also meant: to speak idly and to talk like an ass. This quatrain relates to the Cold War, after America has developed the Bomb.

Chapter 4

The Lessons Learned of Secrecy and Denial

Stealing Land for a New Israel Requires Strong Allies

Near to one high bridge to plain spacious,	*Près d'un grand pont de plaine spatieuse,*
Them great lion through forces of Caesar ones:	*Le grand lyon par forces Cesarées:*
Will beat down out of city unmerciful,	*Fera abbatre hors cité rigoureuse,*
Through fear ways to enter it being official supervisors.	*Par effroy portes luy seront referées.*

Note: Originally listed as quatrain number 33 in Centurie I. In this quatrain, the word *Près* appears accented, whereas it is most frequently unaccented. This proves that the accent marks are to be applied by the reader when they are absent. Only when they appear is one limited to only using a letter with an accent. The name *Casarée* is the correct French spelling for *Caesarea Maritima*, which is a Mediterranean costal fortress city built in what is now Israel, and named in honor of Caesar. It was in that city the Romans massacred many Jews, leading to the Jewish rebellion that lost many more Jewish lives to the might of Rome. This appears to be a statement about the British Protectorate powers in the Middle East, from League of Nations Mandate, which allowed illegal Jewish immigration to flourish, until the beginning of World War II. The United States would assume this power, indirectly, following that war.

The share loose of scope ones husband will be yourself wearing a miter,	*Le part soluz mary sera mitré,*
Returning battle will transport above them yourself oiled:	*Retour conflict passera sur le thuile:*
For five rent assist one to betray will be entitled	*Par cinq cens un trahyr sera tiltré*
Narbonne & Condiment by reason of cost to them use of oil.	*Narbon & Saulce par coutaux avons d'huile.*

Note: Originally listed as quatrain number 34 in Centurie IX. If one looks at this quatrain as

Chapter 4 - The Lessons Learned of Secrecy & Denial

one of the series explaining Israel becoming a nation in 1948, it begins to make sense. The main theme is about the British being given the right of Protectorate over several dominions of the fallen Ottoman Empire. That was them "loosely sharing" *a marriage*, or union, where the Brits acted as *husband* in that relationship. The word *miter* comes from Latin (mitra), which means, "headband, or turban". This is an imaged from the movie Lawrence of Arabia, which was set during World War I. Line two is then telling of the major *Return* (capitalization) of battle, which would be WW2. During that war, the use of *oil* became vital, in the area of transportation. Line three is then telling of the *five* vassals in the Middle East, under the League of Nations Mandate (which ceased to be an organization). Of those *five* (Syria, Lebanon, Palestine, Transjordan, and Mesopotamia), only one was not entitled to the value of their *rent assist* (land given to subjects after service rendered). The reason is then in line four, as the cost to them for the *use of oil*.

Libra will oversee to govern the Western land ones,	*Libra verra regner les Hesperies,*
With heaven, & country to uphold there government of one absolute prince:	*De ciel, & terre tenir la monarchie:*
To Asia compelled ones nothing neither will see lost ones,	*D'Asie forces nul ne verra peries,*
Which seven not possessing for course the sacred principality.	*Que sept ne tiennent par rang la hierarchie.*

Note: Latin: *Hesperia* = *the western land.* Originally listed as quatrain number 50 in Centurie IV. With a time of date stated as 12:00 PM, on July 4, 1776, when the Declaration of Independence was ratified by a closed session of the Continental Congress, the Sun is in the sign of Cancer, conjunct the Mid*heaven*, with the Rising Sign being *Libra*. This identifies the "sign" of the United States.

Lamentations, proclamations, & bemoaned ones, howling terrorist,	*Pleurs, cris & plaints, hurlement effraieur,*
Inward conceit discourteous, fierce, black, & hardened of heart sense and spirit:	*Cœur inhumain, cruel, noir, & transy:*
Geneva, the isles of Tortured ones them larger side ones,	*Leman, les isles de Gennes les maieurs,*
Kindred to pour out hastily, ill-desiring after something with not one given thanks for a benefit.	*Sang espancher, frofaim à nul mercy.*

Note: Originally listed as quatrain number 81 in Centurie VI. Line one is using words that are indicative of the pro-Israeli defense of the State of Israel. The capitalized *Pleurs*, as *Lamentations*, is a reference to the biblical book that recounts the sufferings of people who lost everything God had given them. By the end, having stolen back that land, the Jews of the modern Israel make cries of *"terrorist"*, when someone tries to revenge a wrong. The whole quatrain reads as an explanation of how stolen land could have ever been supported in 1948.

The Epic Poem Prophecied by Nostradamus

Unheard of before ordinance country new to enjoy,	*Nouvelle loy terre neufve occuper,*
Near to Syria, Judea, & Palestine:	*Vers la Syrie, Judee, & Palestine:*
A great empire barbarous to be collapsed,	*Le grand empire barbare corruer,*
Having which Phebé (goddess of the Moon) its time ended.	*Avant que Phebés son siecle determine.*

Note: Latin: *corruo = fall down, collapse.* Myth: *Phoebe = Artimis, the moon.* Originally listed as quatrain number 97 in Centurie III. That was Great Britain as the protectorate of that region, prior to the re-creation of a State of Israel.

Munich Olympics, 1972

Year revolved to the great number seventh	*Au reuolu du grand nombre septiesme*
Will suddenly show at the time Games to Sacrifice,	*Apparoistra au temps Jeux d'Hecatombe,*
Not distant from the great age thousandth,	*Non esloigné du grand eage milliesme,*
That them entered ones will be going forth from their fallen.	*Que les entres sortiront de leur tombe.*

Note: Originally listed as quatrain number 74 in Centurie X. In line one we have the word *septiesme*, which is a cleanly spelled word meaning *seventh*. However, with the word *sept* meaning both *seven* and *September*, this word could represent September as well. The 1972 Munich Olympics (the focus of this quatrain) was marred by the Israeli Olympic team massacre by Black September, the Palestinian terrorist organization. A "hecatomb" is a sacrifice of 100 oxen, by priests, for ceremonial purposes to honor the gods.

Gymnastic kind captive for hostage,	*Gymnique sexe captive par hostaige,*
Will issue from darkness guardians to betray:	*Viendra de nuit custodes decevoyr:*
The principal commander of the camp betrayed by his national language:	*Le chef du camp deceu par son langaige:*
Will relinquish from there easy, will make pitiful to see.	*Lairra à la gente, fera piteux a voyr.*

Note: Originally listed as quatrain number 41 in Centurie IV. Nostradamus uses the word "*lairra*" on three occasions, also found in quatrains II-81 and V-54. However, this is the only capitalized version. The translation is still debatable, although evidence shows "*laïer*" to be an older form (Occitan) of "*laisser*." If the OF word "*aïrer*" (meaning, "to chase, to anger")

Chapter 4 - The Lessons Learned of Secrecy & Denial

conjugated into the future tense as "*aïrra*", or "*ayrra*", the word could be read as, "*L'ayrra*", becoming, "Them will chase", or "Them will anger." Either translation makes this quatrain apply to the deaths that occurred at the Munich airport, as a result of the 1972 Olympics massacre.

Shah of Iran

From the city of the sea & tribute-paying,	*De la cité marine & tributaire,*
There headiness ruined will embrace the satrapy:	*La teste raze prendra la satrapie:*
To expel corrupt who then will be against,	*Chasser sordide qui puis sera contraire,*
For fourteen years will hold there violent bloody government.	*Par quatorze ans tiendra la tyrannie.*

Note: Latin: *satrapes = governor of a Persian province.* Originally listed as quatrain number 13 in Centurie VII.

Rain, hunger, contention in Iran not ceased,	*Pluie, faim, guerre en Perse non cessée,*
There belief in too much great will betray the monarch:	*La foy trop grande trahira le monarque:*
By reason of there concluded in France entered into,	*Par la finie en Gaule commencée,*
Secret forewarning on to one to be fixed.	*Secret augure pour à un estre parque.*

Note: Originally listed as quatrain number 70 in Centurie I. While Gaul was all of what is today France, it covered more territory than only modern France. Switzerland, Belgium, and part of Germany were also part of Roman Gallia.

Him great Royal to gold, from brass amplified,	*Le grand Royal d'or, d'airain augmenté,*
Broken there agreement, by youthful open contention:	*Rompu la pache, par jeune ouverte guerre:*
People tormented by reason of one chief complained against,	*Peuple affligé par un chef lamenté,*
With lineage barbarous will be veiled country.	*De sang barbare sera couverte terre.*

Note: Originally listed as quatrain number 19 in Centurie V. This feels like a reference to the Shah of Iran, where the agreement with the United States was broken when the students (*youthful open contention*) overtook the American Embassy during the Islamic Revolution.

35

The Epic Poem Prophecied by Nostradamus

Ayatolla Khomeini

A long time ago without of the kingdom placed into hazard travel,	*Loin hors du regne mis en azard voiage,*
Great army will use in defense of itself them will occupy,	*Grand ost duyra pour soy l'occupera,*
Him head man will keep them his party lost liberty pledge,	*Le roy tiendra les siens captif ostage,*
At one's coming back all country will make havoc.	*A son retour tout pays pillera.*

Note: Originally listed as quatrain number 92 in Centurie VIII. The use of "*hostage*" in line three makes this match the American Hostage Crisis in Iran, 1979. It happened after the Shah ran off and the Ayatolla Khomeini returned from exile.

A principal commander to Scotland with six from Germany,	*Le chef d'Escosse avec six d'Alemagne,*
Through men of sea East ones subject:	*Par gens de mer Orientaux captif:*
Will be crossing them Gibraltar & Spain,	*Transverseront le Calpre & Hespaigne,*
At hand in Iran unused the new chief cowardly.	*Present en Perse au nouveau roy craintif.*

Note: Latin: *Calpe = Rock of Gibraltar.* Originally listed as quatrain number 78 in Centurie III. The word *Escosse* has traditionally been translated as meaning "Scottish," however, while the word *Escossois* does mean "Scottish, from Scotland", that word is not what was written. The word *escosse* is clean Old French, both with and without an accented *e* at the end, meaning: the husk, hull or cod of beans, peas, etc, or the actions unhusked, shelled or hulled.

Saddam Hussein

Them languishing (or failing) in garment of citizen,	*Le deffaillant en habit de bourgois,*
Will come the King to tempt from his displeasure:	*Viendra le Roy tempter de son offense:*
Fifteen soldiers there more-part V (five)-slag-people,	*Quinze soldats la pluspart Vslagois,*
Time second in place & leader to his wealth.	*Vie derniere & chef de sa cheuance.*

Note: Originally listed as quatrain number 64 in Centurie IV.

Chapter 4 - The Lessons Learned of Secrecy & Denial

He will enter sordid, wicked, disgraceful,	*Il entrera vilain, méchant, infame,*
Tyrannizing there Mesopotamia,	*Tyrannisant la Mesopotamie,*
All friends made from adulteress-born Mistress,	*Tous amis fait d'adulterine Dame,*
Earth horrible black from physognomy (general appearance).	*Terre horrible noir de phisonomie.*

Note: Originally listed as quatrain number 70 in Centurie VIII. *Physonomy* was a medieval science for determining the nature of creatures (including man), by looking at the physical features displayed. It was the brainchild of someone named Psysonomias.

Together with them dark Greedy & red,	*Avec le noir Rapax & sanguinaire,*
Toll paid with the helm of barbarous Nero one,	*Ysseu du peaultre de l'inhumain Neron,*
In the midst of two rivers public power sinister warlike	*Emmy deux fleuves main gauche militaire*
Will be crushed by United him to wax bald one.	*Sera meurtry par Joyne chaulveron.*

Note: Latin: *rapax* = rapacious. French: *chauver* = to wax bald. Originally listed as quatrain number 76 in Centurie IX. The word *Neron* can also be *N'eron*, where the negative is about either a *heron* (wading bird) or *hero-one*. The word *peaultre* was used in Old French to state "the stern of a ship." The word *peautre* translates as "pewter." The word *gauche* typically means "left," but also has a negative connotation, such as *sinister*. The word *chaulueron* is translated as *l'chauveron*, meaning "him to wax bald one".

Tasked to murder most wicked ones adulterers,	*Tasche de murdre enormes adulteres,*
Great enemy of all them type humane	*Grand ennemy de tout le genre humain*
Who will be of small value than forefathers, hoofed ones, not priests	*Que sera pire qu'ayeulx, oncles, ne peres*
Into iron, fire, water, spiritless & beastly.	*En fer, feu, eau, languin & inhumain.*

Note: Originally listed as quatrain number 10 in Centurie X.

The Epic Poem Prophecied by Nostradamus

Moammar Gaddafi

One the crown device promotion,	*Un coronnel machine ambition,*
Himself will take possession of there more mighty furnished with arms:	*Se saisira de la plus grande armée:*
Towards one's chief devised trick,	*Contre son prince fainte invention,*
And detected will be beneath then thicket.	*Et descouvert sera soubz la ramée.*

Note: Originally listed as quatrain number 62 in Centurie IV. The English definition for the word *coronel* is both as *colonel* and as: iron head of a tilting spear, divided into two, three or four blunt parts. Both definitions can apply in the main theme statements. However, the Old French word "coronne" means the "l" can be removed to form a simple anagram, "*l'coronne*". the spelling, as published, give a feel for Colonel Gaddafi.

Prince Libyan wealthy (and powerful) as West	*Prince Libyque puissant en Occident*
Of France to Arabian will come in such manner to inflame:	*Francois d'Arabe viendra tant enflammer:*
Learned ones of them letters will make condescending,	*Scavans aux lettres fera condescendent,*
The language Arabic into French to translate.	*La langue Arabe en Francois translater.*

Note: Originally listed as quatrain number 27 in Centurie III. In line two it is important to remember that Osama bin Laden is a Saudi *Arabian.*

The World Becomes Aware of Islam and *Fatwa*

WITHIN there family of the translator to Quagmire,	*DANS la maison du traducteur de Bourc,*
Being the grants obtained ones over there domain,	*Seront les letters trouvées sur la table,*
Shady, reddish, white, hazard will keep from courts of law,	*Borgne, roux, blanc, chanu tiendra de court,*
Which will transform to the new policeman.	*Qui changera au nouveau connestable.*

Note: Originally listed as quatrain number 1 in Centurie IX. Research shows that the male name *Bourke* comes from Old French and means "fortified settlement." However, the word *bource* is clean French for "quagmire." A website that traces family names states

Chapter 4 - The Lessons Learned of Secrecy & Denial

the name *Bourc* to be from Normandy, meaning bastard. In the days of Nostradamus a *constable* was an important captain of the garrison at a fortress or a general at war.

The great copy of writing that will pass them mountain ones,	*La grand copie que passera les montz,*
Saturn in Sagittarius returning to the fish Mars:	*Saturne en l'Arq tournant du poisson Mars:*
Poison ones kept secrets beneath self willfulness ones from salmon ones:	*Venins cachés sous testes de saulmons,*
Their chief hanging with rank to war ones.	*Leur chief pendu a fil de polemars.*

Note: *French: (from Greek) polemos = war.* Originally listed as quatrain number 48 in Centurie II. The play on Salmon Rushdie's name is interesting, as this quatrain shows how Satanic Verses came. It more applies to Osama bin Laden's rise, due to the Soviet invasion of Afghanistan. Both place the timing to 1988.

Chapter 5

Diametrically Opposite Sects & Religions & Reigns

The Final Corruption of a "Christian" Reign

The Murder of Lady Diana Spencer

Considering not to intend to consent to the divorce,	*Pour ne vouloir consentir au divorce,*
Which then after will be acknowledged undeserving,	*Qui puis apres sera cogneu indigne,*
Him chief to the Isles will be rejected through virtue,	*Le roy des Isles sera chassé par force*
Set in his place who from head man of a party not will keep pledge.	*Mis à son lieu qui de roy n'aura signe.*

Note: Originally listed as quatrain number 22 in Centurie X. Possibly about King Edward VIII who abdicated to marry Mrs. Simpson, the divorcee from America. That made Elizabeth be in line to be Queen. However, it could also fit the intrigue surrounding Prince Charles' decision to allow Diana to divorce him.

The divine sickness will overtake the great prince,	*Le divin mal surprendra le grand prince,*
One little before will enjoy woman married:	*Un peu devant aura femme espousée:*
His draw well & trust in one touch will appear thin,	*Son puy & credit à un coup viendra mince,*
Advice will die because there head razed.	*Conseil mourra pour la teste rasée.*

Note: Originally listed as quatrain number 88 in Centurie I. Sounds perfect as a fit for Prince Charles and his "uncle" Lord Montbatten, who was assassinated before Charles met Diana. Montbatten told him to look for someone young and naive.

Chapter 5 - Diametrically Opposite Sects & Religions & Reigns

Him son Royal will despise there mother,	L'enfant Royal contemnera la mere,
Sight, root ones hurt ones, uncivil, against obedient,	Oiel, piedz blessés, rude, inhobeissant,
Unheard of before with lady unacquainted & patrimony most despiteful,	Nouvelle à dame estrange & bien amere,
Being murdered ones of those belonging to himself more to five estimates.	Seront tués des siens plus de cinq cens.

Note: Originally listed as quatrain number 11 in Centurie VII. In Old French the words *"inobedient"* and *"desobïessant"* both meant, *"disobedient"*. In Latin, the prefix, *"in-"*, means, *"into, on to, towards, against"*, and *"until"*. This quatrain could be saying a Royal child is responsible for *five* murders, which would be worthy of comparing to the Jack the Ripper history. Since a *Pope* (a Royal) cannot be married (with *lady*), this quatrain is about the British Royal family. It seems to fit Prince Charles, prior to his marriage to Diana Spencer.

Them Unfortunate ones wedding will be celebrating,	Les Malheureuses nopces celebreront,
Upon stately rejoicing, but there conclusion miserable,	En grande joye, mais la fin malheureuse,
England & mother daughter-in-law will be despising,	Mary & mere nore desdaigneront,
Him Diana death & wife of a son more piteous.	Le Phybe mort & nore plus pyteuse.

Note: Greek: *Phoibe > Phoebe = Artemis;* Roman equivalent = *Diana.* Originally listed as quatrain number 55 in Centurie X.

Younger royal from burning to most affectionate violent desire,	Puysnay royal flagrand d'ardant libide,
In regard of himself to receive the fruit, of cousin bred of the same kind,	Pour se jouyr, de cousine germaine,
Raiment of wife at the church with Dried up subject,	Habit de femme au temple d'Arthemide,
Cheating fellow with to grow by reason of ignoble with the Mayborn.	Allant murdry par incognu du Maine.

Note: Latin: *libido = whim, violent desire.* Mythology: (spelling: th > t), *Artemis = Diana = goddess of the hunt.* Originally listed as quatrain number 35 in Centurie X. In French, the

The Epic Poem Prophesied by Nostradamus

combination of words, *cousine germaine*, means "first cousin." Sounds like could be Diana's murder or sex with Randy Andy (Prince Andrew). The place *Maine* is a province in France, whose capital city is LeMans (west of Paris). The "name" *Maine* can be broken into *Mai-ne*, or May-borne. Quatrain X-85 has its main theme offer the word "larthemide", which may relate to the same meaning as here. This quatrain could be an indication of Diana being raped, as if it was a ceremony to ensure a royal lineage, because Charles could not impregnated her himself. Diana's younger brother, Charles Spencer, was born in May 1964.

Lady in extreme anger through rage of adultery,	*Dame en fureur par rage d'adultere,*
Will come to her prince to beseech earnestly not of to tell:	*Viendra à son prince conjurer non de dire:*
But a note notorious will be there vituperated,	*Mais bref cogneu sera la vitupere,*
Which will be put seventeen at martyrdom.	*Que seront mis dixsept à martire.*

Note: Originally listed as quatrain number 59 in Centurie VI. Lady Diana Spencer became engaged to Prince Charles in 1981 (first date in 1980). From that time, until her death in 1997, the last seventeen years of her life were controlled by the British royal family.

Lady in the absence of her noble captain,	*Dame à l'absence de son grand capitaine,*
Will be entreated to affections from the Second to the throne,	*Sera priee d'amours du Viceroy,*
Adulterated oral assurance given & unfortunate taste of what is to come,	*Faincte promesse & malheureuse estraine,*
One with another them public authorities with the high prince Counsel to the King.	*Entre les mains du grand prince Barroys.*

Note: Originally listed as quatrain number 9 in Centurie VII. The word *hansel* (from the word *estraine*) means the first present of the New Year. As such, it is the first gift of a series. The root is *hand*, meaning coming from the *hand*, with *sell* being a gift, or a shake upon which a first agreement is made.

There queen Servant beholding her daughter pale,	*La royne Ergaste voiant sa fille blesme,*
For one affection unto inwardly the stomach enclosure,	*Par un regret dans l'estomach encloz,*
Proclamations pitiful ones being in that time of Anglo determination	*Cris lamentables seront lors d'Angolesme*

Chapter 5 - Diametrically Opposite Sects & Religions & Reigns

As well to them come of the same stock marriage without it be perfected.	*Et au germains mariage fors clos.*

Note: Originally listed as quatrain number 17 in Centurie X. Another translation of the word *blesme* is "dead colored." The word *regret* actually is stated to mean: desire, will, affection, *stomach* or humor unto, such that when it is followed by the combination *l'estomac enclos*, it means an emotionally upsetting moment which turns the *stomach* making one sick. In 1661, or 103 years after Nostradamus had this quatrain published, the French play writer Molière (his stage name) wrote, "*The School for Husbands*", in which a character's name is *Ergaste*. Accordingly, *Ergaste* was a "valet" (or a slave) to his master, the character *Valère* (Italian for "to be of worth"). The Falklands War (between Britain and Argentina) ended on June 14, 1982. Prince William was born on June 21, 1982, during a period of *Anglo determination*.

Him father & sons being from to make mature ones jointly	*Le pere & fils seront meurdris ensemble*
The principal person within his admiral's flagship	*Le prefecteur dedans son pavillon*
There mother in Towers with a son belly will contain swollen.	*La mere à Tours du filz ventre aura enfle.*
Small craft greenness to leaves butterfly.	*Caiche verdure de feuilles papillon.*

Note: Originally listed as quatrain number 75 in Centurie VIII. In the 1611 French-English Dictionary by Randle Cotgrave, the listing for "*Caiche*" states, "As the Italian, "*Catzo*"; *membre viril*." The idiom, "*membre viril*" means "*male organ*", where "*viril*" means, "*manly*". In general, *caiche* denotes a "*male*." In Italian, the word "*cazzo*" (pronounced "*catzo*") is [at best] slang, where "*prick*" is the least vulgar translation possible. Prince Charles was in the Royal Navy, between the years 1971 and 1976. Prince Andrew, served on the HMS Invincible, the *lead ship* of its class of anti-submarine aircraft carriers. Andrew was on that ship when it was dispatched to the Falklands War, in April, 1982. Prince William of Wales was born on June 21, 1982. He became a "*butterfly*," out of his mother's cocoon.

From Castle fig yards daylight to edge of evening,	*De Castillon figuieres jour de brune,*
To wife infamous will be born sovereign prince	*De feme infame naistra souverain prince*
Above not from stocking ones through country him born after father's death,	*Surnom de chausses perhume luy posthume,*
At any time King not had been so worse one his country.	*Onc Roy ne feut si pire en sa province.*

Note: Originally listed as quatrain number 9 in Centurie X. A *Chastillon* is the diminutive form of *castle*. This is telling of the birth of Prince Harry to Diana.

The Epic Poem Prophesied by Nostradamus

When the adulterer wounded besides strike will hold	Quand l'adultere blessé sans coup aura
Crushed there wife & them son through despite,	Meurdry la femme & les filz par despit,
Female stricken the child will smother:	Femme assommee l'enfant estranglera:
Eight servile ones caught, they to stop breathing without time to breathe.	Huit captifz prins, s'estouffer sans respit.

Note: Originally listed as quatrain number 63 in Centurie VIII. Shows how Diana was using the children to hurt Charles. It also indicates Diana was pregnant at the time of the death. It also indicates *eight* servants were threatened to remain forever silent.

First son widow unhappy marriage,	Premier filz vefve malheureux mariage,
Besides blank ones children two Islands in disagreement,	Sans nulz enfans deux Isles en discord,
Before eighteen not coming together time,	Avant dixhuit incompetant eage,
With the other nearby more humble will be the contract.	De l'autre pres plus bas sera l'accord.

Note: Originally listed as quatrain number 39 in Centurie X. There are similarities to quatrain X-09, VIII-63, and X-55, but the use of malheureux connects this to the offspring of Charles and Diana (X-55). This could identify the time when the two boys come of age, into their "inheritance". The use of nulz, can mean Charles is impotent, thus not the father. The other nearby would be Prince Andrew, probably the father of Prince William. Prince William was born in 1982, meaning that 18 years would be in the year 2000.

Prosperous in the kingdom to France, happy with life	Heureux au regne de France, heureux de vie
Simple stock death madness & violent snatching,	Ignorant sang mort fureur & rapine,
By no sycophants will be thrust into malicious emulation,	Par mon flateurs sera mys envie,
King stolen too much from faith upon kitchen.	Roy desrobé trop de foy en cuisine.

Note: Originally listed as quatrain number 16 in Centurie X. One definition of *mort*, as death (versus "dead") is: "departure out of this life." Following the happiness of an age of prosperity, which includes the French people (i.e.: the West), the *unskilled*, or *unlearned* (of the third world) are kept away from this fortunate age, creating *fury* within third world nations. A "sycophant" is defined as, "A servile self-seeker who attempts to win favor by flattering influential people", which

Chapter 5 - Diametrically Opposite Sects & Religions & Reigns

would describe people that are commonly referred to as "paparazzi". In the case of Diana Spencer and Dodi Faud, said to have been chased by photographers is now said to be a lie, as they were "no flatters". The use of "malicious emulation", where the obsolete definition of "emulation" is, "jealous rivalry", means this rivalry has turned "deliberately harmful."

Him son to the kingdom through the father's side taking,	*L'enfant du regne par paternelle prinse,*
Deprived of will be in respect of to yield over unto:	*Expolié sera pour le delivrer:*
Compared with the snare Trasimene the sky-color received of,	*Aupres du lac Trasimen l'azur prinse,*
There crew surety by reason of too much powerful himself to make drunk.	*La troupe hostaige par trop fort s'enyurer.*

Note: Originally listed as quatrain number 39 in Centurie VI. *Trasimene lake* was where Hannibal conquered the Romans under Flaminius in 217 B.C. It is also known as the Lake of Perugia and is in the Umbrian region of peninsular Italy. The battle is still recognized as one of the most successful ambushes in history. The battle as *Trasimene* was a *trap*, into which the Romans fell. Nostradamus mentioned "*Lac Thrasmien*" in quatrain VIII-47, again as a comparison to a historic event of a successful *trap* being set. The main theme can be seen as reference to the British throne, as that is the only kingdom, where a son can inherit it, in the tale of *The Prophecies*. The only son (prince) ever in need of being taken by the father's side is Prince William (and Harry), as a child last through divorce. The secondary theme is the dilemma Prince Charles was faced with, in respect of *delivering* the children back to his custody.

Above him palace in the rock from the windows	*Sur le palais au rochier des fenestres*
Will be forcibly carried away ones them two young ones royals,	*Seront ravis les deux petits royaux,*
To transport attention given Paris Denis abbey ones,	*Passer aurelle Luthece Denis cloistres,*
Nun, bad fines of alienation by a lord, to swallow green ones plum pits.	*Nonain, mallods, avaller verts noyaulx.*

Note: Originally listed as quatrain number 24 in Centurie IX. If line one is referencing *the rock* as *Gibraltar*, there is a Caleta Palace Hotel there. However, Scotland's Royal Castle Rock is another possibility as a site. Paris was originally named "*Lutetia Parisii*", due to the Gaulish tribe of *Parisii* that lived there. This mutated to *Lutèce*, and some say later *Luthece*.

The Epic Poem Prophesied by Nostradamus

Letters obtained ones to the queen them put into a chest ones,	*Lettres trouvees de la roine les coffres,*
Not at all with signed besides someone title of the causer	*Point de subscrit sans aucun nom d'hauteur*
For there police will be hidden corner ones biddings,	*Par la police seront cachez les offres,*
That one not will understand who will be the lover.	*Qu'on ne scaura qui sera l'amateur.*

Note: Originally listed as quatrain number 23 in Centurie VIII. This is about the letters stolen from Diana Spencer's home shortly after her death, before it was publicly announced, but her butler, who was charged with theft, but eventually all charges were dropped because Queen Elizabeth had a return of memory that she ordered him to take things. The police were certainly involved, but no letters were concretely exposed.

Heart to the loving apparent of love stolen,	*Coeur de l'amant ouvert d'amour furtive,*
Within them current of water will act to take away forcibly the Mistress,	*Dans le ruysseau fera ravyr la Dame,*
The half harm will imitate weariness,	*Le demy mal contrefera lassive,*
The father with two will take from body to the soul.	*Le pere à deux privera corps de l'ame.*

Note: Originally listed as quatrain number 25 in Centurie VIII. This is linked to quatrain VIII-23, where Diana's letters are stolen. The lover is whom she truly loved, and who is the father of her two children. One lover was Prince Andrew, aka "Randi Andy."

This one of the lineage splattered the aspect of a man,	*Celuy du sang resperse le visaige,*
To the victim close unto offered up in sacrifice:	*De la victime proche sacrifiée:*
Making a loud noise in England forewarning through presage,	*Tonant en Leo augure par presaige,*
Thrust into line of a pedigree with death then for the fiancée.	*Mis estre à mort lors pour la fiancée.*

Note: Latin: *respersi* = sprinkled, splashed; *victima* = animal offered in sacrifice, victim; *tono* = to thunder. Originally listed as quatrain number 98 in Centurie II. This appears to be about Prince Charles, who had Diana Spencer killed so (for one reason minimally) he could wed Camilla. Diana was a sacrificial lamb.

Chapter 5 - Diametrically Opposite Sects & Religions & Reigns

The government seized a King will invite to a feast,	*Le regne prins le Roy conviera,*
There mistress taken to dead them taking the oath at hazard,	*La dame prinse à mort ljurez à sort,*
Then whole time with queen son one will defame,	*La vie à royne filz on desniera,*
Both his concubine to the mighty from the spouse.	*Et sa pellix au fort de la consort.*

Note: Latin: *pellexi = enticed, decoyed, seduced.* Originally listed as quatrain number 77 in Centurie IX. This reads like Charles denying any involvement with Diana's death to the Queen; but the first two lines seem like some one is channeling the past from the spirit of Diana. The reference to "Both" can include Camilla. This could also be a focus after the attacks on London and the death of Queen Elizabeth.

Them run-away ones & outlawed ones countermanded ones,	*Les fuitifs & bannis revoquez,*
Priests & boys great had furnished years those high ones shafts:	*Peres & filz grand garnisant les haultz puits:*
Him tyrannous father & they his own ones choked ones,	*Le cruel pere & les siens suffoquez,*
His sons more worse submerged in a draw well.	*Son filz plus pire submergé dans le puits.*

Note: Originally listed as quatrain number 53 in Centurie IV. Quatrain V-97 uses the words "*suffoque*" and "*revoque*", with variations of the same words appearing in this quatrain. In line two, the words "*haultz puits*" remind me of the movie *Troy*, where the royal family had escape routes planned, which took them through *shafts* to a exit far from the castle. These were only designed for "*those noble ones.*"

Into place of wedded them girls sliced their throats,	*En lieu d'espouse les filles trucidées,*
Murder with noble responsibility not will be witnessed him:	*Meurtre à grand faulte ne sera superstile:*
Within themselves wells clothed them overwhelmed with water ones,	*Dedans se puys vestules inondées,*
The wife extinguished through ladle of Poison.	*L'espouse estaincte par hauste d'Aconile.*

Note: Originally listed as quatrain number 71 in Centurie IV. This is another seeming to tell of Jack the Ripper, or one like him. It appears wells or extinct volcano mounds of earth (hills, clots of earth) are where the bodies are disposed, either fully *clothed* (as *vestu-les*), or along with *letters* (*vestules*). If *letters* is the meaning, then the use of a Latvian word would indicate someone formerly of the Soviet Union. There is a *wife* as well, who seems to know of the murders, and eventually becomes another victim.

The Final Corruption of a "Christian" Religion

The Murder of Pope John Paul I

The law Moorish one will see to decay (or wax feeble),	*La loy Moricque on verra defaillir,*
Following one different from the former many more leading aside,	*Apres une autre beaucoup plus seductive,*
Russia before others will grow to end,	*Boristhenes premier viendra faillir,*
Forgiveness ones & form of speech one more alluring.	*Pardons & langue une plus attractive.*

Note: French: *morisque* = Moorish dance. Roman: *Borysthenes* = *Dnieper River*. Originally listed as quatrain number 95 in Centurie III.

Hercules Pope to my Rome & of Year risen dregs,	*Hercules Roy de Romme & d'Annemarc,*
With Long staff three Guide one surnamed,	*De Gaule trois Guion surnommé,*
To quake the Italy & the wave of saint Mark,	*Trembler l'Italie & l'vnde de saint Marc,*
Chief above everything monarch exceedingly spoken of.	*Premier sur tous monarque renommé.*

Note: Originally listed as quatrain number 33 in Centurie IX. If it were not for the capital *A* in *Annemarc*, it would be easier to transform *d'Annemarc* into Denmark, as from *Danemarc*. This is certainly still an option for line one. As for the name *Guyon*, a quietist Catholic named (Madame) Jeanne-Marie Motte-*Guyon* wrote poetry and inspired many with her preaching about mystical experiences (late 17th century, to early 18th century). Today the modern French word *Guion* means, "Screenplay or script." In the center of Rome is *San Marco*, which is the basilica name for *saint Mark*. The Year 1978 was when *three* popes occupied the same seat, separately. Pope Paul VI and Pope John Paul I were both *Italian*, unlike Pope John Paul II.

In the sacred ones churches being done ones scandals,,	*Aux sacréz temples seront faicts escandales,*
Calculated ones will be through promotions & praises:	*Comptéz seront par honneurs & louanges:*
From one who they engraved with silver, of gold the broaches,	*D'un que on grave d'argent, d'or les medalles,*

Chapter 5 - Diametrically Opposite Sects & Religions & Reigns

There end will be in tortures quite unusual ones.	*La fin sera en tourmens bien estranges.*

Note: French: *scandale = cause of sin*. Originally listed as quatrain number 9 in Centurie VI. It is interesting that the spelling *escandales* makes it apply to *escandal*, a "mariner's sounding [measuring] plummet [lead ball on a line]." The reference is then specific to scandals in the Roman Catholic Church, as the church symbolized as the barque [boat].

Sights barred, uncovered ones of ancient judgment,	*Yeux clos, ouverts d'antique fantasie,*
The vestment of the singular ones being thrust into naught:	*L'habit des seulz seront mis à neant:*
Him great monarch will punish their madness,	*Le grand monarque chastiera leur frenaisie,*
To bear away suddenly from the churches the revenue of the monarchy through owing.	*Ravir des temples le tresor par devant.*

Note: Originally listed as quatrain number 12 in Centurie II. The word *seul* also means: singular, only and oneself. The plural indicates unmarried ones. The French word for "soul" is "ame." The French phrase, "mettre à neant" meant, "to antiquate, to abolish, to avoid, to make void, to ruin, to subvert, to raze, to overthrow." The word frenesie was clean Old English, from Old French, from the Latin version, spelled pherensia, which meant "madness, frenzy". The 1555 Albi edition spells the word frenesie, with the 1557 Utrecht edition spelling it frenaisie, the proper French spelling. This tells of the times leading up to Pope John Paul I, when the losses of paying Catholics in the world placed the Church in economic danger.

Him great Prelate one light following his dream,	*Le grand Prelat un jour apres son songe,*
Shown the meaning of the wayward from one's judgment:	*Interpreté au rebours de son sens:*
From there Gascony he will appear suddenly one monk,	*De la Gascoigne luy surviendra un monge,*
Which will act to pick out them great Bishop with feeling.	*Qui fera eslire le grand Prelat de sens.*

Note: Originally listed as quatrain number 86 in Centurie VI. Gascony becomes a reference to the Knights Templar, and their suppression by King Philip IV of France, which would lead to the Avignon Papacy. The word *monge* is Gascon. In French it is spelled "*moine*," which means *monk*. Gascony is in southwest France, from the Atlantic (at Bordeaux) to the Pyrenees, dividing Aquitaine.

The Epic Poem Prophesied by Nostradamus

The one who will have government of there great cope (alb),	Celuy qu'aura gouvert de la grand cappe,
Will be induced with some crime to bring to completion:	Sera induict a quelque cas patrer:
Them twelve red ones will be arriving to soil the sheet,	Les douze rouges viendront souiller la nappe,
At the bottom of homicide, murder themselves will come to perpetrate.	Sous meurtre, meurtre se viendra perpetrer.

Note: Latin: *patronus* = *a protector, defender*. Originally listed as quatrain number 11 in Centurie IV. The word *cappe* has clear meaning as an ecclesiastical garment. The 1555 Albi edition shows the Roman numeral for *douze*, as XII., with a period mark denoting the end of the numeral. Roman numerals would carry a clear indication of Rome being where the twelve were. All editions beyond the 1555 copies show *douze*. The use of color, as *rouges*, means those who have no religious values, which are usually communists. However, organized crime can be equally non-religious, while acting as if so.

One King angered will be at the seat-rotten ones,	Un Roy iré sera aux sedifragues,
Regarding interdicted ones being harness of discord:	Quant interdicts seront harnois de guerre:
There poison imbued with the sugar on strawberries,	La poison taincte au sucre par les fragues,
By bodily fluids murdered ones, cause of death, telling shut up, to draw near together.	Par eaux meurtris, mors, disant serre, serre.

Note: Latin: *sede* = *a seat, throne, chair; fragmen* = *a breaking*. Latin: *succresco* = *to increase, match; fragro* = *to emit a smell, especially sweet, fragrant*. Originally listed as quatrain number 94 in Centurie VI. The Vatican is referred to as the Holy See (Holy Seat). The word *sedifragues* is translated from Italian, the language of Rome's country. The word *interdict* is a Roman Catholic Church word, meaning, "An ecclesiastical censure that excludes a person or district from participation in most sacraments and from Christian burial."

For the universal world will be forged one absolute prince,	Par l'univers sera faict un monarque,
Who in agreement & life not will be at length:	Qu'en paix & vie ne sera longuement:
While itself will cast away there fisherman barque,	Lors se perdra la piscature barque,
Will be governed into more great loss.	Sera regie en plus grand detriment.

Chapter 5 - Diametrically Opposite Sects & Religions & Reigns

Note: Latin: *piscator = a fisherman*. Originally listed as quatrain number 4 in Centurie I. The definition for a *barque*, in English, is the same as for *bark*, meaning : A sailing ship with from three to five masts, all of them square-rigged except the after mast, which is fore-and-aft rigged. It is the symbol for the Catholic Church and the reason church officials wear miters and the main church seating room is called a nave.

One great King received one with another them public powers to one United,	*Un grand Roy prins entre les mains d'un Joyne,*
Not far from Easter (feast of) chaos blow to denomination:	*Non loin de Pasque confusion coup cultre:*
To perpetrate servile ones lightning upon the ship's mast	*Perpet. captifz fouldre en la husne*
In that time which three brothers themselves will be wounding & murder.	*Lors que trois freres se blesseront & murtre.*

Note: Latin: *perpetis = continual, unbroken*. French: *husine > usine = manufactured*. Originally listed as quatrain number 36 in Centurie IX. Due to the use of *King* being seen as either Jesus or a pope, due to the other references to *Monk, Easter* and *friars*, this quatrain refers to the murder of Pope John Paul I. The main attempt on Pope John Paul II's life occurred on May 13, 1981 (with another on May 13, 1982). In 1981 Easter fell on April 19th (April 11th in 1982). Less than one month's time can be seen as "not far from" that date. The words *trois freres* appear in another quatrain, and need to be seen as referencing *three Christian nations*, and not three individuals who are related.

The enemy great ancient lamentations murder with poison	*L'ennemi grand viel dueil meurt de poison*
Them notable ones by reason of immeasurable ones brought into subjection ones:	*Les souverains par infiniz subjuguez:*
Peters to pour down wet, kept secret ones beneath the fleece of wool,	*Pierres plouvoir, cachés soubz la toison,*
On dead principle causes of the matter upon vain are brought forth evidences of proof.	*Par mort articles en vain sont allegués.*

Note: Originally listed as quatrain number 47 in Centurie II. In line three, when Nostradamus wrote *under the fleece of wool* it is saying: under sheep's clothing.

The Epic Poem Prophesied by Nostradamus

Prelate insatiably lusting from ambition cheated,	*Prelat avare d'ambition trompé,*
Ought not will be who mightily will grow to have an opinion:	*Rien ne sera que trop viendra cuider:*
His apostles & him good office overtaken,	*Ses messaigers & luy bien attrapé,*
Everything to the quite contrary to observe, whom the staff cutting to pieces.	*Tout au rebours voir, qui les boys fendroit.*

Note: Originally listed as quatrain number 93 in Centurie VI. The word rien used without a negative (ne) means, "something, anything." Typically, Rein ne would be read as "nothing", but those rules do not apply here. The word *bois* (i=y) most typically means "wood," thus the following word, *fendroit* (from fender, meaning to crack, cut, slit, cleave, divide) would indicate cracked wood of some kind. However, the word *bois* also meant a staff or spear, thus made out of wood. The following verb indicating a cuting or piercing from the wood, along with the religious context, give the image of the Church becoming the ones who speared the body of Christ to ensure he was dead, while on the cross.

By him dying from the singular ruler of Rome,	*Par le trespas du monarque latin,*
Those who he will have through realm assisted ones:	*Ceulx qu'il aura par regne secouruz:*
The light will yield a radiant luster, divided it booty taken,	*Le feu luyra, divisé le butin,*
There death common to the daring ones not overthrown ones.	*La mort publique aux hardis incoruz.*

Note: Latin: *incorruptus* = *not corrupted, untainted, unspoiled unimpaired.* Originally listed as quatrain number 21 in Centurie V. In modern French, the word *latin* is not found capitalized in the English-French dictionary, although it translates into English in the capitalized form. By it not being capitalized by Nostradamus, it shows less importance, such that the language or people are not greater than the one speaking or being of those.

Close to the Rhine from the mountain ones Noric race,	*Aupres du Rin des montaignes Noriques,*
Will be born one great to people mightily late arrived:	*Naistra un grand de gens trop tard venu:*
Who will maintain WOUNDED-ROME & Hungaro-Slavic ones,	*Qui defendra SAVROME & Pannoniques,*
Whom one not will perceive who he will be become.	*Qu'on ne saura qu'il sera devenu.*

Chapter 5 - Diametrically Opposite Sects & Religions & Reigns

Note: Mid-High German: *rin > Rhine = to flow, run*. History: *Noricum = between Alps & Danube*. Latin: *SAU(CIA)-ROMA = WOUNDED ROME*. Originally listed as quatrain number 58 in Centurie III. In the breakdown of *SAVROME*, the Romans made a "U" look like a "V." This means "SAUROME" can be the spelling to solve. With line one stating the general location and line two speaking of a lineage aligned with *the ship*, or barque of ROME, the result is the Holy Roman Empire. That was a land without kings, which depended on Rome to anoint Emperors over vast regions of Eastern Europe. Especially in the Pannons (Pannonia), which were basically Austria, Hungary, and Yugoslavia.

Through the death to the very old pope,	*Par le trespas du tresvieillart pontife,*
Will be chosen of Rome to principal part time:	*Sera esleu Romain de bon aage:*
That he will be spoken which the see much out of tune,	*Qu'il fera dict que le siege debiffe,*
Both long will restrain & with stinging workmanship.	*Et long tiendra & de picquant ouraige.*

Note: Originally listed as quatrain number 56 in Centurie V. Pope John Paul II died at the age of 85, which is very aged. Pope Ratzinger was 78 when he was made pope. The purpose of aage is not to define Ratzinger's age, but to state that both John Paul II and Benedict would be the popes of the time of the end of the world, according to the story of Nostradamus. This could relate to the last pope, according to Saint Malachy – Peter of Rome.

After the see held seventeen years,	*Apres le siege tenu dixsept ans,*
Five will be altering upon resembling passed fully about crossway:	*Cinq changeront en tel reuolu terme:*
In that time will be the one chosen to very same opportunity,	*Puis sera l'un esleu de mesme temps,*
Whom to the ones of Rome not will be mightily agreeable unto.	*Qui des Romains ne sera trop conforme.*

Note: Originally listed as quatrain number 92 in Centurie V. Pope John Paul II took office in 1978, and did not die until 2005, twenty-seven years later. Pope John Paul IIs seventeenth year was then 1995. This makes it possible that some "body doubles" held the last ten years of the pope's reign, with Ratzinger chosen to be his replacement.

In land unheard of before riches having King begun in	*En terre neufve bien avant Roy entré*
Declining subjective ones it will be growing to cause reception,	*Pendant subges luy viendront faire acueil,*
His treachery will occupy resembling encountered	*Sa perfidie aura tel rencontré*

The Epic Poem Prophesied by Nostradamus

Which in the citizens state holy day & entertainment.	Qu'aux citadins lieu de feste & recueil.

Note: Latin: *perfidia* = *faithlessness, treachery.* Originally listed as quatrain number 74 in Centurie VIII.

Roman Pope defender of yourself to come near unto,	Romain Pontife garde de t'approcher,
To there summoned to appear who two rivers water,	De la cité que deux fleuves arrouse,
Your kindred will arrive ones near to there to spit.	Ton sang viendras au pres de la cracher.
You & them hold until will have much reputation in the world the reddish.	Toy & les tiens quand fleurira la rouse.

Note: Originally listed as quatrain number 97 in Centurie II.

That one who would be well within the government,	Celuy qu'estoit bien avant dans le regne,
Having chief red adjoining in there holy government:	Ayant chef rouge proche à la hierarchie:
Biting & unmerciful, & one will cause so much to fear,	Aspre & cruel, & se fera tant craindre,
Will follow to sacred kindgom.	Succedera à sacree monarchie.

Note: Originally listed as quatrain number 57 in Centurie VI. This quatrain refers to Pope John Paul II, since he was a *leader* in the Polish church, when it was *red* and he *succeed*ed being *sanctified* as the Vatican *monarchy* and was a cardinal *well before* being elected pope.

The Final Corruption of a "Christian" Sect

The Assassinations of John and Robert Kennedy

There sister eldest to the island British,	La sœur aisnée de l'isle Britannique,
Fifteen years before him brother will enjoy first appearing:	Quinze ans devant le frere aura naissance:
By reason of his given by word in return for verified,	Par son promis moyennant verrifique,

Chapter 5 - Diametrically Opposite Sects & Religions & Reigns

Will follow with the government of balance.	*Succedera au regne de balance.*

Note: Originally listed as quatrain number 96 in Centurie IV. In line four, the word *balance* is defined as also representing the astrological sign of Libra. This is interesting when one considers the natal chart of the United States. While many argue the precise time the birth of the nation occurred, with a basic time of noon used, on July 4, 1776, in Philadelphia, PA., the Ascendant, or Rising (notice the last word in line two) Sign is Libra. The *eldest* of Great Britain is, of course, the USA. This is about the political rise of John F. Kennedy, who was born in 1915.

Chief with beauty in such manner gracefully,	*Prince de beauté tant venuste,*
With the leader brought, him second exploited betrayed:	*Au chef menee, le second faict trahy:*
There summoned to appear with the weapon of gun powder, figure gloomy,	*La cité au glaive de poudre, face aduste,*
For excess great murder him principal commander from the head man of a company detested.	*Par trop grand meurtre le chef du roy hay.*

Note: Latin: *venuste [adv.]* = charmingly. Originally listed as quatrain number 92 in Centurie VI. The *beautiful Prince charming* sounds precisely like John F. Kennedy, and the press terming the White House as Camelot. During the campaign of 1960, Nixon was the vote *leader*. The *second* to the *leader*, if the leader were a President, would be the Vice President. Still, this line can have multiple meanings, as Jack Kennedy *brought* his brother Bobby, who became his *assistant*. Line four's use of chef as "head man of a company" then names the one who ordered the assassination: J. Edgar Hoover.

The trembling so strong in the month of May,	*Le tremblement si fort au mois de May,*
Saturn goat, Jupiter Mercury in the ox,	*Saturne caper, Jupiter Mercure au bœuf,*
Venus likewise crab, Mars into Nun (Virgo)	*Venus, aussi cancer, Mars en Nonnay*
Will fall hail then more big that one egg.	*Tombera gresle lors plus grosse qu'un oeuf.*

Note: Originally listed as quatrain number 67 in Centurie X. The astronomy dates the greatest measured earthquake, which occurred in Chile on May 22, 1960. At that time, Saturn was at 17 Capricorn 57.5, with Jupiter at 2 Capricorn 54, with both in Capricorn the whole month of May. Thus, Saturn he-goat, Jupiter. Mercury was in Taurus between May 4 and May 19, thus after Saturn and Jupiter. After that timing (into line three), Venus would enter into Cancer on June 23, 1960, with Mars going into Virgo between June 29 and August 17, 1961. This spans the time of John Kennedy's inauguration, and greatest challenges of his presidency, being the Bay of Pigs and the

The Epic Poem Prophesied by Nostradamus

Cuban Missile Crisis. Line four can then be seen as the Berlin Crisis of 1961, where Berlin was an egg in East Germany, which was part of the larger West Germany.

The Morals of the day world with fortress of Light	La Meuse au jour terre de Lucembourg
Will discover Saturn & three in the urn (Aquarius),	Descouvrira Saturne & trois en lurne,
Mountain & absolute, city, warned to appear & fortified,	Montagne & pleine, ville, cite & bourg,
The-gold-branch surrounding treason by reason of voting urn.	Lorrain deluge trahison par grand hurne.

Note: Originally listed as quatrain number 50 in Centurie X. A *bourg* was a town without walls of defense. The *land* that would become the country called Luxembourg is actually the world's last remaining Grand Duchy and its independence was not assured until the 19th Century. Saturn was in the sign of Capricorn, along with the Sun, Mercury, and Jupiter, on January 1, 1961. The Sun went into Aquarius the day after the Kennedy inauguration (20th), with Mercury going into Aquarius on the 15th. Venus was in Aquarius on the 1st, leaving for Pisces on the 6th. The *mountain* of line three is Cuba.

Murdered conspired will come upon plain bringing to pass,	Mort conspiree viendra en plain effect,
Charge of gun delivered up & journey to death,	Charge donnee & voiage de mort,
Elected, created, admitted by his followers overthrown,	Esleu, cree, receu par siens deffait,
Lineage with integrity formerly him by reason of regret.	Sang dinnocence devant soy par remort.

Note: Originally listed as quatrain number 87 in Centurie VIII. The word Charge (especially capitalized) can also mean "Dignity," or "An Office." The office given would be the Office of President, to JFK. Also, the word devant means "before, formerly", as an adverb; but, as the present participle of the verb devoir, it means "owning." The dual meaning is owning the sacrifice of the faultless, ahead in his future and the loss of the young ahead of their normal time.

Him successor will avenge his handsome brother,	Le successeur vengera son beau frere,
Will trouble government at the bottom of covert with revenge,	Occuper regne souz ombre de vengeance,
Murdered hindrance his parentage dead dishonored,	Occis obstacle son sang mort vitupere,
Continual opportunity Amorica will maintain there France.	Long temps Bretaigne tiendra avec la France.

Chapter 5 - Diametrically Opposite Sects & Religions & Reigns

Note: Originally listed as quatrain number 26 in Centurie X. This is about Bobby Kennedy, who saw the shadow government was at work in the assassination of his brother, Jack. He became troublesome to the possibility that should he become elected president he could expose the covert operations that were regularly carried out. He too was assassinated, with it later made known that his father, Joe, and his brother, including Bobby, had lived lives far from the pure, clean lives that had been projected. This level of dishonor spread to Ted, as he too was involved with a killing he could not explain. All of this left the Kennedy line unwilling to attempt another presidential campaign, which means Ted Kennedy's run in 1980 was more designed to keep Carter from a second term. Line four then states the shadow government would be free to rule undercover.

There lady by herself with the government continuing behind,	*La dame seule au regne demourée,*
With unique perished before others in the rank of honor:	*D'unic estaint premier au lict d'honneur:*
Seven years will be from grief looked far into,	*Sept ans sera de douleur explorée,*
After continual living at the reign of great fortune.	*Puis longue vie au regne par grand heur.*

Note: French: *vnic = unique*. Originally listed as quatrain number 63 in Centurie VI. Line two draws a strong image of the eternal flame at John Kennedy's burial site in Arlington Cemetary. The *bed of honor* is the lying in State at the Capitol Rotunda. The Warren Commission's report on the investigation of Kennedy's death was released on September 24, 1964, which supported the lone gunman theory, while suppressing evidence. This could make *Sept* translate as *September*.

Chapter 6

The State of the World before the Dominoes Fall

We Are the Champions of the World

The great empire will be suddenly transferred,	Le grand empire sera tost translaté,
Upon state low whose wealth swiftly will come to rise in height:	En lieu petit qui bien tost viendra croistre:
Credit thoroughly most bottom scarcely a county	Lieu bien infime d'exigue compté
Where at the center of will come to place its absolute rule.	Ou au milieu viendra poser son sceptre.

Note: Latin: *imfimus* > *inferus* = lowest. Originally listed as quatrain number 32 in Centurie I.

Under cloak devised of to expel from servitude,	Soubz ombre faincte d'oster de servitude,
Populous & summoned to appear them will seize one's rights it very same:	Peuple & cité l'usurpera luy mesmes:
Worse will act on commons with young rotten,	Pire fera par fraulx de jeune pute,
Distributed unto in the land reading them incorrectly neighbor.	Livré au champ lisant le faulx proesme.

Note: French: *putain* = whore, *puterie* = whoring, *putier* = whore-monger. Originally listed as quatrain number 5 in Centurie V.

Them two united ones not will be possessing lastingly,	Les deux uniz ne tiendront longuement,
Both within thirteen years to the Barbarous satrapy:	Et dans treze ans au Barbare satrappe:

Chapter 6 - The State of the World Before the Dominoes Fall

With the two sides factions being such losing,	*Aux deux costez seront tel perdement,*
That one will wish well unto the Small Ship & its cloak.	*Qu'un benyra le Barque & sa cappe.*

Note: Originally listed as quatrain 78 in Centurie V. The *two united ones* are, of course, the United States of America and the United Kingdom. A *satrapy* is defined as: A nation, state, territory, or area controlled as if by a satrap. It also is a clearly recognized division of power known in Iran (Persia). Line four's relationship to the secondary theme statement means that the *Small Ship* (*Barque*) is related to *That one*, being the *Barbarous satrapy*, or Iran. The ship referencing is a submarine and the ampersand marks the most important aspect of that ship – its cloaking capability. The less than 13 years is between January 1991 (Gulf War) and March 2003 (Iraq War), which is more than 12 years, but *within thirteen years*. Papal capes (a mantum) had gone out of style recently, but Pope Ratzinger has begun wearing one again, as reported in April 2008.

More not will be the great in false sleep,	*Plus ne sera le grand en faulx sommeil,*
The unrest will grow to take peace:	*L'inquietude viendra prendre repos:*
To raise cut lengths of rod from gold, turquoise, & fine silver gilded with gold,	*Dresser phalange d'or, azur, & vermeil,*
To subject Africa there to wear away until at the bone.	*Subiuger Afrique la ronger jusques os.*

Note: Originally listed as quatrain number 69 in Centurie V. When the Latin phalanga(e) is read, carrying rods become reminiscent of the Ark of the Covenant, which is said to have been hidden in Ethiopia. The Ark was layered in gold. Turquoise has been mined in Iran for over 7,000 years; but it is also found other places, such as Egypt, Turkey, and the American west. The flag of Eritrea (nation on the horn of Africa, next to and north of Ethiopia) has blue, red, and a gold leaf seal on it (along with green).

The world near to the end period,	*Le monde proche du dernier periode,*
Saturn yet long in coming will be of returning:	*Saturne encor tard sera de retour:*
Celebration of transfer empire to wards nation of Black,	*Translat empire devers nation Brodde,*
The sight uprooted with Narbonne by reason of Round-about (or Goshawk).	*L'oeil arrache à Narbon par Autour.*

Note: Latin: *translat = celebration of transfer.* Latin: *Narbo = Narbonne.* Originally listed as quatrain 92 in Centurie III. The word *brod* is a common name found in Slavic nations, meaning "ford." The word *Autour* also means a short-winged hawk, which makes it a perfect description of a Blackhawk helicopter. A helicopter has short wings and blades that go *round-about*.

The Epic Poem Prophesied by Nostradamus

Scythe in standing water conjunct towards them Sagittarius,	*Faulx a l'estang joinct vers le Sagitaire,*
Upon its height AUGURED of the exaltation.	*En son hault AUGE de l'exaltation.*
Plague, famine, death from hand military,	*Peste, famine, mort de main militaire,*
The age (or 100 year century) approached to renewal.	*Le siecle approche de renovation.*

Note: Latin: *auger* = *augur, interpreter*. Originally listed as quatrain number 16 in Centurie I. In the Català language, *Sagitari* is spelled with one t. The word AVGE (AUGE) first translates to "trough," but also translates to MANGER. The all-caps call for an important translation, and since Christ was born in a manger, highly exalted, that is my choice. Saturn went from Scorpio (standing water) into Sagittarius in November 1985. It was conjunct the Sun, as the Sun went into Sagittarius about the same time.

Two turns around made of the malific scythe-bearer,	*Deux revolts faictz du maling falcigere,*
To sign of rulership & times forged exchanging:	*De regne & siecles faict permutation:*
A mutable sign with its face so force upon,	*Le mobil signe à son endroict si ingere,*
In the two equals & with affection unto.	*Aux deux egaux & d'inclination.*

Note: Latin: *mobilis* = movable, rapid.; *falcifer* = carrying a scythe. Originally listed as quatrain number 54 in Centurie I. The *malific scythe* is the planet Saturn. Line one is referring to the planets Saturn and Mars, as both are called the "malifics," Saturn the Greater Malific, and Mars the Lesser Malefic. The glyph for Saturn is a scythe shape, as it is known as the Grim Reaper, or Father Time. Saturn rules Capricorn and Aquarius. Mars rules Aries and Scorpio. The mutable signs are Gemini, Virgo, Sagittarius, and Pisces. The word endroict can mean direct, which in astrological terms means movement forward. Thus, forward motion would be facing an upcoming sign. When two planets are equal ones, they are in conjunction, which means their inclination is the same degree, within a 5 degree orb. This quatrain is then telling of a time when Saturn and Mars will be conjunct in the sign of Sagittarius, about to enter Capricorn. Such a placement took place in February (13-29) 1988.

General of Aries, Jupiter, & Saturn,	*Chef d'Aries, Juppiter, & Saturne,*
God without end which ones changing ones?	*Dieu eternel quelles mutations?*
Moreover through wearisome age one's ill-willed opportunity restored,	*Puis par long siecle son maling temps retourne,*

Chapter 6 - The State of the World Before the Dominoes Fall

Gaul, & Italy what one's sudden stirrings?	*Gaule, & Italie quelles esmotions?*

Note: Latin: *Juppiter* = *Jupiter*. Originally listed as quatrain number 51 in Centurie I. The planet that is the *general* of *Aries* is Mars. *Gaul* can be read as France.

After consent sedition civil, more great themselves prepared,	*Apres grant trouble humain, plus grand s'apreste,*
Them great rehash the times beginning anew again:	*Le grand mouteur les siecles renouvelle:*
Rain, blood, milk, famine, weapon & plague,	*Pluye, sang, laict, famine, fer & peste,*
In the sky heeded light, current of water outstretched sparked.	*Au ciel veu feu, courant longue estincelle.*

Note: Originally listed as quatrain number 46 in Centurie II. In line two, a mouteur is seen as a gristmill word. However, as moteur, it can represent a motor, including one at a grist mill. Line three shows a weapon that is importantly a contagion, which progresses through a series of occurrences. First, it falls as rain, then it is absorbed into the blood, which comes out as milk to the young, such as livestock. This in turn reduces the food sources, to the point that there becomes an extreme shortage of food, or famine.

Mars us could be led by its energy martial,	*Mars nous menasse par sa force bellique,*
September before time will act it blood to spill:	*Septante foys fera le sang espandre:*
Increased & waste to the Clergy,	*Auge & ruyne de l'Ecclesiastique,*
As well more those who both a matter will be wanting to understand.	*Et plus ceux qui deux rien voudront entendre.*

Note: Originally listed as quatrain number 15 in Centurie I. *Septante* is read as *Sept-ante*, thus *September before*.

Clergy of Rome the year millennium six votes & new,	*Clerge Romain l'an mil six cens & neuf,*
To the principal commander with twelve months prolific election	*Au chef de l'an feras élection*
Of one whitish & obscure from there Company descended,	*D'un gris & noir de la Compagnie yssu,*
Who ever not will have been as hurtful.	*Qui onc ne feut si maling.*

The Epic Poem Prophesied by Nostradamus

Note: Latin: *censeo = to form or express an opinion of a person, to estimate.* Originally listed as quatrain number 91 in Centurie X. Most wrongly read line one as stating the year 1609. The word *neuf* can also mean "nine." Pope John Paul II's death in 2005 is the main theme statement. Counting 2000 to 2005 is six years. In February 2005 the pope was hospitalized, released and expected to die. He died on March 31, with Pope Ratzinger elected on April 19th, waiving the 5-year beautification period for determining a saint on May 9, 2005. Time Magazine predicted on January 2, 2005 that Ratzinger was first in line to be pope, should John Paul II die (7 :1 odds).

When them sepulcher with the great Roman devised,	*Quand le sepulchre du grand Romain trouvé,*
The day after will be chosen pontiff:	*Le jour apres sera esleu pontife:*
From the senate but little ones it not will be verified,	*Du senat guieres il ne sera prouvé,*
Poisoned his kindred in the sacred communion cup.	*Empoisonné son sang au sacré scyphe.*

Note: Latin: *scyphus = drinking cup, goblet.* Originally listed as quatrain number 65 in Centurie III. Line four's use of *Empoisonné* ties this to the murder of Pope John Paul I, making this quatrain identify the plot to name his successor the following day, although Vatican law detailed a waiting period before such matters should be considered. Still, it refers to something found in the tomb of John Paul II, which will indicate his connection to that murder.

By reason of Mars much disagreeing will be there government of the absolute prince,	*Par Mars contraire sera la monarchie,*
From the great fisherman into sedition ruinous:	*Du grand pescheur en trouble ruyneux:*
Youthful obscurity red will seize the holy government,	*Jeune noir rouge prendra la hierarchie,*
Them traitors will be traveling daylight loaded with blasts of fog.	*Les proditeurs iront jour bruyneux.*

Note: Originally listed as quatrain number 25 in Centurie VI. On the day that Pope John Paul I was murdered, Mars was at 5 degrees of Scorpio, the sign it rules. With Mars were Venus and Uranus. Mars is symbolic of volatile energy. The word *trouble* also includes a usage as "*molestation,*" which specifies one of the troubles the Catholic Church faces today. The word *hierarchie* also includes the definition "holy government." This represents the beginning of Pope John Paul IIs reign. Line four tells this "*holy government*" will last until the attacks on Rome.

Chapter 7

Closing the Century of Gold

Pre-existing Conditions

Saddam Hussein Still in Power

The stratagem grudge will be excellent	*Le stratagesme simulte sera rare*
There death in manner that will not be ruled by country:	*La mort en voye rebelle par contrée:*
For the return to them voyage Barbarous	*Par le retour du voyage Barbare*
Will be commending there protested before entrance.	*Exalteront la protestante entrée.*

Note: This quatrain was originally number as quatrain 82 in the short Centurie VII. The French comes from the 1630 Lyon edition, which included five extra quatrains in *Centurie Septiesme*, as well as other Centuries and Presages. The word *protestante* is correctly translate into the capitalized version of Protestant; but protestant is the present participle form of the verb "*protester*", as, "protesting, denouncing, and openly declaring." Line one is referring to the *strategem* created by the Bush administration to *return* troops to Iraq, due to supposed hidden weapons of mass destruction.

Him third day above others worse some not will have had acted Nero-one,	*Le tiers premier pys que'ne feit Neron,*
Empty spaces honest that kindred civil to scatter abroad,	*Vuidex vaillant que sang humain respandre:*
To build again will forge them furnace one,	*R'édifier fera le forneron,*
Age of gold, departed from life, new king great a danger.	*Siecle dor, mort, nouveau roy grand esclandre.*

Note: Originally listed as quatrain number 17 in Centurie IX. The main theme statement can be read as Jesus resurrecting on the third day, such that a third of the world's population claims to be Christian. Just as Nero burned Rome and blamed it on the Christians, such an atrocity will pale to what is written of in this quatrain. Line two can be seen as speaking of the trust America affords

The Epic Poem Prophesied by Nostradamus

everyone, particularly those passing through empty spaces, such as the air lanes airplanes fly in. The new king great is George W. Bush. His danger will be found coming on September 11, 2001.

Late an absolute prince oneself will grow to repent,	*Tard le monarque se viendra repentir,*
From not to have thrust into at death his adversary:	*De n'avoir mis à mort son adversaire:*
More will come riches with more eminent to allow of,	*Mais viendra bien à plus hault consentir,*
That everything his lineage of killed will act to ruin.	*Que tout son sang par mort fera deffaire.*

Note: Originally listed as quatrain number 36 in Centurie I.

Nine years a realm them barren in agreement will restrain,	*Neuf ans le regne le maigre en paix tiendra,*
After he will fall into thirst so bloody:	*Puis il cherra en soif si sanguinaire:*
Because him great people without faith & liberty will die,	*Pour luy grand peuple sans foy & loy mourra,*
Killed by one much more affable.	*Tué par un beaucoup plus debonnaire.*

Note: Originally listed as quatrain number 9 in Centurie II. Iraq was sanctioned for nine years under Saddam Hussein, following the Gulf War (1991), until before September 11, 2001. Saddam Hussein would fall in 2003, when the people of Iraq would lose their freedom to an armed occupation. This was *Because him* (Saddam Hussein) was allied with the former Soviet Union, or the *great people* of Russia. Saddam Hussein would then be killed by one much more affable, since anyone would be that, when compared to Saddam Hussein.

The Burning Bush Plots Revenge

To the great empire will attain all one other	*Au grand empire parviendra tout un autre*
Goodness far removed more of exceeding good fortune:	*Bonté distant plus de felicité:*
Directed by one proceeded from not far off from the helm,	*Regi par un issu non loing du peaultre,*
Sinks down governments mighty made unhappy.	*Corruer regnes grande infelicité.*

Note: French: *peaultre > peautre = stern of a ship*. Latin: *corruo = fall down, collapse*. Originally listed as quatrain number 67 in Centurie VI. The stern of a ship is the rear part, which means part of the same ship the bow, or front part, was attached. The words "*issu du peaultre*" are also found

Chapter 7 - Closing the Century of Gold

in quatrain IX-76, referencing Neron, which is about Saddam Hussein. That connects these two quatrains.

From the water signs in trine aspect to one another will be born,	*De l'aquatique triplicité naistra,*
To one which will forge a Thursday for its feast:	*D'un qui fera le jeudy pour sa feste:*
His public voice, praise, government, one's authority will increase,	*Son bruit, loz, regne, sa puissance croistra,*
On whole earth & sea in the Middle Eastern ones stormed.	*Par terre & mer aux Oriens tempeste.*

Note: Originally listed as quatrain number 50 in Centurie I. The translation possible for l'aquatique, as water signs, is due to it being a symbolic term of astrology. The word triplicité is further evidence, as this word is directly related to astrology, as the division of the zodiac into four elements, each with three signs: water, fire, earth, and air. Each sign of the same element is 120 degrees from the others (a trine aspect). The capitalization of *Oriens* means a name for people of the east, which are equally Middle Easterners and Asians. Afghanistan, Iraq, Syria, and North Korea all fit that distinction.

A year following uncovered ones for to overwhelm,	*L'an ensuyvant descouverts par deluge,*
Two head men of parties chosen ones the first not will retain	*Deux chefs esleus le premier ne tiendra*
Of to delay pretense for the one two a help,	*De fuyr umbre à l'un deux le refuge,*
Ruined house which chief will stand in.	*Saccagée case qui premier maintiendra.*

Note: Originally listed as quatrain number 4 in Centurie IX. The word esleus is a word that specifically applied to "Assessors of Townships", which in essence means they were elected to serve the Prince, for each town, with pay rendered by the people to them, to determine revenues needed for the township's security and continued maintenance. Generally, today those would be called "government officials".

BY. SEEING IT AS IT IS. ONE TO DECAY, to ruin great debate,	*PAR. CAR. NERSAF, à ruine grand discorde,*
Neither the one nor the other not will have election,	*Ne l'un ne l'autre n'aura election,*
Born ravenous to the people will have good will & harmony	*Nersaf du peuple aura amour & concorde*
Rare weapon, Commander of the regiment might public defense.	*Ferrare, Collonne grande protection.*

The Epic Poem Prophesied by Nostradamus

Note: Latin: *colonia* = *colony*. French (as anagram): *Collonne* > *Colonnel* = *Colonel*, defined as "Commander of the rgeiment." Originally listed as quatrain number 67 in Centurie VIII. The all-cap words *PAR.* and *CAR.* are abbreviations, as noted by the period marks that follow each. The words *Parallel* and *Character* are common words that would be so abbreviated, both in English and French. The manufactured word *nersaf* is in lines one and three, meaning each requires a separate translation.

There natural in so honorable chief not base	*La naturelle à si hault non bas*
A late return will cause angry ones satisfied ones,	*Le tard retour fera marris contens,*
Them Reopened-put forth not will be without contention	*Le Recloing ne sera sans debatz*
In filling & losing all one's opportunity.	*En empliant & perdant tout son temps.*

Note: French: *R'esclos* = *Reopened* + Latin: *ingenero* = *to generate*. Originally listed as quatrain number 84 in Centurie X. If the *-ing* ending is an intentional use of English, *Recloing* (Old French spelling *esclos* is now *éclos*) can simply mean *Reopening*, and through language use that translation would indicate an event in an English speaking country.

Neither will be only one a very long time with to bring an action for,	*Ne sera saoul jamais de demander,*
Great Faulty-one will get its government	*Grand Mendosus obtiendra son empire*
Much of the assembly of judges will act to recall a former command,	*Loing de la cour fera contremander,*
Great-number-of-people-worse, From-pierce, Created-ones, Novice there unworthy.	*Pymond, Picard, Paris, Tyrron la pire.*

Note: Latin: *Mendosus* = *full of faults, inaccurate, making mistakes*. Originally listed as quatrain number 45 in Centurie IX. The word *Picard* is a clean word naming a Romance language similar to French, spoken in the region of France known as *Picardie* (close to Belgium). The name *Paris* could obviously mean the capital city of France. The title *Mendosus* fits George W. Bush.

Commissioned one suddenly will appear in its high government,	*Mandosus tost viendra à son hault regne*
Bringing back one few of Unwilling-ones,	*Mettant arriere un peu de Nolaris:*
The red whitish, them masculine in the interregnum,	*Le rouge blaisme, le masle à l'interregne,*

Chapter 7 - Closing the Century of Gold

Him youthful doubted & terror foreign ones.	*Le jeune crainte & frayeur barbaris.*

Note: Latin: *mando* – entrust, to order, to commission; *Nolo* = be unwilling, wish not to + *aris* = star; *barbaria* – a foreign country. Originally listed as quatrain number 50 in Centurie IX. Also relating to *Nolaris* : Latin: *Nolo* – to be unwilling, wish not to, refuse, *-aris* – of or relating to. An *interregnum* is defined as: the government between the death of one prince and the election of another. The use of *Mandosus* parallels the use of *Mendosus*, where the one full of faults has changed into a *Commissioned one*. this brings to mind the image of George W. Bush landing on an aircraft carrier deck, in a pilot's jumpsuit, announcing "Mission accomplished." One of his faults was being absent without permission, while in the Air National Guard; but as a pilot he was a *Commissioned* officer.

Aquarius wanderer without advice from oneself the same	*Urnel Vauclle sans conseil de soy mesmes*
You daring cowardly through fear caught overcome,	*Hardit timide par crainte prins vaincu,*
Having the fellowship of many whores whitish ones,	*Accompagné de plusieurs putains blesmes,*
To the descendant of Hannibal with the prisoners convicted.	*A Barcellonne au chartreux convaincu.*

Note: French (as anagram): *Vauclle > l'Vaucrer* = them To wander. Originally listed as quatrain number 14 in Centurie X. In modern French, the past participle verb *vaincu* means "defeated party," which adds depth to the Old French definition of "over-mastered." In politics the "over-mastered" are those of the "defeated party" that can do nothing to avert the legislation of the current ruling party. There are communes in France named Barcelonne (Drone department) and Vaucelles (Lower Normandy, Calvados department).

Them old in years disappointed with the main point of a matter hope	*Le vieux frustré du principal espoir*
He will come forward in the world to the principal commander to one's government	*Il paruiendra au chef de son empire*
Twenty month will retain him rule with great to have might	*Vingt mois tiendra le regne à grand pouvoir*
Tyrant, unmerciful in relinquishing one of smaller value.	*Tiran, cruel en delaissant un pire.*

Note: Originally listed as quatrain number 65 in Centurie VIII. The Old French word, *tiran*, meant: any string, lace, line or cord, which pulled at one end closes at the other the thing it is fastened to. Of course, with the "t" at the end left off [Provincial abbreviation?], and the "i" changed to a "y," *tiran* becomes Tyrant. As a secondary meaning one finds a "puppet Tyrant." The word cruel also translates as "tyrannous." Sort this to the George W. Bush rises to power series. Also, from October 2001, until May 2003, was *20 months* and when Bush announced

67

The Epic Poem Prophesied by Nostradamus

"mission accomplished" [banner announcement]. Osama bin Laden would be the *one abandon*ed, in lieu of Saddam Hussein becoming the Bush vendetta focus.

The Tyrant without a Land Waits for His Moment

Will be born of the deep waters & alleged not examined,	*Naistra du goulphre & cité immesuree,*
Risen from parents unknown ones & full of obscurity:	*Nay de parents obscurs & tenebreux:*
That which there possibility to the great chief revered,	*Qui la puissance du grand roy reveree,*
Will intend to destroy by THE last year & Eastern.	*Voudra destruire par Rouan & Eureux.*

Note: Latin: *parens = a parent.* Arpitan: *Rouana = Roanne.* Originally listed as quatrain number 84 in Centurie V. The last two capitalized words of line four have consistently been translated to be misspelling of the French cities – Rouen and Evreux. However, the city Roanne is spelled Rouana in Arpitan. Still, a word that was old when Old French was the standard language, oüan, is listed as meaning, "the last year." When an R- is seen as a prefix, Re-, those possibilities surface. Obviously the context, when understood, does not have much to do with France, meaning Eur is perhaps best translated as an abbreviation for Europe, with eux clean French, meaning "them, they." The bin Laden wealth is tied to the European connections.

With a name cursed such like delivered will be,	*D'un nom farouche tel proferé sera,*
Because them three secure ones will be enjoying destiny the fame:	*Que les trois seurs auront fato le nom:*
Then great people through language & forged will accustom,	*Puis grand peuple par langue & faict duira,*
More that none other will have talk of people & reputation.	*Plus que nul autre aura bruit & renom.*

Note: Latin: *Fatum – divine utterance, destiny, fate.* Originally listed as quatrain number 76 in Centurie I. Mythology knows the *three sisters* as the Fates, or the Moirae, who were also called the Daughters (of Zeus) of Necessity. They were: Clotho ("spinner"), Lachesis ("allotter"), and Atropos ("inevitable"). Each, in order of presentation, came at – birth, life and death, deciding the time of birth, length of life and time of death. Also, the *great people of language*, which most importantly is the language the people speak *made from the* common language of all is reference to the Romantic Languages of France, Spain and Italy, whose different languages are based on Latin. The word *renom* also means: exceedingly spoken, especially abroad.

Chapter 7 - Closing the Century of Gold

Towards them red ones sect ones oneself will be flexing,	*Contre le rouge sectes se banderont,*
Spirit, emotion, weapon, cord for peace himself will undermine,	*Feu, eau, fer, corde par paix se minera,*
To the edge to perish these who will be conspiring against,	*Au point mourir ceux qui machineront,*
All out one who a vast number of people above all will destroy.	*Fors un que monde sur tout ruynera.*

Note: Originally listed as quatrain number 51 in Centurie IX. Line one can be seen from two directions. First, Contre shows action Against, which becomes two opposing forces coming Towards each other. Thus, Towards shows how this action leads to one side being more like the other, through moving towards something, when against it. The color red is Nostradamus' way of indicating communism (the sect without religion), thus one Against communism, while going Towards communism, is a movement Towards socialism. Line two is stating that weapons will be sold by the former Soviet Union, particularly naval *fire*.

From soldier simple will come forward in the world in empire,	*De soldat simple parviendra en empire,*
To robe brief will thrive to there outstretched	*De robe courte parviendra à la longue*
Valiant with the weapons upon church where more bad,	*Vaillant aux armes en eglise ou plus pyre,*
To vex them priests like the water done the sponge.	*Vexer les prestres comme l'eau fait lesponge.*

Note: Originally listed as quatrain number 57 in Centurie VIII. This quatrain has regularly been applied to Napoleon, incorrectly. Randle Cotgrave lists the idiom "robbe courte", as the way to state, "gens de robbe," such as, "noblemen, gentlemen, soldiers, and officers." An idiom like this is secondary to the individual words being understood separately first. The line four words, comme l'eau fait l'espongne, is reminiscent of Jesus on the cross, being given wine vinegar on a sponge. Historically, the Roman soldiers would blend wine vinegar with water to drink (called posca).

Upon the midnight leader to the army	*Sus la minuict conducteur de l'armee*
Himself them will be safe, suddenly slipped out of sight,	*Se saulvera, subit esvanouy,*
September years after there renown not found fault with,	*Sept ans apres la fame non blasmee,*
With his returning neither will say never heard.	*A son retour ne dira oncq ouy.*

Note: Originally listed as quatrain number 4 in Centurie X. This quatrain seems to relate best with the leader who has made a name for having slipped out of sight, which would be Osama bin Laden.

The Epic Poem Prophesied by Nostradamus

Line three's Sept ans, as September year ones, where that is indicative of those planning September 11, 2001, makes him the best fit, since he took credit for the attacks. Only Muslims will find no fault with that renown, and be silent about his returning. This quatrain would then identify the conducteur as Osama bin Laden, and connect this quatrain to *the conducteur de l'armée*, mentioned in quatrain VII-39.

Chapter 8

The Day the Earth Stood Still

Prelude to the 21st Century

Deeply in long time the whole sum will be ordered	*Avant long temps le tout sera rangé*
Us spurs an age quite sinister:	*Nous esperons un siecle bien senestre:*
The state of the masked ones & of the only ones wealth exchanged,	*L'etat des masques & des seulz bien changé,*
Few will be finding what has one's place intended to be.	*Peu trouveront qu'a son rang veuille estre.*

Note: Originally listed as quatrain number 10 in Centurie II. This is a general quatrain that connects to any generally indicating a "century", such as "century of gold", which was the 20th century. This is further identified as a sinister century, where the state of the masks will have long existed, then being more exposed.

There substantial decay snare that will be acting them decrees,	*La grande perte las que feront les lettres,*
Deeply in them round of Leto complete:	*Avant le cicle de Latona parfaict:*
Light great inundated by waters more through having no experience ones kingdoms,	*Feu grand deluge plus par ignares sceptres*
Which from continual age neither themselves will see improved.	*Que de long siecle ne se verra refaict.*

Note: Mythology: *Lato/Latona* = mother of Apollo and Diana. Originally listed as quatrain number 62 in Centurie I. The word *ignares* is Latin, where *ignarus* means: ignorant, inexperienced in and unknown. *Latona* is the Roman name for the Greek goddess Leto, who was the daughter of Titans. She is the mother of Apollo (the Sun) ans Diana (the Moon). *Latona*'s mother, Phoebe, was the epitet of the full moon.

71

The Epic Poem Prophesied by Nostradamus

You will see ones suddenly & late to forge great ones transformation,	*Vous verrés tost & tard faire grands change,*
Horrors worst ones, & states of revenge:	*Horreurs extremes, & vindications:*
That so there moon government by one's angel,	*Que si la lune conduicte par son ange,*
Them heaven themselves drawing near to the dispositions.	*Le ciel s'approche des inclinations.*

Note: Latin: *vindicatio = defending, avenging.* Originally listed as quatrain number 56 in Centurie I. Sudden transformation of the great ones, means many (if not all) Western nations. The moon is synonymous with Islam, although the lack of capitalization makes it simply Arab, rather than the spiritual aspect of the religion of Arabs. Drawing heaven near means taking one to the edge of death.

One few after no point of a weapon long interval,	*Un peu apres non point longue intervalle,*
By sea & country will be caused great sedition:	*Par mer & terre sera faict grand tumulte:*
Much more mighty will be contest belonging to ships,	*Beaucoup plus grande sera pugne navalle,*
Fires, animals, which will be making to assault.	*Feus, animaux, qui plus feront d'insulte.*

Note: Latin: *pugna = fight, battle, contest.* Originally listed as quatrain number 40 in Centurie II. In line four, the word *feus* can be seen as *fire ones*, where fire symbolizes spirit. Then *animaux* can be seen as Latin, "anima-us," meaning both anima and animus – breath of life and the rational soul. For a rational soul to cause such a war and promote such vengeance, both become insults of the ways of man to God.

September 11, 2001

To the big town without walls Queens will be coming unto with Consumptions	*Du bourg Lareyne parviendront droit à Chartres*
Also will be acting nearby to the sea Flourishing delay,	*Et feront prés du pont Anthoni pause,*
September considering there peace crafty like weasels,	*Sept pour la paix cauteleux comme martres,*
Will be causing entrance to furnished with weapons to settle an account conclusion.	*Feront entree d'armee à Paris clause.*

Chapter 8 - The Day the Earth Stood Still

Note: Latin: *Ant(e)* = *Before*. French: *honni* = *disgraced, reproached, shamed*. Originally listed as quatrain number 86 in Centurie IX. There is a place in France, not far from Paris, named Bourg-la-Reine. You will see the absence of hyphens in what Nostradamus wrote. Perhaps it was not the style in the 16th Century to hyphenate multi-word cities, but in any case, the name Bourg-la-Reine means Queen Borough.

Many much before resembling ones private factions,	*Beaucoup beaucoup avant telles menées,*
Those of Middle East of there merit belonging to the moon:	*Ceulx d'Orient par la vertu lunaire:*
The year millennium September votes will be causing mighty ones brought in ones,	*Lan mil sept cent feront grands emmenées,*
Bringing under submission almost the grunting of pigs Northern.	*Subjugant presque le coing Aquilonaire.*

Note: Originally listed as quatrain number 49 in Centurie I. The word *menée* can also mean: practiced, guided, directed, managed and moved. When the main theme line states *Many much before*, who are like ones later, this is signaling a link to the past, from the future. Add to this the translation of *coing* as the grunting of pigs, and one has a link here to a later series of quatrains and a "human genetic abberation." This form of man may be what many mistake as aliens today.

Him Pope will propose within city new to enter	*Le Roy voudra dans cité neufve entrer*
By reason of adversaries to win by assault the one will approach	*Par ennemys expugner l'on viendra*
Captive without restraint lying to report unto & to perpetrate,	*Captif libere faulx dire & perpetrer,*
Head man of a party on the outside to be, far from enemies will maintain.	*Roy dehors estre, loin d'ennemys tiendra.*

Note: Originally listed as quatrain number 92 in Centurie IX. This quatrain is dependent on identifying the "*Roy*" of line one. If it is a *Pope*, this could be in reference to the papal visit of John Paul II to Israel and Jordan, which took place in May 2000. If this is about the papal visit to Arab-Jewish land, this could be reason for the attacks of 9-1-1. If "*Roy*" is translated as "*Chief*", it would then indicate Osama bin Laden and the planning for the attacks of September 11, 2001.

The Epic Poem Prophesied by Nostradamus

Within the Islands they young zealots transported,	*Dedans les Isles les enfans transportez,*
Those two from September will be in desperation,	*Les deux de sept seront en desespoir,*
Those of the terrorist into will be supported ones,	*Ceux du terrouer en seront supportez,*
Name shovel taken with the leagues slipped aside the trust.	*Nom pelle prins des ligues fuy l'espoir.*

Note: Originally listed as quatrain number 64 in Centurie VIII. September 11, 2001 attacks took place in pocket areas, or important *Islands*, such as New York City and Washington, D.C., with Manhattan itself being an *Island*. While the word *enfans* is the plural of *enfant*, it can denote more than *youths*, or *children* and *infants*. The word fan is related to fanatique, which makes the word bear the meaning of *zealots*, while also being young and impressionable.

The year millennium new votes not sooner than nine September month	*L'an mil neuf cens nonante neuf sept mois*
Of the sky will approach one substantial Chief a terrorist	*Du ciel viendra un grand Roy d'effrayeur*
To raise him great Head man of a party English-masters.	*Resusciter le grand Roy Dangolmois.*
Advent after War to govern for principal point of the matter fortune	*Avant apres Mars regner par bon heur*

Note: Originally listed as quatrain number 72 in Centurie X. The "name" *d'Angolmois* should be seen as an anagram - *Angli-domos*. The *Advent* (Christian season) *after* September 11, 2001 began on December 2nd, and lasted until December 24th. By that period of time the UN had supported the occupation and war in Afghanistan, by resolution (December 20, 2001), after the battle of Tora Bora. This quatrain does not have line four end with any punctuation. A period ends line three.

Large galleys well furnished ones all cage captive,	*Triremes pleines tout cage captif,*
Time principal point of the matter to hurt them courteous instead of anguish of mind:	*Temps bon à mal le doux pour amertume:*
Prey with barbarous ones too much suddenly being forward ones,	*Proie à barbares trop tost seront hatifz,*
Desire from to behold to make moan for at the blast there fleeced.	*Cupid de veoir plaindre au vent la plume.*

Note: Latin: *cupido* = longing, desire for power, ambition. French: *cage* > *c'age*. Originally

Chapter 8 - The Day the Earth Stood Still

listed as quatrain number 97 in Centurie X.

Placed into a plain kettles to depraved ones,	Mys en planure chaulderons d'infecteurs,
Ordain, sweetness & oil, & set up above kilns	Vin, miel & huyle, & bastis sur fourneaulx
Will be plunged ones without hardly told evil agents	Seront plongez sans mal dit mal facteurs
September smoke recorded in the public roll of the boundary waters.	Sept fum extaint au canon des borneaux.

Note: Latin: *fumo* = smoke. French: *born+eaux* > *borne* = limit, *eaux* = waters. Originally listed as quatrain number 14 in Centurie IX. The word *planure* is referencing flat, wide-open land, as one would find at an airport, where airplanes land and take-off on a plain. The word *plonge* can also mean "dived." This means line three has taken the reader from the flat plains of line one to an elevation, from which a *Being* could be *plunged*.

Suddenly at unawares sprang the terrorist will be high,	Subit venu l'effrayeur sera grande,
To the principal ones of the affair kept secret ones:	Des principaulx de l'affaire cachés:
Likewise lady in hot embers more not will be that surveyed on a piece of ground.	Et dame en braise plus ne sera en veue.
This few with little being them substantial ones molested ones.	Ce peu à peu seront les grans fachés.

Note: French: *principe-aux=a beginning with them*. Originally listed as quatrain number 65 in Centurie V.

Cries, weeping ones, the weapons will be coming together with knives	Cris, pleus, larmes viendront avec couteaux
Seeming to make holes in the ground will be delivering up last assault	Semblant fouyr douront dernier assault
The rundle impaled ones to ground high ones broadways,	Lentour parques planter profons plateaux,
Sparkling thrust back ones & murdered ones from piercing leap.	Vifs repoulsez & meurtrys de prin sault.

The Epic Poem Prophesied by Nostradamus

Note: Originally listed as quatrain number 82 in Centurie X. The letters in line one, *l armes*, have consistently been translated as larmes, meaning tears or teardrops. That translation becomes a repeating of the word written before it, since *pleurs* means tears. When one realizes the "L" must be separated, making it *l'armes*, it becomes *the weapons* or arms, which matches the following use of *knives*. The word *plateaux* meant "flat and thin stones," which sounds like stones for skipping across water. Still, in English we define "plateau" as "elevated land" or "leveled off." Both terms would apply to an airplane leveled off *to plant* itself into the elevated tower ahead of it.

Five & forty degree ones sky will consume with fire,	Cinq & quarante degrés ciel bruslera,
Fire warned will appear by official report to there great alleged new,	Feu approcher de la grand cité neufve,
Moment great flame broken into many pieces cast here and there will leap,	Instant grand flamme esparse sautera,
In regard one will propose of the Robbers to make evidence produced.	Quant on voudra des Normans faire preuve.

Note: French: *app* = (abbv.) *appel* = call; *roucher* = to rush. Originally listed as quatrain number 97 in Centurie VI. Following the ampersand in line one, *forty degree* refers to all of the *ones* at that degree of latitude. New York City (Manhattan) is at 40*46', Boston is at 42*21.5', Washington DC is at 38*53.7' and Somerset, PA is at 40*00.7'. When the capitalized first word, *Five*, is then seen as a range (+/-) from 40 degrees, all of the locations are easily accounted for and two are at 40 degrees (the first and last crashes). The use of grand in line two shows how each word has individual meaning, separate from the flow of words surrounding them. As such, grand is in the masculine case, whereas la, cité (as a noun), and neufve are all in the feminine case. The same occurs in line three, where grand (masc.) is followed by flame (fem.). In both cases, the correct spelling would be grande, which it is not. The word grand has specific meaning that grande does not cover.

There mighty death to city bordering on the sea,	La grande peste de cite maritime,
Neither will stop who killed nor may be revenged:	Ne cessera que mort ne soit vengée:
Of the lawful kindred through value taken judged unto death without crime,	Du juste sang par pris damne sans crime,
From the great lady by reason of seeming other than it is not outraged.	De la grand dame par feincte n'outraigée.

Note: Originally listed as quatrain number 53 in Centurie II. This is telling of non-stop war following September 11, 2001. So many innocent will die for the false reasons of the United States of America.

Chapter 8 - The Day the Earth Stood Still

Him great out-crying without shame hazardous,	*Le grand criart sans honte audacieux,*
Will be elected commander of the army:	*Sera esleu gouuerneur de l'armée:*
There audacity from his full of controversy,	*La hardiesse de son contentieux,*
A bridge dashed in pieces, alleged from terror fallen in a swoon.	*Le pont rompu, cité de peur pasmée.*

Note: Originally listed as quatrain number 81 in Centurie III. This quatrain sounds like post-911, when Bush changed and wrangled to get America into the bombing-invasion of Baghdad-Iraq. Still, the presence of *audacieux* in line one makes it have a capabilitiy of telling about Barack Obama, whose book that was promoted throughout his presidential campaign is titled *The Audacity of Hope*. The word *hardiesse* then also translates as *audacity*.

Chapter 9

United We Stand

A Declaration of War Against Ghosts

When there litter from the whirlpool shed forth,	Quand la lictiere du tourbillon versée,
Also will be figures with their own covering secret ones:	Et seront faces de leurs manteaux couvers:
The republic for inhabitants of a country new ones vexed,	La republique par gens nouveaux vexée,
In that time whites & reds will be dooming with the upside down.	Lors blancs & rouges jugeront à l'envers.

Note: Originally listed as quatrain number 3 in Centurie I. The word *lictiere* meant "litter," particularly of horses, but also the dung of horses ("old dung"), or manure. The word *tourbillon* was specifically used to indicate a whirlpool in water, as opposed to a whirlwind of air. The translation of *republic* to *commonwealth* has to be understood as being from an early 17th Century perspective. Certainly it can stand for a *republic*, like the one in France, or the one for which we stand in the USA; but, it can *likewise* represent a communist nation, such as the former Soviet Republic.

The head man of London by reason of government the spirit-rich	Le chef de Londres par regne l'americh
The isle of Scotland will tempt by reason of the frozen,	L'Isle d'Escosse temptera par gellée,
King Rebellious. will be having one so false antichrist,	Roy Reb. auront un si faulx antechrist,
Who them will thrust into everyone inwardly there mixture.	Que les mettra tretous dans la meslée.

Note: French: *ame* = soul, spirit; *riche* = rich, wealthy, opulent. Latin: *tempto* = to prove, test by attack; *ante* = before + *Christus* = Christ. Originally listed as quatrain number 66 in Centurie X. Certainly, the word *americh* could easily be a way of indicating "America," as the New World had already been discovered and named by 1555. Since those early times, America has been promoted as the land of dreams, for those filled with the *spirit* to become *rich*. The word *antechrist* is French for "antichrist," but they spell it with the "before" prefix.

Chapter 9 - United We Stand

The Revenge in Afghanistan

From the realms vassals under to there Balance,	*Des regions subjectes à la Balance,*
Will be acting to disturb them mountain ones through substantial warfare	*Feront troubler les monts par grande guerre*
Lost liberty ones all sex one's own & everything state of two,	*Captifz tout sexe deu & tout bisance,*
Which one will shout at the dawning land with region.	*Qu'on criera à l'aube terre à terre.*

Note: Originally listed as quatrain number 70 in Centurie V. The word *Balance* is astrological, meaning the sign of Libra. Libra is the rising sign of the United States of America's birth chart, and thus the face it wears to the world – as a nation being fair and balanced.

This one who will occupy there accusation of to ruin,	*Celui qu'aura la charge de destruire,*
Temples, & factions, changed ones through opinion:	*Temples, & sectes, changés par fantasie:*
More at the rocky ones who to the living ones will grow to hurt,	*Plus aux rochiers qu'aux vivans viendra nuire,*
Of speech finely set forth to those attention gotten ones filled ones.	*Par langue ornée d'oreilles ressaisies.*

Note: Originally listed as quatrain number 96 in Centurie I. If the occupation is seen as Afghanistan, with the Temples being those ancient Hindu shrines destroyed by the Taliban sect, that destruction would be only to rocks. That makes the statement, who to the living ones will grow to hurt, meaning the harm to human life, to those who occupy. The Language finely set forth then is representative of political talk, where nothing of real meaning is actually said. That would be the continued speeches about why forces should stay as occupiers.

Over them battle from the horses speedy ones,	*Sur le combat des chevaulx legiers,*
One will proclaim him great increasing upset:	*On criera le grand croissant confond:*
With darkness to rush mountains, garments of shepherds,	*De nuict ruer monts, habits de bergiers,*
Abysses red ones inwardly a tunnel about a camp secret.	*Abismes rouges dans le fossé profond.*

Note: Originally listed as quatrain number 7 in Centurie VII. Line one appears to be indicating that

The Epic Poem Prophesied by Nostradamus

a major event *Before* is one recounting a *battle* of calvary. It must be realized that modern calvary consists of tanks and helicopters, rather than fast horses. The word *croissant* can be translated several ways, with each appropriate. If is the present participle of "to cross," being *crossing*; but, it can also state "crescent" or "moon shape", indicating Islam. It also means, separately, "growing, increasing, waxing bigger and bigger."

After battle to the wounded the graceful speaking,	*Apres conflit du lesé l'eloquence,*
For few of time themselves woven caused peace:	*Par peu de temps se tramme faint repos:*
Point of the matter the one not admitted them, great ones in setting at liberty,	*Point l'on n'admet les, grands à delivrance,*
With the enemies are restored with purpose.	*Des ennemis sont remis à propos.*

Note: Originally listed as quatrain number 80 in Centurie II.

Wanted Dead or Alive

From the mountain Royal will be born to one home-born,	*Du mont Royal naistra d'une casane,*
That which cave & reckoning will come to play the tyrant,	*Qui cave, & compte viendra tyranniser,*
To raise troops with there marching of soldiers the year millennium,	*Dresser copie de la marche Millane,*
Favorable ones, Fleur-de-lis of gold & nations to consume.	*Favene, Florence d'or & gents expuiser.*

Note: Latin: *casa* = cottage, hut, cabin; *copia* = [mil] troops, forces; *faveo* = to favor / *florens* = flourishing. Originally listed as quatrain number 32 in Centurie VII. The emblem of Bosnian Muslims (Bosniacs) is a gold fleur-de-lis. The French also have gold fleur-de-lis on their coat of arms. However, the Florence coat of arms has a red fleur-de-lis on it.

Him great pilot by reason of Head man of a party will be directed,	*Le grand pilot par Roy sera mandé,*
To set aside there rank for more honorable calling to attain unto:	*Laisser la classe pour plus haut lieu attaindre:*
September years after will be banded-against,	*Sept ans apres sera contrebandé,*
Barbarous furnished with arms will come Venice to fear.	*Barbare armée viendra Venise caindre.*

Chapter 9 - United We Stand

Note: Originally listed as quatrain number 75 in Centurie VI. The word *caindre* is translated as *craindre*, meaning *to fear*. As "*ceindre*" it means, "wrap around." This is a perfect breakdown of the growth of Osama bin Laden, as first a CIA operative in Afghanistan against the Soviets, and then to him setting aside that honor to become a Muslim "Musab". September is the date he will forever be known for (911), which was the final blow that caused the West to band together against him. The use of Venise, in line four, which is a clean French spelling for Venice, Italy, has double meaning, although the primary meaning comes from the anagram, *se-Veni*. Being "wrapped around" is aligned with the quatrains that tell of the 3-pronged invasion of Italy, where one point is near Venice.

In that time that the one who with nothing not given place,	*Lors que celuy qu'a nul ne donne lieu,*
To outlaw will desire reckoning embraced, not caught:	*Abandonner vouldra lieu prins, non prins:*
Fire unused before for bled ones, anointed with bitumen in Chariot-place,	*Feu neuf par saignes, bitument à Charlieu,*
Will be in Fifth one Whale ones recovered.	*Seront Quintin Balez reprins.*

Note: Originally listed as quatrain number 29 in Centurie IX. There is a town in Iran named Baliz, which is not far from the border with Afghanistan. *Bitumen* is a pitch from the Dead Sea, in the area historically known as Palestine, which is a natural tar substance. Due to the nature of this quatrain, and the air of Osama bin Laden, bitumen can mean Arab oil. *Charlieu* is a French commune, in the Loire Department, in the northern end of the Rhone-Alps Region. In other words, it is insignificant to the meaning of this quatrain, other than as a general hint of France as a target. It best is read as a manufactured word.

From the bridge Hospitable, & there great Russia,	*Du pont Euxine, & la grand Tartarie,*
One head man of a party will be who will come to oversee there Western Europe:	*Un roy sera qui viendra voir la Gaule:*
Will pierce through Alania & the Armenia,	*Transpercera Alane & l'Armenie,*
Also in Byzantium will leave bleeding Beaten down with a pole.	*Et dedans Bisance lairra sanglante Gaule.*

Note: Greek: *Euxinus* = *Hospitable*. Originally listed as quatrain number 54 in Centurie V. The single word, *Euxine*, is a form of the Latin word "Euxinus," which by itself is an epithet for the Black Sea. This means the lower case *pont* can carry its French translation, as "bridge," making line one be about a bridge at the Black Sea. This could indicate the Bosporus & Dardanelles straits, connecting the Black Sea with the Mediterranean Sea. *Tartary* is an old name for Russia at the Black Sea and NE. Tartary is an old name for Asia, from north of the Caspian Sea, and east to the Pacific Ocean. It was divided into several sections (Mongol Tartary, Cathay Tartary, East Tartary [Manchuria], Turkistan, and Muscovite Tartary [Russia, north of the Black Sea]), but Russian

The Epic Poem Prophesied by Nostradamus

Tartary and Turkistan bordered the Black Sea. That area was referred to as Little Tartary. Armenia is surrounding Mount Ararat, as part of eastern Turkey, but exists as a remnant nation between Iran, Turkey, Georgia, and Azerbaijan. The second use of Gaule has to mean more than simply France, as it covered parts of Belgium, Switzerland, and Germany. In essence, it means Western Europe.

The army lodged with the church of the virgin pure,	*Le camp du temple de la vierge vestale,*
Not removed far away to Gentile nation & mountain ones Pyrenees:	*Non esloigné d'Ethne & monts Pyrenées:*
Him great training east kept secret destructive power there harmful,	*Le grand conduict est caché dens la male,*
North violently sent forth ones flown ones & vines rudely handled ones.	*North. getés fluves & vignes mastinées.*

Note: Latin: *dens = tooth, destructive power, envy, ill-will.* French: *fluvius = flowing water, a stream.* Originally listed as quatrain number 17 in Centurie II.

At what time torch burning from fire inextinguishable,	*Quand lampe ardente de feu inextinguible*
Will be devised at the temple of the Vestal Virgins,	*Sera trouvé au temple des Vestales,*
Child get hold of spirit, emotion going along through hundred in a commune:	*Enfant trouvé feu, eau passant par trible:*
To come to ruin water Nîmes, Toulouse to tumble down them open markets standing on pillars.	*Perir eau Nymes, Tholose cheoir les halles.*

Note: Latin: *tribus = div. of Roman people.* Originally listed as quatrain number 9 in Centurie IX. The main theme statement is about an eternal flame, such as the one that another quatrain stated would go out, referring to the temple of Vesta, and the hearth flame. In Roman mythology all new infants (children) had to be carried around the hearth before they could be accepted into the home. The French city of Nîmes is named for it healing spring, and also a sacred wood, made holy by the spirit Nemausus. This name is said to be from a Celtic tribe that founded the city, prior to the Romans encountering it. In Occitan Toulouse is spelled "Tolosa."

Them five alien ones begun in ones within a temple,	*Les cinq estranges entrés dedans le temple,*
Their race will issue from there region to not hold holy:	*Leur sang viendra la terre prophaner:*

Chapter 9 - United We Stand

In the people of Toulouse will be quite solid copy,	*Aux Thoulousains sera bien dur exemple,*
Of one who will approach one's laws to ruin.	*D'un qui viendra ses loix exterminer.*

Note: Originally listed as quatrain number 45 in Centurie III. Notice how Thoulousains has a "Th" replaced by a "T". The same occure with prophaner, where the "ph" is replaced with an "f". This is a system of phonetics, which is similar to the interchangeability of a "y" and an "i", and an "x" and an "s". The city of Toulouse is in southwestern France, halfway between the Atlantic and the Mediterranean.

Who will have been by reason of potentate of the Eastern Roman Empire,	*Qu'aura esté par prince Bizantin,*
Will be taken away through chief of people of Toulouse.	*Sera tollu par prince de Tholoze.*
There loyalty with Foix by the principal ones of Tolentino	*La foy de Foix par le chef Tholentin*
He will deceive not denouncing the spouse.	*Luy faillira ne refusant l'espouse.*

Note: Originally listed as quatrain number 39 in Centurie VIII. The city of *Toulouse* is in southwestern France. The city Foix lies south of Toulouse, near Andora and Spain, in the Pyrenees. The city of Tolentino is in Italy, east of the Adriatic port of Ancona. Saint Nikolas of Tolentino was known for healing abilities there. The Italian city (Adriatic coast), Tolentino, is historically known to be associated with a treaty forced by Napoleon upon Pope Pius VI, which extremely limited the power of the Roman Catholic Church.

Beneath Work made of rushes to the dangerous strait	*Dessous Jonchere du dangereux passage*
Will act to pass the last born his company of soldiers,	*Fera passer le posthume sa bande,*
The mountain ones buried under the Pyrenees to proceed without its carriage of an army	*Les monts Pyrens passer hors son bagaige*
With Alike-depict will make hostile incursions on owl in encamped.	*De Parpignam courira duc à tende.*

Note: Originally listed as quatrain number 11 in Centurie X. A *Jonc* is a bulrush, which is a marsh reed. Bulrushes are then found in wetland areas, along river deltas. Baby Moses was found among the bulrushes in an Ark of Bulrushes, formed with reeds, slime, and pitch. *Jonchere* is defined as "a place strewn with bullrushes." As an anagram, *Par pingam* becomes a statement in Latin, as "Like seeing paint", "seeing draw", "Match stain", or "Alike depict". It then becomes reminiscent of cave painting found in the Pyrenees, with Perpignan the closest big airport to many of those sites.

The Epic Poem Prophesied by Nostradamus

Him deputy at the threshold of the door,	*Le lieutenant à l'entrée de l'huys,*
Will fell them great of Perpignan,	*Assommera le grand de Parpignan,*
In themselves proposing to secure in Region along the Rhone River,	*En se cuidant saulver à Monpetruis,*
Will be disappointed bastardly from Lusignan.	*Sera deceu bastard de Lusignan.*

Note: Originally listed as quatrain number 24 in Centurie VIII. *Parpignan* can be seen as the southwestern France city of Perpignan. There is no place actually named Monpertuis, although there is a vineyard known as Domaine Monpertuis. That vineyard is part of the Cotes du Rhone grape-growing region, primarily between Marseilles and Avignon, with the Chateauneuf du Pape being where the Domaine Monpertuis is primarily harvested. This is near Orange, France. However, when seen as Mon-pertuis, which is clean French for "My hole" or "My center", it reads as Nostradamus identifying his region of Provénce, and in particular the St. Remy-Salon area. Lusignan is in western France, in the department of Vienne. It is 25 km southwest of Poitiers.

Crescent-shaped hidden in the deep ones obscurity,	*Lune obscurcie aux profondes tenebres,*
Its brother time past from stain rust-colored:	*Son frere passe de couleur ferrugine:*
The great hidden continual under them subterfuges,	*Le grand caché long temps soubz les latebres,*
Will give a little heat unto weapon there coast bloody.	*Tiedera fer dans la plaie sanguine.*

Note: Originally listed as quatrain number 84 in Centurie I. The secondary theme statement identifies the Moon is Arabs, who are the brothers of Jews. A "red heffer" is one born of a white and black parent, and was one designated as to be sacrificed at certain occasions. The color of this is "dun" or "rust-colored", as stated in the Bible's use of Latin, *ferriginis*. The word "dun" is defined as: An almost neutral brownish gray to dull grayish brown.

Near from them she sleeps by sea Tyrrhenian hedged in,	*Proche del duero par mer Tyrrene close,*
Will arrive to pierce them great ones mountain ones Pyrenees	*Viendra percer les grans monts Pyrenees*
There public authority more short & its full of holes exposition,	*La main plus courte & sa percee gloze,*
In Carcassonne will manage one's devices (or led ones).	*A Carcassonne conduira ses menees.*

Note: Originally listed as quatrain number 62 in Centurie III. The Tyrrhenian Sea is along the western coast of Italy, inside the curve created by the three islands: Sicily, Sardinia, and Corsica.

Chapter 9 - United We Stand

Carcassonne is a southwest France commune, near the Mediterranean Sea, in the Department of Aude, in the region known as Languedoc.

Quite close together with the great ones mountain ones Pyrenees,	*Bien contigue des grans monts Pyrenees,*
One in opposition to the eagle great troops to direct:	*Un contre l'aigle grand copie adresser:*
Opened veins, forces driven forth ones,	*Ouvertes veines, forces exterminees,*
Which until in Pau him principal commander will come to pursue.	*Que jusque à Pau le chef viendra chasser.*

Note: Originally listed as quatrain number 70 in Centurie IV.

In around to the mountains Pyrenees great rout	*Autour des monts Pyrenees grand amas*
From people foreign to help head man of a party new:	*De gent estrange secourir roy nouveau:*
Nearby with Garonne to great temple of the Farmhouse,	*Pres de Garonne du grand temple du Mas,*
One Roman general them will fear in the water.	*Un Romain chef le craindra dedans l'eau.*

Note: Originally listed as quatrain number 1 in Centurie VI. Approximately 45 miles (120 kilometers) east of Bordeaux (at the mouth of the Garonne River), is a small commune name Le Mas. It is doubtful the word Mas is referencing that town. However, in Nîmes, France, there is a temple called the Maison Carrée, which translates to "Squared House". Still, Nîmes is near Marseilles, and on the Mediterranean, the opposite direction from the flow of the Garonne.

Chapter 10

Divided We Stand Alone

The Worst Laid Plans of Eagles and Lions

Them two contained ones being united ones likewise,	Les deux contens seront unis ensemble,
Regarding there majority in War will be united:	Quant la pluspart à Mars seront conjonict:
A great from Africa into terrorist & trembling:	Le grand d'Affrique en effrayeur &tremble:
Two-man court for the order divided.	Duumvirat par la classe desjoinct.

Note: Latin: *duumviratus = of commission of two men*. Originally listed as quatrain number 23 in Centurie V. The main theme does not have to infer two who are contained, meaning able to hold their own, although also being restrained, united together. It can simply mean that both of the two are likewise related, as simply as having united be part of their names. Thus, the English and Americans are likewise of the same blood, with one being named the United States, and the other the United Kingdom. A unification of the two contained is not found a certainty in line one.

Him great monarch who will forge band of soldiers,	Le grand monarque que fera compaignie,
With that two head men of parties united ones through concord:	Avecq deux roys unis par amitié:
Alas what a short breath will act there noble family,	O quel souspir fera la grande mesgnie,
Children Narbonne in the round about who pity.	Enfants Narbon à l'entour quel pitie.

Note: Originally listed as quatrain number 99 in Centurie I. In Occitan, Narbonne is spelled Narbona, while the Romans named the town Colonia Narbo Martius (Colony Narbo of Mars).

The deceiver will be thrust into the cave,	Le seducteur sera mis en la fosse,
As well fastened ones until to some opportunity,	Et estachez jusques à quelque temps,

Chapter 10 - Divided We Stand Alone

A cleric together with him chief with his crosier	*Le clerc uni le chef avec sa crosse*
Piercing direct will provoke them restrained ones.	*Pycante droite attraira les contens.*

Note: Latin: *ercisco > hercisio = to divide an inheritance*. Originally listed as quatrain number 95 in Centurie VIII. The word "*crosse*" also meant "a Bishop's staff, which would only be the translation if other preceding words were of religious theme (which they are not). The word *fosse* can meant *grave*, but is clearly a word stating a round hold (not rectangular) and specifically a long hole, like a trench or moat. This appears to lend towards more of a military usage.

The terrible war that upon the west its provided	*L'orrible guerre qu'en l'occident sapreste*
A year succeeding will come there epidemic disease,	*L'an ensuiuant viendra la pestilence,*
So massive abominable that young aged, born beast,	*Si fort horrible que jeune vieulx, ne beste,*
Blood, fire, Mercury, Mars, Jupiter in France.	*Sang, feu, Mercure, Mars, Jupiter en France.*

Note: Originally listed as quatrain number 55 in Centurie IX. The word orrible is a correct spelling of "horrible", in Middle English. This usage is then designed to show where horror will prevail. The alchemical references to planets mean that mercury (Mercure) applied to grain (Mars) silos can be the source of line two's pestilence. Mercury, Mars, and Jupiter will all be in the sign Cancer, when the Sun ends its time in Cancer, before going into Leo, in July 2013. With France's Republic born on July 14, 1789, France is a Cancer Sun sign nation, and on July 14, 2013 Mars will enter Cancer, conjuncting Jupiter in Cancer, while Mercury will be retrograde in Cancer (but not in aspect).

The advisors to the chief private conspiracy,	*Les conseilliers du premier monopole,*
Them conquerors seduced ones in respect of the Land of honey:	*Les conquerants seduits pour la Melite:*
Roamed ones, Brownish considering theirs laying out an end of an axis:	*Rodes, Bisance pour leurs exposant pole,*
World will be necessary them followers of a cause with excuse.	*Terre faudra les poursuivants de fuite.*

Note: Catalan: *Melite = Malta*. Originally listed as quatrain number 49 in Centurie II. The source for the name Malta is Greek, *meli*, meaning "honey." The name Malta represents "the Land of honey." The word "Rodes" is rooted in the French verb "roder," meaning "to roam, wander." Capitalized and with the plural added to the past participle, *rodé*, it becomes synonymous with the Jews. Thus, the Land of honey is the Promised Land.

The Epic Poem Prophesied by Nostradamus

There peace themselves almost arrived at with one quarter, & the contention	La paix sapproche d'un costé, & la guerre
Never not had been there legal proceedings so substantial,	Onques ne feut la poursuite si grande,
To find fault with man, female, lineage guiltless for whole earth	Plaindre homme, femme, sang innocent par terre
As well this will be to France in every bit combined together.	Et ce sera de France à toute bande.

Note: Originally listed as quatrain number 52 in Centurie IX.

The race of the great made ruinous	Le circuit du grand faict ruineux
Them name seventh of the fifth will be:	Le nom septiesme du cinquiesme sera:
To one third more great the foreign warlike.	D'un tiers plus grand l'estrange belliqueux.
Motovun, Lutecia Parisorum (Paris), Aix not will defend.	Monton, Lutece, Aix ne garantira.

Note: Originally listed as quatrain number 88 in Centurie II. *Motovun* is a city atop a high hill (mont) on the coast of Croatia. Its Italian name is *Montona* d'Istria.

Them tormented ones through sin from a single stain,	Les affligez par faulte d'un seul taint,
Countermining with party adverse,	Contreminant, à partie opposite,
To the Bound-together people will send word of that forced on against one's will,	Aux Lygonnois mandera que contraint,
Will be of to make restitution unto them great end of time to Land of honey.	Seront de rendre le grand chef de Molite.

Note: Originally listed as quatrain number 98 in Centurie IX. It becomes tempting to change *Lygonnois* into the name of the people of Lyon, but that name is Lyonnaise. The *–nois* ending has to be seen as a standard indication of "the people of". The use of *Molite* here is similar to the use of *Melite* previously, in quatrain II – 49, but the two words are spelled differently. As an anagram, *Melito*, it retains the meaning of sweetness, as honey.

Chapter 10 - Divided We Stand Alone

Him rule with two left quite little will be sustaining,	Le regne à deux laissé bien peu tiendront,
Three years September month times past will be making there war	Trois ans sept mois passéz feront la guerre
Them two vestal virgins in opposition will be revolting,	Les deux vestales contre rebelleront,
Conqueror then sail to Harmonic land.	Victor puis nay en Armonique terre.

Note: Latin: *armonia* = *harmony*. Originally listed as quatrain number 95 in Centurie IV. Lines one and two seem to be addressing the beginning of the Geo. W. Bush years. Interestingly, the word *laissé*, if broken into "lais se," says, "bush himself." The *Harmonious soil* is another way of saying "Balanced land," which becomes another reference to the land of the Balance. This is the USA astrological chart, with the sign of Libra on the Ascendant.

Those who will be using risked to destroy,	Ceulx qui auront entreprins subvertir,
Peerless government powerful & unconquerable:	Nompareil regne puissant & invincible:
Will be acting by reason of deceit, nights three to warn,	Feront par fraulde, nuicts trois advertir,
In regard of him more great at table will read Bible.	Quant le plus grand à table lira Bible.

Note: Originally listed as quatrain number 83 in Centurie V. The main theme is a good summary of those who attacked America on September 11, 2001, with line two summarizing the mighty status of the USA. With the second line being the country attacked, line four is about the leader of the USA, George W. Bush, who was known as a "reborn'Christian", thus a Bible reader. Line three is then the warning Bush gave to Saddam Hussein, three days before the begin of the second Iraq War.

War Against Iraq

In warned to appear new thinking of in defense of to condemn,	A cité neufve pensif pour condemner,
The bird of prey in the sky them arrives to exhibit:	Loisel de proye au ciel le vient offrir:
After victory with war prisoners to pardon,	Apres victoire à captifs pardonner,
Cremona & Mantoa mighty ones hurtful ones will occupy suffered.	Cremone & Mantoue grans maulx aura souffert

89

The Epic Poem Prophesied by Nostradamus

Note: Originally listed as quatrain number 24 in Centurie I. Line four does not end with any punctuation, per 1555 Lyon copy observed. Both *Cremona* and *Mantua* are in the Lombardy region of northern Italy. The word *crémone* translates as (window) lever. The root meaning for the name of the town Cremona is "the high ground."

Within there city of Fertile turf murderer	*Dans la cité de Fert sod homicide*
Proposition in pleading & acted penalty bull to rant not to smite,	*Fait, & fait multe beuf arant ne macter,*
Returning ones even again ones with the reputations to bear	*Retours encores aux honneurs dartemide*
Both in Vulcan body dead ones to bury.	*Et à Vulcan corps mort sepulturer.*

Note: Originally listed as quatrain number 74 in Centurie IX. Artemide was the Italian name for the Greek goddess Artimis. Artimis is also known as Diana in Latin, being the Moon goddess. Vulcan was the Roman name for the god of fire (Hephaestus in Greek).

There great bound & sect crusader,	*La grande bende & secte crucigere,*
Itself will govern in Iraq:	*Se dressera en Mesopotamie:*
From the neighboring flood band of soldiers fleet,	*Du proche fleuve compaignie legiere,*
Which such like law will repute upon enemy	*Que telle loy tiendra pour ennemie.*

Note: Latin: *tellus* = land, soil, county, world. Originally listed as quatrain number 61 in Centurie III. The word *crucigere* is further defined as: an order of friars who wear crosses on their habits. This represents a Crusader, of the particular kind that thrives on protecting Israel. This places the main focus on the regions that supplied protective forces to send to the Holy Land (i.e.: Christian nations). The secondary theme narrows the place where the mighty bound as Iraq. Line three is then stating the support from Syria and Iran, in the present Iraq War, where the laws, or rules of war make this type of mercenary warfare difficult to uphold law outside of Iraq.

For two faiths honorable, through two times brought to bottom	*Par deux fois hault, par deux fois mis a bas*
The sunrise likewise the sunset will enfeeble	*L'orient aussi l'occident foyblira*
One's enemy following many contentions,	*Son adversaire apres plusieurs combats,*
By sea pursuit, hunted after in the need will err.	*Par mer chasse, chasse au besoing faillira.*

Note: Originally listed as quatrain number 59 in Centurie VIII.

Chapter 10 - Divided We Stand Alone

The young monarch accused falsely,	*Le jeune prince accusé faulsement*
Will place in sedition the army lodged & upon debates:	*Mettra en trouble le camp & en querelles:*
Murdered him general because them supporting,	*Meurtry le chef pour le soustenement:*
Absolute rule to quiet: after to mend ones troubled with the king's evil.	*Sceptre apaiser: puis guerir escroueles.*

Note: Originally listed as quatrain number 10 in Centurie IV.

The great most supreme power each year duty to remain	*Le grand Empire chacun an devoir estre*
One over the others them will come to acquire,	*Un sur les autres le viendra obtenir,*
More scarce with time will be one's dominion & to remain,	*Mais peu de temps sera son regne & estre,*
Two years with the navies themselves will have power to endure.	*Deux ans aux naves se pourra soustenir.*

Note: Originally listed as quatrain number 32 in Centurie X. Line four begins with the capitalized first word Two, which stands alone to identify Two empires, one which was above the other to come. These Two will have years in which they will consecutively have dominion over others; and this will be through both having naval power. These Two are Great Britain and the United States of America.

Wave Goodbye to Saddam

Touching there crow upon whole sum of brick joined,	*Quant la corneille sur tout de brique joincte,*
Continuing September times not will cause that to proclaim:	*Durant sept heures ne fera que crier:*
Death argued to come from kindred standing image of metal stained,	*Mort presagée de sang statue taincte,*
Tyrant murdered, with the God ones people to pray.	*Tyran meurtri, au Dieux peuple prier.*

Note: Originally listed as quatrain number 55 in Centurie IV. The word *brique* also meant anything composed to form a *brick* shape, such as: a plate, leaf or wedge of metal. This could then be applied to the black color of a *crow*, becoming a 16th Century description of a 20th Century Stealth Bomber. In that sense, the *crow* upon everything *brick* would be a heavy bombing raid. Baghdad faced this in the Iraq War of 2003; and the reasoning given for this war was something *Lasting* (from *Durant*), as Saddam Hussein had refused to go along with the sanctions imposed

91

The Epic Poem Prophesied by Nostradamus

following the 1991 Gulf War. *September* became the *times* that made a second Iraq war seem necessary. However, it would later be proclaimed that was not the case. Saddam Hussein was tried in a court by his own people, with his *Death* argued to come. He also had statues erected in his own honor, which became *stained* from his actions. He certainly was a *Tyrant*, who ended up hung without any right to appeal, as his people wanted him out of the way.

Soldier Barbarous the great King to strike,	*Soldat Barbare le grand Roy frapper,*
Wrongfully not sent far away from killed,	*Injustement non esloigné de mort,*
The greedy mother to the deed business will be	*L'avare mere du fait cause sera*
Conspirator & government into great should again have died.	*Conjurateur & regne en grand remort.*

Note: Originally listed as quatrain number 73 in Centurie VIII. The word *remort* is the 3rd past conditional of the Old French verb *remourir*, which is like *re-mourir* (re-to die).

Commander deceit after soon at that time will die, will arrive,	*Mabus puis tost alors mourra, viendra,*
To people & animals without reason a hideous overthrow:	*De gens & bestes une horrible defaite:*
Moreover everything in blow there revenge one will note,	*Puis tout à coup la vengence on verra,*
Fire extinguishing, public legal authority, drought, famine, until will run the comet.	*Cent, main, soif, faim, quand courra la comete.*

Note: Latin: *cento [war]* = coverings to ward off missile or extinguish fires. Originally listed as quatrain number 62 in Centurie II. The word *Mabus* is translated as an anagram, becoming *Musab*. The historic character named *Musab* holds a heroic place in Islamic lore; and, this historic person's actions are a close match to the way Muslims see Osama bin Laden. However, when *Mabus* is seen as *M'abus*, the abbreviation of "M" makes less sense as a reference to Nostradamus, as "Me", or "Myself". It therefore must be seen as the abbreviation Me , rather than Me, which is the standard abbreviation for Maistre (or Maître).

The ignominy stinking detestable,	*L'honnissement puant abhominable,*
Following the feat will be happiness:	*Apres le faict sera felicité:*
Great pretty well avoided, in regard of not being friendly,	*Grand excusé, pour n'estre favorable,*
That in agreement God of the sea not will be incensed.	*Qu'a paix Neptune ne sera incité.*

Chapter 10 - Divided We Stand Alone

Note: Originally listed as quatrain number 90 in Centurie VI. The first line uses two French words that have an "aspirated h", in honnissement and abhominable. This quatrain is an exact fit for the way the world would not dare stand in the way of the United States, after the events of September 11, 2001, due to its immense anger, which went along with its superior naval powers, in particular the "earth quaking" (Neptune) powers of its weaponry.

One's legal public authority last by reason of Liberty ones blood-thirsty,	*Sa main derniere par Alus sanguinaire,*
Not themselves will have power on the sea to support:	*Ne se pourra par la mer guarantir:*
Between two rivers to fear hand military,	*Entre deux fleuves craindre main militaire,*
Him black the wrathful he will cause repentance.	*Le noir l'ireux le fera repentir.*

Note: Originally listed as quatrain number 33 in Centurie VI. The word *Alus* is translated as a form of the word *aleu*. The line three identification of "*Between two rivers*" is reference to the Firtile Crescent of Mesopotamia, now Iraq. This will become the initial focus of the next quatrain's main theme, repeating, "*Between two rivers.*"

Between two rivers themselves will observe closed,	*Entre deux fleuves se verra enserre,*
Barrels & kegs united ones in to hold a course forwards,	*Tonneaux & caques unis à passer outre,*
Eight bridges dashed in pieces ones principal commander with so many pierced with an iron blade,	*Huict pontz rompus chef à tant enferre,*
Children accomplished ones are those ordering into the knife of a plow.	*Enfans parfaictz sont jugurez en coultre.*

Note: Latin: *iugum = yoke*. Originally listed as quatrain number 55 in Centurie VIII. Line two appears to be surrounding an ampersand with two words of the same meaning. A "tun" was basically any barrel that was known to hold wine, or liquids. A *caque* seemed to be for salted meats, but still a barrel. However, when the importance of the ampersand separates the two words, *Barrel ones* brings forth the image of "fish in a barrel" and the *vessels* that follow are the ships that represent the fish, going into the enclosed barrel, passing beside those who will soon take aim. The use of *Enfans*, as a capitalized first word in line four, must be known for its idiom in Old French, which was, "*Enfans perdus*". This was described as meaning, "in war, (ordinarily) gentlemen of companies, reserved for, and exposed unto, all desperate services." In other words, soldiers who are put in the worst positions are nothing more than babes, of the lowest ranks. Thus, *Enfans* means the children who serve in the military as a service, for a job, or because adults told them it was a fine profession.

The Epic Poem Prophesied by Nostradamus

There death quick to the principal personage	*La mort subite du premier personnaige*
Will have transformed & thrust into one another in the government:	*Aura changé & mis un autre au regne:*
Swiftly, long in coming arrived to so eminent & lowest part of an age,	*Tost, tard venu à si haut & bas aage,*
That country & sea will be fitting who the one them to dreaded.	*Que terre & mer faudra que lon le craigne.*

Note: Originally listed as quatrain number 14 in Centurie IV.

The sovereign excellent with pity & mercifulness,	*Le prince rare de pitié & clemence,*
Will come to change through death great familiarity with:	*Viendra changer par mort grand cognoissance:*
For substantial peace a government labored,	*Par grand repos le regne travaillié,*
In that time then the great uddenly will be beaten.	*Lors que le grand tost sera estrillé.*

Note: Originally listed as quatrain number 17 in Centurie VII.

By reason of slanderer false accusation to after born,	*Par detracteur calomnié à puis nay,*
In as much as will be repeating allegations heinous ones & warlike ones:	*Quant istront faictz enormes & martiaulx:*
There lesser party hesitant with the first-born,	*La moindre part dubieuse à l'aisnay,*
Both suddenly at the realm will be thrust into ones unequal ones.	*Et tost au regne seront faictz partiaulx.*

Note: Latin: *dubius = doubtful, hesitating, wavering.* Originally listed as quatrain number 95 in Centurie VI. This sounds strongly like the false accusations of weapons of mass destruction [*martial ones*], aimed at Saddam Hussein by Geo. W. Bush. Hussein (*the inferior party*) was *hesitant* to adhere to the weapons inspectors, with only *partial ones* completed. The *eldest* Bush, who was the president that set the sanctions, combines with his son president, so that *Both* target taking over the *government* of Iraq.

Chapter 10 - Divided We Stand Alone

Him near, son of the mule skinner will come forward in the world,	*Le prochain, fils de l'asnier parviendra,*
As worthy promoted until unto in the government from luck:	*Tant eslevé jusques au regne des fors:*
His rude reputation one everyone there will doubt,	*Son aspre gloire un chascun la craindra,*
More his children of the realm cast ones without.	*Mais ses enfants du regne getés hors.*

Note: Originally listed as quatrain number 11 in Centurie II.

Chapter 11

Not Turning the Other Cheek

Unification Church and the Moon People

Exhibition, Sun-flow, Tarascon of SIXTY DEGREES the arch,	Salon, Mansol, Tarascon de SEX. l'arc,
Where east still standing even yet the pyramid:	Ou est debout encor la piramide:
Will be coming to distribute unto them chief Denmark,	Viendront livrer le prince Dannemarc,
Ability to recover land shamed at the temple of Diana.	Rachat honni au temple d'Artemide.

Note: Originally listed as quatrain number 27 in Centurie IV. In astrological terminology *L'arc* is commonly used to state Sagittarius, the sign of the Archer. The small French town Tarascon gets its name from the defeat of a monster called the Tarasque (amphibian, armadillo-wolf-like prehistoric dinosaur), which terrorized the locals. Christianity (the saint Martha from Palestine) tamed the animal and saved the people in 48 AD.

Istria from mount Big rod to cut asunder & Aventine,	Istra de mont Gaulsier & Aventin,
Which through the gap will warn the army:	Qui par le trou advertira l'armee:
Between two strongholds will be seized the booty,	Entre deux rocz sera prins le butin,
From SIXTY DEGREES sun-flow to deceive there renown.	De SEXT. mansol faillir la renommee.

Note: Originally listed as quatrain number 57 in Centurie V. *Gaul* was actually western Europe, as a Roman name (Gallia), including France, northern Italy, Belgium, Luxembourg and western Germany. *Gaulsier* splits to become *Gaul-sier*, which means: Gaul-to cut asunder; but, the similarity to the word, *gaultier*, meaning "idiot," could also play a role in the translation here. Aventine is the name of one of the Seven Hills of Rome. The all-caps SEX, followed by mansol, is repeated in quatrain IV-27.

Chapter 11 - Not Turning the Other Cheek

There tempest deceiving concealing simplicity,	*La trombe faulse dissimulant folie,*
Will cause Byzantium one altering of rules:	*Fera Bisance un changement de loix:*
Istria with Egypt who desires what the one at liberty	*Hystra d'Egypte qui veult que l'on deslie*
Statute transforming monies & fine metals.	*Edict changeant monnoyes & aloys.*

Note: Originally listed as quatrain number 40 in Centurie I. This quatrain mentions Hystra, which is a "silent H" away from matching quatrain V-57's first word, Istra. Both are the peninsula that juts into the northern Adriatic, surrounded by two gulfs, as part of modern Croatia, near its border with Slovenia, all parts of the former Yugoslavia. This also links Egypt here, to the SEXTILE (60-degrees) arc from the pyramid in quatrain IV-27. Other quatrains will connect to these as well.

At the dawning of the daylight at the second song from the cock,	*Au point du jour au second chant du coq,*
Those from Tunis, to Fez, & with Béjaïa (Algeria):	*Ceulx de Tunes, de Fez, & de Bugie:*
By reason of them Arabs captive the King Morocco,	*Par les Arabes captif le Roy Maroq,*
The year millennium six estimates & September, of Liturgy.	*L'an mil six cens & sept, de Liturgie.*

Note: Originally listed as quatrain number 54 in Centurie VI. The Algerian port city named Béjaïa is called Bougie, or Bugie. It represents the center of the Barbary Coast, which along with Algiers, was a menace to ships on the Mediterranean after the Moors and Berbers were banished from Spain. Line three is accurate for the historical event that occurred in the Moroccan war for independence from the French, between 1953 and 1955. However, the current King of Morocco is Mohammed VI, who took the throne in 1999.

Close to the youthful the ancient in years angel to bow down,	*Auprès du jeune le vieux ange baisser,*
As well them will come to vanquish to the ending	*Et le viendra surmonter à la fin*
Ten years well matched ones with more decrepit to hold under	*Dix ans esgaux au plus vieux rabaisser*
From three two the one the eighth burning angel.	*De trois deux l'un huitiesme seraphin.*

Note: Hebrew: *serapim = fiery serpents*. Originally listed as quatrain number 69 in Centurie VIII. The word "seraphim" is defined as: (Christianity) The first of the nine orders of angels in medieval angelology. These orders include: Seraphim; Cherubim; Thrones; Dominion; Virtues;

The Epic Poem Prophesied by Nostradamus

The Powers; Principalities; and, Archangels. If *three* is the third highest order, The Powers, these were the angles said to be created by God on day *two* of Creation. *The one* leader of The Powers is the Archangel Camael, with Archangels being the *eighth* order of angels. The Powers main purpose is to be on guard against a possible invasion by the legions of Hell to heaven or earth.

At the end of a time to the world a great This-beaten-one will be,	*Au chef du monde le grand Chyren sera,*
More pierced following loved shrieking feared:	*Plus oultre apres aymé criant redoubté:*
His public voice & renown the heavens will surpass,	*Son bruit & loz les cieulx surpassera,*
As well with the singular title victor able to bear much assault fully pleased.	*Et du seul tiltre victeur fort contenté.*

Note: Originally listed as quatrain number 70 in Centurie VI. The above translation is as *C'hier-on*, from the Old French word "*hire, hier,* and *hié*" meaning "rammed, beaten." The prefix chir- , with the variant chiro- has the function of combining form and is Latin for "hand." It is seen in the word chiropractic, which is the practice of healing with the hands. In this usage, *Chyren* becomes Chiren, with the Latin ending –en an abbreviation of –ent, meaning "they shall see" precedes "hand." *Chyren* is an enigma of The Prophecies, as it is repeated. If the "h" is unnecessary (silent), the word "cirer" ("to wax") might be at its root. Still, phonetically, Chiren can sound like Iran.

There beard frizzled & black by engine,	*La barbe crespe & noire par engin,*
Will vanquish then nation fierce & arrogant:	*Subjuguera la gent cruele & fiere:*
Him great THIS BEATEN ONE will deliver from the distance,	*Le grand CHYREN ostera du longin,*
All them lost liberty ones by Selene banner.	*Tous les captifs par Seline baniere.*

Note: Originally listed as quatrain number 79 in Centurie II. In this quatrain and quatrain VI – 70, the use of *CHYREN*, when seen as "ciré (o)n," or (more properly) WAXED ONE, or WAXEN ONE, shows a character of MAJOR proportions in the theme of the end of the world, while being ONE who, "increases gradually in size, number, strength, or intensity," as the definition for the verb form of "wax" means. This makes the title synonymous with a lunar definition, which clearly would fit the likes of Osama bin Laden. Additionally, when the word "waxen" is used as descriptive of bin Laden, this also fits. "Seeming to lack vitality or animation" would be an apt characterization of the stoic look portrayed by bin Laden. Stoic is defined as, "One who is seemingly indifferent to or unaffected by joy, grief, pleasure, or pain," and this easily could also be described as a waxen look.

Chapter 11 - Not Turning the Other Cheek

Through all Asia Minor substantial designing for slaughter,	*Par toute Asie grande proscription,*
Same ones in Mysia, Lycia, & Pamphilia:	*Mesmes en Mysie, Lysie, & Pamphylie:*
Lineage will turn out by reason of abolition of wrongs,	*Sang versera par absolution,*
From one lusty obscure well furnished with offense against rulers.	*D'un jeune noir rempli de felonnie.*

Note: Originally listed as quatrain number 60 in Centurie III. The word *proscription*, as defined from its Latin spelling means: public notice of outlawry. The word *outlawry* is defined as: the act or process of outlawing or the state of having been outlawed; and, defiance of the law. Mysia is in Asia Minor, in northwestern Turkey, on the shores of the Sea of Marmara. Lysia is in Asia Minor, in southwestern Turkey, on the shores of the Gulf of Antalya and the Mediterranean Sea. Pamphillia is just east of Lysia, on the shores of the Gulf of Antalya.

Him great Satyr & Tiger to Caspian,	*Le grand Satyre & Tigre de Hyrcanie,*
Gift presented with those from the Ocean:	*Don presente à ceulx de l'Ocean:*
One principal commander of fleet will venture forth Persian Gulf Iran,	*Un chef de classe istra de Carmanie,*
Who will seize land in the Tyrrhenian Marseille.	*Qui prendra terre au Tyrren Phocean.*

Note: Latin: *Oceanus = father of the Nymphs.* Originally listed as quatrain number 90 in Centurie III. The word *Satyre* has two separate definitions in Old French. One was as a "monster, half man and half goat." The other definition of the word *Satyre* was of an "Invective, or vice-rebuking poem." This is a denunciatory poem, using abusive language. The name *Hyrcania* is the area around the Caspian Sea, in northern Iran and is associated in history to the Persian Empire. The name means, "Land of the Wolves" and the Caspian Sea was previously name the Hyrcanian Sea. *Carmania* was the land now known as Iran and Afghanistan, both fertile and desert.

After stayed in a place will be setting sail in Epirus,	*Apres sejourné vogueront en Epire,*
Him great help will come towards Antioch:	*Le grand secours viendra vers Antioche:*
The dark hair curled will hold strong with the empire,	*Le noir poil crespe tendra fort à l'empire,*
Beard of brass it will hale ruddy at spit.	*Barbe d'ærain le roustira en broche.*

Note: Originally listed as quatrain number 74 in Centurie I. The land known as Epirus now

The Epic Poem Prophesied by Nostradamus

covers western Greece and southern Albania. It bordered on the Adriatic Sea. *Antioch* is an ancient Turkish city, near the Mediterranean coast, on the river Orontes. This river flows through Turkey, south to Syria and Lebanon.

Near to Serbia one in regard of to assault Hungary,	*Près de Sorbin pour assaillir Ongrie,*
The herald from Budapest his will arrive to give intelligence of,	*L'heraut de Bude les viendra advertir,*
Leader Byzantine, the Exhibition of Croatia	*Chef Bisantin, Sallon de Sclavonie*
Has law of Arabs them will approach to transform.	*A loy d'Arabes les viendra convertir.*

Note: Originally listed as quatrain number 62 in Centurie X. The word "Sorbin" is rooted in the German word, "Sorbe," meaning: a member of a Slavic people inhabiting the region of Lusatia in eastern Germany and southwest Poland. This is often mistaken as a possible double translation as Serb. In Latin *Sorbus* is the genus of a family of rose trees and the French word "sorbe" means "sorb fruit" from any of these trees. These trees are known as "service" trees, which can be a connection to the Slavic name meaning "servant" or "slave." Hungary is spelled as *Ongria* in the Occitan language. *Buda* is the ancient name for the western part of the city of Budapest. The word *Sclavonie* is Esclavonia, which was close to Hungary, but part of present-day Croatia, formerly Yugoslavia. Croatia is a "Fancy room" (with Sallon = l'Salon) for Christianity (Byzantine).

Beaten, Vienna, Perished, the state of Scarbantia (ruins)	*Betta, Vienne, Emorie, Sacarbance*
Will be willing to give to the Barbarians parts of Central Europe and the Balkans,	*Voudront livrer aux Barbares Pannone,*
By long spear & fire, enormous violence,	*Par picque & feu, enorme violence,*
Them warned ones uncovered ones by discrete wise woman.	*Les conjurez descouvers par matronne.*

Note: Originally listed as quatrain number 61 in Centurie X. The first word, is a simple anagram, where the vowels are swapped, *Batte* becomes Beaten or Beat you (Bat-te). The capitalization means a very serious beating has occurred. This relates to the manufactured word in quatrain V – 57, Gaulsier, where it is read as Gaule-sier, and Gaule means a "big rod" or "long pole", and Gaulé means "beaten black and blue." This is the biblical, "I will beat you with an iron rod", form of destruction. It could be possible that *Sacarbance* is an anagram for Scarbantia, which was in ancient *Pannonia*, now the city of Sopron, Hungary.

Chapter 11 - Not Turning the Other Cheek

Inwardly Hungary through Bohemia, Navarre,	*Dedans Hongrie par Boheme, Navarre,*
Both for standard devised ones seditions:	*Et par banniere fainctes seditions:*
By flowers of lily country notwithstanding there barred,	*Par fleurs de lys pays pourtant la barre,*
Against Orleans will effect turbulent stirrings.	*Contre Orleans fera esmotions.*

Note: Originally listed as quatrain number 89 in Centurie V. Bohemia is part of what is now the Czech Republic, next to Germany (west), Austria (south) and Moravia, which borders Slovakia. Navarre is the Basque region of Spain on the western slopes of the Pyrenees Mountains, to the Bay of Biscayne, with Pamplona the capital. As an anagram (*Navrera*) would mean, "*Will wound.*" The city of *Orleans* is 80 miles southwest of Paris, in the department of Loiret.

The pretense of the government of Navarre not undoubted	*L'ombre du regne de Navarre non vray*
Will cause there a direct way to heaven from tough lowly born,	*Fera la vie de fort illegitime,*
The observed promised an uncertainty to Cambrai,	*La veu promis incertain de Cambray,*
Chief Orleans will give wall orderly.	*Roy Orleans donra mur legitime.*

Note: Originally listed as quatrain number 45 in Centurie X. The place *Navarre,* as an anagram, would mean, "*Will wound,*" when changed to *Navrera*. The word *Cambray* is clean French for "cambric", finely woven linen, made from cotton. The flax used today comes from Egypt and America. This, however, was not invented until 1593, or after the death of Nostradamus. In this case *Cambray* becomes *Cambrai*, which is the cleanly spelled name of a northern French city, with a history of power over the lowlands of Europe, due to the Bishopric of Cambrai.

Him religious Empire will come upon Germany,	*Le saint Empire viendra en Germanie,*
Arabs will be finding degrees apparent ones,	*Ismaëlites trouveront lieux ouverts,*
To understanding will be wanting even as there Iranian,	*Anes vouldront aussi la Carmanie,*
Them ones in to sustain with country hidden ones.	*Les soustenens de terre tous couverts.*

Note: Originally listed as quatrain number 31 in Centurie X. Carmania is the ancient name for Iran/Afghanistan/Persia, but primarily was the satrapy along the Strait of Hormoz. The Achaemendid Empire is also known as the Persian Empire, which was that of Cyrus the Great. The image of line two is a secondary theme of learning the knowledge of the West, so that Iran will be equal. Line four then furthers this educational purpose as also being to maintain a covert presence in the lands

The Epic Poem Prophesied by Nostradamus

of their enemies.

Persecuted will be to God the Congregation of Christians,	*Persecutee sera de Dieu l'Eglise,*
Both them religious ones temples will be deprived of ones:	*Et les saincts temples seront expoliez:*
The child there by itself will lay naked on smock,	*L'enfant la mere mettra nud en chemise,*
Being Muslims with the Heaven ones re-allied ones.	*Seront Arabes aux Polons raliez.*

Note: Originally listed as quatrain number 73 in Centurie V. In line four the word *Polons* can equally be translated to "Paul ones," as "Pol" had dual uses, as Paul and as pole. Line three seems to be metaphorically stating that the *mother* is the Catholic Church, which reveres Mary like no other. Further, the *infant* is baby Jesus. A *chemise* is a *smock* as well as a "shirt," but a *smock* is defined as a woman's undergarment, which makes line three support the main theme of prosecution, such that for people to see Jesus the Church had to hide its services.

With the Enemy the adversary faith promised:	*A Lennemy lennemy foy promise:*
Bred themselves will keep them servile ones retained ones,	*Ne se tiendra les captifs retenuz,*
Taken stricken down dead & the remainder in smock	*Prins preme mort & le reste en chemise*
Condemned his remnant because direct line of a pedigree endured.	*Damne le reste pour estre soustenus.*

Note: Latin: *premo = to press, press together, strike down.* Originally listed as quatrain number 1 in Centurie X. As the first quatrain of a Centurie, the printer (1566 and 1568 Lyon editions) would make the first letter in a large floral box set, where in this quatrain the first letter, A, is also the first word, thus capitalized. Still, the second letter was always capitalized, even as the beginning of a new word, or the continuation of the word begun by the large block letter. This reaffirms the importance of capitalization to the word in normal text. Thus, in this quatrain, the preposition A is an important direction, with L'ennemy being the most important focus of that direction. The enemy the adversary faith promised means those prophesied to come from the holy word of God. Line three is very reminiscent of the Star of David the German made the Jews wear on their clothes to readily identify themselves as Jewish.

Nephew & blood to the sacred new issued from,	*Nepveu & sang du saint nouveau venu,*
Through him family name kept alive vaults & buried	*Par le surnom soustient arcs & couvert*
Being hunting ones put to death driven away ones uncovered,	*Seront chassez mis à mort chassez nud,*

Chapter 11 - Not Turning the Other Cheek

Upon red & black will be converting their young.	En rouge & noir convertiront leur vert.

Note: Originally listed as quatrain number 30 in Centurie X. Feels like Holy Blood Holy Grail, or the Raider's of the Lost Arc, until it gets to line four. Line four seems like money is being made, but then again, to Nostradamus green was either a color or plant life. Green must relate to the vaults & buried of line two, and the uncovering of line three. Still, red is non-religious, and black is Muslim, and those will be converting.

At his most glorious taken more there desert frankincense,	A son hault pris plus la lerme sabee,
Of human flesh by death in ashes to put:	D'humaine chair par mort en cendre mettre:
Has the island Lighthouse of Alexandria by corsairs disturbed,	A l'isle Pharos par croisars perturbee,
At that time that to Roamed ones will manifest himself solid spirit.	Alors qu'a Rodes paroistra dur espectre.

Note: Originally listed as quatrain number 16 in Centurie V. The word lerme has to be seen as l'erme, meaning la has to be seen as a preposition, and not an article. Old French used the idiom, "terres ermes, which were lands that "lie in waste, desert, untilled." The word sabé is also shown as an idiom, "Haleine sabée," which translated as, "a fragrant sweet-smelling breath," with haleine meaning "breath." Therefore, all translations of l'erme as l'herme are references to land. Also, in Latin, the word "saba" is defined as, "a town in Arabia, famous for perfumes." Arabia is also famous for desert sand. The Bible refers to Saba as Sheba, and it was on the southern peninsula of Arabia. In line three, the island Pharos is referencing Alexandria Egypt, where the Lighthouse of Alexandria, on the peninsula (island), was one of the Seven Wonders of the World. The word spelled croisars is not a French word meaning "Crusaders". It can be seen as implying someone dedicated to the cross, but only on a secondary basis. The spelling Rodes is Catalan for Rhodes, the site of the Colossus of Rhodes, another of the Seven Wonders of the World. Two leaders of Alexander the Great, who took control of the Aegean shipping lanes after his sudden death, commissioned both structures, and they established an alliance between Alexandria and Rhodes. However, the French meaning of Rodes comes from the verb roder, meaning, "to roam, or wander." As a capitalized verb, "Wanderers" equates to the Jews.

Chapter 12

Expanding Terrorism

Homeland Insecurity

From there sixth light glistening sky-born	De la sixiesme claire splendeur celeste
Will come to thunder so strong in there large town borne of fire:	Viendra tonner si fort en la bourgongne:
Moreover will be produced a thing contrary to nature from very-hideous beast,	Puis naistra monstre de tres-hideuse beste,
March, April, May, June great within to divide & cut away.	Mars, Apvril, May, Juin grand charpin & rongne.

Note: Astronomy: *6th heavenly light = Jupiter.* French: *charpi = tossed, pulled out, hackled (as a thick lock of wool).* Originally listed as quatrain number 80 in Centurie I. In astrology, during the times of Nostradamus, there were seven orbs in the heavens: two luminaries, and five planets. Counting the luminaries as numbers one (Sun) and two (Moon), the planets were numbered from Mercury (fastest) to Saturn (slowest), with Saturn being the seventh light. This makes Jupiter number six. This may relate to the two quatrains with abbreviated words in all-caps, SEX. and SEXT., as both could mean SIXIESME. Those both talked of rockets taking off. The word *bourgongne* is read as an anagram, *bourg-n'onge*, where *n'onge* is Old Slavic for "born of fire."

Thunderbolt into Town-without-walls-born-of-fire will make crime monstrous,	Foudre en Bourgongne fera cas portenteux,
That by reason of policy not could to do:	Que par engin ne pourroit faire:
With their senate sexton made crippled,	De leur senat sacriste fait boiteux,
Will act to have insight in the enemies the matter.	Fera scavoir aux ennemis l'affaire.

Note: Originally listed as quatrain number 76 in Centurie II. This presentation of Bourgongne is consistent with the anagram presentation in quatrain I-80, where it became *bourg-n'ogne*. The word *bourg* is defined as "a town without walls." Line three gives an indication that Bourgongne can be any place governed by a senate of citizens, where sacristy represents the places where sacred vessels, records, and furnishings are Christian. Thus, London, New York, Washington, D.C., and

Chapter 12 - Expanding Terrorism

Rome are all possibilities.

Two great ones brothers will be chased ones from Spain,	Deux grans freres seront chassés d'Espaigne,
The eldest put down by reason under them mountains Pyrenees:	L'aisné vaincu soubz les monts Pyrenees:
To grow red sea, rhone, blood theme from Germany	Rougir mer, rosne, sang leman d'Alemaigne
Narbonne, them Béziers, the people of Agde contaminated ones.	Narbon, Blyterre, d'Agath contaminees.

Note: Originally listed as quatrain number 94 in Centurie IV. The two great brothers cannot be the United States and Great Britain, as the British is the father of America. However, the French and the Americans are brothers in having republics, without royalty. In that sense, the first born would be the Americans; but France is the eldest of the two nations. The Catalan translation of the Wikipedia article on Béziers shows the *"en francès"* spelling of the Latin antiquity *Baeterrae*, to be *biterrois*.

The Arabian king to pass mountain ones born of the Pyrenees,	L'Aemation passer montz Pyrennees,
At War Narbonne not will make resistance,	En Mars Narbon ne fera resistance,
By sea & land will act as great directed,	Par mer & terre fera si grand menee,
Captive not holding land sour as continuing.	Cap. n'ayant terre seure pour demeurance.

Note: Mythology: *Emathion = an Arabian king*. Originally listed as quatrain number 64 in Centurie IX. *The Arabian king* is Osama bin Laden. This quatrain includes the abbreviated and capitalized word *Cap.* The spelling of *Pyrennees* matches the letter of Henry II, which is shown as *Pyren-nees*. That means *ones born of the Pyrenees*.

To the port of Agde three foists will be entering	Au port de Agde trois fustes entreront
Carrying the infect not belief in & pestilence	Portant l'infect, non foy & pestilence
Passing along the sea soldier thousands will be stealing,	Passant le pont mil milles embleront,
Also the bridge to dash to pieces in third endeavor against.	Et le pont rompre à tierce resistance.

Note: Originally listed as quatrain number 21 in Centurie VIII. *Agde* is a port city on the Mediterranean Sea, at the Canal du Midi, in the Herault department. The people of Agde are called

The Epic Poem Prophesied by Nostradamus

Agathois, which links this quatrain, and its talk of *l'infect* and pestilence to the abbreviation in quatrain IV – 94 (*L'Agath.*) and its talk of *contaminees*. The use of third in line four is reference to quatrain IV – 94 listing *Narbonne, Béziers, and from Agathois* as where the infections will be dispersed. A *foist* is defined as: a light galley, meaning small ships or large boats. However, the word *fuste* is also used to denote a "cask", and as a past participle verb, "stocked", "branchless" and "ransacked."

Near to Parpan the red ones detained ones,	*Pres de Parpan les rouges detenus,*
Those of the soldier's rank of by reason of to sink ones led ones far away.	*Ceux du millieu parfondrez menez loing.*
Three thrust into fragments & five sick endured ones	*Trois mis en pieces & cinq mal soustenus*
For them landlord & prelate to Town-grease.	*Pour le seigneur & prelat de Bourgoing.*

Note: Originally listed as quatrain number 15 in Centurie IX. There is a commune named *Parpan* in Switzerland. If split, as *Par-pan*, with *pan* French, derived from Latin *pannus*, it could mean, *For rag,* or *By reason of piece of cloth.* It gives the impression of Perpignan. The word *Bourgoing* is split, as *Bourg-oing.*

At the side left in the face of a thing of Glass	*Au costé gauche à l'endroit de Vitry*
Will be watched ones them three red ones to France,	*Seront guettez les trois rouges de France,*
Everything cast into a heavy sleep red, black not bruised,	*Tous assommez rouge, noir non murdry,*
By reason of the Britons revived at assurance.	*Par les Bretons remis en asseurance.*

Note: Originally listed as quatrain number 58 in Centurie IX. Line one, with the capitalization of *Vitry* seen as important *Glass*, begins to sound like one watched from a satellite, as a "looking glass" would be much too large to hold in one's hands. A Latin spelling of "murder" is *murdri*. The commune known as *Vitry* was a Merovingian villa of importance, now in the Pas-de-Calais department, in the northern region bordering Belgium.

Into place openly will enjoy one's tent,	*En lieu libere tendra son pavillon,*
Likewise not will propose upon city ones to embrace dignity:	*Et ne vouldra en citéz prendre place:*
Waters, This acre the island the voice, mount the one Horseman,	*Aix, Carpen l'isle volce, mont Cavaillon,*

Chapter 12 - Expanding Terrorism

Through all its states will deface with his footprint.	Par tous les lieux abolira la trasse.

Note: Latin: *libero = to set free, liberate*. Originally listed as quatrain number 76 in Centurie V. The word *pavillon* can also mean an Admiral's flag on the commanding ship, as well as a tabernacle. The *Volcae* were the "river people" of Celtic Gaul, located west of Provence, in the area where *Aix*, *Carpentras* and *Cavillion* are located. The French town of Cavaillon is not far from Aix-en-Provence. All places can be read based on the meaning behind the names. The word "*aix*" refers to natural springs or a water source. The word *Carpen* can be seen as *C'arpent*, or *This acre*. The lower-case word, "*volce*," can be seen as an anagram, "*l'voce*," with voce derived from Latin, *vox* – voice. The word *Cavaillon* can be seen as *l'on Cavalier*, or *the one Horseman*. Still, as *il l'on Cava* (from the verb *caver*), it identifies, "he the one Will cave."

Albi & Castres will be forging new league,	Albi & Castres feront nouvelle ligue,
Nine people of Arrien Lisbon & Portuguese,	Neuf Arriens Lisbon & Portugues,
Carcassonne, Toulouse will be destroying their underhanded laboring for office	Carcas, Tholosse consumeront leur brigue
In regard of capital strange thing bred contrary to nature to Lauragaise.	Quant chief neuf monstre istra de Lauragues.

Note: Originally listed as quatrain number 5 in Centurie X. The word *neuf* equally means *nine* and "new." The word *Arriens* could be from the word arriere, meaning ones fallen behind, or ones far from. The place *Lauraguez* is listed as a part of Languedoc, which is the province containing the communes listed in this quatrain (Albi, Castres, Arrien, Carcassonne, and Toulouse).

Wine tart there table upon will be largely extended,	Vin sur la table en sera espandu,
Him third part not will contain this one that it would intend:	Le tiers n'aura celle qu'il pretendoit:
Two time of the black to Parma brought down,	Deux fois du noir de Parme descendu,
Perugia to Pisa will be this that it would think.	Perouse à Pize sera ce qu'il cuidoit.

Note: Originally listed as quatrain number 5 in Centurie VII. In France 40% of the wines produced for market fall into a category known as "*vin de table*" or "*vin de pays*." These are known in English as "table wines." They are below the category of "quality wines" and the table wines are restricted from having sugar added to increase the alcohol content during fermentation. The word *pizé* shows in the Cotsgrave 1611 dictionary, defined as, "*whence; murailles de pizé, earthen walls.*" The word "*muraille*" means "a rampier, a wall," leaving *pizé* to translate as *earthen*. The use of *third*, and the possibility of *Wine* being laced with something intended to harm, connects this quatrain to quatrain IV-94 and VIII-21, where contaminants and infectious elements will be presented in France.

The Epic Poem Prophesied by Nostradamus

The great to swarm themselves will advance bees,	Lou grand eyssame se levera d'abelhos,
That not known gift you one seated to avengers:	Que non sauran don te siegen venguddos:
From back of the neck laid in ambush, them row beneath there trails,	Denuech l'embousque, lou gach dessous las treilhos
City to drag along five targets not bare.	Ciutad trahido per cinq lengos non nudos.

Note: Originally listed as quatrain number 26 in Centurie IV. This language is possibly Provençal French, but at times it seems closer to Portuguese and Spanish, so it may be Occitan or Catalan. It appears to be clearly about a surprise attack in the water. The bees of line one would be aircraft from an aircraft carrier. The back of the neck becomes the word neck is defined as, "A relatively narrow elongation, projection, or connecting part." In nautical terms, a neck would be a "strait", or the "bottleneck" where two larger bodies of water come together. Line four is them a celebratory exercise, where the defeated is paraded so that all may see. We have seen this happen in Iraq, particularly when the Blackwater "contractors" were drug through the streets.

By not Lamb to circle town open,	Par Arnani tholoser ville franque,
Bound together innumerable one him mountain Adriatic,	Bande infinie par le mont Adrian,
Transported over river, Dived by bridge there hiding hole	Passe riviere, Hurin par pont la planque
Bayonne an entry every Two hours crying.	Bayonne entrer tous Bihoro criant.

Note: Latin: *Hadria = the Adriatic Sea.* Originally listed as quatrain number 86 in Centurie VIII. The word Arnani is seen as Latin, "Arna-ni." Bihora is Spanish for "two hours." There is a county of Romania named Bihor, and Old French named a heron *bihoreau*.

The buried will come forth from the grave,	L'ensevely sortira du tombeau,
Will make with chains to unite them sturdy to the bridge:	Fera de chaines lier le fort du pont:
Poisoned with roe of barbel,	Empoysonné avec oeufz de barbeau,
Great to Lorraine by reason of the Marquis with the Sea.	Grand de Lorraine par le Marquis du Pont.

Note: Originally listed as quatrain number 24 in Centurie VII. The word *barbeau* was specifically defined (as "sea barbel [catfish]") to be a term of Bourdeaux France. An alternate translation of *barbeau* is "little beard," but this does not seem to match the words before it, *egg* or *Poisoned*. The main theme clearly says The buried will come forth from the grave, but this does not mean bones will get up and walk around. The capitalization of The connects importance to someone or

Chapter 12 - Expanding Terrorism

something that was buried. An earthquake, or other form of earth disturbance (even heavy rains and floods), will have the same effect. Still, line three assists in this determination by stating the dead were poisoned by caviar. To know that the dead might have to be exhumed, for the purpose of an autopsy. Some black caviar comes from "barbel sturgeon."

Stake, Verona, Vicenza, Bound fast-devoured,	*Pau, Verone, Vicence, Sarragousse,*
From lances far ones soil ones themselves lineage waterish ones:	*De glaisves loings terroirs se sang humides:*
Plague so substantial will grow with there great shell,	*Peste si grande viendra à la grand gousse,*
Neighboring ones assistance, & a long way off the medicines.	*Proches secours, & bien loing les remedes.*

Note: Originally listed as quatrain number 75 in Centurie III. *Sarragousse* is a misspelling and not Saragossa, Spain. The Old French verb *sarrer* is the same as the modern French verb *"serer"*, of which the passé simple 3rd person form is *"serra"*. This then reverts to *sarra*, meaning, "closed, compacted, etc." By seeing the capitalization of an Old French word meaning *Stake (Pau)*, it is possible to see how two side-by-side provinces could be "staked" as "off limits", due to a plague.

Rankness substantial will come forth from Lausanne,	*Puanteur grande sortira de Lausanne,*
That one not will understand the beginning to the act,	*Qu'on ne saura l'origine du fait,*
The one will set without everything there inhabitants far distant,	*L'on mettra hors tout la gent lointaine,*
Light seen in the sky, people alien defeated.	*Feu veu au ciel, peuple estranger desfait.*

Note: Originally listed as quatrain number 10 in Centurie VIII. The city of *Lusanne* is in the French-speaking part of Switzerland, on the shore of Lake Geneva, 50 km northeast of Geneva.

Geneva & Langres by those of Castrated ones & the Deceit,	*Geneve & Langres par ceux de Chartres & Dolle,*
Likewise for Grenoble captive at the Montelimar:	*Et par Grenoble captif au Montlimard:*
Wheat, There-sound of cunning wrought,	*Seysset, Losanne par fraudulente dole,*
Them will be dealing treacherously with for gold sixty mark.	*Les trahiront par or soyxante marc.*

Note: Originally listed as quatrain number 42 in Centurie IV. In line one Geneve and Langres are properly spelled cities: one in Switzerland and one in northeastern France. The spelling of *Chatres*,

The Epic Poem Prophesied by Nostradamus

implies Châtres, which is not the same as Chartres. There are four communes in France that go by Châtres, with two others that include Châtres in the name, in six different departments. Châtres in Aube is closest to Langres and Geneva. The word "*chatre*" is from the Latin "*castro*" and Old French "*chastrer*," meaning "to castrate." This makes *Chatre-s* become "*Castrated ones*." Since the commune Dôle is not spelled *Dolle*, it becomes an anagram for "*le Dol*," with "*dol*" meaning, "deceit, fraud, guile, craft, trumpery, treachery, falsehood, and wiliness." There is a commune named Montelimar, south of Lyon, where the Roubion River joins the Rhone. It is, however, misspelled, with no "d" at the end, "nor an "e" after "mont". *Losanne* becomes *La sonne*, "There sound." There was an Old French word, spelled *seissete*, which meant, "a pale red wheat," one that is known to be grown in the Languedoc region of southern France.

Them worthy of silver from Diana & Mercury	*Le tant d'argent de Diane & Mercure*
The images in the lake will be devised ones,	*Les simulacres au lac seront trouvez,*
Him potter seeking clammy earth fresh,	*Le figulier cherchant argille neufve,*
It & them his own from gold being shortened ones.	*Luy & les siens d'or seront abbrevez.*

Note: Latin: *figulus = worker in clay, potter.* Originally listed as quatrain number 12 in Centurie IX. In Old French the word "diane" is defined as meaning (in the phrase "a la diane) in the morning. Still, the reference leading to the capitalized names surrounding the ampersand in line one is to silver. One is the alchemical relation of silver to the Moon (Diana), with the other being the alchemical Quicksilver relating to Mercury. The capitalization of Mercury means the liquid state, as a poisonous metal, is the final focus. The silver from Diana means the money, or blessed wealth, allowing one to buy large pools of Mercury. Mercury compounds have uses in photography, where images and pictures connects to this use.

Nearby with Black, & neighboring to white wool,	*Pres de Rion, & proche à blanche laine,*
Aries, Taurus, Cancer, Leo, the Virgin:	*Aries, Taurus, Cancer, Leo, la Vierge:*
War, Justice, the Ground will burn great plain,	*Mars, Jupiter, le Sol ardera grant plaine,*
Spear & warned to appear ones, decrees conveyed away ones in largest church ceremonial candle.	*Boys & citez, lettres cachez au cierge.*

Note: Originally listed as quatrain number 35 in Centurie VI. I can find no evidence that the constellation named Orion was ever termed Rion. It is, however, a perfect anagram for Noir, and a balance for the presence of blanche in the line. When black and white are seen leading to wool, it brings to mind sheep. It is then important to realize the description of Jesus in The Revelation, where John said his hair was white, like white wool. Still, when laine (wool) is seen as breaking sown into l'haine, where the "h" is "silent", or in the case of the word "ain", was instructed to seek "haim", it becomes the "hatred" that exists between Jews and Muslims and Christians. Line one

Chapter 12 - Expanding Terrorism

places focus on all three groups, who come near in the Middle East. Also note that the French way of writing "Virgo" (la Vierge) actually translates to "the Virgin," which can very easily then not refer to an astrological sign, but to the Virgin Mary. The use of great means (primarily) the USA, thus a great plain is identifying "middle America".

Value there meat of animals cud chewing	*Soulz la pasture d'animaux ruminant*
Through them conduits to the brain ventricles grass covered in polish	*Par eux conduicts au ventre helbipolique*
Soldiers kept secret ones provided with weapons public voice directing,	*Soldats cachez let armes bruit menant,*
Not long distance off tested by attack ones from city Opposite-pole-like.	*Non long temptez de cite Antipolique.*

Note: Originally listed as quatrain number 13 in Centurie X. When ventre is seen as coming from Latin, such that brain ventricles are a possibility, this makes the secondary theme be close to "mad cow" disease. With line four ending by stating, "city Antipolic", it becomes easy to find the French city near Nice, named Antibes, as a potential city, as it was named "Antipolis". Still, the French ending, -ique, means it would have to be something "like" Antipolis. That makes it better as simple a city, where a sneak attack by that city's own government would seem to be one coming from the opposite pole ones.

From Nîmes, to Arles, & As if to come to set at nothing	*De Nysmes, d'Arles & Vienne contemner*
Not yielded unto with submission everything in the edict this Westerner:	*N'obey a ledit Hespericque:*
To the industrious considering them great to overthrow in judgment,	*Aux labouriez pour le grand condamner,*
Six discharged from ones in apparel this burning (celestial).	*Six eschappez en habit seraphicque.*

Note: Originally listed as quatrain number 94 in Centurie X. There are multiple places named Vienne, or have Vienne in their names, in France, with the closest to Nîmes and Arles being Vienne, Isère, near Lyon. This makes the present subjunctive form of "venir" the primary focus, as it is vienne. Another possibility then become the important Austrian city, Vienna, which is spelled Vienne in French.

The Epic Poem Prophesied by Nostradamus

Garden to the large numbers of people compared with city strange,	Jardin du monde aupres de cité neufve,
Inwardly a passage of the mountain ones excavated ones	Dans le chemin des montagnes cavées
Will be possessed of & thrust far in to there Tank,	Sera saisi & plonge dans la Cuve,
Venting an ill savor by operation waters sulfur empoisoned ones.	Beuvant par force aux soulfre envenimées.

Note: Latin: *cavea* = *a hollow place, cavity*. Originally listed as quatrain number 49 in Centurie X. It is hard not to see "*city new*" as anything other than New York City. The word *Beuvant* is derived as *Drinking* due to the word "*beuvailler*," meaning "to drink excessively," as referencing alcoholic consumption. The word can be seen as a manufactured word, which captures this excessive drinking, as *Beu-vant(er)*. This translates as "Drunk-boast." The word *soulfre* meant "brimstone" as well as *sulfur*.

Good Lord what most ugly & sinister torment,	O quel horrible & malheureux tourment,
Three innocent ones who one will come with to yield over:	Trois innocens qu'on viendra à livrer:
Poison mistrusted, damage defending treason,	Poyson suspecte, mal gardé tradiment,
Placed into horror by reason of executioners made to be drunk ones.	Mis en horreur par bourreaux enyvrés.

Note: Originally listed as quatrain number 68 in Centurie I.

Chapter 13

Mediterranean Woes

Eroding the Edges

September year ones will be Philippine. luck thriving,	*Sept ans sera Philip. fortune prospere,*
Will pull down with the Arabs the doing,	*Rabaissera des Arabes l'effaict,*
Moreover one's noon entangled wayward business	*Puis son midy perplex rebors affaire*
Themselves a stake in play onion will engulf its mighty.	*Jeusne ognyon abysmera son fort.*

Note: Originally listed as quatrain number 89 in Centurie IX. The Old French word *Philippine* is defined as: an edict whereby Philip the Fair assumed to himself the absolute bestowing and disposal of Royal Benefices [land grants]. Philip the Fair was Philip IV of France, who made edicts against the Jews (banishment) and Catholic Church (the captive papacy at Avignon), as well as a seven year period (1306 – 1314) which ended with the last Grand Master of the Templars being burned at the stake in Paris. Philip himself also died in 1314. All of his edicts were designed to establish strict financial controls for the Kingdom of France, to strengthen its wealth. The ancient Greek settlement, to which Paul wrote letters to the early Christian church there, was Philippi, making the people there *Philippians*. The word "*en-jue*" is listed, while being an idiom, as meaning, "a stake in play." This obviously means a stake being gambled. This relates to *prospere*, where it relates to chance and luck. An *onion* is a metaphor for something wrapped in many layers, which have to be removed to tell if there is a sweet heart or a rotten core.

This one who in Sparta Lame not is able to rule,	*Celuy qo'en Sparte Claude ne peut regner,*
He will cause so much by reason of manner deceptive:	*Il fera tant par voye seductive:*
That to the short, out-stretched, them will act to spin a web,	*Que du court, long, le fera araigner,*
Who against Chief will forge his perspective.	*Que contre Roy fera sa perspective.*

Note: Latin: *claudo = to close, shut up, make inaccessible*. Originally listed as quatrain number 84 in Centurie VI. The reference to *Sparta* here seems to match the story of Lycurges told in the Letter to Henry II. Claudius of Rome was afflicted with some kind of disability, which may be the source of his being called Claudius. However, Plutarch wrote of Agesilaus – the lame king of

The Epic Poem Prophesied by Nostradamus

Sparta, who broke Lycurgus' rule to never fight the same enemy too often. Diopithes, a Spartan prophet of sorts, remembered an oracle saying, "if the Spartans ever made a lame man king, they would experience many unexpected troubles and storms of war."

From the (Gulf of) Ambracia & to the region of Thrace,	De l'Ambraxie & du pays de Thrace,
People of sea hurt & relief French,	Peuple par mer mal & secours Gaulois,
Continual in Provence there footprint	Perpetuelle en Provence la trace
With traces with their order & liberties.	Avec vestiges de leur coustume & loix.

Note: Originally listed as quatrain number 75 in Centurie IX. French: *Ambracie* = Ambracia, the ancient city in Greece and the Gulf off its shores. This city and gulf are now known as Arta. It was founded by the mythological king *Ambrax*. This appears to be the original settlement of coastal *Provence* by the Greeks. The line from *the Gulf of Arta to the region of Trace*, would cut through the northern half of the mainland of Greece. Ambracia was aligned with Corinth. The French of the southeast will send them assistance after a natural disaster.

With darkness traveling along a chief nearby to one Corridor-born,	De nuict passant le roy pres d'une Andronne,
This one to those of Cyprus & principal spy:	Celuy de Cipres & principal guette:
Him head man of a party failed the public authority fled from Rose-born,	Le roy failli la main fuict long du Rosne,
Them conspired against ones they will be journeying with death to place.	Les conjurés l'iront à mort mettre.

Note: Latin: *Andron* = *Corridor*. Originally listed as quatrain number 17 in Centurie V. In Greek, an Andron was a room in a house specific for males to gather, with couches, where wine and food would be served. There is a forest in southwest France named *Andronne*. This does not seem to be the focus of the main theme.

At this time there will be deceived Cyprus ones,	En ce temps la sera frustré Cypres,
With its assistance, from those of sea Aegean:	De son secours, de ceulx de mer Egée:
Aged in years destroyed ones, more for virile ones & delivered ones	Vieux trucidés, mais par masles & lyphres
Deceived their chief, chief's wife more abused.	Seduict leur roy, royne plus outragée.

Chapter 13 - Mediterranian Woes

Note: Latin: *trucido* = *to slaughter, massacre, destroy.* Phonetics: *ph* = *v* ; *livre* = *delivered.* Originally listed as quatrain number 89 in Centurie III.

Through fire & weapons not big distance away to there sea-black,	*Par feu & armes non loing de la marnegro,*
Will spring from Persia of a vessel to take by force Trabzon:	*Viendra de Perse occuper Trebisonde:*
To quake Fatal ones Mytilene, Land lively tempo,	*Trembler Phatos Methelin, Sol alegro,*
With lineage Arabian of Adriatic hidden wave.	*De sang Arabe d'Adrie couvert onde.*

Note: Latin: *fato* = *fate, fatal; adria* > *Hadria* = *Adriatic Sea.* Originally listed as quatrain number 27 in Centurie V. In Spanish, "*mar Negro*" means the Black Sea. In Latin the Black Sea was not known as such, since that particular name cannot be dated earlier than the 13th Century. Ancient Greeks and Romans simply called it "*the Sea*" (pontos), but then began calling it "inhospitable sea," or "*Pontos Axeinos,*" due to the difficulties navigating it and the shores being filled with savage tribes. Once settled this mutated to the "Hospitable Sea," but the Persian-Iranian word, "*Axsania,*" meaning "*dark*" began its translation as the Black Sea. Since there is a lack of capitalization, marnegro carries the "color" black, which represents Islam. As a form of Latin *mare-nigro*, or the Spanish *mar-negro*, one is able to see a "sea of Muslims." In French, the word *negre* meant, "a negro, Moor." A "*Moor*" is a Muslim evicted from Spain, living along the North African coast. *Mytilene* is an island off the coast of Turkey, in the Aegean Sea. Due to the severe misspelling, it could be an anagram from Greek, "*n'Thelemi,*" meaning, "not Philosophy of will." The use of *Perse* can mean both Persia and the United Nations Security Forces, whose helmets are Sky-blue colored. *Trebizonde* is a Turkish city on the Black Sea. The word *Phatos* must be seen phontically as *Fatos*. In Greek, Pathos is one of three modes of persuasion in rhetoric, which go along with Ethos and Logos.

There company of soldiers forceless the little hill will possess	*La bande foible la tertre occupera*
Those with the importance rank will be making horrible exclamations,	*Ceux du hault lieu feront horrible crys,*
The big flock of kindred wedge will trouble,	*Le gros troupeau d'estre coin troublera,*
Tumbled down nearby 500th rebel unearthed ones them crying out ones.	*Tombe prés D. nebro descouvers les escris.*

Note: Hebrew-Greek: *Nebro* = *rebel, the name of an angel from the underworld.* Originally listed as quatrain number 56 in Centurie VIII. In line four a capitalized *D* is written, followed by a period, making it an abbreviation, especially since the following word is not capitalized. Interestingly, *D.* is an acceptable abbreviation (in English) for "Died"; it may not be so typical for Latin, although "decido" means: to fall down, to fall dead, die. However, the Roman numeral "*D*" represents 500, and numerals were followed by period marks, usually denoting "th."

The Epic Poem Prophesied by Nostradamus

A mighty Arabian will march quite deeply in,	*Le grand Arabe marchera bien avant,*
Treacherously dealt with will be on them people of Byzantium:	*Trahy sera par les Bisantinois:*
The ancient Wandered ones he will come to the owing,	*L'antique Rodes luy viendra au devant,*
As well more substantial disease through southern wind people of the Balkans.	*Et plus grand mal par austre Pannonois.*

Note: Catalan: *Rodes = Rhodes.* French: *Rodé-s = Wandered ones (Jews).* Originally listed as quatrain number 47 in Centurie V. The Ladino language is said to be a mix of Romantic languages: Castilian (Spanish), Hebrew, Turkish, some French and Greek, as a variant of Latin. Speakers today are now almost exclusively Sephardic Jews (originating from Iberia – Port./Spain). In Old French the verb *"roder"*, meaning: to roam, wander, rogue abroad, would make *Rodes* translate as (in line three context) *The ancient Wanderers*, which could indicate the Hebrews. Rhodes has a history of Jews in its populace.

Far from his land King will lose the battle,	*Loing de sa terre Roy perdra la bataille,*
Nimble evaded pursued follower seized	*Prompt eschappé poursuivy suivant prins*
Ignorant taken beneath there gilded stitch,	*Ignare prins soubz la doree maille,*
Under devised clothes & the enemy beguiled.	*Soubz fainct habit & l'ennemy surprins.*

Note: Originally listed as quatrain number 14 in Centurie VI. Because the main theme statement says the defeated will be far from home, this reads like attacks on land-based military personnel, following the surprise naval attacks in the Persian Gulf. Lines three and four seem to be telling of modern body armor worn by the military in Iraq and Afghanistan.

The more mighty ship out of from the port of Zadar,	*Le plus grand voile hors du port de Zara,*
Nearby to Byzantium will make its usurping,	*Pres de Bisance fera son entreprinse,*
With enemy ruin & the friend not will be	*D'ennemi perte & l'ami ne sera*
A third at two will cause great robbed & taken.	*Le tiers à deux fera grand pille & prinse.*

Note: Originally listed as quatrain number 83 in Centurie VIII. Zadar is located in the Dalmatian portion of Croatia, which is a part of the former Yugoslavia and a port city on the northeastern coast

Chapter 13 - Mediterranian Woes

of the Adriatic Sea.

The Wandering people will be begging relief,	*Les Rodiens demanderont secours,*
By reason of the angle of its heirs given over.	*Par le neglet de ses hoyrs delaissée.*
The empire Arabian will be restored one's course	*L'empire Arabe revalera son cours*
Through Western Land ones there cause recovered.	*Par Hesperies la cause redressée.*

Note: Latin: *revalesco* = *to be well again*. Originally listed as quatrain number 39 in Centurie IV. The word *neglet* is not French, as the word *negliger* is French for "to neglect." Since one does not have the right to simply add letters, without some language making that act excusable, *neglet* becomes apt for being seen as a simple anagram. The letters *neglet* become *englet*, which is the same as *anglet*, meaning, "an angle or corner."

Hanging that general commander, chief, wife to head man of a party will usurp,	*Pendant que duc, roy, royne occupera,*
Leader Byzantium of the captive in Only Thrace:	*Chef Bizant du captif en Samothrace:*
Before the assault the one the other will fall to its food supply,	*Avant l'assault l'un l'autre mangera,*
Savage hard will go after from the lineage there footprint.	*Rebours ferré suyvra du sang la trasse.*

Note: Originally listed as quatrain number 38 in Centurie IV. *Bisant* is accurately represented as a clean French word, meaning *Encoring*. The spelling *Bizant* is Serbo-Croatian for Byzantium. Samothrace is an island in the northern Aegean Sea, and part of Greece. It is the only island that is part of Thrace. Mainland Thrace borders Turkey. The word *Samo* is Serbo-Croatian for "just, simply, only, merely, and solely."

With the calmed Leader upon pulling away by violence the leaving,	*Au chalmé Duc en arrachant l'esponce,*
Ship Arabian-like to behold, sudden detected:	*Voile Arabesque voir, subit descouverte:*
Tripoli Chios, & those from Trabzond,	*Tripolis Chio, & ceulx de Trapesonce,*
General commander caught, Black Sea & there warned to appear uninhabited.	*Duc prins, Marnegro, & la cité deserte.*

The Epic Poem Prophesied by Nostradamus

Note: Originally listed as quatrain number 55 in Centurie VI. The word *duc* also meant, "owl." In Old French the word *Arabesque* meant "Arabian-like," but the lower case *arabesque* is defined as "an intricate or elaborate pattern or design." *Tripoli* is the Lebanese port Tripoli. *Chios* is the fifth largest Greek islands, five miles off the coast of Turkey. Chios is the fifth largest of the Greek islands, near the Turkish mainland. The Empire of Trebizond covered most of the north coast of Turkey, or the southern Black Sea coast. *Trebizond* is in Turkey, on the coast of the *Black Sea*.

Ambassadors of there Tuscany national language,	*Ambassadeurs de la Toscane langue,*
April & May Alps & sea to pass:	*Avril & May Alpes & mer passer:*
This one with stupid fellow will marry the declaration,	*Celuy de veau expousera l'harangue,*
Whole age of France not happening to wipe away.	*Vie Gauloise ne venant effacer.*

Note: Originally listed as quatrain number 20 in Centurie VII. The use of expousera leads one to see the translation as "will expose," when the French for "to expose" is "exposer," without a "u". However, when the "x" is seen as interchangeable with "s", the word espouser becomes the root verb to translate. Still, "exposure" is intended to be seen, as a secondary meaning. The surrounding of an ampersand with Alps & sea, where the lower case sea is less likely to be the Mediterranean Sea, makes the "Maritime Alps", the border mountains between southeastern France and Italy come into view. The use of veau as a slang name for stupid person is a value judgment that makes more sense about Frances decision to send troops to Italy. This is talking about the diplomatic union between France and Italy, which will precede the outbreak of total war. Line four is stating that the French *arriving* in Italy will *not* be for the purpose of war against that nation, or *to abolish* the Italians. This is showing a call for desired military occupation.

Through there pounced again with spirit head man of a party troubled,	*Par la responce de dame roy troublé,*
Ambassadors will be despising their living:	*Ambassadeurs mespriseront leur vie:*
Them great its brothers will be imitating twice as much,	*Le grand ses freres contrefera doublé,*
By reason of dues will be dying indignation, hatred, envy.	*Par deus mourront ire, haine, envie.*

Note: Originally listed as quatrain number 85 in Centurie I. The word "*reponce*" translates as the past participle of the verb "responcer," meaning "to pounce again." The word written in the main theme statement, *dame*, most certainly can be translated as "lady," however the combination with "*roy*" makes it more likely to be a splitable word, as "*d'ame*," meaning "of spirit."

Chapter 13 - Mediterranian Woes

Them ancient in years singular ruler expelled from his rule,	*Le vieux monarque deschassé de son regne,*
With the Middle Eastern ones its relief will journey to inquire after:	*Aux Orients son secours ira querre:*
Because terror from the cross will fold her standard,	*Pour peur des croix ploiera son enseigne,*
Into Mitylene will march in regard of harbor & country.	*En Mitilene ira pour port & terre.*

Note: Originally listed as quatrain number 47 in Centurie III. The lack of capitalization of *monarque* probably represents a dictator, or leader who gained control of a country through a military coup. This means chased away becomes a form of revolution, or another military coup. *Mitylene* is the main city on the Greek island of Lesbos, in the Aegean Sea. Obviously, this would be a strategic location for military deployment to the *East*, should hostilities there escalate, with no Arab nations willing to provide land and sea bases of operations for America or Great Britain.

Entry deep through there great Queen caused	*Entree profonde par la grand Royne faicte*
Will bring to pass a state mighty which cannot be come into:	*Rendra le lieu puissant inaccessible:*
The army of the three lions will be destroyed,	*L'armee des troys lyons fera deffaite,*
Causing inwardly case hideous & most fearful.	*Faisant dedans cas hideux & terrible.*

Note: Originally listed as quatrain number 16 in Centurie VII. The *army of the three lions* would be connected to those forces in Iraq, from multiple perspectives. However, the 1568 Lyon edition gives a hint that *des troys* can also be read as *destroys*. In this case, the word destroict becomes an important secondary hint, as it means, "strait, narrow place, or passage". This connects well to the main theme statement in quatrain I – 85.

There mighty made queen at what time themselves will behold vanquished,	*La grande royne quand se verra vaincu,*
Will act excess of masculine courage:	*Fera exces de masculin courage:*
Over horse, flowing water will hold on course everything cloud,	*Sus cheval, fluve passera toute nue,*
Consequence of weapon: to loyalty will cause much violence.	*Suite par fer: à foy fera outrage.*

Note: Originally listed as quatrain number 86 in Centurie I. Line three can be very symbolic. First of all, it brings about the image of Joan of Arc, riding on her horse in armor, showing masculine

The Epic Poem Prophesied by Nostradamus

courage. Still, in that sense, a horse has military applications, as armored cavalry (chevalerie). Thus, when preceded by Sus (capitalized, thus of greater importance) an Over horse becomes a military airplane, or helicopter. Line three is then observing the damage, while also delivering weapons of its own.

There made a queen Grecian of beauty ugly-like,	*La Dame Greque de beauté laydique,*
Prosperous made from legal matters too many to number,	*Heureuse faite de procs innumerable,*
Out of translated adjoining with the realm Hispanic,	*Hors translatee proche au regne hispanique,*
Taken in war catching to die death unfortunate.	*Captive prinse mourir mort miserable.*

Note: Originally listed as quatrain number 78 in Centurie IX. The *Lady* (on more than one occasion in the quatrains) will be seen to identify with the statue called Lady Liberty (Statue of Liberty). In Randal Cotgrave's 1611 dictionary, he shows the idiom, "*beauté Grecque,*" which he defines as, "a foggy plumpness, or fatness of body; (for the Grecians hold the fat body the fairest.)" With *beauté* following Greque, in line one, this can be see as descriptive of something other than the commonly expected appearance of beauty. The Statue of Liberty is made to look like Greek statues, where it appears men posed as women for sculptors, thus making the women have a masculine, "ugly-like" appearance.

Until in the depths there great vault frame defaced,	*Jusques au fondz la grand arq demolue,*
By reason of end of a time lost liberty, the friend taken before:	*Par chef captif, l'amy anticipé:*
Will rise with lady front figure wearing long hair,	*Naistra de dame front face chevelue,*
In that time through deceit general commander, with dead caught.	*Lors par astuce duc, à mort attrapé.*

Note: Originally listed as quatrain number 9 in Centurie V. The word *demolue* is seen as an anagram, "*demoule.,* which means, "form spoiled, broken mould, or frame defaced." In line two, where it states, "the friend anticipated", relates to quatrain VIII-83, where it states, "the friend not will be".

By reason of impatience feigned from sudden turbulent stirrings coming from God,	*Par fureur faincte d'esmotion divine.*
Will be there woman to the great mighty broken:	*Sera la femme du grand fort violee:*

Chapter 13 - Mediterranian Woes

Doomed ones friendly unto ones to give judgment against such science,	*Juges voulans damner telle doctrine,*
Victim with the multitude of people unlearned devoted to death.	*Victime au peuple ignorant imolee.*

Note: Latin: *victima = an animal offered in sacrifice, victim.* Originally listed as quatrain number 72 in Centurie VI. The word *femme* means *woman*, but it can also mean "wife." As "wife" it makes one see the *wife of the great* become visible as Hilary Clinton, the *wife* of former president *of the great* U.S.A. If this is indeed a reference to her, line one's main theme statement of separated event (ending with a period) is preceding her rise by a faked religious *fury*.

For land Attica head of the wisdom,	*Par terre Attique chef de la sapience,*
Whose from present is there rose to the world:	*Qui de present est la rose du monde:*
Bridge ruined & its great pre-eminence,	*Pont ruyné & sa grande preeminence,*
Will be from unlooked for & shipwreck to the waves	*Sera subdite & naufrage des undes:*

Note: Latin: *Atticus = belonging to Attica.* Originally listed as quatrain number 31 in Centurie V. *Attica* was the Roman district of Greece containing Athens. In line three the capitalized first word, *Pont*, cannot be overlooked as being the root of the reason the pope is called a Pontiff. The Latin word pontifex comes from *pons facere*, meaning a pontiff was a "bridge builder." With the Bridge *destroyed* or *ruined*, there will be no more builders of bridges. That moniker was because of the Latin root, thus French, meaning a Bridge to God. The use of *preeminence*, a title bestowed upon a Pope, makes this idea confirmed. The preeminence was only by the Grace of God, through a holy connection (bridge) to God.

Above them center to the great world there rose,	*Sur le milieu du grand monde la rose,*
Considering unheard of before feats blood common scattered abroad:	*Pour nouveaux faicts sang public espandu:*
Has to speak truth men will hold entry into perfected,	*A dire vray on aura bouche close,*
Then with the necessity of will arrive long in coming the expected.	*Lors au besoing viendra tard l'attendu.*

Note: Originally listed as quatrain number 96 in Centurie V. This quatrain's use of "great world there rose" makes it connect to quatrain V-31, which applied it to Greek philosophy and the Bridge Christianity found in the Greek acceptance of all philosophy, while becoming the center of the Eastern Church. The translation of *attendu* is as "expected." The attachment of the article *"le"* to this past participle verb makes it a noun, as *the one*, or *him* awaited or "expected" to arrive. This quatrain is certainly stating the pre-conditions that will arise before the need for Christ to return.

The Epic Poem Prophesied by Nostradamus

God, the firmament everything a most holy word in the wave,	Dieu, le ciel tout le divin verbe à l'unde,
Carried by vermillion ones shaven ones in Byzantium:	Pourté par rouges sept razes à Bisance:
Towards them grease ones three values from Trebizond,	Contre les oingz trois cens de Trebisconde,
Two laws will be setting, horror, then faith.	Deux lois mettront, & horreur, puis credence.

Note: Latin: *verbum = a word.* Originally listed as quatrain number 36 in Centurie VII. Line two appears to be referring to seven representatives of the Eastern Orthodox Church in Trabzon, formerly part of the Byzantine Empire. The sepling, *Bisance*, can be seen as "*Bis-ance*," or "Blackish state." Turkey is Muslim, thus "black" in Nostradamus terms, but its acceptance of Christians (in its desire to join the EU) makes it blackish. The word *oing* refers to "hogs" grease, and may have some importance as the stuff used in anointing, rather than oil. The spelling, *Trebisconde*, is Italian, with a "*c*" that needs to be taken and placed at the beginning, as "*c'Trebisonde*." It means Trabzon, a city in eastern Turkey, with a strong history with the Byzantine culture, and also the empire known as *Trebizond*. The empire was an extension of the Byzantine Empire.

Three hundreds will be to one to covet & bargain struck,	Trois cens seront d'un vouloir & accord,
Which in regard of to spring at the end with them designation:	Que pour venir au bout de leur attaincte:
Twenty months following everything & court recitals of things done,	Vingt mois apres tous & recordz,
To their head man of a party treacherously dealt with imitating hatred devised.	Leur roy trahy simulant haine faincte.

Note: Latin: *simulo = to make like, make copy of.* Originally listed as quatrain number 37 in Centurie V.

The ambassador cast out on two-oar-banked ships,	L'ambassadeur envoyé par biremes,
Has half course of obscure ones repulsed ones:	A mi chemin d'incogneuz repoulses:
From salt abundance will be issuing four largest ships,	De sel renfort viendront quatre triremes,
Twisted strings & chains into Black Sea trussed up ones.	Cordes & chaines en Negrepont troussés.

Note: Latin: *biremis = two oared, boat or ship; triremis = having three banks of oars.* Originally listed as quatrain number 21 in Centurie II. The 1611 Randal Cotgrave dictionary shows "*my-*

Chapter 13 - Mediterranian Woes

chemin", in particular as, "*à my-chemin*", as an common idiom, or hyphenated word, meaning "half-way" or "in the mid-way". Since Nostradamus did not hyphenate here, it has to be seen as two words. This being so, when attached to the series of quatrains telling of serious earthquake-related changed (mirrored here in line three's *repoulses*, and line four's *troussés*), the mid-point of a journey is not as important as the path to take being reduced by one-half. The use of *repulses* is like "aftershocks", or *re-pulses*.

The great god to the Sea from the deep of there sea,	*Le grand Neptune du profond de la mer,*
Of people Characterized by treachery & lineage of France put among:	*De gent Punique & sang Gauloys meslé:*
The Islands with stock considering them long in coming to row,	*Les Isles à sang pour le tardif ramer,*
More it will hurt than the concealed evil kept secret.	*Plus luy nuira que l'occult mal celé.*

Note: Originally listed as quatrain number 78 in Centurie II. In the 16th Century the planet Neptune was still over 200 years from being discovered. Therefore, the reference to *Neptune* is to the god of the sea. Carthage is now modern Tunis in Tunisia, North Africa.

A general who will have governed people innumerable,	*Le chef qu'aura conduit peuple infini,*
A distance away from his sky, to advised ones & national language unaccustomed:	*Loing de son ciel, de meurs & langue estrange:*
Five thousand into Crete & Thessaly limited,	*Cinq mil en Crete & Thessale fini,*
The end of a time soon gone secured at marine barn.	*Le chef fuyant sauvé en marine grange.*

Note: Originally listed as quatrain number 98 in Centurie I. This chef could be the same one mentioned in the series about the loss of a "general" or "head man of a party," leading to a "queen" taking the lead. Quatrain V-09 and IV-38 talk of a "*chef Bisance captif,*" with the indication being Greece.

Chapter 14

The Power of Nature

And Great Earthquakes Shall be in Diverse Places

One year bound unto the bickering Italianesque people,	*Un an devant le conflit Italique,*
Come from the same stock, French, Spanish ones in place them forcible:	*Germains, gaulois, hespaignolz pour le fort:*
Will fall the school family to commonwealth,	*Cherra l'escolle maison de republique,*
In what place, out of set almost nothing, being suffocated cause of death.	*Ou, hors mis peu, seront suffoqué mors.*

Note: Originally listed as quatrain number 39 in Centurie II. The word *devant* means "*before*," but is also the present participle of "*devoir*," meaning, "*having*." In 1611, the capitalized word Germain was not identified as a French word for the name of the people that live in Germany, as it is today. It was a word stating, "come of the same stock, bred of the same kind; near of kin, and of all-one race."

The ten Calends to April with made Gothique,	*Le dix Kalendes d'Avril de faict Gotique,*
Revived again by ordinary attendants evil ones:	*Resuscité encor par gens malins:*
A fire lost, gathering of a hunting party diabolical,	*Le feu estainct, assemblée diabolique,*
Hunting them pit to them of Lover & Selene.	*Cherchant les or du d'Amant & Pselyn.*

Note: Phonetics: *Ps = s,* thus *Pselyn >Selin.* Originally listed as quatrain number 42 in Centurie I. The word *Gotique* is a correctly spelled, functional word, which does not translate as "Gothic." *Gotique* is an Indo-European language, particularly as Germanic language, specifically an East Germanic language spoken in parts of Crimea (Black Sea Russia) up until the 17th Century. It is now an extinct language. A Calend is from the Latin word, Kalendae, which was the first day of a Roman month. *The ten Calends* could then be both, the tenth day of the month, with the month in question being stated as *April*, or the tenth firsts of ten months before the month of April (i.e.: July). Actually, the *Re-* of *Resuscité* states *again*, and is part of the translation used: *raised up again.* It

Chapter 14 - The Power of Nature

would then become redundant to write a word duplicating "again." In the Ukraine there is a Psel River, which could possibly figure into the translation of *Pselyn*.

There stately mountain around to seven races of men,	*La grande montaigne ronde de sept stades,*
Following peace, warfare, hunger, inundation surrounding	*Apres paix, guerre, faim, inundation:*
Will roll along big distance away suddenly undoing high ones delivered together ones,	*Roulera loing abysmant grans contrades,*
Same self ones ancients, & great foundation of.	*Mesmes antiques, & grand fondation.*

Note: Latin: *inundatio* = inundation, flood; *contrado* = deliver together, wholly. Originally listed as quatrain number 69 in Centurie I. The word *stade* refers to a place for races, by men or horses, which could be performed in a stadium. It is possible to see a "*stately mountain*" as Mount Olympus. According to Friedrich Blumenbach (1752 – 1840), there were five basic races, white, yellow, brown, black, and red. In reference to John Hunter's theory (1775), there were seven races of men, which were: black, blackish, copper-colored, red, tawny, brownish, and white.

Unfathomable potter's clay white to breed up to a rock,	*Profonde argille blanche nourrir rochier,*
Who from one immense depth will flow forth milky-white here born,	*Qui d'un abysme istra lacticineuse:*
Upon feeble hindrances neither them will be daring to strike,	*En vain troubles ne l'oseront toucher,*
Simple ones to abide at the bottom country full of clay.	*Ignorants estre au fond terre argilleuse.*

Note: Latin: *lacticinium* = milk-food. Originally listed as quatrain number 21 in Centurie I. Fat mould is a soil type with a high clay content, but tends to retain more moisture than sandy-clay soil. It then must be noted that quatrain IX-12 also mentioned argille, in line three, where Nostradamus wrote, "Le figulier cherchant argille neufue," or, "The potter searching potter's clay new." In French, the idiom "en vain" means, "in vain; idly; to no purpose." Line one can be read as like Genesis 2:7, where "God formed man of dust". The Hebrew word for "dust", "aphar", can also mean, "clay". From seeing that, "to breed up to a rock" means a man form that will lead to Peter, the rock of Jesus, who would form the Churches of Christ. Again, Nostradamus uses "white" as a color symbolizing Christianity. Iran has an 8,000-year history of pottery manufacturing.

The Epic Poem Prophesied by Nostradamus

Inwardly many nights there ground will tremble,	*Dans plusieurs nuits la terre tremblera,*
Before them taken opportunity two makes known consequence:	*Sur le prins temps deux efforts suite:*
Corinth, Ephesus with the two seas will swim,	*Corynthe, Ephese aux deux mers nagera:*
Debate themselves uproar by both courageous ones to struggling with.	*Guerre s'esmeut par deux vaillans de luite.*

Note: Originally listed as quatrain number 52 in Centurie II.

Religion with the fame from the merchandise will surmount	*Religion du nom des mers vanicra*
On the other side the sect son Lunatic foolish,	*Contre la secte fils Adaluncatif,*
Faction obstinate forsaken will doubt	*Secte obstinée deplorée craindra*
With the two wounded ones by Alpha particles & Aleppo.	*Des deux blessez par Aleph & Aleph.*

Note: Originally listed as quatrain number 96 in Centurie X. The word "Adaluncatif" is not a word, meaning it is an anagram. The translation above is it being changed to, "*Lunatic fada.*" *Aleph* is the letter A in the Hebrew alphabet. It represents God in some ways, but its mention here clearly identifies the *Faction obstinate forsaken* as the Jews, who along with Islam are the *two Against the sect* of the *son* Jesus Christ. The word *blessé*, used in line four, also means, "whose skin is fretted off", which means, "worn off, or eroded off." This could be the result of radiation that effects anyone near its release.

Nearby to the great river substantial dike town ground wasted,	*Pres du grand fleuve grand fosse terre egeste,*
In fifteen offices will be the water distinguished:	*En quinze pars sera l'eau divisee:*
There city seized, light, stock, outcries, bickering to thrust into,	*La cité prinse, feu, sang, cris, conflit mettre,*
Likewise the more part touched in the coliseum.	*Et la plus part concerne au collisee.*

Note: Latin: *egestio = wasting.* Originally listed as quatrain number 80 in Centurie IV. The word in line one, *egeste*, is the root of a French word, "*egestion.*" That word means, "a voiding, evacuation, casting out of excrements and odors." I imagine the Latin sums it up more eloquently, but for *the great* who run their nation by the Potomac *River* to find the *grave* of the *great* ones that believe election equates to ownership, the death of both nation and leaders will be the final bodily movement, and that is a *wasted* nation of peoples. This quatrain tells about Hurricane

Chapter 14 - The Power of Nature

Katrina. In Latin the word "*collis*" means "high ground." While the French word "*collizee*" leads to "*colisee*," meaning *coliseum*, the element of high ground cannot be overlooked as to why the coliseum was chosen to house the people of New Orleans.

Great Signs Shall There be from Heaven

Deeply in what might happen them transforming government,	*Avant qu'advienne le changement d'empire,*
It will come to pass one account aptly miraculous:	*Il adviendra un cas bien merveilleux:*
An open piece of ground changed, a pillar of purple rock,	*Le champ mué, le pillier de porphire,*
Placed, transferred above the rock not eye light.	*Mis, translaté sus le rochier noilleux.*

Note: Originally listed as quatrain number 43 in Centurie I. The word *porphyry* is defined as "Rock containing relatively large conspicuous crystals, especially feldspar, in a fine-grained igneous matrix." In the Old English dictionary it was said to be, "a dark red marble spotted with white." The Latin-Greek root leads to the word, "purple." As a manufactured word, *noilleux*, also can split to become "n'oiel lux." This translates as, "*no eye light*," meaning the inscriptions on the porphyry are in the dark, unseen, but felt. That, indeed, would be a *very marvelous* event to witness.

False to interpret will issue from description of a place,	*Faulx exposer viendra topographie,*
Will be them earthen pots from the tombs uncovered ones:	*Seront les cruches des monumens ouvertes:*
To sprout out sect devised study of wisdom,	*Pulluler secte faincte philosophie,*
As whites, blacks, & considering ancient ones green ones.	*Pour blanches, noires, & pour antiques vertes.*

Note: Originally listed as quatrain number 14 in Centurie VII. This is about an archeological discovery, which connects this to the series about the result of an earthquake. Some group of people will use this uncovering to promote a false agenda. With the current focus on "green" technology, some connection could be made to the ancients, and the proposition that an ancient civilization (Atlantis possibly) used crystals for power. Still, with the element of "*green ones*" following "*whites*" and "*blacks*," the possibility of evidence of lizard aliens (like in the TV series *V*) could be discovered.

The Epic Poem Prophesied by Nostradamus

There order the banished person the one before them else arcade	*La voye auxelle l'une sur l'autre fornix*
From the large vessel to measure out saving reward & broom,	*Du muy doser hormis brave & genest,*
The piece of evidence of emperor him model of excellence	*L'escript d'empereur le fenix*
Viewed upon the one this who to no man another not is.	*Veu en celuy ce qu'à nul autre n'est.*

Note: Latin: *fornix* = arch, vault, arcade, [mil] arched sally port; *desero* = to abandon, forsake, desert. Originally listed as quatrain number 27 in Centurie VIII. A "sally port" is defined as, "A gate in a fortification designed for sorties." The word "sortie" is defined as, "an armed attack, especially from a place surrounded by enemy forces." Thus, a *fornix* is an arched gateway, through which attacks upon an enemy would flow. However, in esoteric terms, a *fornix* is one of a series of arches, such that an *arcade* is such a series, forming a gallery. Seen in this light, this quatrain becomes one telling of the discovery of the tomb of Adam, the Son of God, the first priest of the "one God", in an arching lineage to the broom. The word broom, as "new broom", can be defined as, "a newly appointed official, etc., eager to make changes." This saving reward would be Jesus Christ.

With the foundation of there new sect,	*Au fondement de la nouvelle secte,*
Will be them bones from the great of Rome invented ones:	*Seront les oz du grand Romain trouvés:*
Tomb in marble will be seen suddenly closed,	*Sepulchre en marbre apparoistra couverte,*
Earth to quake upon April, badly upon whips.	*Terre trembler en Avril, mal enfouetz.*

Note: Originally listed as quatrain number 66 in Centurie VI. This quatrain seems to link to quatrain VII-14, where line three states, "To sprout out sect devised study of wisdom". It also matches quatrain I-42, where it mentions the Calends of April. The word enfouetz is close to the Old French word "enfoue," when means: converted or turned into fire. Still, as a manufactured word it cleanly translates and more closely fits the context. The combination mal enfouetz can also translate and mean, "evil to whip ones"; but this would only act secondarily to describe the people of Rome, in line two. This quatrain, when connected to quatrain VIII-27, makes it possible to see the Adam big vessel become here the tomb of Saint Peter, who began the new sect that would become the Roman Catholic Church.

At the forth pillar they consecrated to Saturn.	*Au quart piller lon sacre à Saturne.*
By reason of quaking earth & inundations of waters opened	*Par tremblant terre & deluge fendu*

Chapter 14 - The Power of Nature

Beneath the structure of the building Lead of Saturn found earthen vessel	*Soubz l'édifice Saturnin trouvee urne,*
Of gold takeing suddenly carried away & then given back.	*D'or Capion ravy & puis rendu.*

Note: Latin: *capiō* = *I capture, sieze, take*. Originally listed as quatrain number 29 in Centurie VIII. When one sees the "Lead" (metal) meaning in Saturnin, line three leading to *D'or* (To gold) in line four is the quest of an alchemist.

From vein in a quarry of stone rock with embedded crystals deep the fragment found	*De fin porphire profond collon trouvée*
Lowest part of there omen writings capitoline:	*Dessoubz la laze escriptz capitolin:*
Bone hair wreathed Roman power verified,	*Os poil retors Romain force prouvée,*
Rank to move often at the gate to Mytilene.	*Classe agiter au port de Methelin.*

Note: Originally listed as quatrain number 32 in Centurie IX. The word *capitolin* is clean French for Capotiline, which is the name of one of Rome's seven hills. In Latin, the word *Capitolina* means, "of the Capitol," which was reference to the temple of Jupiter located there. On Capitoline Hill is found the Temple of Jupiter, which was the site of the capitol of Rome, known as *Capitolium*. A *capitolinus* was a superintendent of games in honor of Jupiter Capitolinus. The translation of Methelin is questionable, but if the "h" were turned upside down, it would resemble a "y." Mytilene it is a port city on the island of Lesbos, in the Aegean Sea. It is the seat of the Orthodox Church, and was a place visited by the Apostle Paul.

In regard of the inscription D. M. found,	*Quant l'escripture D. M. trouvee,*
As well vault ancient with brightness detected,	*Et cave antiqué à lampe descouverte,*
Law, head man of a company, & chief Ulpian experimented,	*Loy, roy, & prince Ulpian eprouvee,*
Tabernacle queen & general leader under there buried.	*Pavillon royne & duc soubz la couverte.*

Note: Originally listed as quatrain number 66 in Centurie VIII. Carved in tombstones of ancient Romans are the initials *D. M.* I believe this stands for *Deus Manes*, or something similar, meaning Gods Spirits of the Dead. One source explains DM actually states "to god's MANES." The Latin word "*mane*" means, "*remain.*" In other words, *D. M.* represents, *To God these Remains.*" There was a Roman named Domitius Ulpianus, called *Ulpian*, who was a jurist and writer of law. His death has been estimated at 228 A.D. The last *Tabernacle* (upper case T) was during the time of

129

The Epic Poem Prophesied by Nostradamus

Solomon, a *king*, before he built the first Temple for the Ark of the Covenant (the *Law* of God). A lower case *queen*, when following the capitalized (thus religious) Tabernacle, sounds like a High Priestess of some kind.

That which will open a sepulcher found,	*Qui ouvrira le monument trouvé,*
As well not will come he brings forth quickly,	*Et ne viendra le serrer promptement,*
Diseased it will grow & born will have strength proved,	*Mal luy viendra & ne pourra prouvé,*
Surely preferable bound unto chief of Britain whereas a Norman.	*Si mieux doit estre roy Breton ou Normand.*

Note: Originally listed as quatrain number 7 in Centurie IX. The edition of the 1568 Lyon manuscript reviewed is difficult to read, due to print bleed from the opposite page. The word in line two shown as "*serer*" is either that or "*seror*," with both being derived from the Latin word "*serō*," meaning, "I sow, plant, beget, bring forth, produce, found, establish, scatter, spread, disseminate, propagate, excite, cause, and/or produce." The two regions of modern France, known as Brittany and Normandy, are the northernmost land parts of France, across the English Channel from England. England ruled these regions during Roman times, and beyond. The "*roy*" of this quatrain links to the "*roy*" of quatrain VIII-66.

By reason of a fifth & one mighty Hercules	*Par le cinquieme & un grand Hercules*
Will be issuing from him temple to discover to public authority warlike,	*Viendront le temple ouvrir de main bellique,*
One Merciful, a Jule & the people of Ascanius withdrawn ones,	*Un Clement, Jule & Ascans reculez,*
The span, key, eagle, not will have had contained ever so great grudge.	*Lespe, clef, aigle, neurent onc si grand picque.*

Note: Latin: *clementia* = *mildness, gentleness, mercy.* Originally listed as quatrain number 27 in Centurie X. In Mythology: For the fifth labor, Eurystheus ordered Hercules to clean up King Augeas' stables. We have seen *stable* in quatrain VII – 14 and *a fourth pillar,* in quatrain VIII – 29. *Un Clement* can very well refer to *Clement I*, who was the 4th Pope and Bishop of Rome, between 88 and 99 AD. He died in the Crimea (a Russian penninsula in the Black Sea). There was also a Pope Julius I, who led between 337 and 352 AD.

Chapter 14 - The Power of Nature

From the Triumvir will be found ones them bones,	Du Triumvir seront trouvez les os,
Searching after secret treasure puzzling,	Cherchant profond tresor ænigmatique,
Those of thereabouts not being at peace,	Ceux d'alentour ne seront en repos,
This to excavate marble & lead metallic.	Ce concaver marbre & plomb metalique.

Note: Latin: *aenigma = a riddle, mystery.* Originally listed as quatrain number 7 in Centurie V. A *Triumvir* is defined as, "a board or commission of three." Line three is primarily a statement that supports the finding of bones in line one, by stating the country will be agitated, and far from tranquility. On a secondary level, the spirits of the dead will have been disturbed from their rest. The correct spelling of "metallic" in Old French was "metallique", with two "l"s. The word written only has one "l".

King exposed will finish the massacre,	Roy exposé parfaira L'hecatombe,
Following to have invented its beginning,	Apres avoir trouvé son origine,
Land flood to set open of marble & lead there tomb	Torrent ouvrir de marbre & plomb la tombe
To a noble Roman with symbol of power of Medusa.	D'un grand Romain d'enseigne Medusine.

Note: Latin: *Medus > Medi > Medes = [poetically] the Persians.* Originally listed as quatrain number 84 in Centurie IX. The French word *hecatombe* was defined as the "sacrifice wherein 100 beasts are killed." It is a term of ritual sacrifice. In Latin, *hecatombe* is translated as "hecatomb," meaning "large-scale slaughter" also. The 1568 Lyon edition clearly shows a capital "L" before hecatombe, meaning it is not an ordinary sacrifice or slaughter. The word *Corrente*, in Old French, meant, "a strait of violently running waters that were dangerous to sailors (i.e.: Gibraltar & Magellan)." Some editions print this word, which is not too different from the French word "*Torrent.*" The Greek word "medousa" means, "guardian, protector." The gorgon, or female monster named Medusa, had a head full of snakes and anyone who looked upon her would turn to stone. Perseus beheaded Medusa, and used her head as a weapon, until giving the head to the goddess Athena, who placed it on her shield, as her own protection. The island of Sicily, and other villages of Europe, have flags and shields picturing Medusa's head. Medusa was one of three sisters (the only mortal one), born of gods (Titans), and all were said to have yellow wings, snakes for hair, brazen hands, and impenetrable scales (lizard women).

The Epic Poem Prophesied by Nostradamus

Temples made holy ones first form Roman,	*Temples sacrés prime façon Romaine,*
Will be throwing back them honeycomb foundations:	*Rejetteront les goffres fondements:*
Taking theirs laws first ones & humane ones,	*Prenant leurs loix premieres & humaines,*
Following of, not whole sum from the devout ones the refinements.	*Chassant, non tout des saints les cultements.*

Note: Originally listed as quatrain number 8 in Centurie II. Line two is stating a secondary theme of an earthquake tossing back the earth, which will have had covered underground honeycombs as the groundwork below a building. Line three is talking about the laws of the Jews, sent through Moses, by God, to His people. However, this is of Rome, so the Roman Catholic Church would only take the first Ten Commandments, leaving the rest for the Jews. Those were, for the most part, humane and gentle, because they had no punishments of death for not obeying them. The word *cultements* does not exist, although *culte* is French, and *–ment* is a French ending, meaning, "-ly" or "-ing". Thus, it could mean "worshiping". However, in Latin the word *culter* means, "knife; (weapon/ sacrificial/ hunt); pruner-edge; spear point; and/or plowshare." The addition of a *–ment* ending can make this "knifing ones." This could be an indication of human sacrifice.

Branch of sect ones great penalty to the complainer:	*Secteur de sectes grand peine au delateur,*
Beast into arena for public games, ordered them sport theatrical:	*Beste en theatre, dressé le jeu scenique:*
From the performance ancient made noble the contriver,	*Du faict antique ennobli l'inventeur,*
Through sect ones vast numbers of people confused & divided into factions.	*Par sectes monde confus & schismatique.*

Note: Originally listed as quatrain number 45 in Centurie I. The word "schism", from which one becomes *schismatic*, is defined as a division or separation into factions, while also being specifically a formal breach of union within the Christian Church. It means "disunion" and "discord." This quatrain is stating that Christianity, as it is known today, was the creation of Romans, after true Christians were killed as sport. The rest since has been devised through lore, whereas the contriver was the Emperor who ordered them sport.

From the kings & potentates will be raising up images of a man,	*Des rois & princes dresseront simulacres,*
Prophecy ones, trusted ones elevated ones pagan priests of Rome:	*Augures, creuz eslevés aruspices:*
Horn, animal offered in a sacrifice with prayers, & to sky blue, from eager,	*Corne, victime dorée, & dazur, dacre:*

Chapter 14 - The Power of Nature

Interpreted ones will be them examined entrails of the sacrificed.	*Interpretés seront les extipices.*

Note: Latin: *victima = animal offered in sacrifice, victim*. Originally listed as quatrain number 26 in Centurie III. Line one is making the point that God commanded, "You shall not make for yourselves idols, nor shall you set up for yourselves an image", where "*set up image*" is the same verb as "*raise up image.*" The word, *aruspice*, is defined as, "A priest in ancient Rome who practiced divination by the inspection of the entrails of animals." The idiom "*azur d'acre*" is said to have meant, "natural azure, as it is taken out of the mine." When this quatrain is read along with quatrain I-45, the examined entrails of line four seems more like those of the Christians thrown to the lions for sport. In line four, the word *extispices* is found in Latin, meaning [plural of], "a soothsayer predicting from the entrails of a victim." The Old French word *extipiscine* meant, "divination, or soothsaying by the inspection of the entrails of beasts."

Them bones of the feet & with the hands chained ones,	*Les os des pieds & des mains enferréz,*
By reason of race extended while resided:	*Par bruit maison long temps inhabitee:*
Will be through dreamed ones emptying disinherited ones,	*Seront par songes concavant deterréz,*
House wholesome & without public voice dwelt abroad.	*Maison salubre & sans bruit habitée.*

Note: Originally listed as quatrain number 41 in Centurie VII. The word *deterrez* can equally mean *disinherited* as it can mean "disinterred", meaning dug up from the ground. The use as *disinherited* actually means not left any land. This quatrain tells of the foreign treatment of Jews, who are the "disinherited ones," or the "left landless ones". Due to the main theme statement beginning with "Les os", showing the importance of "Bones" discovered "chained", this is a statement of Jewish persecution that will be discovered. While bones were discovered in the Nazi concentration camps, they were not in shackles. Therefore, this is about the discoveries made after the future earthquake, which shows Roman treatment of Jews.

At the bottom of them ancient ones large buildings undefiled ones,	*Soubz les antiques edifices vestaulx,*
Not removed far away from aqueduct utterly decayed:	*Non esloignez d'aqueduct ruyne:*
From Ground & Silver are the radiant ones metals,	*De Sol & Lune sont les luisans metaulx,*
Burning lamp Trajan from gold entailed.	*Ardante lampe Trajan d'or burine.*

Note: *Trajan > Trajanus = Trajan (a Roman Emperor)*. Originally listed as quatrain number 66 in Centurie V. The alchemical metals associated with the Sun and the Moon are gold and silver. Thus, line three can be read, "*To Gold & Silver are the shining ones (the luminaries) metals.*" The

The Epic Poem Prophesied by Nostradamus

primary use of "*sol*", in French, was as "soil" or "ground", with "the Sun" being the capitalized version. Latin has *Sol* primarily shown as "the sun". Still, both gold and silver come from the ground. Marcus *Ulpius Trajanus* was the Emperor of Rome between 98 ans 117 AD. The name Ulpius relates to quatrain VIII-66, where line three, following a mid-line ampersand states, "Prince Ulpian". The use of bruiné as "entailed" can carry the meaning of an "inherited" lamp, or one passed down from the engraved original source.

In that time that serpents will be coming to encompass a hundred square meters,	Lors que serpens viendront circuir l'are,
The stock Trojan disquieted by reason of them Spanish ones:	Le sang Troyen vexe par les Espaignes:
Of them great reckoning upon will be thrust into loss,	Par eulx grand nombre en sera faicte tare,
General escaped, hidden in the standing pools inwardly the blood drained ones.	Chef fuict caché aux mares dans les saignes.

Note: Originally listed as quatrain number 19 in Centurie I. Modern French has the word *are* as functional and translated as "are", as 100 square meters, or a measure of area. Also, when talking about the Trojans and Spanish in the same breath, "Spanish" is best translated as "Spain ones," and thus not Spaniards. This could be the oldest civilization in Europe, the Basques.

Poisonous reptiles let go to another fangs there cage of iron,	Serpens transmis dens la caige de fer,
In what place them children encompassing jurisdiction to the chief are undertaken:	Ou les enfans septains du roy sont pris:
Them aged in years & fathers will be delivering out of lowest part from evil,	Les vieux & peres sortiront bas de l'enfer,
Before to depart this life to see one's profits from hard work dead & cries.	Ains mourir voir de son fruict mort & crys.

Note: Latin: *dens* = *a tooth*. Originally listed as quatrain number 10 in Centurie I. This quatrain links to quatrain I-19, as both quatrains mention "*serpens*" in the main theme statement. Here, the word is capitalized. These are figurative "snakes", which are given more detail here as being "*caged*" in "*iron*," the word that symbolizes "*weapony*." The "*enfans*" of this quatrain also connects this to quatrain VIII-55, where "*Enfans*" is line four's capitalized first word.

134

Chapter 14 - The Power of Nature

Another Major Quake Soon Follows

Them trembling to land with Will grind like a mortar,	*Le tremblement de terre à Mortara,*
This axis charges holy George with half pair to sink ones,	*Cais.ch. seront verongne demy perfondrez,*
Accord lulled asleep, there warfare will stir up,	*Paix assoupie, la guerre esveillera,*
Within temple at feast of Easter engulfed ones drowned ones.	*Dans temple à Pasques abysmes enfondrez.*

Note: Originally listed as quatrain number 31 in Centurie IX. The town of *Mortara* is located in the Lombardy region of Italy, in the Pavia Province, between the Agogna and Terdoppio rivers. The word Mortara may be best translated as from the French word mortiers, meaning, "mortar (small bowl used for grinding)," becoming, "will grind." The word abbreviated as *Cais.*, is translated as *C'ais*, with *ais* French, from Latin *axis*, meaning, "board or plank." The abbreviation "ch." Is listed in the Harper Collins French Concise Dictionary as being standard for either, "*charges, chauffage, cherche,*" where "responsibilities" is one translation possibility. The word perfondrez is translated as *per fondre-z*, meaning, "pair to sink ones." *Saint George* is the patron saint of England, as well as other places; but he is also considered the patron saint of soldiers, archers, cavalry, and chivalry. England celebrates a national day of recognition for *Saint George* on April 23, each year. The flag of *Saint George* is the same for the Red Cross (a red cross on a white field). Easter Sunday will occur on April 24, 2011, April 8, 2012, April 20, 2014, and April 5, 2015.

Nautical rowed will invite the shadows,	*Nautique rame invitera les umbres,*
With the great Empire then will come to prick forward:	*Du grand Empire lors viendra conciter:*
There sea Aegean from the kindred peoples them encumbered ones,	*La mer Aegée des lignes les encombres,*
Encumbering the surge of the sea Tyrrhenian-born of the moved upon the waves ones.	*Empeschant l'onde Tyrrenne defflotez.*

Note: Latin: *nauticus = of a sailor, nautical; Tyrrhenia = Etruria (Italy).* Originally listed as quatrain number 95 in Centurie V. Interestingly, the Old French word *encombre* is different from the verb "*encombrer*" and the past participle form, "*encombré.*" For the base word meaning, *encombre* is referred to the word "*encombrier,*" meaning, "encumbrance, pesterance, trouble," etc. *Encombre*, however, meant, "rubbish or ruins of falling and decayed buildings," which perfectly fits the context here.

The Epic Poem Prophesied by Nostradamus

By reason of summoned to appear at liberty of there great sea Muslim,	Par cité franche de la grand mer Seline,
Whose port calls again ones in the gullet the stone:	Qui porte encores à l'estomach la pierre:
English fleet will approach beneath in that place blasted with mist,	Angloise classe viendra sous la bruine,
One branch to seize from the mighty uncovered warfare.	Un rameau prendre du grand ouverte guerre.

Note: Originally listed as quatrain number 35 in Centurie V. When one sees a *city freed of the great*, meaning an occupation has been lifted, a *sea Seline* could very well be a *sea* named after "themselves" and their "lineage," which would be the sea Persian, or Persian Gulf. But, since the *English fleet* is still around in line three, it might be the Arabian Sea or Aegean Sea or the Mediterranean Sea. The name *Angloise* is the feminine of "English," therefore meaning "Englishwoman" specifically. Ships are referred to in the feminine gender. Still, if the word is seen as a two-word anagram, combining French and Latin, it could become *Ango* (Latin) – *lisé* (past part. of the verb *liser*) where *Ango* means, "to press tightly; to strangle, throttle; to hurt, distress; to torment, make anxious." The verb *liser* means, "to list, or border a garment; also to coast along by a country."

Shipwreck to order near the wave Adriatic.	Naufraige a classe pres l'onde Hadriatique.
There country stirred up over anger land thrust into:	La terre esmeuë sus l'air en terre mis:
Egypt shaky growth Islamic,	Egypte tremble augment Mahometique,
The King of Arms himself to yield with to proclaim east committed.	L'Herault soy rendre à crier est commis.

Note: Originally listed as quatrain number 86 in Centurie II.

An army lodged Samos by reason of ones from Europe will depart,	Le camp Asop d'Europe partira,
Themselves uniting close unto with the island submerged:	S'adjoignant proche de lisle submergée:
To Strait fleet battalion of soldiers will turn up,	D'Arton classe phalange pliera,
Center to the world more substantial voice substituted.	Nombril du monde plus grand voix subrogée.

Note: Latin: *artus* = *narrow, tight, close*. Originally listed as quatrain number 22 in Centurie II. The word *Asop* is questionable, but it is clearly designed to bring Aesop to mind. Therefore, Samos becomes an option, where Aesop lived. When Turkey is seen as another reference, *Aesop* becomes

Chapter 14 - The Power of Nature

synonymous with Greece and one part of Europe that is *adjoining* and *neighboring* Turkey. Further, the word *classe*, meaning "order, rank, class," fits as "rank" because the word *phalange* is defined as: battalion of soldiers (8,000 to 18,000 men) ranked so they may encounter the enemy in every way. The *Navel of the world* is defined, according to Greek Mythology, as the Apollon at Delphi, such that: The shrine of Apollon at Delphi has a stone depression that is called the *Navel of the World*; the depression is covered by a stone known as the Omphalos, which literally means "Navel."

One realm great will change from death abandoned of company,	*Un regne grand demourra desolé,*
Close to the Ebro oneself will be acting calling soldiers to report:	*Aupres del Hebro se feront assemblees:*
Mountain ones Pyrenees him will be restoring comforted,	*Monts Pyrenees le rendront consolé,*
In that time then in May will be countries quaked ones.	*Lors que dans May seront terres tremblees.*

Note: Originally listed as quatrain number 88 in Centurie VI. This relates to quatrain IX-83, which tells of an earthquake at 20 degrees of Taurus. The Sun is at that degree in that sing during the month of *May*. However, the main theme is stating that something has already caused One great to stay abandoned. This means one earthquake has already occurred, and this is In that time of a second quake. The focus of this quatrain is an army of soldiers raised by Osama bin Laden.

Foundation twenty bull so strong land to quake,	*Sol vingt Taurus si fort de terre trembler,*
The great arena filled will wreck,	*Le grand theatre rempli ruinera,*
The atmosphere, sky & world to darken & to trouble,	*L'air, ciel & terre obscurcir & troubler,*
While that the infidel god & profane will sail forth.	*Lors infidelle dieu & sainctz voguera.*

Note: Originally listed as quatrain number 83 in Centurie IX. Astrologically, the Sun reaches 20 degrees of the sign Taurus around the 10th – 12th of May each year. Incidentally, Taurus is an *earth* sign. The lower case spelling of *taurus* makes it more translatable as "bull." Also, note the word *theatre* in this quatrain. While it may represent a physical coliseum or stadium, remember the description of people acting religious, putting on theatrical plays, in quatrain I – 45. The word *impeach* is defined as, "To challenge the validity of; try to discredit." The word "*sainct*" is said to have a "contrary" meaning, such that its use (in obvious sarcastic situations) means, "profane".

The Epic Poem Prophesied by Nostradamus

A great arena themselves will come to set straight,	*Le grand theatre se viendra redresser,*
The dice cast, & them nets well near spread ones:	*Le dez geté, & les rets ia tendus:*
More than needed them first into mirror will come to tire,	*Trop le premier en glaz viendra lasser,*
By reason of arc ones will have had seriously debilitated ones from times already cut asunder ones.	*Par arcz prostrais de long temps ja fendus.*

Note: Originally listed as quatrain number 40 in Centurie III. The use of theatre in line one connects this quatrain to quatrain IX-83, where the same word is used in the secondary theme statement.

Again being them sacred ones churches dishonest ones,	*Encor seront les saincts temples pollus,*
As well the robbed upon ones them by counsel of citizens Rotunda in good liking,	*Et expillez par senat Tholossain,*
Saturn two three cycles the gone fully about ones,	*Saturne deux trois cicles revolus,*
In April, May people of unheard of before rising agent.	*Dans Avril, May gens de nouveau levain.*

Note: Greek: *tholos* = dome. Catalan: *Tolosa* = Toulouse. Originally listed as quatrain number 72 in Centurie IX. A *Tholos* is an ancient Greek building, which were circular and included columns. The ruins of three are most noted in Athens and Delphi. It can be assumed that *people of fresh leaven* will have a new cause to rise up about. The U.S. Senate meets at the Capitol Building, where overhead is the round dome of the Rotunda.

The chief Arabian Iron, Foundation, Islam, Lion,	*Le prince Arabe Mars, Sol, Venus, Lyon,*
Reign of Church by sea will fall down under a burden:	*Regne d'Eglise par mer succombera:*
Towards there Persia quite near to a million,	*Devers la Perse bien pres d'un million,*
Byzantium, Egypt in decay. serpent. will usurp.	*Bisance, Egypte ver. serp. invadera.*

Note: Latin: *ver.* is accepted as the abbreviation of the word *versus* = *act of turning [version]*; *serpo* = *to creep, crawl, advance slowly*. Originally listed as quatrain number 25 in Centurie V. The astrological symbolism of the *Lion* is the sign of Leo. The *Sun* passes through the sign of Leo between the 22nd of July and the 22nd of August (roughly).

Chapter 14 - The Power of Nature

A third portion of the world at the bottom of War comprehended,	*Le tiers climat soubz Aries comprins,*
The year millennium September estimates twenty & seven in October:	*L'an mil sept cens vingt & sept en Octobre:*
Him head man of a party with Persia on those of Egypt seized:	*Le roy de Perse par ceux d'Egypte prins:*
Battle, death, decay: in there cross great disgraceful reviling.	*Conflit, mort, perte: à la croix grand opprobre.*

Note: Originally listed as quatrain number 77 in Centurie III. The word *climat* is further defined as, "a clime, a division in the sky, or portion of the world, between North and South." This indicates three climates: North, Equatorial, and South. Line one is indicating one of these areas that has become dominated, due to warlike actions. Line two then identifies the climate as the one that reacted in September, 2001. On October 7, 2001, Geo. W. Bush ordered American forces to strike at al-Qaeda camps in Afghanistan, making a televised announcement of those actions on that day.

Chapter 15

Fanning the Flames of War

Eastern European Unrest

Balkans

Enter Plain field, Siena, Spring, Struck,	*Entre Campaigne, Sienne, Flora, Tustie,*
Six months unheard of before days neither will cry one iota:	*Six moys neufz jours ne ploura une goutte:*
The unusual national speech upon world Croatia,	*L'estrange langue en terre Dalmatie,*
Will make haste upon: laying waste there country everything.	*Courira sus: vastant la terre toute.*

Note: Originally listed as quatrain number 84 in Centurie II. The word *Campaigne* is a cleanly spelled word in Old French, meaning a *Plain field*. The word *sienne* is also a properly spelled word in Old French, as the feminine form of "sien," meaning, "his own or belonging to himself." However, as a capitalized name, *Sienne* is correctly spelled French for the Italian city of *Siena*. That city is located in the province of *Tuscany*. The goddess *Flora* represented "Spring." In Catalan and Occitan the word "*Tusti*" is a first person indicative past "*preterit*", meaning, "struck, hit." The *land Dalmatia* is now part of the nation Croatia, which is on the Adriatic Sea coast and was once part of the former Yugoslavia. It borders Italy to the northeast. The word *vastant* has a French ending (-ing English), but the Latin words, "vastus" or "vasto," can actually be the true meaning of the root, "laying waste, ravaging, preying upon." Still, the use of *widening* could be to mean that the government of Yugoslavia will expand to once again include Croatia.

The year that them brothers to the lily will be at an age,	*L'an que les freres du lys seront en aage,*
The one of them will hold there mighty Romania:	*L'un d'eux tiendra la grande Romanie:*
To quake the mountains gaping hidden entry to a place	*Trembler les monts ouvert latin passage*
Capitulation to eat against fortress to Armenia.	*Pache marcher contre fort d'Armenie.*

Note: Originally listed as quatrain number 50 in Centurie V. The main theme statement referencing brothers can be a religious relationship, due to the word *frère* also meaning friar, or

Chapter 15 - Fanning the Flames of War

priest, thus indicating Christianity. The word *latin* can also mean "Latin," or in this case, Italian. The mountains opened will reveal elaborate tunnel systems and underground strongholds. *Romania* and *Armenia* are separated by the Black Sea, and/or Turkey and Russian-Georgia.

And Ferdinand blonde will be to the coat,	*Et Ferdinand blonde sera descotte,*
To abandon there flower to pursue a Macedonian.	*Quitter la fleur suyvre le Macedon,*
With the great need of will mistake one's route,	*Au grand besoing de faillira sa routte,*
Both will step towards them Myrmidon.	*Et marchera contre le Myrmidon.*

Note: Greek Myth: *Myrmidon = soldiers of Achilles [ant-men].* Originally listed as quatrain number 35 in Centurie IX. The word *descotte* is read as *des-cotte*, meaning, "to the coat," usually as a coat of arms. The name *Ferdinand* is perhaps most important as Archduke Franz Ferdinand, the heir to the Austro-Hungarian throne was assassinated in Serajevo (then Serbia), leading to the beginning of World War I. The use of *blonde* could be a reference to the Germanic race (he was Bohemian). Line three makes a reference to the act that led to the assassination, as their driver went down the wrong street, and while backing up the assassin recognized him and killed both he and his wife. The *Myrmidon* would then represent the military soldiers who swarmed into battles, after a declared war on Serbia. Austria, Hungary, and Germany all declared war on each other, due to the triple alliance they had with Serbia.

In the times of the lamentation that him cat singular ruler	*Au temps du dueil que le felin monarque*
Will make war upon the young Macedonian,	*Guerroyera la jeune Æmathien,*
Western Europe to stagger to endanger there small sailing vessel	*Gaule bransler perecliter la barque*
To attempt wise judgment to the west entertainment through courteous speeches.	*Tenter phossens au ponant entretien.*

Note: Originally listed as quatrain number 58 in Centurie X. The use of *felin*, meaning *cat*, can be seen as a *lion*, symbolizing the *monarch* of England. The word *perecliter* has been translated as the word *pericliter*. The actual spelling presented makes *pere* stand out for the purpose of seeing "father" in *jeopardy*. The moniker *la barque* is used to name the *small ship* that the pope pilots, in the transport of souls to Heaven. It is because of this that a "nave" of a church is designed to look like a boat and why the mitered hat is shaped like the bow of a boat. Therefore, the *small ship* in line three is a reference to the Vatican. Seeing *phossens* as a phonetic spelling of the Latin word fossa (fossens), it becomes a "trench, ditch, or channel."

The Epic Poem Prophesied by Nostradamus

Reunified Germany

Next unto will arrive from the furthest from good ones countries,	*Apres viendra des extremes contrées,*
Prince German, over him throne of gold:	*Prince Germain, dessus le throsne doré:*
There servitude & water met with ones	*La servitude & eaux rencontrées,*
There lady served, her time more not adored (or honored).	*La dame serve, son temps plus n'adoré.*

Note: Originally listed as quatrain number 87 in Centurie II. The word *Germain* (in the lower case) meant, "come from the same stock, near of kin, of all one race." It still can be seen as German, when capitalized. The current pope is a *Prince German* (Ratzinger). Notice that if this is indeed referencing Germany, there presently a *lady* (lower case common) *serv*ing as their Chancellor (Angela Merkel). The part of *Germany There* in *servitude* would be the former East Germany.

From land feeble & poor kindred,	*De terre foible & pauvre parentele,*
On the tip of something & agreement will come unto within the empire.	*Par bout & paix parviendra dans l'empire.*
Extended opportunity to govern a youthful female,	*Long temps regner une jeune femelle,*
Who never at realm not upon will have had helped one so bad.	*Qu'oncq en regne n'en survint un si pire.*

Note: Originally listed as quatrain number 28 in Centurie III. Following the previous quatrain, East Germany was a *feeble land*, as was the whole of reunified Germany afterwards for some time. The reunion is here said to be *poor*. It is a *peace* generated *For the end* of the West. The *empire* (lower case) is the modern nation of Germany, which is the collection of principalities formerly considered part of the Holy Roman Empire. Again, Germany has recently elected its first *female* leader, who is relatively *young* (born in 1954), but the reunified Germany is *young* still. In her experience under Helmut Kohl, she was appointed minister of women and youth. She was elected in September 2005 (ran and lost in 2001) and won by a narrow margin. Although she received the majority, it was less than 50% of the total vote. She was reelected in 2009, with the next election in 2013.

Then that soldiers extreme wrath mutinous,	*Lors que souldarts fureur seditieuse,*
Contrary to their general will be with night weapon to shine:	*Contre leur chef feront de nuict fer luire:*
Enemy to Rome should be by reason of public authority raging,	*Ennemy d'Albe soit par main furieuse,*

Chapter 15 - Fanning the Flames of War

In that time to afflict Rome & the highest ones to beguile.	Lors vexer Rome & principaulx seduire.

Note: Latin: *Albe* = *Alba Longa*. Originally listed as quatrain number 68 in Centurie VI. *Alba Longa* is the oldest city of Latinum, approximately 12 km southeast of *Rome*. It is the legendary birthplace of Romulus and Remus, the founders of Rome. In the day of Nostradamus Italy was an ununified group of *principalities*. This quatrain tells of *sediti*on of the military, which will happen in Italy; but, because the sedition will be over the use of nuclear *weapon*s, the impact could be global in the West.

Large number itself draws near to arriving from Croatia,	Amas s'approche venant d'Esclavonie,
The Anointing old city will destroy:	L'Olestant vieux cité ruynera:
Stronghold desolated will observe its Romania,	Fort desolee verra sa Romanie,
Then there mighty flame to extinguish not will understand.	Puis la grande flamme estaindre ne scaura.

Note: Originally listed as quatrain number 82 in Centurie IV. The word Olestant is questionable. The German word Olest is the 2nd person subjunctive of Olen, meaning, "to oil." As Oiling, the meaning would be Anointing. The land known as *Esclavonie* was located east of Croatia, south of Hungary, and west of *Romania*, where Serbia (what became left over of the former Yugoslavia) is now. The country *Romania* was named after Rome, as part of the Holy Roman Empire, making line two's *ancient city* become Rome. The Romanians called themselves *Rûmans*, which meant "Bondsman". A "bondsman" is a male held in bondage, or a slave.

Conflict Barbarous upon there Horn black,	Conflict Barbar en la Cornette noire,
Race spread abroad to tremble there Croatia,	Sang espandu trembler la d'Almatie,
Substantial Islam will thrust into one's promontory,	Grand Ismaël mettra son promontoire,
Frog ones to shake relief Portugal.	Ranes trembler secours Lusitanie.

Note: Originally listed as quatrain number 60 in Centurie IX. *Lusitania* was an ancient Roman province, located in present northern Portugal and northwestern Spain.

Chapter 16

Fearing Ones Neighbors

Western Europe Acts Defensive

Italy

Them exiled ones at Time will be arriving,	*Les exilés en Secile viendront,*
For to release from hunger the people harsh:	*Pour delivrer de faim la gent estrange:*
At the moment in time to the day them the seals it will be failing,	*Au point du jour les celtes luy faudront,*
There whole age stay in judgment: King themselves ranked.	*La vie demeure à raison: Roy se range.*

Note: Originally listed as quatrain number 71 in Centurie II. The urge is to translate the capitalized *Secile* as Sicily. Certainly, I see this as a secondary intention, as Sicily will be one of the islands of *exile* in the future. However, it is spelled properly at other times and is not done so now. It is then a perfect anagram for *Siecle*, meaning, "Time, Season, Age, and/or Century." The lack of capitalization makes *celtes* less likely to actually be a reference to the Celts or their language, other than as a secondary reference to Europe in general, particularly France. The word *faudront* appears to be the future tense of the word "*falloir*" (to be necessary, to have to), with an *–ont* ending creating, "will be making necessesary," or "will be having to." It means the "ont" at the end is a compound addition, of the third person plural form of *avoir*, which is added to the future form, "*faudra.*" The word *range*, as *rangé*, refers the reader to look up "*rengé*". Both words mean the same, but there is no *range*, only *rang* and *ranger*. This quatrain is saying that the French will be facing difficulties the same as the Italians, following the invasions; but, the French will have it a little better.

Paternal will bedew from there Sicily outcry,	*Paterne orra de la Sicile crie,*
All them making ready for from the gulf of Trieste,	*Tous les apprest du goulphre de Trieste,*
Which themselves will learn until in the triangular land,	*Qui s'entendra jusques à la trinacrie,*
To in such manner with ships slipped aside, evaded the horrible plague.	*De tant de voiles fuy, fuy l'horrible peste.*

Chapter 16 - Fearing One's Neighbors

Note: Originally listed as quatrain number 84 in Centurie VIII. The Sicilian city Palermo is spelled the same way in French, Catalan, Portuguese, and Italian. The word *Paterne* is the feminine form for *Paterno*, in Italian, meaning "Paternal, Fatherly." *Trieste* is a northeastern Italy city and port, near the border with Slovenia. It is at the head of the *Gulf of Trieste*, in the Adriatic Sea. Slovenia actually surrounds this land, with only a narrow strip along the coast being in Italy. *Trieste* keeps Slovenia from having a larger coastal area.

Principal great return profit the potentate of Fishery	*Premier grand fruit le prince de Pesquiere*
More after will arrive riches & unmerciful despiteful,	*Mais puis viendra bien & cruel malin,*
Within Venice will let slip its renown high-minded	*Dedans Venise perdra sa gloire fiere*
Likewise lay with evil by reason of more joined Islam.	*Et mys à mal par plus joyne Celin.*

Note: Phonetics: *C > S / Celin > Selin = Selene*. Originally listed as quatrain number 31 in Centurie VIII. In French the word "*pesquer*" leads to "*pescheur*," (fisherman) where "*pesche*" means "fishing." The French ending "–ere" acts to place the root word in "the state of" by adding an "-ry" ending in English. The *First* of the *great*, being the West, led by the *great Fishery* in Rome, would have the *Prince* be Paul, with the *fruit* the Church that he built, in honor of the Prince of Peace (Jesus). Line one is referencing the Vatican. *Celin* is a form of "Selene," a repeated characterization of the Moon/Islam.

Within the islands with five streams in one,	*Dedans les isles de cinq fleuves à un,*
By reason of an increasing to the great not Healer Muslim:	*Par le croissant du grand Chyren Selin:*
Through them blasted ones by burning mists from the air wrath upon the one,	*Par les bruynes de laër fureur en l'un,*
Six escaped ones, hidden ones bundles of linen cloth.	*Six eschapéz cachéz fardeaux de lyn.*

Note: Originally listed as quatrain number 27 in Centurie VI. The translation of *Chyren* is as Chiron, a mythological figure who was known as a *Healer*. The meaning of the Greek root is "Hand." When the *Chy* of *Chyren* is seen as the Greek letter "chi," it becomes pronounced with a "hard h" sound, as Kuh-ren. This makes Iran be similar in sound and become a nation closely related to the *Selin* moon of Islam. If phonetics allows "ch" to become "c," the spelling "*Cyren*" is close to "Cyrene," which indicates an ancient Greek colony that settled what is now in Libya.

The Epic Poem Prophesied by Nostradamus

Them exiled ones exempted ones in the islands.	*Les exiles deportés dans les isles.*
In the exchanging from one more tyrannous monarch	*Au changement d'une plus cruel monarque*
Will be crushed by beatings ones: & set two to the sparks,	*Seront meurtrys: & mis deux des scintiles,*
Who of to tell not being remained ones enclosed ones.	*Qui de parler ne seront estés parques.*

Note: Originally listed as quatrain number 59 in Centurie I. The correct spelling of "scintille" includes two "l"s. However, it appears to rhyme with "isle" only one "l" was used to convey the meaning. Still, this could be an anagram.

One King will be who will give the opposition,	*Un Roy sera qui donra l'opposite,*
Them the exiled ones elevated ones over the government:	*Les exilléz eslevéz sur le regne:*
From race swimming there people pure horse liberator,	*De sang nager la gent caste hyppolite,*
Likewise will flourish continual under such standard.	*Et florira long temps soubz telle enseigne.*

Note: Originally listed as quatrain number 52 in Centurie V. The word donra is not the correct spelling for the 3rd person future tense of donner (to give), as that is "*donnera*". It does act as an anagram for the Catalan-Occitan word of the same meaning, "*donar.*" It is interesting to realize that the name *Hyppolyte* (capitalized) comes from Greek mythology, as a queen of the Amazon warriors, with a special belt she wore to protect her, given to her by Ares (the god of war). Hercules' ninth labor was to gain possession of Hyppolyte's belt (or girdle). Since the word here is not capitalized, this can only apply as a secondary meaning, which in Greek meant, "horse liberator." One other consideration could be Hippolytus of Rome. He was considered to be the first antipope; but, he was later martyred and deemed to be a saint.

Elected will be with Sable born sounding speech,	*Esleu sera Renad ne sonnant mot,*
Making him holy apparent in the eyes of the world living bread of barley,	*Faisant le saint public vivant pain d'orge,*
To play the tyrant after so much of one cast,	*Tyrannizer apres tant à un cop,*
Thrusting with base of the more substantial ones over the deepest part of the mouth.	*Mettant à pied des plus grans sus la gorge.*

Chapter 16 - Fearing One's Neighbors

Note: Originally listed as quatrain number 41 in Centurie VIII. The 1568 Lyon edition shows Renad in line one, while the 1566 edition (and also later ones) shows Renard. From French Medieval literature comes the peasant-hero *fox* character *Renard* (or *Renart* [various spellings], which is the French word for *Fox*. While many stories were constructed with this character, and repeat characters being bears, wolves and other fable symbolic comparisons to known human beings, *Renard* was known to make fun of the false piety presented by the royalty and clergy. However, the misspelling acts as an anagram, "*d'Rena*," which is Italian for "with Sable," a black fur of heraldry. The use of Italian would indicate the Vatican (royal realm in Italy), with black symbolizing Islam. The aspect of *barley bread* is biblical, as it represents the unleavened bread of nature, of which Jesus passed out to the multitude.

One with another a large number in the islands spared ones,	*Entre plusieurs aux isles deportés,*
The one direct line of a pedigree ship with two fangs into there deepest part of the mouth:	*L'un estre nay à deux dents en la gorge:*
Will be perishing from hunger them trees grazed ones,	*Mourront de faim les arbres esbrotés,*
In respect of them new Pope voice of acclamation that is welcoming edict made.	*Pour eux neuf roy nouel edict leur forge.*

Note: Originally listed as quatrain number 7 in Centurie II. The word "*dents*" means "teeth," but is equally meaningful as "fangs." It depends on the animal imagery desired to convey. The word *gorge* translates as "throat," but is said to be "most properly" the bottom or deepest part of the mouth." The translation also includes, "the upper part of the breast, in a woman." The word is repeated in quatrain VIII-41. With the two words separated, "fangs to there breast" brings out a strike of death, much as the form of suicide Cleopatra chose. The word *nouel* initially appears to be novel, but actually is *nouël*. It is a word similar in meaning to "noel," as it refers to feasts and singing at Christmas. However, in general it means a "a voice of acclamation, or congratulation used by the people welcoming such as are gracious with them."

The child will grow to two teeth upon the breast	*L'enfant naistra à deux dentz à la gorge,*
Stones in Tuscia through rain will be falling into:	*Pierres en Tuscie par pluie tomberont:*
Almost nothing from years after not will be corn nor barley,	*Peu d'ans apres ne sera bled, ne orge.*
In respect of to fill those who from hunger will be failing.	*Pour saouler ceux qui de faim failleront.*

Note: Originally listed as quatrain number 42 in Centurie III. The words, "*dents en la gorge,*" were in quatrain II-07, and "*sus la gorge*" in quatrain VIII-41. That last quatrain also used the word "*orge*," which is found here as well. This links the three quatrains together. *Tuscia* is the precise translation of *Tuscie* and Tuscia is comparable with the province of Viterbo today. Viterbo is the northernmost province of the Lazio region, bordering on the Tuscany region (to the north) and the

147

The Epic Poem Prophesied by Nostradamus

Rome province (to the south). The name Tuscany is derived from *Tuscia* and is related to the Latin word, Tuscus, referring to the Etruscan people.

For them appetite from ordinance wholly devoted to worldly delights,	*Pour le plaisir d'edict voluptueux,*
One will mix there poison within the alloy of precious metals:	*On meslera la poyson dans l'aloy:*
Arrived ones will be upon continual journey so valiant,	*Venus sera en cours si vertueux,*
Which will darken with the gold everything in law	*Qu'obfusquera du soleil tout à loy.*

Note: Originally listed as quatrain number 72 in Centurie V. The word *soleil*, as "the *sun*", also carries the alchemical metal value, as *gold*. The word *aloy* carries the primary usage as "allay," particularly of gold and silver, for coins, or the process of working with metals.

Them citizens from Iraq,	*Les citoyens de Mesopotamie,*
Angered ones encountering friends to northeast Spain:	*Yrés encontre amis de Tarraconne,*
Games, agreeable ones, banquet ones, whole nation drowsy	*Jeux, ritz, banquetz, toute gent endormie*
Vicar to the rose-born, seize city, those of Ausones.	*Vicaire au rosne, prins cité, ceux d'Ausone.*

Note: Originally listed as quatrain number 22 in Centurie VII. The place known as Mesopotamia is modern Iraq. Tarragona (*Tarraconensis* people live there) is a port city on the Mediterranean part of Catalonia, in northeast Spain. The word *rit* is a form of the verb *rire*, meaning, "to laugh," but is used to indicate those "agreeable." The capitalized *Vicar* acts as the Bishop of Rome, the Vicar to Jesus, the *Pope*.

Greece

The horrible plague European Turkey & Western Greece,	*L'horrible peste Perynte & Nicopolle,*
Them not Peninsula will hold & Marine tempest,	*Le Chersonnez tiendra & Marceloyne,*
There Northern Greece will empty the Both ends strong,	*La Thessalie vestera l'Amphipolle,*
Disease unknown & a refusal to Anthony.	*Mal incogneu & le refus d'Anthoine.*

Chapter 16 - Fearing One's Neighbors

Note: Originally listed as quatrain number 91 in Centurie IX. *Heraclea Perinthus* (aka: *Perinthe*) is located in what is now Turkey, called *Marmara Ereğli,* in the region of Thrace. It was founded as a Greek colony, with its renowned being its resistance to Phillip II of Macedonia in 340 BC. *Nicopolis* is in Greece, in the region of Epirus, on the Adriatic coast. The name *Nicopolis* is Greek for "city of victory." The ancient Greek city of *Chersonesos* was located in the southwestern part of Crimea, on the shores of the Black Sea, near where present day Sevastopol, Ukraine is located. The name in Greek simply means "peninsula". *Thessaly* is a region of Greece, bordering on the north to Macedonia, to the west to Epirus, to the south to Central Greece and the Aegean Sea to the east. The city of *Amphipolis* is located in ancient Greece, on the edge of the regions of East Macedonia and Thrace, on the Aegean Sea coast. It is interesting to note that Trace and Epirus were considered part of Turkey before the start of World War I, with Thessaly an independent entity, between "Turkey" and "Greece". The question here becomes *Antoine* and who that is. If it is French World War I general Francois Anthoine, this quatrain could be referencing the poor decisions to break up the Ottoman Empire following a stalemate war.

The enemy thoroughly instructed, itself will return disordered,	*L'ennemy docte se tournera confus,*
Great camp ill at ease, & broken by reason of ambushes,	*Grand camp malade, & defaict par embusches,*
Mountain ones Pyrenees & Tunisian will be feat repulse,	*Monts Pyrenees & Pœnus luy seront faict refus,*
Adjoining with the river discovering ancient ones sedges.	*Proche du fleuve descouvrant antiques oruches.*

Note: Originally listed as quatrain number 99 in Centurie VI. The word *oruches* can only be seen as an anagram for "*rouche*," meaning, "rush, sedge."

The great Highly praise worthy from the title to feat corrupt,	*Le grand Antoine du moindre de faict sordide*
With Louse-disease at its furtherest eaten away:	*De Phthyriase à son dernier rongé:*
One who from bullet will intend to be greedy,	*Un qui de plomb voudra estre cupide,*
Going along them favor of elected will be thrust far into.	*Passant le port d'esleu sera plongé.*

Note: Originally listed as quatrain number 88 in Centurie IV. The spelling of *Antoine* is different than the spelling found in quatrain IX-91, where *Anthoine* is the French proper name "Anthony". *Antoine* is pronounced An-twon, and it is French meaning, "beyond praise", or "highly praise worthy." The Latin word "*pythisis*" means, "consumption." This is related to tuberculosis, and stems from the Greek word, "*phthinein,*" which means, "waste away." The name *Phintriase* is a questionable translation. As *Phythias*, one needs to know the mythological story of Damon & Pythias, which is a story about trust. Phythias was *plunged* overboard upon his return to save his friend Damon and had to swim and run to get back in time. Obviously, this is a parallel story.

The Epic Poem Prophesied by Nostradamus

After victory to furious talk,	*Apres victoire de rabieuse langue,*
The heart tested in quiet & repose:	*L'esprit tempté en tranquil & repos:*
Victor bloody by battle feat preached unto,	*Victeur sanguin par conflict faict harangue,*
To roast the tongue & there flesh & them stone of the fruit.	*Roustir la langue & la chair & les oz.*

Note: *Latin: rabies = madness, rage, fury; tempto = to prove, try, test.* Originally listed as quatrain number 56 in Centurie IV. The choice of *rabieuse* can be seen as suggestive of *"rabbi"*, thus hinting in the main theme of anger against Jews.

Chapter 17

A Return to French Glory

By the Process of Elimination

Land Indo-European near to the mountains will tremble,	*Terre Italique pres des monts tremblera,*
Lyon & cock not more than needs entered into a league together ones:	*Lyon & coq non trop confederés,*
Into place with terror the one the other themselves will assist,	*En lieu de peur l'un l'autre s'aidera,*
By itself the one Clean & Celtic peoples patient ones.	*Seul Castulon & Celtes moderés.*

Note: Originally listed as quatrain number 93 in Centurie I. The word *confederéz* also meant "in friendship", which would also apply specifically for the British-French longtime cold relationship. The word *Castulus* has to be rooted in the Latin word *Castus*, meaning, "pure, moral; chaste, virtuous, pious; and, sacred." This splits to say, "the one Pure," from *Castu-l'on*. It then indicates *the one Chastised*. I see *Castulon* as Israel, or more specifically Jerusalem. This quatrain tells that an earthquake in Italy will make *Castulon* all by itself, while the French guard Italy.

From the undefiled French will deliver out of the call of soldiers to duty.	*De castel Franco sortira l'assemblee.*
The ambassador not sporting will cause division in the church:	*L'Ambassadeur non plaisant fera schisme:*
Those with River will be in there mingled,	*Ceux de Ribiere seront en la meslee,*
Likewise to the great gulf will be denying the entry.	*Et au grand goulphre desnieront l'entrée.*

Note: Originally listed as quatrain number 16 in Centurie IX. The word *Franco* is a common surname in Portugese and Spanish which derives from the word "Frank", in reference to the Germanic tribe of the Franks, who invaded the modern-day France during the Migration period. During that period the Germanic Franks migrated into northern France, in the regions of Champagne, Picardy (including the area now Paris) and Normandy. Also, the Old French word "ribe" meant "a coast, etc.", as in sea coast, river-water bank, referring one to the word, "rive." The word Ribiera is Portuguese, with the same meaning. This could make Ribiere be a reference to the Duero River.

The Epic Poem Prophesied by Nostradamus

To shout victory from the great Islam increasing bigger,	*Crier victoire du grand Selin croissant,*
By reason of them ones of Rome will be the Eagle acclaims:	*Par les Romains sera l'Aigle aclamé:*
This Ticino, Milan, & Genoa not there approve of,	*Tuccin, Milan, & Gennes n'y consent,*
Moreover for them self-same King substantial earnestly cried unto.	*Puis par eux mesmes Basil grand reclamé.*

Note: Spanish: *aclamé* = acclaims, applauds. Originally listed as quatrain number 78 in Centurie VI. It has been common for the name *Gennes* to be translated as "Genoa," the Italian city, making it appear to continue a string of Italian cities in line three. However, the correct spelling is "*Gênes*" (Gennes?). The word *Basil* comes from the Old French "*basile*", from the Medieval Latin "*basilicum*," meaning "royal." However, there was a Greek Christian leader who was bishop of Caesarea named *Basil*. He lived in Cappadocia after 370 A.D. He was a vigorous opponent of Aryanism, who became a saint known as "Basil the Great." The word "Aryanism" is defined as, "The doctrines of Arius, denying that Jesus was of the same substance as God and holding instead that he was only the highest of created beings, viewed as heretical by most Christian churches."

Them exiled ones by reason of rage, hatred hidden,	*Les exiles par ire, haine intestine,*
Will be acting with the Pope great private confederacy against:	*Feront au Roy grand conjuration:*
Unknown will be placing enemy ones for there undermined,	*Secret mettront ennemis par la mine,*
Likewise one's old his own ones contrary to them sedition.	*Et ses vieux siens contre eux sedition.*

Note: Originally listed as quatrain number 13 in Centurie I. The phrase *haine intestine* calls for an understanding of "inward *hatred*," as the word *intestine* is further defined as meaning: intestine (guts), inward, privy, hidden, rancorous, and deadly." In line three, the word *mine* is a term that is referencing the underground digging for ore; thus, it could easily be seen as being intended to mean "underground."

Within them island ones so terrible insurrection,	*Dedans les isles si horrible tumulte,*
Wealth one not will listen to which one warlike labored for underhandedly:	*Bien on n'orra qu'une bellique brigue,*
So many great will be from the plunderers the wronged,	*Tant grand sera des predateurs l'insulte,*
That one itself will come to rank in the mighty alliance contracted.	*Qu'on se viendra ranger a la grand ligue.*

Chapter 17 - A Return to French Glory

Note: Originally listed as quatrain number 100 in Centurie II. In line three the word *insulte* also means, "triumph over, wrong, rejoice at, and leap for joy."

Mars reared up at its more secret sudden fear,	*Mars eslevé en son plus haut beffroy,*
Will cause to shrink them Allobroges from France:	*Fera retraire les Allobrox de France:*
There people of Lombardy will make as great terror,	*La gent Lombarde fera si grand effroy,*
With those of the Eagle contained within the limits of at the bottom of the pair of weights.	*A ceux de l'Aigle comprins soubz la balance.*

Note: Originally listed as quatrain number 42 in Centurie V. Line one is a timing element. An *honorable* place for Scorpio is its sign of rulership (Aries or Scorpio) or the sign of Exaltation (Capricorn, especially at 28 degrees). Mars enters Scorpio on August 23, 2012 [total eclipse the following November]. The spelling *beffroy* is found in the 1557 Utrecht edition. The word *baffroy* is an alternate spelling for the same general meanings. The *Allobroges* unsuccessfully tried to keep Hannibal from crossing the Alps. They were independent, yet allied with the Roman presence near their area of control. The word *Lombarde* is the feminine of "*Lombard*," meaning one "of Lombardy. The Lombard people would migrate in stages to eventually cover the region of northern mainland of Italy, including the peninsula region known as Lombardy. *The Eagle* is the USA, but can also represent France; but the balance is indicative of America.

With the belt of Spacious there great cavalry,	*Au cainct de Vast la grand cavalerie,*
Neighboring at Ferrara hindered to the military supply lines:	*Proche à Ferrare empeschee au bagaige:*
Quickly in Turin will be making like practicing birds of prey,	*Prompt à Turin feront tel volerie,*
That within the fortress will be bearing away suddenly their hosts.	*Que dans le fort raviront leur hostaige.*

Note: Latin: *vastus* = *huge, vast, immense, monstrous, empty, unoccupied, wasted, deserted.* French: *vaste: vast, huge, wide, broad, large, spacious, desolate, uninhabited, wild.* Originally listed as quatrain number 27 in Centurie VII. The use of *cavalry* in a modern sense includes tanks, personnel carriers, and helicopters, with all assigned to rapid advancement elements of an army. The use of *hostage* can be seen as being rooted in *host*, which is a synonym for "army". Thus, a *hostaige* can be seen as "one of a host", in particular one who is being "hosted" in a foreign country.

The Epic Poem Prophesied by Nostradamus

The passage to Blaye through La Rochelle & the English	L'entrée de Blaye par Rochelle & l'Anglois
Will strain through beyond them great Arabian king,	Passera outre le grand Aemathien,
Not large distance away from Agen will wait the French,	Non loing d'Agen attendra le Gaulois,
Themselves course Narbonne deceived by maintenance.	Se cours Narbonne decue par entretien.

Note: Originally listed as quatrain number 38 in Centurie IX. This quatrain gives a very clear visual with the aid of a map of French Aquitaine. Both *Blaye* and *La Rochelle* were areas developed first by the *Santones* people of ancient *Gaul*. The people of the Charente-Maritime Department of France, which includes La Rochelle, Rochefort, and Saintes, are called *Anglois*. The English, in general, are referred to as, "*l'Anglais*," but "*Anglois*" was Old French for "Englishman." The spelling of *Aemathien* is different from the earlier spelling, as *Aemathion* (in quatrain IX-64), but should be seen as referring to Osama bin Laden, as representing an *Arabian king*. The 1568 Lyon edition seems to allow for a space between the letters of *Secours*, such that it could be read as *Se cours*. All other editions show "*Secours*," meaning, "Aid, help, assistance." This meaning should be seen in support of "*Themselves*" taking a "*course*" to "*relieve Narbonne*."

Order of France through buttress from great protection,	Classe Gauloise par apuy de grand garde,
Of the mighty god of the Sea & its tridents soldiers:	Du grand Neptune, & ses tridens souldars:
Eaten away ones Provence considering to support substantial company of soldiers,	Rousgée Provence pour soustenir grand bande,
More War Narbonne by reason of javelins & darts.	Plus Mars Narbon par javelotz & dards.

Note: Originally listed as quatrain number 59 in Centurie II. The word *apuy* has been taken as a provincial spelling of "*appui*," which in modern French means, "support." The Old French equivalent, "*appuy*", is the source of *buttress*. The word *buttress* is defined as, "Something that serves to support, prop, or reinforce." This fits the context of this main theme statement perfectly. *Neptune's trident* was a three-pronged weapon that sent forth amazing streaks of lightening. The word *rousgée* can only be seen as a combined form of "*rousse* (or *roux*)" and "*rouge*," both associated with the color "red." *Provence* is a southern region of France, bordering the Mediterranean, from Marseille to Italy. The word *bande* has multiple meanings. One important secondary meaning is that of being "bandaged," showing the injury received from trying to *hold out*. The word *javelot* is of Celtic origin and the word from which the French word "javeline" is the diminutive.

Chapter 17 - A Return to French Glory

An everlasting age for them discerning far off to the day	*Jamais par le descouvrement du jour*
Not will come forward in the world in the sign bearing a scepter	*Ne parviendra au signe sceptifere*
Which whole sum his seat ones neither may be in place of residence,	*Que tous ses sieges ne soient en sejour,*
Carrying from the cock with the THIEVISH having let go.	*Portant au coq du TAG amisere.*

Note: Latin: *sceptrifer* = *scepter-bearing*. Originally listed as quatrain number 61 in Centurie VIII. In line two it can be assumed that the sign scepter-born is either Sagittarius or Pisces, both ruled by Jupiter, whose glyph is a scepter. Both signs have religious meanings, with Pisces the true sign of Christ. Line one then can be seen stating, through discovering of the light of day, the "dawning of the sun." When one realizes the connection (symbolic) between Jesus Christ, Christianity, and the Sun, the element of true royal rule (from the bloodline of Jesus Christ) will keep all common mortal men from truly attaining to the sign Pisces, instead surrounding themselves with the dogma of Sagittarius. Line three points out the mortal limits of all humanly Kings and kings, by stating *being* in the present subjective, where wishing for such lasting glory fills those with one-time power. The word *siege* can also translate as "throne." Line three points out the mortal limits of all humanly Kings and kings, by stating being in the present subjective, where wishing for such lasting glory fills those with one-time power. The word "*coq*" can also translate to mean, "Saint Peter's fish." This is a Biblical reference to a fish caught by Peter, which had a coin in its mouth.

In the lake Fucine from Bénac the waterside,	*Au lac Fucin de Benac le rivaige,*
Taken to the Léman at the port of the Gold-scenario:	*Prins du Leman au port de l'Orguion:*
Ship with three arms foretold warfare figure,	*Nay de troys bras predict belliq image,*
For three crowns to the mighty Endymion.	*Par troys couronnes au grand Endymion.*

Note: Originally listed as quatrain number 73 in Centurie II. While not stated as fact, Lake Fucine, site of the Battle of Fucine Lake (89 BC), in Italy, was a lake with no natural source. Therefore, the Roman may have named it "Counterfeit Lake" due to this. The word "Benac" refers to Lake Garda, the largest lake in Italy, which was formerly known as *Lago Benaco*. Lake Garda is in northern Italy, between Venice and Milan. Lake Fucine was in central Italy, southwest of Rome. Line three is stating a "*Trireme*", where it is a "Ship with three" banks of oars. An oar is then seen as an arm. These are generally large *ships*. In Greek mythology, *Endymion* was a shepherd so lovely the Moon goddess Selene fell in love with him, and asked Zeus to keep him forever young and asleep. Selene saw he was adorable sleeping in his cave. In Greek, Endymion translates as "in dive," or "to dive in." Line four is stating that the souls of three long-dead tyrants will be reborn, arising from their great sleep, as *Endymion* was not dead, only forever sleeping. Nostradamus mentions several such lost leaders, Nero and Hannibal, to name two.

The Epic Poem Prophesied by Nostradamus

Of Rome to have force will be to the whole sum at bottom,	*Romain pouvoir sera du tout abas,*
Its great neighbor to follow the example of their footsteps:	*Son grand voisin imiter ses vestiges:*
Covert ones hatreds secular ones & debates,	*Occultes haines civiles & debats,*
Will be delaying with the buffoons theirs follies.	*Retarderont aux bouffons leurs folies.*

Note: Originally listed as quatrain number 63 in Centurie III. Line one is stating the main theme of the weakness of the Italian (i.e.: Vatican as well) state. Line two is then making a comparative secondary theme statement about France (rather than Switzerland, Austria or Slovenia); but, all of the above fit just as well. Line three is stating the elements of immigration of Muslims (or refugees) into both Italy (in particular) and France, with hidden cells (illegal immigrants), hated cells (the known beggars on the streets, bilking the Western systems) and the citizens of those nations, having immigrated legally. All of these issues will raise *debates* over limits and restrictions. Line four is stating these immigrants will tie up the court systems, simply for the purpose of delaying until time to show they were only using the Western systems of freedoms against the West.

Him great will be born with not Verona & not Vicenza,	*Le grand naistra de Veronne & Vincence,*
Which will bring forth one surname quite vile	*Qui portera un surnom bien indigne*
Who in Venice will want to make vengeance,	*Qui à Venise vouldra faire vengeance,*
Him same self taken subject of the observation & presage.	*Luy mesme prins homme du guet & signe.*

Note: Originally listed as quatrain number 33 in Centurie VIII. The French spelling for Verona, Italy is "*Verone*", with one "*n*." Likewise, the Italian city of Vicenza is correctly spelled as *Vicence*, with only one "*n*". A surname is a family name or last name.

Naples, Florence, To aid & By all means,	*Naples, Florence, Favence, & Imole,*
Will be upon large highways dividing land to resembling trouble:	*Seront en termes de telle fascherie:*
That in respect of to serve to the unhappy from Unwilling,	*Que pour complaire aux malheureux de Nolle,*
Found fault with of to have proposition at its principal commander mockery.	*Plainct d'avoir faict à son chef moquerie.*

Note: Originally listed as quatrain number 74 in Centurie III. The line one main theme statement

Chapter 17 - A Return to French Glory

is saying that Naples (south of Rome) will be the site of a first occurrence, followed then by a separate occurrence in Florence (north of Rome). Both cities are generally along the western coast of Italy. The Italian city named Faenza, is known for pottery (fine china), which is internationally called "faience", with some stating the French form of this word is "favence". If this is true (could not be verified), then the implication would be that Naples and Florence would be as breakable as fine china. The word Imole tantalizes to make it represent the Italian commune Imola; but that city is spelled the same in French, Catalan, Latin, and Occitan. In Latin the word imo bears the same meaning as the word immo, meaning the double "m" can be averted, allowing imole to become immole. It is interesting to note that the word, terme, is also defined as used to denote: a cross-way; a great highway.

Bemoaned Milan, wept Lucca, Flowering,	*Pleure Milan, pleure Luques, Florance,*
That sound great Leader before them chariot will show in quantity,	*Que ton grand Duc sur le char montera,*
To alter the seat of justice nearby to Venice themselves profited by,	*Changer le siege pres de Venise s'avance,*
In that time which Column in Rome will transform.	*Lors que Colomne à Rome changera.*

Note: Originally listed as quatrain number 64 in Centurie X. The word pleure does not translate as, "tear". Old French for "tear" was "pleur". However, the word spelled "pleùre" meant, "a thin and smooth skin wherewith the inside of the ribs is covered." The name Milan is a correct spelling for the city in Italy. However, it is not in the same province as the other two Italian cities (Tuscany). In Old French, the word Milan meant, "kite, puttock, or glede", all of which are birds of prey, similar to eagles and hawks. Additionally, the word "puttock" can also nautically be used to mean the same as a "futtock," which means, "ribs of a ship."

Him by reason of nephew great through forces will prove.	*Le nepveu grand par force prouvera.*
An accord forged from the heart without courage:	*Le pache faict du coeur pusillanime:*
Weapon rare & Cast it Leader will analyze,	*Ferrare & Ast le Duc esprouvera,*
For in that time that in the evening will be the act of many parts in one play.	*Par lors qu'au soir sera le pantomime.*

Note: Originally listed as quatrain number 73 in Centurie IV. When nepveu is seen as an anagram, the lone "p" then acts as the abbreviation for the word "par". Line three is thought to be stating two Italian communes, "Ferrara & Asti," which are in two different northern regions. *Ferrare* is a correct French spelling for Ferrara, but *Ast* is missing the "i". Because both surround an ampersand, making both related as similarities or opposites, one cannot be a city and the other nothing related. For this reason, *Ferrare* is a manufactured word, read as *Fer-rare*, becoming *Weapons-rare*. The Old French word, *ast*, is defined as used in the phrase, "*Armes d'ast*," which meant: weapons to be cast, as darts; and, it then referenced a search of the word "*armes*," where the same usage furthered:

The Epic Poem Prophesied by Nostradamus

any weapons that are usually hurled or cast at an enemy; or, as *"armes d'hast"*: such weapons as have long heads and handles, such as darts, javelins, pikes and spears.

In Lucca blood & milk will come to rain,	*En Luques sang & laict viendra plouvoir,*
A little before transforming from officer of much authority:	*Un peu devant changement de preteur:*
Great plague & warfare, famine & drought will cause to heed	*Grand peste & guerre, faim & soif fera voir*
Far off, in what place will die their potentate curate.	*Loing ou mourra leur prince recteur.*

Note: Originally listed as quatrain number 19 in Centurie III. A *preator* was a Roman judge, or officer of great authority among the Romans. With that word, combined with the Italian commune *Lucca*, line two is saying someone, who was previously *almost nothing before*, will become something great. The word *recteur*, either as *curate*, rector, or parson denotes someone of religious authority, especially as *prince*.

In there wide level piece of ground will be so continual rain,	*En la campaigne sera si longue pluye,*
Also in then Naples so great drought:	*Et en la Pouille si grande siccité:*
Cock will see the Eagle, the wing badly supplied,	*Coq verra l'Aigle, l'aesle mal accomplie,*
For Lyon thrust into will be upon extremity.	*Par Lyon mise sera en extremité.*

Note: Originally listed as quatrain number 52 in Centurie III. TThere are editions that capitalize campaigne, which would make it become an indication of "Campagna", a commune in the province of Salerno, in the "Campagnia" region of Italy, along the Tyrrhenian Sea coast, on the western peninsula. In Old French, the word "Pouille" meant both "louse" and "Naples, Italy." Obviously, there was some distrust of the people in Naples. In modern French, the word Pouilles (s at the end) means, "Apulia, Italy." The Apulia region is on the Adriatic coast of the peninsula, to the heel of the peninsula. Either way, the focus is to southern Italy.

There great Brittany contained within the limits of the England	*La grand Bretagne comprinse l'Angleterre*
Will come by water in sort secret with to overwhelm:	*Viendra par eaux si hault à inunder:*
The degree of kindred strange to Ausonia will make War,	*La ligue neufve d'Ausonne fera Guerre,*
That against them they themselves will be coming to bend a bow.	*Que contre eux ils se viendront bender.*

Chapter 17 - A Return to French Glory

Note: Originally listed as quatrain number 70 in Centurie III.

A general from Ausonia with the Spain ones will march,	Un chef d'Ausonne aux Hespaignes ira,
By sea will make stay in Marseille:	Par mer fera arrest dedans Marseille:
Before his death one extended time will linger,	Avant sa mort un long temps languira,
After one's departure from this life the one will observe great miracle.	Apres sa mort l'on verra grand merveille.

Note: Originally listed as quatrain number 86 in Centurie III. The name *Ausonne* is incorrectly spelled, as the correct spelling for Ausonia (ancient region of Italy, settled by the Ausones) only contains one "n". The use of the abbreviation of "de", as d'Ausonne, would make this possible as an anagram, where the extra "n" becomes the abbreviated "prefix", as *ne d'Ausone*. The Ausones were a tribe in the regions now Lazio (Rome) and Campagna (Naples). The Roman destroyed a town named Ausonia in 314 BC. This yields no connection to Spain, and the quatrain III-70, which also lists *Ausonne*, yields no clear connection to the use of Brittany there.

Within Monaco him Cock will be received,	Dedans Monech le Coq sera receu,
The First rank from France will be apparent	Le Cardinal de France apparoistra
By The orgie one of Rome will be beguiled	Par Logarion Romain sera deceu
Weakness in the eagle, & strength to the French will take beginning.	Foiblesse à l'aigle, & force au coq naistra.

Note: Originally listed as quatrain number 4 in Centurie VIII. *Logarion* is seen as an anagram, as *L'orgia-on*. The word *orgia* is Latin and Italian, from Greek, meaning, "secret rites, mysteries." This is still representative of sexual orgies.

The seven in three month at agreement,	Les sept en trois mis en concorde
In respect of to bring under subjection from the high mountains Apennines:	Pour subjuguer des alpes Apennines:
More there hurried & Ligurian fearful,	Mais la tempeste & Ligure couarde,
Them overcoming upon hasty ones subverted ones.	Les profligent en subites ruines.

Note: Originally listed as quatrain number 39 in Centurie III. The word *profligent* is the Present

159

The Epic Poem Prophesied by Nostradamus

Active Subjunctive, plural form of *profligo*. The Latin word *profligo*, yielding *profligent*, means, *"they see overthrowing."*

The union devised will be scant of continuance,	*L'union faincte sera peu de durée,*
With one changed ones new formed ones there majority:	*Des uns changés reformés la pluspart:*
Within them vessels will be people tolerated ones,	*Dans les vaisseaux sera gent endurée,*
In that time will have Rome one new leopard.	*Lors aura Rome vn nouveau liepart.*

Note: Originally listed as quatrain number 20 in Centurie VI. The main theme line is about the two "United" nations, the United Kingdom and the United States. Line two then states that the "*new formed ones*" will be democratic, rather than monarchic, due to a system based on *majority* will. The use of *Rome* becomes an indication of the promotion of Christianity, while the new formed Christians (those of the Reformation) will be those who have severed direct ties to the Roman Catholic Church. The English coat of arms is multiple lions, which can also be called "*leopards.*"

Certainly France times past beyond sea privet,	*Si France passés outre mer lygustique,*
Quieted you will see in islands & seas shut up on every side:	*Tu te verras en isles & mers enclos:*
Islam adverse, more sea Adriatic,	*Mahommet contraire, plus mer Hadriatique,*
Horses & from blockheads kept secret red-shaven the bone.	*Chevaux & d'asnes tu rougeras les os.*

Note: Originally listed as quatrain number 23 in Centurie III. Here Nostradamus is telling the French people what it will be like in their distant future (now & times past), after the seas will all be sailed and the major land will be divided amongst the powers that be, only the islands will be within France's reach. *Contrary* to the sea, will be the rule given to France in Asia Minor, and the rule it will take in French-Africa. The word *Hadriatique*, while certainly being the Latin spelling for the *Adriatic* Sea, that sea was named after the Roman emperor Hadrian, making that sea named because of characteristics relating to Hadrian. Hadrian was a horseman and was depicted riding a horse on coins and had a monument built in his honor, after his death, showing him at the helm of a 4-*horse* chariot. That Hadrian had a history that was anti-Jewish, actually the first to call Jerusalem a Roman city, forbidding the Jews from worshiping there, and quelling a Jewish uprising. The first part of line four may be referencing this "characteristic" of Hadrian, which took place beyond the *Adriatic* Sea. The word *os* also means "the stone (pit) of a date or olive."

Chapter 17 - A Return to French Glory

From the adventure substantial chaos	*De l'entreprinse grande confusion*
Detriment to inhabitants of a country, riches innumerable:	*Perte de gens, thresor innumerable:*
Held one's peace not must again strain.	*Tu ny dois faire encor tension.*
France has truly to declare burden that must be able to be remembered.	*France a mon dire fais que sois recordable.*

Note: Originally listed as quatrain number 24 in Centurie III. The word *entreprinse* also means, "enterprise, action, adventure, and encroachment upon." The word *perte* also means, "damage, decay and ruin," which becomes the *treasure* of Western Europe. Besides its *people*, is represents the ancient decaying ruins, which will be destroyed, along with the people when the attacks begin. No value can be placed on these *loss*es. In the definition of the Old French word *record*, in parenthesis past "*witness*" was written, "that remembers well the thing he witnesses." This quatrain sums up why Eastern Europeans will be willing to fight as mercenaries. The West of Europe did not feel it "owed" (alternate translation of *dois*) anything to free the East, after it achieved "peace," and later to find "*wealth*." France is one of those most wealthy, and Nostradamus is calling for France to remember there is a heavy load that has been born by the East, at their expense.

Inhabitants of a country from around Tarn, Disinclined, & Garonne,	*Gens d'alentour de Tarn, Loth, & Garonne,*
Watched ones them mountain ones Apennines to transport:	*Gardés les monts Apennines passer:*
Belonging to you grave near to Rome & with Ancona,	*Vostre tombeau pres de Rome & d'Ancone*
The black hair frizzled will make trophy to raise.	*Le noir poil crespe fera trophée dresser.*

Note: Originally listed as quatrain number 43 in Centurie III. It is assumed that the word *Loth* means *Lot*, where *th > t*. The Lot River is called the *Olt*, in both Occitan and Catalan. All three names: *Tarn*, *Lot* and *Garonne* are rivers; but, the first two are smaller, east to west feeder rivers, emptying into the major *Garonne*, which runs north to the Atlantic Ocean, from the southern Pyrenees Mountains. It represents southwestern France, in particular a region once possessed by the English. As such, the word *loth* is a Middle English version of "loath," and the translation is based on that. The name Garonne comes from ancient Aquitanian (similar to Basque language), which basically means, "source from rock". The name Ancona comes from Greek, and means, "elbow." The "black hair frizzled" is a theme repeated in other quatrains.

The Epic Poem Prophesied by Nostradamus

By reason of dead there France will embrace journey in to act,	Par mort la France prendra voyage à faire,
Fleet on sea, footing mountains Pyrenees,	Classe par mer, marcher monts Pyrénées,
Spain upon sedition, to march nation soldier-like:	Espaigne en trouble, marcher gent militaire:
To them more mighty Of spirit-ones into France fetched unto ones.	Des plus grand Dames en France emmenées.

Note: Originally listed as quatrain number 2 in Centurie IV. The word Dames is translated as *D'ames*. Still, line four could be a secondary meaning reference to women in the military, as line three ended with a colon. This sorts to the preparation at Bordeaux and signals that Spain will already become unstable, causing the French to march their border with Spain, before sending troops to Italy.

From Sens, to Autun will be coming until at the Rhone	De Sens, d'Autun viendront jusques au Rosne,
For to pass beyond towards them mountains Pyrenees:	Pour passer outre vers les monts Pyrénées:
There kindred to deliverto the Mark of Ancona,	La gent sortir de la Marque d'Anconne,
By land & sea them will pursue with mighty ones traps for ravenous beasts	Par terre & mer le suivra à grans trainées.

Note: Originally listed as quatrain number 74 in Centurie II. The word Sens is both a clean French word and a correctly spelled name of a commune in the French Department of Yonne. Sens is north of Autun, which is in the Department of Saône-et-Loire. The major rivers of Saône-et-Loire are the Saône and the Loire, with the Saône running north-south, running into the Rhone River, in the convergence at Lyon. The word sens means, "sense, understanding, and judgment." The word Rosne is a Provencal spelling, more applicable today for denoting the Petit Rhone. The spelling, Ros-ne can be translated as "Rose-born," which gives a total religious meaning to the main theme line (along with "judgment" translated). Still, line one would then literally be from understanding that which is between Auton and Lyon, meaning the Saône River. In Latin, Ancon was representative of the Italian town on the Adriatic Coast, Ancona. In Catalan, the word March is spelled Marques. A March is derived from the Latin word Marca, and is the term for a border area, or frontier. The March of Ancona was a region of eastern Italy, with the name Ancona derived from its Greek settlers, with a name meaning, "elbow." There is history associated with that location. The word trainee means, "a train for a wolf, or any such wild and ravenous beast", and, it refers to the word "trainement." That word means, "a trailing, drawing or dragging along." However, the word "traine" means, "a drag-net or draw-net", such that trainees are those ones laying a trap for such beasts are to be caught.

Declining that the eagle & the cock at Savona	Pendant que l'aigle & le coq à Savone

Chapter 17 - A Return to French Glory

Being equal ones Sea East country & Hungary,	*Seront unis Mer Levant & Ongrie,*
The army in Naples, By go-between, March to muscle of the elbow.	*L'armee à Naples, Palerne, Marque dancone.*
Rome, Venice by Barbarous horrible outcry.	*Rome, Venise par Barb' horrible crie.*

Note: Originally listed as quatrain number 9 in Centurie VIII. The commune of Savona is in the province of Liguria, which is the western coastal province of Italy, bordering with France, just where the Italian peninsula begins to jut south. The Ligurian Sea is off this coast, and Genoa is east of Savona. The Greek word *ancone* means, "elbow," with *ancon* the Latin word meaning the elbow muscle. Ancona is a port city at the point of an "elbow" bend on Italy's Adriatic coast. Quatrain II-74 also mentions "*Marque d'Anconne*", with an extra "*n*". The "March of Ancona" is a term dated to the Middle Ages, as a march designating a political division of the Papal States. As a Papal State, a "rector", who was accountable to the Pope, ruled Ancona. The word *Barb'* must be seen as including a printer's mark for abbreviation. The translation is from *Barbare*.

The bird to prey fast running in there to the left,	*L'oyseau de proye volant à la senestre,*
Deeply in battle done with the French trimming:	*Avant conflict faict aux Françoys pareure:*
The one virtuous will take the one doubtful disaster,	*L'un bon prendra l'un ambigue sinistre,*
The severed farm animal stomach (honeycomb tripe) will hold for good prediction of things to come.	*La partie foyole tiendra par bon augure.*

Note: Originally listed as quatrain number 34 in Centurie I. The Old French word *pareure* leads to the spelling "*parure*," which is defined as meaning, "a decking, tricking, trimming; also, array, apparel, attire." This means a *battle with them in French attire*, or uniforms. The word *senestre* means "left", being synonymous with "*gauche*," while also translating as "sinister." The 1568 Lyon edition clearly shows *foyole* in line four, which is the Italian word, "*foiolo*," which means tripe made from the second and third parts of ruminating animal stomachs. The implication is seeing the entrails of animals (cows), cut open in the field of battle, acting as an omen, as in days long past.

Them joined ones for ease of the great band of soldiers,	*Les assemblés par repos du grand nombre,*
On land & sea advice contradicted:	*Par terre & mer conseil contremandé:*
Well-nigh to the Autumn Genoa, Nice from the pretense	*Pres de l'Automne Gennes, Nice de l'ombre,*
By open pieces of ground &, towns the principal commander contra-banded.	*Par champs &, villes le chef contrebandé.*

The Epic Poem Prophesied by Nostradamus

Note: Originally listed as quatrain number 64 in Centurie V. The word *contrebandé*, is derived from its Old French meaning, where neutral forces were called upon to get between two belligerent parties, to calm them down. Otherwise, the word means an illegal, untaxed substance, as contraband. There is also a clear mark, like a comma, following the ampersand in line four, and before the word "*villes.*" It apparently was placed there on purpose, because it has its own space between the ampersand and the word "villes" It almost looks like a "*j*", which only appears in the Roman numeral usage of *The Prophecies*, possibly as a sign indicating "-th." For example, *xiiij.* appears in a quatrain in the 1555 edition, and in the 1568 edition as *xxvij.de Juing*, at the end of the letter to Henry. However, those examples have dots over the "i" and "j," and this mark does not. One must read this as the ampersand marking an important time of separation or pause, if a comma is the intention.

The conductor of the army of France,	*Le conducteur de l'armée Francoise,*
Thinking to spend idly the most special battalion of soldiers:	*Cuidant perdre le principal phalange:*
By reason of upon paved from porphyry & of slate,	*Par sus pavé de lavaigne & d'ardoise,*
Himself will discharge through Genoa people foreign.	*Soy profondra par Gennes gent estrange.*

Note: Originally listed as quatrain number 39 in Centurie VII. The word *parfondra* is the 3rd conjugation, derived from the word *fondre*, and *parfondu*. It is a process used in the making of glass, or possibly the assembly of stained glass, where lead is melted. This should be seen as relating to the word *lavaigne*, which is split into *lava-igne*, thus heated lava turned to porphyry.

Everything at them on all sides of there mighty warned to appear,	*Tout à l'entour de la grande cité,*
Will be soldiers encampments on open pieces of ground & enclosed towns	*Seront soldatz logez par champs & ville*
To deliver up the assault Paris, Rome instigated,	*Donner l'assaut Paris, Rome incité,*
Over the sea at that time will be achievement great bereaved of all.	*Sur le pont lors sera faicte grand pille.*

Note: Originally listed as quatrain number 30 in Centurie V. The encamped soldiers are clearly stated, in other quatrains, to be in Italy. Line three is stating that the capitals of France and Italy will have "encouraged" the attacks on their soil by their actions to place French troops in Italy. The move will be because of Muslim instabilities seen as threatening. All sides means from Eastern Europe, North Africa, and the Middle East, as well as from east, west, and south shorelines.

Chapter 17 - A Return to French Glory

Near to Ticino them inhabitants from Loire,	*Pres de Thesin les habitans de Loyre,*
Garonne & Saône, Seine, Silvering, & Gironde:	*Garonne & Saonne, Seine, Tain, & Gironde:*
Beyond the mountains will be advancing promontory,	*Outre les monts dresseront promontoire,*
Battle given Pau that substantial, overflowed by water surge of the sea.	*Conflict donné Pau granci, submergé onde.*

Note: Originally listed as quatrain number 79 in Centurie VI. The use of the West Lombard spelling for the Ticino River is an indication of the focus placed on the Lombard provinces, particularly Milan, and where the Ticino reaches the Po River. Those inhabiting near the Ticino from the Loire River areas, would have to be French. Line two is the stating more places where French troops came from, and also where the French people have less defenses.

The Sail as Mesh of net port Marseille inclined,	*Voille Symacle port Massiliolique,*
Inwardly Venice carriage of a man to proceed with the Slavic peoples:	*Dans Venise port marcher aux Pannons:*
To divide from the gulf & secret feelings people of the Adriatic,	*Partir du goulfre & sinus Illirique,*
Waste to Age, people of Liguria blows from cannons.	*Vast à Secile, Ligurs coups de canons.*

Note: Latin: *sinus [in a coastline]* = bay, gulf / *Illyrii* = people on the Adriatic [i.e.: non-Italian /Macedonian]; *vasto* = to empty, lay waste, devastate, ravage, prey upon. Originally listed as quatrain number 28 in Centurie IX. The word Symacle can also generate the word mascle (French macle), which is a blazon of heraldry, in a diamond shape, where the mesh of a net is the symbol on a flag, or other standard bearer. The ancient city of Marseille was called Massilia, in 300 AD. The name Pannonia comes from the Illyrian language.

Him light yellow in the disgrace gallows will arrive to give over,	*Le blonde au nez forche viendra commettre,*
By reason of a war & will follow after on the outside of:	*Par le duelle & chassera dehors:*
The banished ones within will cause to pardon,	*Les exiles dedans fera remettre,*
At the places marine ones giving over them more chance.	*Aux lieux marins commettant les plus fors.*

Note: Originally listed as quatrain number 67 in Centurie II. The word *nez* also means "nose." The Old French word *forche* is the diminutive for the word meaning "fork." The word fourche

The Epic Poem Prophesied by Nostradamus

(acceptable variation of forche) translates as "gibbet", which is a, "T-shaped structure for hanging a person until dead."

To mind of government state of defenses in public disgraces,	*D'esprit de regne munismes descriées,*
As well will be peoples stirred up ones against their King:	*Et seront peuples esmeuz contre leur Roy:*
Peace, achievement unheard of before, profane ones laws impaired ones,	*Paix, faict nouueau, sainctes loix empirées*
Plundered places never had been in so very-harsh order.	*Rapis onc fut en si tresdur arroy.*

Note: Latin: *rapio = to seize, snatch, tear away.* Originally listed as quatrain number 23 in Centurie VI. As a future quatrain, the only *King* who will hold any responsibility for national weapons and *munitions* is one yet to take power in England.

Milan, Ferrara, Turin, & the Eagles,	*Milan, Ferrare, Turin, & Aquilleye,*
Cape-born, Calibria afflicted ones by people Celtic:	*Capne, Brundis vexés par gent Celtique:*
By reason of the Lion & battalion defending the frontier	*Par le Lyon & phalange aquilee*
Regarding Rome will have the end of a time ancient British.	*Quant Rome aura le chef vieux Britannique.*

Note: Latin: *Brundisium = a seaport in Calibria [Brindisi, Italy].* Originally listed as quatrain number 99 in Centurie V. The French word *Cap* means cape, as in an area of land meeting the sea. It also means a promontory or hill outstretched into the sea. The promontory of Brindisi is the "heel" of the "boot" of Italy. In the upper-case, the name *Aquilee* is the coastal city known now as Aquiliea, in the province of Udine, Italy.

The mighty Prelate Celtic to King doubted,	*Le grand Prelat Celtique à Roy suspect,*
Of night through continual journey will depart out of from the realm:	*De nuict par cours sortira hors du regne:*
For commander much yielding to his great Chief, Brittany,	*Par duc fertile à son grand Roy, Bretaigne,*
Brown-state in This-nearby & Tunis into suspect.	*Bisance à Cipres & Tunes insuspect.*

Note: Originally listed as quatrain number 53 in Centurie VI. The French spelling for the island "Cyprus" is "*Chypre*." *Cipres* is reference to cypress trees. The *Cypress* tree is tied to ancient Iran, while also being associated with Hades in Greek mythology.

Chapter 17 - A Return to French Glory

With the general Englishman at Nimes mainly sojourning,	Au chef Anglois à Nymes trop sejour,
Towards the Spanish peninsula to comfort Bronze-beard:	Devers l'espaigne au secours Aenobarbe:
Many will be dying through War evident this day,	Plusieurs mourront par Mars ouvert ce jour,
Regarding into Artois to slip star in Barbary horse.	Quant en Artois faillir estoille en barbe.

Note: Originally listed as quatrain number 59 in Centurie V. *Artois* was a separate European country, between Flanders and France, until absorbed by France. Line four, when read quickly, and syntactically, appears to state, "When in Artois will fall a bearded star". A "bearded star" is a comet, which means some form of space dust will make a fiery descent and land in Artois. However, when read according to the systems of Nostradamus, that image dissipates, although it is still valid as a secondary timing element. Line four, as supporting details to the secondary theme (line two), is detailing Aenobarbe, which if a person, is a "star" of the Barbary Coast, traveling to request assistance from France, a former dominator of North Africa. A "star" could be seen as a term meaning, "spur".

A successor of there territory ruled by a General commander will grow,	Le successeur de la Duché viendra,
Greatly more pierced than the sea of Tuscany:	Beaucoup plus outre que la mer de Tosquane:
People of Gaul line of pedigree there Florence will maintain,	Gauloise branche la Florence tiendra,
In its lap from agreement nautical Frog.	Dans son giron d'accord nautique Rane.

Note: Originally listed as quatrain number 3 in Centurie V. The "*sea of Tuscany*" is the Ligurian Sea. The word "*nautical*" is defined as, "Of, relating to, or characteristic of ships, shipping, sailors, or navigation on a body of water." A Frog swims on top of water, as well as under water and also walks on land (i.e.: amphibious). Under the definition of "frog", it is said that the term is "derogatory to a French person", as a Frog is a descendant of Gaul, or person of French ancestry.

From the true branch with flower of lily born of	Du vray rameau de fleur de lys issu
Thrust into & sojourning at a place inheritor of Etruria:	Mis & logé heritier d'Hetrurie:
Its blood ancient from continual outstretched public authority woven,	Son sang antique de longue main tissu,
Will cause Florence to flourish upon the armory.	Fera Florence florir en l'armoirie.

The Epic Poem Prophesied by Nostradamus

Note: Originally listed as quatrain number 39 in Centurie V. The symbolic nature of the *lily* must be seen in the main theme statement. During the Middle Ages, the *lily* was in religious art, particularly in depictions of Jesus. Thus, the *lily* is symbolic of spirituality, with the white lily a reflection of purity. France has the *fleur de lis* as its symbol, due to its royal lineage being from this purity and spirituality. *Etruria* basically covers the region of Tuscany, although it stretched further north and inland that the present-day province. It included what is now Tuscany, Latinum, Emilia-Romagna, and Umbria. The heraldry of *Florence* yields a coat of arms bearing a single red *fleur de lis*. An *armory* is not only a place to store arms, but the place weapons are made, as well as the arsenal produced.

An equal will be upon exile sent back,	*Un juste sera en exil renvoyé,*
By reason of plague in the neighbor ones of Long-needy ones:	*Par pestilence aux confins de Nonseggle:*
Resolution to them red them will be infected,	*Response au rouge le sera desvoyé,*
Chief retiring at there Frog & with the eagle.	*Roy retirant à la Rane & à l'aigle.*

Note: Originally listed as quatrain number 46 in Centurie VI. The word *Nonseggle* is read as an anagram in Italian, *Non-legge-s*, meaning, "*Not law ones*." The use of Italian identifies a *neighbor* of Italy. A colon follows the word, making line three yield the clarification, where the use of the color *rouge* indicates those of Communism, which was a *plague* upon former Catholic Christians. Those "*neighbor ones*" to Italy, are the former Yugoslavia nations of Slovenia and Croatia. The word *Rane* was repeated in quatrain V-03, which links these two quatrains together. *Rane* means *Frog*, which was a slur upon someone French.

Who in the Realm people of Navarre will achieve,	*Qui au Royaume Navarrois parviendra,*
When of Age & Naples will be yoked ones:	*Quand de Secile & Naples seront joints:*
Bigorre & lands through time border one will sustain,	*Bigore & landes par foyx loron tiendra,*
From one which to Spain will be for too much conjoined.	*D'un qui d'Hespaigne sera par trop conjoint.*

Note: Latin: *Neapolis [Naples] = new city.* Originally listed as quatrain number 25 in Centurie III. *Navarre* is a Basque autonomous community in Spain, with its northern border in the Pyrenees. The word *Secile* is read as an anagram, as *Siecle*, meaning, "Century, Age, Time, or Season." The 1568 Lyon edition shows *Bigore* beginning line three, whereas the 1557 Utrecht edition shows *Bigorre*. *Bigorre* was once an autonomous Gascon country in the French Pyrenees, which now makes up the majority of the department *Hautes-Pyrenees*. It was once a part of the *Navarre* holdings. *Landes* is a department in France on the Atlantic Coast, and part of Gascony / Aquitaine, but the lower-case spelling makes it refer to the root meaning, which is "*lands*." *Foix* was a county of southern France, constantly dealing with Navarre, Gascony and Aquitaine. However, its lower-case spelling makes it mean "time ones" from *fois'*, or faith ones, from *foy-s*.

Chapter 17 - A Return to French Glory

An overseer of the government quite cunning,	*Le gouverneur du regne bien scauant,*
Not to allow of well wishing unto with in the deed Kingly:	*Ne consentir voulant au faict Royal:*
Thousand them division by reason of the adverse rumor,	*Mellile classe par le contraire vent,*
Him will release to his more treacherous.	*Le remettra à son plus desloyal.*

Note: Originally listed as quatrain number 45 in Centurie VI. Line two's capitalization of Royal means the secondary theme refers to either an English or Papal decree. Since Britain currently has a Queen, rather than a King, this presently makes a Papal decree seem more likely. However, if the Royal is a reference to a Muslim nation, such as the Crown Prince of Saudi Arabia, line one could be Osama bin Laden, with line two referencing King Abdullah.

The principal commander from Persia will supply all wants mighty pertaining to Iraq,	*Le chef de Perse remplira grande Olchade,*
Fleet Warship towards people Muslim	*Classe trireme contre gent Mahometique*
Of Parthian, & Median, & to make havoc of the Cyclades,	*De Parthe, & Mede, & piller les Cyclades,*
Peace long time to the great port of Ionia.	*Repos long temps au grand port Ionique.*

Note: Originally listed as quatrain number 64 in Centurie III. The word *Olchade* is read as an anagram, *Chaldeo*, meaning, *of Chaldea*. *Parthia* was an ancient empire of Persia, of the Arsacid Dynasty (150 BCE to CE 224). *Media* was one of the conquests of the Parthenians. The *Cyclades* are Greek islands and beyond the scope of *Parthian* conquests. Iona was a part of Greece (Western coast and islands) under Persian dominion, which was the place of the first rebellion, leading to the Golden Age of Greece.

There ship east unaccustomed for them torment of the sea,	*La nef estrange par le tourment marin,*
Will draw near unto as it were touching from port not estrange:	*Abourdera pres de port incogneu:*
For all that presages of bough to strike down with palm of the hand upon,	*Nonobstant signes de rameau palmerin,*
Next unto dead, pillaged, sincere judgment long in coming sprung.	*Apres mort, pille: bon avis tard venu.*

Note: Originally listed as quatrain number 30 in Centurie I. Line three is stating that it has been

The Epic Poem Prophesied by Nostradamus

prophesied that God will strike down and break to pieces those who have turned against Him, just as a potter's vase against stone will break. A rameau, as bough, or branch, shows how the Latin word for "rod" (virga) also translates as "green twig."

There squadron of soldiers within the marine rank,	*La legion dans la marine classe,*
Quicklime, Magnesia sulfur, & pitch will burn:	*Calcine, Magnes soulphre, & poix bruslera:*
Them tedious peace to the settled spacious plain,	*Le long repos de lasseuré place,*
Port Islam, Hercules fire them will destroy unto nothing.	*Port Selyn, Hercle feu les consumera.*

Note: Originally listed as quatrain number 23 in Centurie IV. The Old French dictionary specified a *legion* as being: a squadron of 6830 soldiers, with 730 horsemen and the remaining 6100 footmen. *Magnesia* is a small section of the eastern mainland of Greece. Combined with *sulfur*, this could mean "Greek fire," rather than "magnesium sulfate" (Epsom salt). This is then supported by *Hercules fire* in line four. In the mythology, Hercules soaked a shirt in a poisonous mixture that burned into his skin, causing his flesh to rip off when he tried to remove the shirt. To end his suffering he had them build a funeral pyre, which he set himself into, ending his life. The mortal was burned off by the fire, leaving his immortal self to join with the gods.

Chapter 18

Another Infamous Day in American History

Like Shooting Fish in a Barrell

Between them two singular rulers banished ones,	*Entre les deux monarques esloignés,*
In that time that the Land by reason of Islam light fallen away:	*Lors que le Sol par Selin clair perdue:*
Private hatred mighty amongst both much offended ones,	*Simulte grande entre deux indignés,*
Whom to the Islands & Siena there freedom yielded.	*Qu'aux Isles & Sienne la liberté rendue.*

Note: Originally listed as quatrain number 58 in Centurie VI. The word *Sol*, in French, primarily meant "ground, soil," but capitalized it carries the Latin meaning as "*Sun.*" The use of *Sun*, at all times, must be seen as a reference to Christianity. The capitalization of *Isles* makes it important Islands, of which the Mediterranean Sea Islands (Corsica, Sardinia, Sicily, Crete, Malta, etc.) would relate to Siena, as the Islands of Italy.

Thirty partakers to the order of them ones to entreat	*Trente adherans de l'ordre des quyretes*
Seized ones the net benefits given ones their adversaries,	*Bannys lers biens donnez ses adversaires,*
Whole sum theirs favor will be in regard of ill-deserving ones,	*Tous leurs bienfaits seront pour demerites*
Armed forces of high nests of hawks yielded over unto ones in them pirate ships.	*Classe épargie délivrez aux corsaires.*

Note: Latin: *quirito* = to shriek, scream, cry out. Greek: *eparchia* = rule over. A *Corsair* was a pirate ship and especially associated with the Barbary Coast, which is now Morocco, Algeria, Libya and Tunisia (from *Berber*).

The Epic Poem Prophesied by Nostradamus

Under one there peace for all will be claimed,	Soubz un la paix par tout sera m clamée,
But not long opportunity robbed & public revolt:	Mais non long temps pillé & rebellion:
By reason of refusal enclosed town world, & sea violated,	Par refus ville terre, & mer entamée,
Deaths & subjects them third to one million.	Mors & captifz le tiers d'un million.

Note: Originally listed as quatrain number 92 in Centurie I. The word *clamée* can also mean, "challenged, demanded, and called out loud." Line four seems to be telling of 333,000 people being subjected to violation. However, when read slower, one can see how *one-third* of a population can become prisoners to a total of *one million* persecutors.

Them great with the thunderbolt fallen from space done by day,	Le grand du fouldre tumbe d'heure diurne,
Grief & prophesied through bringer claimant:	Mal & predict par porteur postulaire:
Ensuing presage tombstone of time nocturnal,	Suivant presaige tumbe d'heure nocturne,
Battle Reims London, Etruscan has the plague.	Conflit Reims Londres, Etrusque pestifere.

Note: Originally listed as quatrain number 26 in Centurie I. An *Etruscan* is anyone from Etruria, which is central-northern Italy, peninsula and mainland.

The Lowest level of a place & the eagle to the victor will be presenting itself,	Le Sol & l'aigle au victeur paroistront,
Backward abandoned weak with the overmastered the one assured:	Responce vaine au vaincu l'on asseure:
By reason of judgment neither cries harness nor will be settling,	Par cor ne crys harnois n'arresteront,
Vengeance peace for dead so finished at the hour.	Vindicte paix par mort si acheve à l'heure.

Note: Originally listed as quatrain number 38 in Centurie I. Randal Cotgrave included, in his translation of *"parvoir"*, "to appear as the day in the morning, or the *Sun* over the mountain." In French, the word *cor* means a hunter's horn. However, in Latin, *cor* translates as "heart." Note also that line four's *the hour* is reminiscent of the Letter of Preface and it coming to the "final hour" of mankind.

Chapter 18 - Another Infamous Day in American History

Him-before-Christ three quite quickly brought to nothing ones,	*L'antechrist trois bien tost annichilez,*
Twenty & seven years kindred will sustain his war,	*Vingt & sept ans sang durera sa guerre,*
Them heretics killed ones, captive, exiled ones,	*Les heretiques mortz, captif, exilez,*
Blood corpse human water funeral pyres to hail earth.	*Sang corps humain eau rogie gresler terre.*

Note: Originally listed as quatrain number 77 in Centurie VIII. This is identifying one leader who will begin a multi-pronged attack, where *three* will *quickly* be *destroyed*. This means *three* committed to Christ, or Christian nations, will fall at the beginning of the final hour of mankind. These will be the *three* that will fall in the invasions in Spain, Italy and France and renounce, or annul their historic position as Christian. This will lead to the subsequent surrender of *Twenty* important allies, if not *Twenty* others falling afterwards. Thus, the identification as *L'antechrist* becomes important as *the Antichrist* (who is to come *before Christ*), who is earlier identified as Osama bin Laden.

At what time them defection from the Sun in that time will be,	*Quand le deffault du Soleil lors sera*
On a plain piece of ground without house or tree daylight the thing bred contrary to nature will be beheld:	*Sur le plain jour le monstre sera veu:*
Everything except that one him will interpret	*Tout autrement on l'interpretera*
Costliness not with guardian idle neither unto him will enjoy gift.	*Cherté n'a garde nul n'y aura pourveu.*

Note: Originally listed as quatrain number 34 in Centurie III. Notice the use of *Soleil* in line one. It is the primary French word for "*Sun*". The primary French used for "*Sol*" is "Soil." Latin has the primary use of *Sol* as Sun. When Nostradamus referred to the *Sun*, he meant Christianity in general, and to Jesus (the Light) specifically. A *default* or *defection from the Sun* indicates a time when Christian values no longer lead a Christian nation. The word *plain* is also translated to mean, "plain piece of ground, without house or tree; and, flat, even smooth, without wrinkles and without rubs." The *guardian not with* is God, making line four hint at Israel being the location of the plain piece of ground. A desert is such a *plain*, but there is a vast series of *plains* along the Mediterranean coast of Israel.

The Epic Poem Prophesied by Nostradamus

The gods will be forging in the humane ones manifestation.	*Les dieux feront aux humains apparence.*
These who they will be authors of mighty battle:	*Ce qu'ilz seront auteurs de grand conflict:*
Before heaven beheld fair weather sword & lance,	*Avant ciel veu serain espée & lance,*
That which towards sinister will be more great afflicted.	*Que vers main gauche sera plus grand afflit*

Note: Originally listed as quatrain number 91 in Centurie I. The similarities surrounding the ampersand in line three are weapons. Neither a sword nor a lance which would have been looked for coming from the *sky* in medieval times.

will be heard ones in the sky them weapons to beat:	*Seront oys au ciel les armes batre:*
This one year same them belonging to God ones enemies:	*Celuy an mesme les divins ennemis:*
Will be wanting laws religious ones unreasonably to examine,	*Voudront loix sainctes injustement debatre,*
Through lightning & war with good reason believers to death thrust into.	*Par foudre & guerre bien croyans à mort mis.*

Note: Originally listed as quatrain number 43 in Centurie IV. The word "*oys*" or "*ois*" the plural past participle of the Old French verb, *ouïr*, meaning, "to hear, to listen." The translation is then "heard ones."

By reason of lightning into the coffer gold & silver melted,	*Par fouldre en l'arche or & argent fondu,*
From two captive ones the one the other will feed:	*Des deux captifz l'un l'autre mangera:*
To there warned to appear them more great dispersed mightily,	*De la cité le plus grand estendu,*
At what time submerged the fleet will swim.	*Quand submergée la classe nagera.*

Note: Originally listed as quatrain number 13 in Centurie III. The word *arche* meant, "coffer, chest, bin; the Ark of Noah, arch of a bridge and the well of the pump of a ship." Line one become reminiscent of the Ark of the Covenant, due to the electrical charge and dissolving-melting capabilities it was known to show. Keep in mind, Nostradamus used the symbolisms of color to include *gold* and *silver*. Gold stands for the Sun (alchemically), thus Christianity. Silver stands for the Moon (alchemically), thus Islam. Still, as valuable metals, gold and silver melted represents an expensive form of lightning, which was placed into a container of some kind. Line two seems to

174

Chapter 18 - Another Infamous Day in American History

describe nuclear fusion, with the release of energy in the process being able to melt metals.

Mightily the firmament bemoaned the Hermaphrodite procreated,	*Trop le ciel pleure l'Androgyn procrée,*
As it were touching from this heaven blood human spilt:	*Pres de ce ciel sang humain respandu:*
Through death more than needs lingering great people recreated,	*Par mort trop tarde grand peuple recrée,*
Late & suddenly comes the assistance expected.	*Tard & tost vient le secours attendu.*

Note: Latin: *androgynus* = *hermaphrodite*. Originally listed as quatrain number 45 in Centurie II. Line one is similar to line two in quatrain III-13, where it states, "From two captive ones the one the other will feed". A Hermaphrodite has both "one" and "the other", which joins in the production known as "procreation". The "thunderbolt" from line one of quatrain III-13 appears in association with rain, which is a time when the sky is found weeping.

The enclosure prone unto substantial extreme misery,	*Le parc enclin grande calamité,*
By reason of them Western & Insubres will cause:	*Par l'Hesperie & Insubre fera:*
A fire upon ship plague & captivity,	*Le feu en nef peste & captivité,*
Mercury into Sagittarius Saturn will decay.	*Mercure en l'Arc Saturne fenera.*

Note: Originally listed as quatrain number 65 in Centurie II. The name *l'Arc* can be referring to an important *arch* (of architecture) or arc (angle of trajectory), as an abbreviation for the verb "*arquer.*" However, *l'Arc* must also be seen as *the Archer*, or the symbol for the sign of *Sagittarius*. The verb *fener* in use, as "*se fener*" means, "to fade, wither, wax deadish, to decay." The meaning of *Mercury will fade*, is its apparent slowing of formard motion, to then appear to go retrograde. *Mercury* will be at 0 degrees of *Sagittarius* on October 29, 2012, move to 4 degrees by November 5, 2012, when it will station retrograde on November 6th, staying retrograde for 20 days. In its apparant backwards motion, it will reenter Scorpio on November 14th. *Mercury* will then slow, stop, and go direct, re-entering Sagittarius on December 11, 2012. It will finally leave the sign of *the Archer* on New Year's Eve. *Saturn*, whose symbol is the scythe, would be acting the grim reaper while in the sign of Scorpio the entire time.

Mighty warned to appear to soldiers given over,	*Grande cité à souldartz abandonnée,*
Never not there you have had deadly insurrection so close unto,	*Onques ny eust mortel tumult si proche,*
Alas! what ghastly calamity themselves drawn near to,	*O quel hideuse calamité s'approche,*

The Epic Poem Prophesied by Nostradamus

All out an offense neither will be forgiven.	Fors une offence ny sera pardonnée.

Note: Originally listed as quatrain number 96 in Centurie VI. Latin: tumultus = uproar, violent commotion, turmoil, panic, impending war. Since the word tumult is spelled in the English manner (without the e at the end), the tumult, sedition, uproar, etc. can be seen as being directed towards Britain and America. Randal Cotgrave detailed the use of "O" in French as, "An interjection of grieving, wondering, wishing, anger, exclamation, derision, contempt, etc.", and then continued, "Sometimes in speeches of wonder and mockery it is not expressed, but understood."

There pillage done at the coast marine,	La pille faite à la côte marine,
About moving quickly young & kinsmen led ones	In cita nova & parens amenez,
Many to Malta for the feat of Messina,	Plusieurs de Malte par le fait de Messine,
Strait tightened ones with iron ones being evil rewarded ones.	Etroit ferrez seront mal guerdonnez.

Note: Latin: *In cito novus* = into motion new [feminine singular]; *parens* = parent, ancestor, but also from *pareo* = to appear, become evident. Originally listed as quatrain number 61 in Centurie IX. Messina is a Sicilian city, at the tip of Sicily closest to the peninsula of Italy's "toe." Malta is an island nation to the southwest of Sicily, between Sicily and the North African coast – east of Tunisia, north of Libya. Between Sicily and Tunisia runs the Strait of Sicily, which turns into the Malta Channel, between Sicily and Malta. Between the narrow strait between the peninsula and Sicily is the Strait of Messina.

Above them rock ones blood one will see to rain down,	Sur les rochers sang on verra plouvoir,
Soil East, Patience Western:	Sol Orient, Saturne Occidental:
Near to Orgon warfare, at Rome great evil to observe,	Pres d'Orgon guerre, à Rome grand mal voir,
Ships of melted ones & seized them having Three-prongs.	Nefz parfondrees & prins le Tridental.

Note: Originally listed as quatrain number 62 in Centurie V. The *Sun* rises in the *East* every day, but *Soil East* would be Asia (including Asia Minor). This would indicate where the *rock ones* would be. Still, line two can equally be stating an astronomical alignment, where the *Sun* is it is opposed by *Saturn*. In the year 2012, Saturn will move from the sign Libra into the sign Scorpio. The Sun will be in the opposite sign of Taurus (the sign opposite Scorpio) in April-May, both in 2013 and 2014. It will be in Aries, opposite Saturn in Libra in March-April 2012. *Orgon* is the name of a town 18 kilometers east of Saint Remy de Provence (where Nostradamus was born). It is known historically as the place where an attempted lynching of Napoleon Bonaparte occurred, on his way to St. Helena (to his final exile). One should recognize the element of the *Trident* being representative of the power wielded by Neptune, god of the seas. From this weapon lightening

Chapter 18 - Another Infamous Day in American History

bolted, on Neptune's command. The word *parfondre* is a combined form word, *par* + *fonder*, and is related to melting.

Neighboring with to drop from higher to lower the armed Crusader	*Proche à descendre l'armée Crucigere*
Will be closely observed by them Ishmaelites	*Sera guettee par les Ismaëlites*
With all fully molten battered ones on ship Again-plundered,	*De tous cottez batus par nef Raviere,*
Prepared set upon ones from ten sharks choice ones.	*Prompt assaillis de dix galeres eslites.*

Note: Latin: *battuo* = to beat, knock. Originally listed as quatrain number 43 in Centurie IX. Ismael was the son of Abraham (through the Egyptian slave girl Hagar), brother of Isaac (God's gift to Abraham, through previously barren wife Sara). Ishmael is commonly believed to be the ancestor of Arab people. The word *Raviere* is read as an anagram, Re-ravie, meaning, "*Again plundered.*"

Them veiled shark sail of ship will convey away,	*Voille gallere voil de nef cachera,*
The mighty fleet will arrive to go beyond there inferior	*La grande classe viendra sortir la moindre*
Ten ships adjoining ones will be turning to jolt,	*Dix naves proches tourneront repousser,*
Great vanquished united ones with oneself to couple.	*Grande vaincue unies à soy joindre.*

Note: Originally listed as quatrain number 2 in Centurie X. The word *unie* also means, "joined together," as well as *united*. The word *joindre* means to join, join up," meaning to combine, and associate. This sounds like the secret kept in line one allows enemy ships to mingle with the *great fleet*. This could only occur with underwater *ship*s, hidden or mixed on sonar with friendly submarines.

Ten thrust out ones, principal commander of ship to put to death,	*Dix envoyés, chef de nef mettre à mort,*
From one having intelligence of, on order warfare open:	*D'un adverty, en classe guerre ouverte:*
Confusion, general, the one themselves stung & bites,	*Confusion, chef, l'un se picque & mord,*
Lyre one, this measure of ground ship ones, cape within there not a place that stands high.	*Leryn, stecades nefz, cap dedans la nerte.*

The Epic Poem Prophesied by Nostradamus

Note: Originally listed as quatrain number 37 in Centurie VII. The principal commander is recognized as being of a ship because it is the flagship, thus marked as such. The word Leryn is read as an anagram, Lyre-n, as "Lyre one." This would be significant as an identification of Iraq, where lyres over 4,000 years of age have been unearthed at Ur. Iran is said to control the Strait of Hormuz, which represents a *cape*. Iran has armed that area with the newest weaponry technology. It certainly is prepared to be a combat zone.

Rare & rain unlooked for most forcible,	*Nouvelle & pluie subite impetueuse,*
Will stop quick two armies of men:	*Empeschera subit deux exercites:*
Stone sky, lights to cause there sea rocky,	*Pierre ciel, feux faire la mer pierreuse,*
The dead of seven land & near the sea hasty.	*La mort de sept terre & marin subites.*

Note: Originally listed as quatrain number 18 in Centurie II. Line one makes a main theme of something falling from the sky (as rain does); but this rain is most forcible, meaning it minimally has to be hail. However, what falls is a rare form, strong enough to halt two armies, which will presumably be at war with each other. A capitalized Stone sky, or heaven, indicates a meteor shower (rain), but causing streaks of lights as they burn into the atmosphere. They will be so numerous they will either make the sea stony, or they will create a sea of stones, or both. The use of seven land can indicate all seven continents will be affected in the event; or it can be the United State, as the September (11th, 2001) land.

Stakes conspired against ones at the feast will be acting bright,	*Seps conjurés au banquet feront luire,*
In opposition to the three the iron, out of to fleet of ships:	*Contre les trois le fer, hors de navire:*
The one them two ranks with the mighty will act to manage,	*L'un les deux classes au grand fera couduire,*
At what time for them heavy hammer. Second rank with the front it shot.	*Quant par le mail. Dernier au front luy tire.*

Note: Originally listed as quatrain number 2 in Centurie V. The 1568 Lyon edition clearly shows *Seps* as the first word, whereas the 1557 Utrecht edition clearly shows *Sept*. The word *Sep* is a synonymous with *pieu*, which means, "stake, post." It is related to the Latin word "*cippus*," which means, "gravestone, or tombstone," but a *Sep* is made of wood. It then is a boundary marker, which can also mark specific sites. While *fer* symbolically means "weapon," as *iron* it draws one to see the Soviet Union, who drew closed the *Iron* Curtain. The number *three* could refer to fleets, from the Latin *classus,* but the use of navire leads to the French translation. Line four's use of *hammer* symbolism also is a connection to the Soviet Union, with their emblem being the *hammer* and scythe.

Chapter 18 - Another Infamous Day in American History

The Naval battle night will be excelled,	*Navalle pugne nuit sera supuree,*
The fire in the ships has the West ruined:	*Le feu aux naves à l'Occident ruyne,*
Made red unheard of before there mighty ship shadowed,	*Rubriche neufve la grand nef coloree,*
Wrath to overcome & victory upon hot blasting mist.	*Ire à vaincu & victoire en bruine.*

Note: Latin: *pugna* = *fight, battle, contest.* Originally listed as quatrain number 100 in Centurie IX. The word *supuree* comes from the Old French word "superer," meaning, "to vanquish, overcome, and surmount." The word *Rubriche* is clean French for "Rubified," which means to turn *red*, but also written in *red* ink. This is an indication that something important will have been *Made* in a communist country, or by communist people. This creation will have then been *shadowed*, or kept from clear observation. Line three shows "*la grand*", where a feminine article would be found to precede a masculine noun. This is further evidence that *la* is to be read as accented (*là*).

Combat by night the valiant commander of a ship of war,	*Combat nocturne le vaillant capitaine,*
Vanquished will flee nobody from nations overthrown:	*Vaincu fuyra peu de gens profligé:*
One's people provoked, public faction not without purpose,	*Son peuple esmeu, sedition non vaine,*
Its own son them will impeach beleaguered.	*Son propre filz le tiendra assiegé.*

Note: Latin: *profligo* = *to overthrow, overcome, ruin.* Originally listed as quatrain number 83 in Centurie IV. Line two, as a separate theme statement, can include more than the people of one ship, or even fleet of ships. The word gens can indicate multiple nations being involved in an area, including some on land. This would be a UN presence situation, where few would have access to escape.

A commander of a ship of war will lead mighty prey,	*Le capitaine conduira grande proye,*
Toward there mountain of the enemy ones neighboring more close unto,	*Sur la montaigne des ennemis plus proche,*
Hemmed in on every side, by reason of fire will make such course,	*Environné, par feu fera tel voye,*
All escaped ones on thirty thrust into spit.	*Tous eschapez or trente mis en broche.*

Note: Originally listed as quatrain number 28 in Centurie VII. The only seaport of Iraq, Qasr, is

The Epic Poem Prophesied by Nostradamus

right at 30 degrees of latitude, which would be the *thirty place*, or place to land at *thirty* degrees, where US naval forces still could be in *place*. The word *broche* typically means "spit" or "to broach" (cook on a spit) food; but, it also means "to stitch [broadly]" or "sew with great stitches." That use would support the theme of American facilities in *place*, or *sewn in* to accommodate naval needs.

One almost nothing owing that the sun themselves hidden,	*Un peu devant que le soleil s'esconse,*
Battle delivered up great populous hesitating:	*Conflict donné grand peuple dubieux:*
Overthrown ones, port for ships marine not caused back forgone,	*Proffligés, port marin ne faict responce,*
Sea & grave upon two foreign ones places.	*Pont & sepulchre en deux estranges lieux.*

Note: Originally listed as quatrain number 37 in Centurie I. The word *responce* refers one to the spelling *reponce*, where is becomes the past participle of *reponcer*, meaning, "to pounce again," where *pounce* was a fine power used to absorb ink on paper. It is rooted in the Latin word for pumice, which is glassy lava, used in a solid form as an abrasive, and in a powdered form to polish. However, from the Latin root "*responsio*" the use of *response* is regarding the Latin translation as, "a reply, answer." The same word appears in quatrain I-38, as the capitalized first word of line two. The word *Pont* is rooted in Latin, from "*Pontus*," meaning "The Sea", but in the capitalized form, it typically meant the "Black Sea." Following the ampersand, which highlighted *Sea*, we see that two seas could also be *graves*. Close to the Persian Gulf are the Arabian Sea and the Red Sea, with the Black Sea mentioned in other quatrains, as to where the British Fleet will be destroyed.

Chapter 19

No More Spanish Armada

Spain is Invaded

From Cattail into devised ones in the Barcelona,	De Caton es trouves en Barsellonne,
Set uncovered ones place ones to pierce again & subverted,	Mys descouverts lieu retrouers & ruyne,
Him great who holds not possesses will want Pair-ample,	Le grand qui tient ne tient vouldra Pamplo
Through the monastery with Pliable iron clad blasted with mist.	Par labbage de Monferrat bruyne.

Note: Originally listed as quatrain number 26 in Centurie VIII. The spelling *Barsellonne* is obviously designed to indicate Barcelona, Spain. The spelling with an "s," rather than a "c," is found in the Ladino language, which is commonly called Judaeo-Spanish. That spelling does have an "a" at the end, as *Barselona*. It then becomes an phonetic anagram, as a French version, *l'Barselone*. Barcelona is the capital of Catalonia, on the Mediterranean Sea coast, but it is also a province, which borders Girona, where a large wetland preserve is located (*Cattail*). The Spanish city of Pamplona was founded as *Pompaelo*, which is similar to the *Pamplo* spelling of the 1568 Lyon edition. Pamplona is the capitol of the former Navarre kingdom, which borders France's Atlantic-Pyrenees Department, next to the Midi-Pyrenees. However, *amplo* is Portuguese meaning, "ample, and/or large." The "P" becomes an abbreviation for "Par," which means "*Pair*" in Spanish. The word *Mouferrat*, as it appears spelled in the 1568 Lyon edition, cleanly separates into *Mou-ferrât*, from the French words *Mou* and *ferrer*, meaning Soft (or Pliable) clad in iron, or some other metal. There is a place named *Montserrat*, which is a mountain near Barcelona, in Catalonia, in Spain. It is the site of a Benedictine abbey, Santa Maria de Montserrat. The name "*Montserrat*" literally means "jagged mountain." That site might play a secondary role in interpretation.

Following with France the upper hand of an enemy belonging to ships,	Apres de France la victoire navale,
Them Barcelona ones, Not-issued-forth ones, the Seal ones,	Les Barchinons, Saillinons, les Phocens,
Ivy of gold, the anvil thrust up together in there the base unto,	Lierre d'or, l'enclume serré dedans la basle,
Those to Toulon in the swindle will be concur with ones.	Ceux de Ptolon au fraud feront consens.

The Epic Poem Prophesied by Nostradamus

Note: Originally listed as quatrain number 3 in Centurie VII. The French spelling for the ancient Turkish city "Phocaea" (now named "Foca") is *Phocée*; and, the people from that city are called "*Phocé*ennes. They were Ionian Greek and not Muslim. They were the founders of the port city, Marseille, France. Their people, in English, are called *Phoc*ians, coming from the Greek mainland place known as Phocis (named after the Greek mythological figure Phocus, the son of Poseidon, who was transformed into a *seal* to help him swim ashore). While this association can be read into secondary meaning, I believe the Latin form of *seal* (*phoca, phoce*) is perfect to develop a marine landing force, such as navy *Seal*s. The word *enclume* not only meant a standard *anvil*, but also the *anvil* bone in the eardrum. In this sense *the enclume* becomes specifically an instrument of sound detection. The word *basle* has been translated as "*l'base.*" For the word *Ptolon*, the *Pt* can phonetically be read as T. A correct Occitan spelling for the city *Toulon* is *Tolon*. This is just east along the coast from Marseille, and is one of the two largest cities in Provence. It is the location of a major French naval base, where the French Mediterranean Fleet is based. Still, as an anagram, *Ploton*, it means, "Clue, Bottom of, Low buffet stool."

To bear Barcelona-born by sea so mighty army,	De Barcelonne par mer si grande armée,
All Marseille from terror will shake:	Toute Marseille de frayeur tremblera:
Islands possessed of with sea support locked up,	Isles saisies de mer ayde fermée,
Your betrayer upon land will float.	Ton traditeur en terre nagera.

Note: Originally listed as quatrain number 88 in Centurie III. Note the differences in spellings in the last two quatrains, where Barcelona is the main focus. There is a commune in southeast France, in the Drone Department, named *Barcelonne*, but it is doubtful that would be a focus prior to *Marseille*. The French spelling *Barcelone* with one "n." Still, it is phonetically accurate, or an anagram, as "*n'Barcelone*" ("not or born Barcelona"). With *Barcelona* and *Marseille* being on the Mediterranean Sea, the Islands would be, generally, all of those in that same sea, but probably the Baleric *Islands* of Spain. Line four is another reference to some amphibious submarine that is capable of coming aground.

From Fez a realm will come forward in the world at those of Europe,	De Fez le regne parviendra à ceux d'Europe,
Departed their warned to appear, & the blade will slice:	Feu leur cité, & lame trenchera:
Them substantial from Asian Minor land & sea with mighty throng of people,	Le grand d'Asie terre & mer à grand troupe,
Which blue ones, sky-colored, emblem of the cross, at death will drive away from.	Que bleux, pers, croix, à mort dechassera.

Note: Originally listed as quatrain number 80 in Centurie VI. The city *Fez* is the third largest in *Morocco*, which is the country that possesses the cape opposite the Rock of Gibraltar, creating the Strait of Gibraltar. Paris' nickname is the "City of Lights." *Blue* is the color of United Nations troops, particularly *light blue*, or *sky-colored*, as shown in the color helmets their soldiers wear.

Chapter 19 - No More Spanish Armada

Still, the word *pers* separately meant "peers." The emblem of the *cross* today is worn by the Red Cross, and is a sign of medical and disaster relief.

There dreaded army of the enemy Narbonne,	*La crainte armée de l'ennemy Narbon,*
Will scare so powerful them Western European ones:	*Effrayera si fort les Hesperiques:*
Perpignan void by reason of the ignorant of ship one,	*Parpignan vuide par l'aueugle d'arbon,*
While Barcelona through sea will yield up them pierced ones.	*Lors Barcelon par mer donra les piques.*

Note: Originally listed as quatrain number 56 in Centurie VI. Narbonne is also on the coast, just north of Perpignan. The word Parpignan is an acceptable spelling for the French town, "Perpignan," because the Latin per is the equivalent of the French par. The city of Barcelona is about 100 miles south of Perpignan (nautical miles).

Difficult year, Narbonne, by reason of them salt to admonish	*Gorsan. Narbonne, par le sel advertir*
Will have touched, there forgiveness Perpignan treacherously dealt with,	*Toucham, la grace Parpignam trahye,*
The town red not thereunto will want to approve of,	*La ville rouge ny vouldra consentir,*
Through importance hasty course cloth whitish living bankrupt.	*Par haulte vol drap gris vie faillie.*

Note: Originally listed as quatrain number 22 in Centurie VIII. The word *Touchames* is in the past historic form, for the verb "*toucher.*" The use of *salt* in line one has a feel of pouring *salt* in a wound. When the idiom, "*salt* of the earth", is recalled, it means, "persons or groups of people considered to be the best of a society." When color is known to be representative of religious beliefs, *gris*, as whitish, becomes those closet o Christianity, although not "clean" Christians. This makes the word preceding it, *cloth*, become religiously related, as "one of the cloth".

By reason of them regions of the mighty stream Guadaiquivir,	*Par les contrees du grand fleuve Bethique,*
Long of Iberia to the realm of Grenada:	*Loing d'Ibere au regne de Granade,*
Cross repulsed ones by people Mohammedans,	*Croix repoussees par gens Mahometiques,*
One of Cordova will betray there delivered wholly.	*Un de Cordube trahira la contrade.*

The Epic Poem Prophesied by Nostradamus

Note: Originally listed as quatrain number 20 in Centurie III. "Around 5.9 million years ago, the connection between the Mediterranean Sea and the Atlantic Ocean along the *Bethic* and Rifan Corridor was progressively restricted until its total closure." (from article on Wikipedia on *Strait of Gibraltar*) The *Bethic* Bridge was a connection between the continents, and the *Bethic* Chain stretches from southern Spain to Portugal, called the Baetic Cordillera mountain system. *Granada* is in the Sierra Nevada mountains, part of the Baetic Cordillera. *Cordoba* is in the Sierra Morena range, along the *Guadaiquivir* River, in the Hispania Baetica.

Light galleys & hatches on the top decks round about to seven ships,	*Fustes & galees autour de sept navires,*
Will be delivery of something given one deadly warfare:	*Sera livree une mortelle guerre:*
Principal commander to Madrid-like will receive blow with force,	*Chef de Madric receura coup de vires,*
Two got safe away ones & five moved ones to land.	*Deux eschapees & cinq menees à terre.*

Note: Originally listed as quatrain number 26 in Centurie VII. The word *Fuste* is defined as "a foist," but this is further defined as, "a light galley that has 16-18 oars on each side and two rowers on each oar." The modern usage of *foist* is negative, as an unwanted thrust upon someone, typically with deceit. The word *galee* is defined as: the tops or scuttles of a galley. We today define a *scuttle* as an opening or hatch with a movable lid in the deck or hull of a ship. As a verb, *scuttles* is the sinking of a ship via open holes allowing in water. The word *navire* can also mean a navy or fleet of ships. The word *Madric* is accepted as *Madrique* and therefore has the root *Madr*, which in French becomes *Madre*. This word means, "wood that is streaked with speckles and knots." As wood, it relates to the tree of Madrid, the *Madr*ono, which is part of the city's emblem. The *-ique* ending is the representative of those of *Madrid, Madrilènes*.

France with five through neglect assaulted,	*France à cinq par neglect assaillie,*
Tunis, Lightning blast turning black encouraged forward ones by Iranians:	*Tunys, Argel esmeux par Persiens:*
Leon, Seville, Barcelonans failed,	*Leon, Seville, Barcelonne faillie*
Not will have there fleet for them Venetians.	*N'aura la classe par les Venitiens.*

Note: Originally listed as quatrain number 73 in Centurie I. The word *Argel* can be seen as a simple anagram, as *l'Ager*, to be the French name for *Algiers*, the capital of Algeria. I see this as secondary, since the anagram *l'Arge* gives more detail as to what is being urged forward (*the Lightning blast*).

Chapter 19 - No More Spanish Armada

There plague them on all sides to Gibraltar-misshapen,	*La pestilence lentour de Capadille,*
One another famine nearby of Sagunto themselves made ready for.	*Un'autre faim pres de Sagont s'appreste.*
Them the knight base born with courageous them of old age	*Le chevallier bastard de bon senille*
In the mighty from Tunis will act to hack the headiness.	*Au grand de Thunes fera trancher la teste.*

Note: Originally listed as quatrain number 50 in Centurie VIII. *Capadille* is a good anagram that identifies a place in Spain, near Barcelona, named *Capellades*. If the Catalan language is the root, which is appropriate for a place in Catalonia, the spelling identifies a male of *Capellades*, a *Capelladi*. *Calpe* is the ancient Greek name for Gibraltar, making the anagram, *Calpe-laid* represent a more important place being named in Spain.

To there favorable Arabia delivered together,	*De la felice Arabie contrade,*
Will take beginning from vast means of authority with law Islamic:	*Naistra puissant de loy Mahometique:*
To torment them Spain to conquer the Granada,	*Vexer l'Espaigne conquester la Grenade,*
Likewise more by sea to there kindred Ligurian.	*Et plus par mer à la gent lygustique.*

Note: Originally listed as quatrain number 55 in Centurie V. The word *contrade* also appears at the end of line four in quatrain III-20, which also deals with Spain. *Granada* has a strong Islamic history, prior to the Inquisition forcing the Moors from Spain. The Alhambra in *Granada* was an Islamic citadel and palace, still considered holy to Muslims. An individual from Liguria is a *Ligus*, meaning to act as a *Ligus* is to be *ligustic*. Still, Old French used the word "*ligustique*," which is translated as the herb "lovage." This was obviously used for cramps and excess gas.

Them descendants of Cimbrians joined ones together with their ones neighbors,	*Les Cimbres joints avecques leurs voisins,*
To thin the population will be coming near the people of Spain:	*Depopuler viendront presque l'Espaigne:*
Inhabitants of a country gathered together ones Aquitaine & people speaking Occitan,	*Gens amassez Guienne & Limosins,*
Will be in league, & their will be making large band of soldiers.	*Seront en ligue, & leur feront compaignie.*

The Epic Poem Prophesied by Nostradamus

Note: Originally listed as quatrain number 8 in Centurie III. *Cimbrians* were a Germanic tribe during Roman times, who was located in northeastern Italy. The Cimbrian Language is not similar to standard Austro-Bavarian German. It is spoken primarily in northeast Italy, in the mainland areas surrounding Venice.

The Byzantine making offering	*Le Bizantin faisant oblation*
After to have Cordova to oneself again held.	*Apres avoir Cordube à soy reprinse.*
His path to follow outstretched peace by state of opportunity,	*Son chemin long repos pamplation,*
Sea current tolerable prey through there Gibraltar seized.	*Mer passant proy par la Colongna prinse.*

Note: Originally listed as quatrain number 51 in Centurie VIII. The Spanish city of Pamplona is the historic capitol of Basque Country, the former Kingdom of Navarra. The word *pamplation* could be referencing a state of Pamplona.

Sea of sunny ones sour not will hold on course,	*Mer par solaires seure ne passera,*
Those of Venus will be holding all them Africa:	*Ceux de Venus tiendront toute l'Affrique:*
Their realm more Soil, Saturn not will employ,	*Leur regne plus Sol, Saturne n'occupera,*
Also will transform there portion Asiatic (or Asian).	*Et changera la part Asiatique.*

Note: Originally listed as quatrain number 11 in Centurie V. The capitalization of Mer makes it be representative of a specific Sea. For Nostradamus, that would most likely be the Mediterranean Sea. The countries with coastlines along the Mediterranean are known as sunny places, both of Europe and of North Africa. Line three uses the capitalized word, Sol, which immediately causes one to see Sun, in support of the sunny ones of the main theme. However, Sol is indicative of a major Land mass, where the people are more dependent on the Soil for their survival. That would be a clarification of line two's Africa, which is the world's second largest continent. The word seure, in line one, is the key word to translate. As sour, this could be a reference to coming changes that would make the Mediterranean less desirable to travel. The statement, "Those of Venus", is reference to those of Islamic religious values.

Chapter 20

Meanwhile in Central Europe

By reason of there victory with the disappointed fraudulent,	*Par la victoire du deceu fraudulente,*
Two orders together, the rebellion Germany:	*Deux classes une, la revolte Germaine:*
One principal commander murdered, & his son in there provoked,	*Le chef meurtry, & son filz dans la tente,*
Florence, Imola instantly encircled ones inwardly Roman.	*Florence, Imole pourchasses dans Romaine.*

Note: Originally listed as quatrain number 77 in Centurie VI. The French word for "Germany" is "*Allemagne,*" although "*Germain*" was Old French (masculine) for a German person. The word *Germaine* is cleanly spelled, meaning, "come of the same stock; bred of the same kind; near of kin; of all-one race." This certainly fits when considering the 45 years East and West Germany were divided by political philosophy, while still sharing the same blood. This means that "*Germany*" has a strong secondary meaning in translation. However, the link to line four's listing of Italian places means those *kin* to the *Roman* Empire of old. The word *tente* is translated as the past tense of the verb "*tenter,*" meaning "to tempt;" but, without the accent over the "e" it means, "tent, or open booth in public market;" also, "a tent for a wound."

Upon a year benefit near not sent away from Venus.	*En l'an bien proche non esloigné de Venus.*
The two more mighty ones of them Asia & with Africa	*Les deux plus grands de l'Asie & d'Affrique*
To the Rhine & actor which one will report arrived ones,	*Du Ryn & hilter qu'on dira sont venus,*
Cries, tears in Malta & faction from Liguria.	*Cris, pleurs à Malte & coste ligustique.*

Note: Originally listed as quatrain number 68 in Centurie IV. If capitalized, the word *hilter* could represent the German town in the Lower Saxony region of Germany. However, as "hister," it would represent the ancient name for the Danube River; and, this would make it fit with the ampersand. The source of the Danube is in the Black Forest region of southwestern Germany. As such, it is part of a continental divide, between the Atlantic Ocean catchment (drained by the Rhine) and the Black Sea catchment (drained by the Danube). The word *ligustique* is actually correctly spelled to represent the "lovage herb" [given in treatment of gas and cramps]; but, *ligurian coast* is the simple connection to *Malta*. The Latin word "ligo," meaning, "to bind together, harness, connect, unite,

The Epic Poem Prophesied by Nostradamus

and bandage," is perhaps the best root to translate from, since it has lower case usage. As *ligus* it would represent the masculine singular, with the French ending *–tique* adding the meaning of "tick" or "like." This would then means from *Malta* to the northwestern *coast* of Italy, all is taken.

Brightness flashed with Lyon readied before,	*Clarté fulgure à Lyon apparente*
Radiant, impression Malta suddenly will be consumed,	*Luysant, print Malte subit sera estainte,*
Itself burnt one, themselves Moors will handle for deceived before,	*Sardon, Mauris traitera decepuante,*
Genoa fire with The waves to cock treacherously dealt with dissembled.	*Genefue à Londes à coq trahy son fainte.*

Note: Originally listed as quatrain number 6 in Centurie VIII. The last word written in line one, according to both the 1566 and 1568 Lyon editions, is "*apparante*". This is mistaken as "*apparent*" or "*apparenté*", which an "e" instead of an "a," and have two very different meanings. It is best understood as a manufactured word, "*appar-ante*". The commune in France named *Sardon* brings nothing to bear towards the meaning of this quatrain. The word *Genefue* appears spelled with an "f," rather than an "s," allowing it to act as an anagram for Geneva. Instead, it acts as *Gêne(s)-fue*, or *Genoa fire*. The French spelling for "London" (England) is "*Londres*," with an "r." There is no "r" found in either the 1568 or the 1566 Lyon editions.

Within them born Danube & to the Rhine will come to vent an ill savor,	*Dans le Dannube & du Rin viendra boire,*
A substantial Arabian not himself upon will be sorry for:	*Le grand Chameau ne s'en repentira:*
To quake from the Rhone & more powerful those with dregs	*Trembler du Rosne & plus fort ceulx de loire*
And nearby from the Alps French him will ruin.	*Et pres des Alpes coq le ruïnera.*

Note: Originally listed as quatrain number 68 in Centurie V. The *Danube* River runs from southern Germany (not far from where the Rhine flows) west to east, through Austria, bordering Slovakia, through Hungary, bordering Croatia, through Serbia, bordering Bulgaria and through Romania, into the Black Sea. Line one is then saying east will come west.

There Breton river will alter to seashore,	*La Celtiq fleuve changera de rivaige,*
More not will maintain the city of Saint Agrippine:	*Plus ne tiendra la cité d'Agripine:*

Chapter 20 - Meanwhile in Central Europe

Everything converted over excepting them ancient in years language,	Tout transmué ormis le vieil langaige,
Hardship, Lion, War, Disease (cancer) into violently snatching away.	Saturne, Leo, Mars, Cancer en rapine.

Note: Originally listed as quatrain number 4 in Centurie VI. There are multiple Agrippine's in history (the elder, the younger, to name two). Randal Cotgrave lists the word, as a "silver powder", which (presumably) when poured on meat leads to lust and lechery. In French, the word Cancre means, "the crab," and the astrological sign Cancer. This makes "Cancer" an anagram for French. Line four is showing how astrology states the timing of events. In July 2006, Saturn had been in the sign of Leo, joined by Mars in Leo in June, with both conjunct. Then the sun went into the sign of Cancer and became the midpoint (*ravine*) between the two the first week in July. This timing does not fit the quatrain's wording. The next time Saturn will be in Leo will be 2034, but Mars will not enter Leo during that period.

There substantial devastation with the sacred ones not themselves removed,	La grand ruine des sacrez ne s'esloigne,
Provence, Naples, the Sicily, See ones & Rubbed over:	Provence, Naples, Sicille, Seez & Ponce:
In Germany, at the Rhine & in Cologne,	En Germanie, au Rin & la Cologne,
Tormented ones to death by reason of all those from Tunisia.	Vexez à mort par tous ceux de Magonce.

Note: Originally listed as quatrain number 43 in Centurie V. The French verb "*poncer*" also meant, "to smooth, to rub over, polish, as with a pumice stone." A *See* is defined as, "The official seat, center of authority, jurisdiction, or office of a bishop." This would specify Vatican City among those cities listed, as well as generally Rome. It represents the western half of Italy. When Seez is capitalized, it stands for the Holy See ones. The period mark after Sicille means it could be an abbreviated anagram, such as representing, "*le Sicilien*." This would act to indicate the Mob's influence (Sicilien Mafia) over the Vatican, with the history of high-ranking officials laundering illegal money through their bank. This would specify Vatican City among those cities listed, as well as generally Rome. It represents the western half of Italy. The word *Ponce* is a slang term in Britain, referring to an effeminate man, or homosexual male. Perhaps, this is referenced to one being too *Polished*, so as to be fussy about one's dress. The Vatican personnel's wearing of flowing robes can be seen as effeminate. The unaccented *Ponce* translates as *Pumice*, and presence of *Pumice* stone would indicate Mount Etna, in *Sicily*. The Mediterranean island of *Minorca* is named for General Magon capturing this strategic location. However, the anagram, *c'Magone* would indicate Tunisia, the home of Hannibal's brother *Magonis*.

The Epic Poem Prophesied by Nostradamus

Mighty with Tunisian for substantial thirst to switch off,	*Grand de Magonce pour grande soif estaindre,*
Will be deprived of his lofty nobility:	*Sera privé de sa grande dignité:*
Those from Cologne even as forcible them will be arriving to find fault with	*Ceux de Cologne si fort le viendront plaindre*
Which there great backs at the Rhine will be violently sent forth.	*Que la grand groppe au Ryn sera getté.*

Note: Originally listed as quatrain number 40 in Centurie VI. The words *Magonce*, *Ryn*, and *Cologne* all appear together in quatrain V-43. Quatrain V-43 also used the verb, *boire*, meaning, "to drink", whereas here we find "*soif,*" which means, "desire to drink, from drought, or thirst." As an anagram, *Magonce* become *ce Magon* or *c'Magone*, which comes from the Latin name of Hannibal's brother, either *Mago* or *Magon*, in Latin. Hannibal and his brother were Carthaginians, which is modern Tunisia. The word *groppe* is the plural spelling of *groppa*, the Italian word meaning, "shoulder, back (of a person), and back, rump (of an animal)."

Life is death to THE GOLD villainous undeserving,	*Vie soit mort de LOR vilaine indigne,*
Will be from Saxony not unheard of before elector,	*Sera de Saxe non nouveau electeur,*
Of Brunswick a chessboard with love pledge,	*De Brunsvic mandra d'amour signe,*
Scythe him restoring unto the people seducer.	*Faulx le rendant au peuple seducteur.*

Note: Latin: *mandra* = a stall, cattle pen; a herd of cattle; a draughtboard (chessboard). Originally listed as quatrain number 46 in Centurie X. *Saxony* is the southernmost part of the former East Germany, bordering on the Czech Republic and Poland. *Brunswick* is in the former West Germany's Lower *Saxony*, which is very near where the old east-west border was located.

With the lagoon sediment & those from themselves Poachers,	*Du lac lyman & ceux de Brannonices,*
All joined ones against the ones of Aquitaine	*Tous assemblez contre ceux d'Aquitaine*
Relevant ones many yet more Swiss ones,	*Germains beaucoup encore plus Souisses,*
Will be excuses with these to Humane.	*Seront defaictz avec ceux d'Humaine.*

Note: Originally listed as quatrain number 74 in Centurie IV. A "liman" is, "the deposit of slime at the mouth of a river, backed up from sediment; slime; or a lagoon at the mouth of a river." The word comes from Medieval Greek, meaning "bay" or "port." The first segment of line one is a perfect fit

Chapter 20 - Meanwhile in Central Europe

for the Gironde Estuary, north of Bordeaux France. However, the indication one gets from seeing "*lac lyman*" is to read it as "*lac Leman*," or Lake Geneva, which is not what is written. Still, that indication can play a role on a secondary level.

The assembly mighty near to the lake with Bourget,	*Lassemblée grande pres du lac de Borget,*
Themselves will be reassembling nearby from the Montmélian,	*Se ralieront pres du Montmelian,*
Occupiers more forwards thoughtful ones will be making forecast	*Marchans plus outre pensifz feront proget*
Chambéry Death-borne battle holy Julian.	*Chambry Moriane combat saint Julian.*

Note: Originally listed as quatrain number 37 in Centurie X. The word "*bourget*" meant "round stool" in Old French. The word *rallier* can also mean, "to make peace between, reconcile, accord, agree." *Montmélian* is in the Department of Savoie, which is in southeastern France, bordering with Italy. *Chambéry* is also in the Department of Savoie. In Piedmontese (the language of northwestern mainland Italy), a "*proget*" is a "template." The name *Julian* has several associations with places in southern France and Italy.

Close to the snare Geneva will be to lead,	*Aupres du lac Leman sera conduire,*
By reason of whore unusual warned to appear desiring to deal treacherously with:	*Par garse estrange cité voulant trahir:*
Deeply in his murder at Antwerp the great consequence	*Auant son meurtre à Auspurg la grand suitte*
Both those of the Rhine there will be coming to invade.	*Et ceux du Ryn la viendront invahir.*

Note: Originally listed as quatrain number 12 in Centurie V. The word *Auspurg* is most likely requiring a secondary translation as "Augsborg", the city in southern Germany.

From them states the lowest part of to the country of Lorraine	*Des lieux plus bas du pays de Lorraine*
Being of them lowlands German ones joined together ones,	*Seront des basses Allemaignes unis,*
Through those with the Picard ones, Norman ones to them itself Maine,	*Par ceux du siege Picards, Normans du Maisne,*
As well in the cantons themselves will be reunited ones.	*Et aux cantons se seront reunis.*

The Epic Poem Prophesied by Nostradamus

Note: Originally listed as quatrain number 51 in Centurie X. The word "liĕux" had its own meaning, which was, "full of lees, dregs, or grounds; thick in the bottom after standing." It means, generally, "sediment". The *Lorraine* is a region of France, bordering with Germany, which has been the focus of hostilities between the two nations, along with the neighboring region, Alsace. The French people that live in those two regions are quite fluent in German and some feel a closer connection to Germany than France. *Picard* is a language closely related to French, spoken in northern France and parts of Belgium. The *Normans* also were part of northern France, who spoke an "oïl" language that still survives regionally in France and Belgium. *Maine* is a province of northern France that is west of Paris and borders to the south of *Norman*dy. It was once the possession of Normandy (11th century). This quatrain is talking about a restructuring of northern Europe, including Belgium and France.

The little ship unheard of before will take the voyages,	*La barque neufve recevra les voyages,*
There & next will be passing over into the impaired,	*La & aupres transfereront l'empire,*
Beaucaire, Arles will be holding back them hostages	*Beaucayre, Arles retiendront les hostages*
Near two columns devised ones from porphyry.	*Pres deux colomnes trouvees de porphire.*

Note: Originally listed as quatrain number 93 in Centurie X. *Beaucaire* is located in southern France, in the Gard Department, in the Languedoc-Roussillon region. *Arles* is east of *Beaucaire*, in the southern coastal department *Bouches-du-Rhone*, in the *Provence-Alpes-Cote de Azure* region. In the lower case, *porphyry* is a purplish-red crystal rock.

Seeing that them columns with lance mighty trembled,	*Quand les colomnes de bois grande tremblée,*
From South managing covered from made red:	*D'Auster conduicte couverte de rubriche:*
So many will waste from abroad great gathered hunting party:	*Tant vuidera dehors grand assemblée:*
To shake Vienna & the country of Austria.	*Trembler Vienne & le pays d'Austriche.*

Note: Originally listed as quatrain number 82 in Centurie I. The columns of line one is reminiscent of the columns found in quatrain X-93. Any use of a color is significant. Thus, one "made red, rubbed red, or grown red" is someone who was not originally red, but later became red. The color red signifies one without religious beliefs, or atheist. When whole countries become red, they are seen as politically communist. The fact that Vienna is close to former communist block nations, causing them to shake, means the fear comes from those turned red.

Chapter 20 - Meanwhile in Central Europe

Dull fellows savage ones from huge longing floods not uncertain,	*Bestes farouches de faim fleuves tranner,*
More share to the army lodged just on the other side Danube will be:	*Plus part du camp encontre Hister sera:*
Into cage with iron the great will be landlords,	*En caige de fer le grand sera treisner,*
When again towards child of Same stock will observe.	*Quand rin enfant Germain observera.*

Note: Originally listed as quatrain number 24 in Centurie II.

Powerless ones galleys will be smooth ones one in company of another.	*Foibles galleres seront unies ensemble.*
Adversaries scythe the more forcible upon with defenses	*Ennemis faulx le plus fort en rampard*
Weak assaulted ones Bohemian shook,	*Faible assaillies Vrarislave tremble,*
Lubeck & Meissen will be upholding uncivil party.	*Lubecq & Mysne tiendront barbare part.*

Note: Originally listed as quatrain number 94 in Centurie IX. In Medieval times, a *galley* was specifically known as a vessel navigating the Mediterranean Sea. They were used for both military and cargo (merchant) purposes. The port city of *Lubeck* was at the border between East and West Germany, during the division of Germany, while in the West. *Meissen* was solidly in East Germany.

Ancient Cardinal for them young ones betrayed,	*Vieux Cardinal par le jeusne deceu,*
Out of his business put in charge of oneself will search into disarmed,	*Hors de sa charge se verra desarmé,*
Arles born discovered ones twice as much are perceived,	*Arles ne monstres double soit apperceu,*
As well drawing off liquid & them sovereign anointed with balm.	*Et liqueduct & le prince embausmé.*

Note: Originally listed as quatrain number 68 in Centurie VIII. It appears the 1568 Lyon edition spells apperceu with only one "p", but the "p" in typeset has a bar at the bottom, designating it as a repeating "p". The French word "liquider", in its modern usage, means, "to liquidate". A balm is made from a Mediterranean herb, which was used to produce a favorable savor or smell, while some had medicinal values.

The Epic Poem Prophesied by Nostradamus

Of night through Nantes the Rainbow will suddenly show itself,	*De nuict par Nantes Lyris apparoistra,*
From the sciences marine ones will be stirring up there rain:	*Des artz marins susciteront la pluye:*
Arabian gulf mighty fleet for will sink,	*Arabiq goulfre grande classe parfondra,*
A monster at Saxony will be produced from bear & sow.	*Un monstre en Saxe naistra d'ours & truye.*

Note: Originally listed as quatrain number 44 in Centurie VI. A capitalized *Iris* means the name of the Goddess of the rainbow. The use of parfondra (as parfondreez and parfondre), which is not a definable word in modern French, is found in quatrains V-62 and IX-15. *Saxony* is in the part of Germany that used to be East Germany. The last word translates as *sow*, which alone appears to be a female pig, and as such could also be a female wild boar (some symbolic heraldry used in Germany). However, a female bear is also called a *sow*; meaning, "*bear & sow*" is like, "son & mother." This could make *sow* be symbolic of "mother Russia."

Torch burning in the sky evening will be seen,	*Flambeau ardent au ciel soir sera veu,*
Near to the end & beginning to the Rhone:	*Pres de la fin & principe du Rosne:*
Hunger, sword: long in coming them seconding privileged,	*Famine, glaive: tard le secours pourveu,*
There Iran returned to invade Greece.	*La Perse tourne envahir Macedoine.*

Note: Originally listed as quatrain number 96 in Centurie II. It is probable that the spelling of *Rosne* is a correct provincial spelling for the "*Rhône*" River. *Pourveu* can also mean, "privileged; a patent, gift, and grant; a Benefice or Bishopric."

Next unto there substantial persecution of the monarchy,	*Apres la grande affliction du sceptre,*
Two adversaries by reason of them being defeated ones:	*Deux ennemis par eux seront defaictz:*
Fleet from Africa with the people of Eastern Europe will come to be produced,	*Classe d'Affrique aux Pannons viendra naistre,*
On sea & world will be horrible ones made ones.	*Par mer & terre seront horribles faictz.*

Note: Originally listed as quatrain number 48 in Centurie V. The capitalization of "Two" means there are two very important adversaries to recognize. One is "the monarchy", and the other is the one who will persecute that royal scepter. The persecutors are found teaming with those of Africa and Eastern Europe, making the persecutor bring extra partners. Of course, the scepter is that held

Chapter 20 - Meanwhile in Central Europe

by the Vatican, or the Pope. That office has led to the defeat of Arab lands, through numerous Crusades, while those of the Middle East have returned defeat onto the Crusaders. Line four supports that secondary theme of past history, by stating the world will be making life difficult for those mercenaries, where the world becomes indicative of the United Nations being unable to help the poor, as intended, due to the most powerful nations being unwilling to approve power to the UN.

There people slave by reason of a fortune warlike,	*La gent esclaue par un heur martial,*
Will come into most glorious rank so much promoted:	*Viendra en haut degré tant eslevee:*
Will be changing potentate, to be produced one not sophisticated,	*Changeront prince, naistra un provincial,*
To hold on course the sea abundance with the mountains rising.	*Passer la mer copie aux monts levee.*

Note: Latin: *copia = abundance, [mil] troops*. Originally listed as quatrain number 26 in Centurie V. The combination "*La gent*" is further evidence of *La* being accented as *Là*, since the word *gent* is masculine, and should be preceded by the article "*Le*". The word *esclave* also meant one whose service had been bought. While slaves were certainly bought, a similar arrangement can be found when mercenaries are hired and ordered like slaves. The word *martial* also includes the astrological association with Mars, as, "born under the planet or being of the humor of Mars." This means being warlike and martial. The word *provincial* is spelled as English, rather than as *Provençal*, which means, "of Provence [France]". The word *levee* had a specific usage as the "levying of soldiers or money."

Drawn out, lineage frogs to move into Croatia,	*Laict, sang, grenoilles escoudre en Dalmatie,*
Conflict yielded, pestilence nearby from one Whale:	*Conflict donné, peste pres de Balenne:*
Proclamation will be mighty through all land of slaves,	*Cry sera grand par toute esclavonie,*
In that time will be produced thing made contrary to nature as it were touching & within Ravenna.	*Lors naistra monstre pres & dedans Ravenne.*

Note: Originally listed as quatrain number 32 in Centurie II. The word "*laict*" is seen as a verb, rather than the noun. Thus *to milk* means to draw out. There is a documented case of thousands of tiny *frogs* raining from the sky in Odzaci, Serbia (northwest of Belgrade), as reported in June, 2005. That region of Serbia (Odzaci) borders Croatia, where *Sclavonia* lies. Still, other quatrains mention *frogs*, which was a slur on French people. This use could indicate French soldiers moving into Croatia, from Italy. From Istria, the peninsula of Croatia, to *Ravenna*, Italy is roughly 90-100 miles, or roughly 120 kilometers.

Chapter 21

Christianity's Defender Attacked

Italy is Invaded

French, central Italy quite few will bring into subjection,	*Gaulois, Ausone bien peu subjuguera,*
Pau, Marne & Seine will commit Gone through the spiral:	*Pau, Marne & Seine fera Perme l'vrie:*
Whom a mighty wall in opposition of they will erect,	*Qui le grand mur contre eux dressera,*
With the least at the wall them substantial will spend idly there whole time.	*Du moindre au mur le grand perdra la vie.*

Note: Originally listed as quatrain number 63 in Centurie II. Line one is stating how quickly France and Italy will surrender. The word spelled *vrie* is found to be a form of the French word *vrille*, meaning, "vine, tendrill, spiral, spin, or tailspin." *Ausone* is either the region of ancient southern Italy, which was the land of the *Ausones*, or it is southern Lazio, and the town named *Ausonia*. Either way, both represent Italy. The Gave-de-*Pau* is the river of *Pau*, such that line two can be focusing on the rivers of three regions of France. Line three and four are talking about a line of defense against the invading Muslims (and mercenaries), which is like a repeating of the Maginot Line.

Mind, strength, reputation them government will transform,	*Cœur, vigueur, gloire le regne changera,*
From all instances contrary to occupying its opponent	*De tous pointz contre ayant son adversaire*
Then France infancy through death will yoke,	*Lors France enfance par mort subjuguera,*
One great protector will be in that time more adverse.	*Un grand regent sera lors plus contraire.*

Note: Originally listed as quatrain number 15 in Centurie III. The word *regent* also meant: Protector or Governor of a Kingdom during an interregnum, or the minority or absence of a Prince. This quatrain suggests that France will have a leader that will want to change France's image as a surrenderer; but, at the first sight of death France will become subjected to domination again.

Chapter 21 - Christianity's Defender Attacked

I cried for Nice, not Monaco, Pisa, not Genoa,	Je pleure Nisse, Monnego, Pize, Gennes,
Savona, Siena, Capua, Modena, Malta,	Savone, Sienne, Capue, Modene, Malte,
Them on high race & sword by reason of gratifications,	Le dessus sang & glaive par estrennes,
Fire to shake world, water disastrous ill report.	Feu trembler terre, eau malheureuse nolte.

Note: Occitan: *Nissa* = Nice; *Monegue* = Monaco. Originally listed as quatrain number 60 in Centurie X. The desire is to make the first two lines practically a string of Italian and coastal French cities. *Nisse* is close to the Occitan spelling "*Nissa*" or "*Niça*," for the French city of *Nice*. Some have seen the principality of Monaco in the word *Monnego*. *Pize* is close to the French spelling "*Pise*," for "Pisa" Italy. The word *Gennes* is clean Old French for (through "*gehenne*") as being *tortured*; but, many see it as close to the old way of spelling *Genoa* (now *Gênes*). *Savone* and *Sienne* both are correctly spelled to represent *Savona* and *Siena*, two Italian cities.

A stirring from feeling heart, roots, & public powers,	Le mouvement de sens cœur, piedz & mains,
Will be from reconciliation of differences. Naples, Leon, the Time:	Seront d'accord. Naples, Leon, Secille:
Sword ones, fire ones, waters moreover to the worthy ones of Rome,	Glaisves, feux, eaux puis aux nobles Romains,
Thrown head over heels ones, death by reason of brain weak.	Plongés tués mors par cerveau debile.

Note: Originally listed as quatrain number 11 in Centurie I.

In those days the star wearing long hair visible,	Durant l'estoille chevelue apparente,
Them three great ones potentates being burden adversaries,	Les trois grans princes seront fais ennemis:
Blasted ones from the sky silent world trembling.	Frappés du ciel paix terre tremulente.
Stake, Resonance waving ones snake upon the end of a matter set.	Pau, Timbre undans serpent sus le bort mis.

Note: Originally listed as quatrain number 43 in Centurie II. The idiom, "estoille chevelu̇e," bore the meaning, "a blazing star," and not, "bearded star." Line one is making the statement of a time when a comet will be visible for some length of viewing. The word *Frappé* also means, "wounded; and, blasted, as if with lightening." The name *Timbre*, makes it possible to translate as *Tiber*. The word *timbre* has Old French roots, meaning "drum." The word *undans* is abbreviated in the 1568 Lyon edition, as *undas*, with a printer's mark over the "a," indicating an "n" minimally follows. It

197

The Epic Poem Prophesied by Nostradamus

could be assumed "nt" follows, making the word become *undant-s*. This acts as the Latin spelling of the French word *ondant*, meaning "*waving.*"

Will be seen suddenly towards them Seven-enterers,	*Apparoistra vers le Septentrion,*
Not large distance from South them starry wearing long hair:	*Non loing de Cancer l'estoille chevelue:*
Suze, Sienne (France), Winter wind, one of Eretria,	*Suze, Sienne, Boeer, Eretrion,*
Will decay from Rome mighty, there night removed from office ones.	*Mourra de Rome grand, la nuict disperue.*

Note: Originally listed as quatrain number 6 in Centurie VI. In Latin, the word *septemtriones* means, "the seven stars of either the Little Bear or the Great Bear." Still, it generally translates as, "the north or the north wind." The idiom "*estoille chevelue*" also appears in quatrain II-43, and as an idiom translates as, "blazing star." There is also a small town named *Suza* in Croatia, near the Hungarian and Serbian border with Croatia. The spelling *Sienne* can be Siena Italy (western side, in Tuscany). The ancient city of *Eretria* was totally destroyed by the Persians in 490 BC.

Fleet of France not drawing near unto from Corsica,	*Classe gauloise n'aproches de Corsegue,*
Less to Sardinia kept secret yourself into will be sorry for things done ones:	*Moins de Sardaigne tu t'en repentiras:*
Not one spared will be dying deceived ones with the helper discontent.	*Trestous mourres frustrés de l'aide grogne.*
Kindred will float, lost liberty not to me will believe ones.	*Sang nagera, captif ne me croiras.*

Note: Originally listed as quatrain number 87 in Centurie III. The word *tu* is the proper spelling of the past participle for the word "*taire,*" meaning, "to be silent, mum, quiet, still, make no noise, conceal and keep secret."

From the Middle East will grow the mind of avenger	*De l'Orient viendra le cœur punique*
To anger Adriatic & them heirs of Rome's Empire	*Fascher Hadrie & les hoirs Romulides*
Accompanied to there fleet Libyan	*Acompagné de la classe Libyque*
Shakes the Maltese, & neighboring ones island ones not troubled with.	*Trembler Mellites, & proches isles vuides.*

Chapter 21 - Christianity's Defender Attacked

Note: Originally listed as quatrain number 9 in Centurie I. The *heirs of Romulus* are Romans and thus Italians. *Milite* is a Greek mythology character, known as a Naiad. She was from Mount Melite, on the island of Phaiakians, particularly Korkya. Corkya is now known as Corfu, a Greek island in the Ionian Sea. However, the island of Malta is also known as *Melite*, which is Greek for honey.

EXCEEDING GREAT. Stake substantial harm upon French will receive,	*GRAN. Po, grand mal pour Gauloys receura,*
Forceless terror to the marine British:	*Vaine terreur au maritin Lyon:*
Well planted with folk innumerable through the sea will proceed,	*Peuple infini par la mer passera,*
Without to free himself a fourth from one million.	*Sans eschapper un quart d'vn million.*

Note: Originally listed as quatrain number 94 in Centurie II. In every quatrain the word *grand* is reference to (specifically) the United States of America or (indirectly) Great Britain, Europe and Western nations of wealth and power. Here, the all-caps elevate the word to a level of *GREATNESS*, beyond that long-held title, as a one-time event of *GREATNESS*, incomparable in modern history. The word *GRAN* is an abbreviation, as the period mark indicates. I select the word *GRANDISSIME* as the full-length meaning of the word, relating to: HUGE, MIGHTY, EXCESSIVE, *EXCEEDING GREAT*. The *marine one Lion* is representing the British hold of Gibraltar, as the British will be without a fleet to defend their holding at this time.

The weak potentate offended, objections & actions against,	*L'impotent prince faché, plaincts & querelles,*
From violent snatching of ones & ravaged, for French & by reason of North Africans:	*De rapts & pillé, par coqz & par libyques:*
Great is on land by sea innumerable ones the ships,	*Grand est par terre par mer infinies voilles,*
Alone Italy will be rejecting Celtic ones.	*Seule Italie sera chassant Celtiques.*

Note: Originally listed as quatrain number 4 in Centurie IV. The words *mer* and *infinies* helps connect this quatrain to quatrain II – 94, where they are repeated.

The fire consumed, the maidens will be giving away,	*Le feu estaint, les vierges trahiront,*
There more great portion from the faction unheard of before:	*La plus grand part de la bende nouvelle:*
Lightening in weapon, spear them only ones King will be guarding	*Fouldre à fer, lance les seulz Roy garderont*

199

The Epic Poem Prophesied by Nostradamus

Etruscan & Corsica, of night throat blade of a sword.	*Etrusque & Corse, de nuict gorge allumelle.*

Note: Originally listed as quatrain number 35 in Centurie IV. The correct French name for Corsica is "*La Corse*," although *Corse* is acceptable, but with alternative translations possible.

Them uncertain stay ones, fire to the sky upon the driven into the ground ones,	*Les fugitifs, feu du ciel sus les piques,*
Battle close unto from ravens themselves sporting ones,	*Conflict prochain des corbeaux s'esbatans,*
To land an outcry help assistance celestial ones,	*De terre on crie aide secours celiques,*
Notwithstanding nearby with the walls will be them soldiers engaged in fighting.	*Quand pres des murs seront les combatans.*

Note: Originally listed as quatrain number 7 in Centurie III. The word *corbeau* also was a name for a "warlike weapon." As such, it was like a grappling hook, which was used to bring down defensive walls.

Before the assault communication pronounced,	*Avant l'assaut oraison prononcée,*
Bird of prey taken to eagle through ambushes beguiled ones:	*Milan prins d'aigle par embusches deceuz:*
Rampart ancient by reason of cannons broken open,	*Muraille antique par canons enfoncée,*
On fire & kindred at mercy few accepted of ones.	*Par feu & sang à mercy peu receuz.*

Note: Originally listed as quatrain number 37 in Centurie III. The word *oraison* typically means "*prayer*," but *communication* with God will be so out of the main focus of nations that it does not set well as preceding a coming sudden battle. In a Holy War, *prayer* would be a standard part of *communication*, particularly for Muslims. However, since the storyline calls for the realization of "*fugitives*" (quatrain III-07) already "*on land*", or *refugees* in European nations, from the Arab world, they would need advance warning, through *communication* lines.

In the overthrown ones from accord them enemies,	*Aux profligéz de paix les ennemis,*
Next unto to have Italy by reason of vanquished:	*Apres avoir l'Italie supperée:*

Chapter 21 - Christianity's Defender Attacked

Black cruel, red will be one appointed to decide matters,	Noir sanguinaire, rouge sera commis,
Fire, race to pour out, water with blood colored.	Feu, sang verser, eaue de sang colorée.

Note: Originally listed as quatrain number 38 in Centurie VI. The word *commis* can also mean, "committed, a committee, assigned, referred to, acted, and forfeited." The word *feu* can also mean, "dead, deceased, departed." The word *supperée* is defined as if "*superée*", with "p" made an abbreviated pre-word, "*par*".

THAT of the remnant from race not scattered abroad,	CELA du reste de sang non espandu,
Venice sends for help to be given:	Venise quiert secours estre donné:
After to occupy quite extended time waited,	Apres avoir bien long temps attendu,
Warned to appear delivery, of something given at the first horn sounded.	Cité livrée, au premier cornet sonné.

Note: Originally listed as quatrain number 1 in Centurie IV. Line one can be reference to Jews, who have settled in every nation of Europe, and elsewhere.

To the more secret of Spain in slowly	Du plus profond de l'Espaigne ensegne
Coming forth from the point of a scabbard & with the frontiers to Europe,	Sortant du bout & des fins de l'Europe,
Troubled ones passing close to the sea from the Aigne,	Troubles passant aupres du pont de Laigne,
Will be defeated by companies of soldiers its great troops.	Sera deffaite par bande sa grand troppe.

Note: Originally listed as quatrain number 48 in Centurie X. The word *ensegne* does not contain an "i" and there is a hint of separation between *en* and *segne*. The word *segne* is the adverb form of the Latin word *segnis*, meaning, "slowly, sluggishly." The commune La Laigne is less than 15 miles (east) of the seaport La Rochelle. The commune Aigne is northeast of Carcassonne, west of Narbonne, in the Herault department of southern France. It a seaport on the Mediterranean.

The Epic Poem Prophesied by Nostradamus

With the provincial governor of France forced to act un willingly to batter at the time of war,	Au duc Gaulois constraint battre au duelle,
There ship them Malta northwest Italian coast not will come near to,	La nef Mellele monech n'aprochera,
Offence charged with a crime, prison continual,	Tort accusé, prison perpetuelle,
His son to govern before killed will appoint a task unto.	Son fils regner auant mort taschera.

Note: Originally listed as quatrain number 91 in Centurie IV. The commune *Melle* is not far from the commune *La Laigne*, which was possibly stated in quatrain X-48.

One provincial governor lusting after his enemy to emulate,	Un duc cupide son ennemi ensuyvre,
Within will have access into holding occupied one's defensive military lines:	Dans entrera empeschant la phalange:
Quickly come ones to base even as it were touching will be arriving to prosecute	Hastez à pied si pres viendront poursuivre
Which there the battle contended nearby to Ganges.	Que la journée conflite pres de Gange.

Note: Originally listed as quatrain number 51 in Centurie IV. The use of duc in line one appears to connect to the duc of quatrain IV-91. The spelling *Gange* is the French name for the *Ganges River*. This is the most eastern reference in *The Prophecies*.

Him fresh achievement will lead on the army,	Le nouveau faict conduira l'exercite,
Neighboring weakened until unto close to the seashore	Proche apamé jusques aupres du rivage
Reaching assistance of people of Milan to choose,	Tendant secours de Milanoise eslite,
Provincial governor eyes secret at Milan weapon with cage.	Duc yeulx prive à Milan fer de cage.

Note: Originally listed as quatrain number 95 in Centurie IX.

Chapter 21 - Christianity's Defender Attacked

In city to enter trained body of soldiers with them denied,	*Dans cité entrer exercit desniee,*
Provincial governor will step in by persuasion,	*Duc entrera par persuasion,*
With the feeble ones portals secretly furnished with arms an arrest made by a bailiff,	*Aux foibles portes clam armee amenee,*
Will be thrusting into fire, death, from kindred spilling out.	*Mettront feu, mort, de sang effusion.*

Note: Originally listed as quatrain number 96 in Centurie IX. In line three, "*armee amenee*", together, can apply the meaning of a Sergeant-at-Arms, who then acts as an agent of the Provincial governor, making arrests as directed by the organization making the appointment. Line four can be read as "brother turning on brother," where relatives and neighbors (the weak ones) turn in each other, simply to save their own lives. Thus, information about "*kindred*" would be "*spilling out*."

Hacked to pieces the middle, will be produced by with two heads,	*Tranché le ventre, naistra avec deux testes,*
Both four arms: some ones years unbroken will have life:	*Et quatre bras: quelques ans entiers vivra;*
Day which Eagle-liberty will celebrate their feasts,	*Jour qui Alquiloye celebrera ses festes,*
Inhabitants in a ditch, Turin, chief Ferrara will ensue.	*Fossen, Turin, chief Ferrare suyvra.*

Note: Originally listed as quatrain number 58 in Centurie I. The Italian city named Fossano, which is in the Piedmont region, not far from *Turin*, is spelled with an "a", with no evidence of *Fossen* being a French name for that city. However, the Piedmontese origin of that city's name is "*fossato*", meaning, "ditch," such that a "*fossan*" is an "inhabitant of a ditch." The Latin word, *fossa*, also means "ditch, trench, channel," as does the French version, "*fosse*." The word has a military application, as "*entrenched*." This makes *Fossen* become an important indication of "*One dug in*." The town of Fossano thus becomes secondary in meaning, such that the main theme is a statement of panic defenses set around cities under attack. The "*two heads*" are then Turin in the west and Ferrara in the east.

On the sand for one hideous deluge,	*Sur le sablon par un hideux deluge,*
From the others sea ones found monster marine ones:	*Des autres mers trouvé monstre marin:*
Near to the place will be made one sanctuary,	*Proche du lieu sera faicte un refuge,*
Holding Savona slave to Turin.	*Tenant Savone esclave de Turin.*

Note: Originally listed as quatrain number 88 in Centurie V. The use of *slave* in line four is

The Epic Poem Prophesied by Nostradamus

reference to Slavic mercenaries assisting the Islamic cause.

Restraints, Antibes, towns round about to Nice,	*Freins, Antibol, villes autour de Nice,*
Will be themselves laid to waste fortress, by sea & on ground,	*Seront vastees fort, par mer & par terre,*
Them grasshoppers land & sea gust of wind favorable,	*Les sauterelles terre & mer vent propice,*
Seized, killed ones, overthrown ones pillaged ones without rule of warfare.	*Prins, mors, trossés pilles sans loy de guerre.*

Note: Originally listed as quatrain number 82 in Centurie III. In 1555, the *brakes* were applied to a horse by pulling on the reins. The word *Frein* meant, "bit to put in a horses mouth." This leads to Latin (as an anagram) "*Freni*", or "*Frenum*", which carries the same meanings. It can also be noted that if the "n" in *Freins* is turned upside down, it becomes a "u", making the word become "*Frejus*," which is another French Rivera city, west of both *Antibes* and *Nice*. A *sauterelle* is also defined as, "a mason's instrument for tracing and forming angles", with it meaning, "*grasshopper*", in modern usage.

The tyrant Siena will occupy Savona,	*Le tyran Sienne occupera Savone,*
A fortress gained will hold division marine:	*Le fort gaigné tiendra classe marine:*
Them two fortified ones by there distress from Ancona,	*Les deux armées par la marque d'Ancone,*
By reason of terrorist him principal commander themselves on searched into.	*Par effraieur le chef s'en examine.*

Note: Originally listed as quatrain number 75 in Centurie I. While the word *Sienne* is the French spelling for the Italian city *Siena*, it is also the feminine spelling for the pronoun "*sein*". Despite the word *tyran* being masculine, and preceded by the masculine article, *Le*, the pronoun, "*His own*" could works as well in the main theme. As such, the word can be broken down to match the masculine form by seeing *Sienne* as *Sien né*, or *His born*. An occupation in *Siena* is then designed as a secondary point of focus. The Old French word "*ancon*" is defined as, "a long and heavy axe, which in old time soldiers used to throw at their enemies, either before or just at their joining together in battle." This can be seen as a secondary meaning.

In the smooth hard-surface through sea Adriatic,	*Au crustamin par mer Hadriatique,*
Will appear one abominable fish,	*Apparoistra un horrible poisson,*
With proportion human & there success aquatic,	*De face humaine, & la fin aquatique,*

Chapter 21 - Christianity's Defender Attacked

Which itself will catch out of from reverse barb of an arrow.	*Qui se prendra dehors de l'amecon.*

Note: French: *ameçon > hameçon = little fish hook.* Originally listed as quatrain number 21 in Centurie III. Line one is describing a submarine's sleek, torpedo shape of metal. A missile or torpedo coming from a submarine is a horrible fish, even though coming from a much bigger fish.

When the fish terrestrial & aquatic,	*Quand le poisson terrestre & aquatique,*
By reason of point of excellence ranging in the sand mixed with small stones will be thrust into:	*Par forte vague au gravier sera mis:*
Its shape unusual smooth & frightening,	*Sa forme estrange suave & horrifique,*
Through sea to the ramparts quite quickly them enemies.	*Par mer aux murs bien tost les ennemis.*

Note: Originally listed as quatrain number 29 in Centurie I. This quatrain matches the verbiage used in quatrain III-21, where a *fish aquatic* is *smooth* and *horrific*. The two clearly link together. A *fish terrestrial* has amphibian characteristics, with the difference being a fish "breathes" underwater, while making short trips onto land. The ampersand highlights it is primarily aquatic. The secondary theme states how it will make beach landings.

Through a torrent which swooped down from Véronne,	*Par le torrent qui descent de Veronne,*
By reason of in that season that at the Pau will lift up on high its beginning:	*Par lors qu'au Pau guindera son entrée:*
One great shipwreck, & not least upon rock as source of water,	*Un grand nauffraige, & non moins en garonne,*
In regard of those of Tortured ones will be marching their country.	*Quant ceux de Gennes marcheront leur contrée.*

Note: Originally listed as quatrain number 33 in Centurie II. The prospect of a waterfall (or *torrent descent*) is better around Véronne, France, than Verona, Italy. The commune *Pau* is named for the river that flows by it, the *Gave de Pau*. The French word, "*pau*," means, "stake." Line one then becomes a predictive marker of spring, when heavy rain, or thaw after heavy snow, causes massive flooding. The first part of line three indicates that the flooding is related to a mighty shipwreck, with the second half explaining it to be cause by rock as the source. The Italian coastal city Genoa is now spelled *Gênes*, which accented the abbreviation, from the spelling *Gennes*. The Old French word, "*genne*," refers one to look up the word "*gehenne*," which means, "racked, tortured."

The Epic Poem Prophesied by Nostradamus

Will arrive at the harbor for ships of Embraced-well,	*Arrivera au port de Corsibonne,*
Near to Ravenna, which will deprive of all there of soul,	*Pres de Ravenne qui pillera la dame,*
Into sea secret legacy from there Ulysses-brave,	*En mer profonde legat de la Ulisbone*
At the bottom of stony crag ketches will be taking away forcibly September before ghosts.	*Souz roc caichez raviront septante ames.*

Note: Originally listed as quatrain number 54 in Centurie IX. This quatrain hinges on two capitalized names, which are not any known names. The word *Corsibonne* gives the initial impression of Corsica (*Corse*, in French). However, that does not match the place *Ravenna*, as it is in a different sea, and the possession of a different country. It then is rooted in French, *Corsi-* (Held body, Embraced) *bonne* (good, well). The use of *Corsi* can also indicate a Corsican. The word *Vlisbon* appears to contain the name "Lisbon", and the history behind the name of Lisbon is relative to Ulysses, as a place he visited in his travels, going by Ulyssippo, then Olissipona, and later Ulishbona. Still, that does little to solve this puzzle. The meaning of the Greek name, *Ulysse*, is "hate, to be wroth against." This then becomes an identifier (as *Ulysse-bon*) for one with "plenty of hate." This image matches the storyline of Nostradamus, where French troops will depart from Corsica for stations in Italy. The French word *caiche* is a nautical term, and it means a small ship with one bridge and one main mast, with a "mizzle mast" near the rudder. The word *septante* can again be meant as "September before," as a secondary clarification of who the attackers will be.

There great army to the battle-line mannerly,	*La grand armee de la pugne civile,*
Because of darkness Parma with the alien found	*Pour de nuict Parme à l'estrange trouvée*
Seventy-nine murdered ones within there enclosed town,	*Septanteneuf meurtris dedans la ville,*
Them strangers transported over ones all with the blade.	*Les estrangiers passez tout à l'espee.*

Note: Originally listed as quatrain number 78 in Centurie IV. In line three, the first word is, "*Septanteneuf*," which means, "Seventy-nine". This, of course, could be split into, "*Sept-ante-neuf*", which would translate as, "September before new." This would act as identifying the "new" version of those led by Osama bin Laden, while still maintaining the objective of attacks on the United States, and its allies, as occurred on September 11, 2001.

Army Celtic in Italy extremely grieved,	*Armée Celtique en Italie vexée,*
To all ones through battle & mighty ruin:	*De toutes pars conflict & grande perte:*

Chapter 21 - Christianity's Defender Attacked

Roman ones flee, oh! Beaten with a club driven back,	*Romains fuis, ô Gaule repoulsée,*
As it were touching to the Ticino, Rubicon fight uncertain.	*Pres du Thesin, Rubicon pugne incerte.*

Note: Latin: *incerto = [as to fact] not knowing.* Originally listed as quatrain number 72 in Centurie II. The Latin name for Gaul is "*Gallia,*" which was primarily what is now France, but also included parts of northern Italy and Belgium. *Ticino*, or *Tessin*, is both a town in extreme northwest Italy, and the river of the same name that flows by the city. The river flows south from Switzerland, and *Tessin* is the name of a Swiss canton. The spelling indicated the Italian *Ticino*, in the Lombardy region, centered around Milan. The river is a tributary of the Po River. There is a commune in the southeast of France, named *Thines*, in the Rhone-Alps region, Ardèche Department, which is a perfect anagram, but disjointed from the theme. In Yiddish, the word *Tishen* means, "Tables", where a "*Tish*" is a Hasidic (with public welcome) gathering around a table, for Sabbath observances. The *Rubicon* is another famous river in northern Italy, although it flows from the Apennines Mountain to the Adriatic Sea, parallel and south of the Po. "Crossing the Rubicon" is a popular idiom meaning to go past a point of no return; but having occurred in 49 BC, by Julius Caesar, no one will remember the significance of crossing a river being the point of no return. Then, north of the Rubicon was Cisalpine *Gaul*.

An eye to Ravenna will be destitute,	*L'œil de Ravenne sera destitué,*
Seeing that at their bases them military wings will be failing:	*Quand à ses piedz les œlles failliront:*
The two from Bresse will be having confirmed,	*Les deux de Bresse auront constitué*
Turin, it Poured out that French will be hurting.	*Turin, Verseil que Gauloys fouleront.*

Note: Originally listed as quatrain number 6 in Centurie I. Borg-en-*Bresse* is a city in southeastern France (former province), in the Rhone-Alpes Department, which borders Italy and Switzerland. It is in the Ain Department, which is the northernmost department in the region, bordering on Switzerland.

At the stronghold castle Vigilant-born & Followed again ones	*Au fort chasteau de Viglanne & Resuiers*
Will thrust hard fast locked them younger of Nancy:	*Serra serre le puisnay de Nancy:*
Within Turin will be hot ones the first ones,	*Dedans Turin seront ards les premiers,*
In that time that from grief Lion will be failed in heart, sense, and vital spirit.	*Lors que de dueil Lyon sera transy.*

Note: Originally listed as quatrain number 3 in Centurie VIII. In German, the "proper" name, *Revier*, is understood to represent the Ruhr region, in particular the mines of the Ruhr. The Ruhr

The Epic Poem Prophesied by Nostradamus

River flows through the Ruhr Valley, to the Rhine River, in western Germany. Nancy is a proper place, being a city in eastern France, west of the German border.

There city mighty the exiled ones will be possessing,	*La cité grande les exilés tiendront,*
Them citizens killed ones murdered ones & driven away ones:	*Les citadins morts, meurtris & chassés:*
Those of the Eagle at Parma will be offering,	*Ceulx d'Aquilee à Parme promettront,*
To show the way for the ranks not followed ones.	*Monstrer l'entree par les lieux non trassés.*

Note: Originally listed as quatrain number 69 in Centurie IV. Friulian is a language of northeast Italy, where *Aquileia* (aka *Aquilegia*) is located near the border with Slovenia, on the Adriatic coast. It is a French from of the Latin form of *aquila, aquilae*, meaning, "eagle, or the Roman legion standard of an eagle."

Chapter 22

Spearheads to Submission

The Italian Campaign

Inward that at Rome high possess given back the soul	Avant qu'à Rome grand aye rendu l'ame
Terrorist mighty with the army foreigner:	Effrayeur grande à l'armée estrangiere:
Of Squadrons, the ambush nearby to Parma,	Par Esquadrons, l'embusche pres de Parme,
Then them two red ones jointly will be causing high price.	Puis les deux rouges ensemble feront chere.

Note: Originally listed as quatrain number 22 in Centurie V. The word *squadron* was said to be reserved to denote "horsemen," whereas a "battalion" was used to represent foot soldiers. In today's mechanized army, "horsemen" would be mobile unites of armored weaponry.

Naples, Palermo, Themselves blinked, Syracuse ones,	Naples, Palerme, Secille, Syracuses,
Fresh violent governors, objects struck by lightning ones fires heavenly ones:	Nouveaux tyrans, fulgures feuz celestes:
Energy to London, Ghent, Brussels, & Over are,	Force de Londres, Gand, Brucelles, & Suses,
Great slaughter, triumph to cause festival days.	Grand hecatombe, triumphe, faire festes.

Note: Originally listed as quatrain number 16 in Centurie II. The main theme of line one appears to be placing focus on the southwestern portion of Italy, below Rome, and including the largest cities in Sicily. However, because *Palermo* and *Syracuse* are both cities on Sicily, it makes no sense to include "Sicily" between them. This means the incorrect spelling becomes, "*Se cillé*," meaning, "*They blinked.*" Line three lists three northern European cities, then one that is either a small town, or an anagram. The word *sues* is the feminine plural past participle of the word *savoir* ("to know"), or a form of the verb *suer*, meaning, "to sweat." However, it makes most sense as "*Sus-es*," which says, "*Over are*," meaning aerial attacks in northern Europe. The word Suses matches the use of *Secille* in line one.

209

The Epic Poem Prophesied by Nostradamus

House of Parliament, hawks, by reason of bird driven away,	*Palais, oyseaux, par oyseau dechassé,*
Quite suddenly following a sovereign accused:	*Bien tost apres le prince prevenu:*
How many who out of river enemy ones denied,	*Combien qu'hors fleuve ennemis repulsé,*
Abroad arrested prolonged with mason's mortar trey upheld.	*Dehors saisi trait d'oyseau soustenu.*

Note: Originally listed as quatrain number 23 in Centurie II. The feel of this quatrain is it is about the English royal family and their rule of Britain. The capitalized *Palais* could be a number of places in London. Certainly, a lower case *prince* is an indication of one awaiting the throne, while a King serves as a Prince. The *river* would be the Thames. Still, this one quatrain needs the support of connecting quatrains to best interpret. Quatrain VIII-30 mentions a lower case *palais*, which could help direct this one.

The eagle pushed on all sides of admiral's flagships,	*L'aigle pousée entour de pavillons,*
By reason of other ones birds to encompass will be hunted after:	*Par autres oyseaux d'entour sera chassée:*
When loud sound from the small boats tube & will be ringing bells	*Quant bruit des cymbres tubes & sonnaillons*
Will be rendering them judgment to them there lady unreasonable.	*Rendront le sens de la dame insensée.*

Note: Originally listed as quatrain number 44 in Centurie II. The "angel of hate" named Sonneillon was made public in a 16th century trial in Aix-en-Provence, where this demon was blamed for the possession of a nun, who faced trial for witchcraft. According to a 1612 list, Sonneillon was the 8th of the First Hierarchy, in the category of Thrones (type of angels). Father Sebastien Michaelis wrote, "Sonneillon is the fourth in the order of Thrones, and tempts men with hatred against their enemies. [Adversary: Stephen]" (ref. www.whiterosesgarden.com/Nature_of_Evil/Demons/DM_Occult_Hierarchy/DM_hells_hierarchy_Father-Michaelis_1612.htm)

Neither with good reason nor bad through battle terrestrial,	*Ne bien ne mal par bataille terrestre,*
Not will arrive unto with them bordering unto ones from Perugia:	*Ne parviendra aux confins de Perouse:*
To rise up against one's sovereign earthen walls, Florence to observe evil being,	*Rebeller pise, Florence voir mal estre,*

Chapter 22 - Spearheads to Submission

Head man of a party night wounded concerning large mule with black coarse stocking.	*Roy nuict blessé sur mulet à noire house.*

Note: Originally listed as quatrain number 36 in Centurie VI. The city *Pérouse* (in French) is *Perugia* in English and it is located in the central part of the peninsula, in the Umbria region, in the province of *Perugia*. Its *neighbors* are the regions of Marche (capitol Ancona), Tuscany (capitol Florence) and Lazio (capitol Rome). *Florence* is a city and province in the Tuscany region. The *King* of Italy is reference to the Pope.

There great busied with in Ravenna substantial trouble,	*La magna vaqua à Ravenne grand trouble,*
Canal ones for fifteen shut up ones with Furnace	*Conduictz par quinze enserres à Fornase*
To Roman will be born two things made contrary to nature with head double	*A Romine naistra deux monstres à teste double*
Blood, fire, deluge, them more high ones to the sword.	*Sang, feu, deluge, les plus grands à l'espase.*

Note: Originally listed as quatrain number 3 in Centurie IX. The word *Fornase* is correctly spelled Italian, meaning *Furnace*, with it spelled "*Forna*ise" in French. It is possible that *Fornase* is an archaic name for Venice, or the surrounding region named for Venice.

Open piece of ground Inflamed my Lord! the most wicked overthrow	*Champ Perusin o lenorme deffaite*
Likewise them battle everything close to Ravenna,	*Et le conflit tout aupres de Ravenne,*
Course of a religious order in that time which one will make there festival day,	*Passage sacre lors qu'on fera la feste,*
Victor vanquished cavalry to feed the not veined.	*Vaingueur vaincu cheval manger la venne.*

Note: Originally listed as quatrain number 72 in Centurie VIII. In antiquity, the region now known as Perugia was named *Perusia*, by the founding Etruscans. This is a possible alternate translation for *Perusin*.

The Epic Poem Prophesied by Nostradamus

Furnished with to battle will make defection,	*Prest a combatre fera defection,*
Principal commander contrary party will obtain there victory:	*Chef adversaire obtiendra la victoire:*
The rear-guard will make defense,	*L'arrieregarde fera defension,*
Them failing ones dead in the white territory.	*Les defaillans mort au blanc territoire.*

Note: Originally listed as quatrain number 75 in Centurie IV. The money aspect of the word *Prest* makes the main theme be about the buying of mercenaries. Soldiers are "on loan" while also receiving money. One does not to train such a soldier, as mercenaries are ready for combat. The *contrary party* of line two is stating that these mercenaries will have been those who were not historically friends and allies before. This secondary theme is one of, "The enemy of my enemy is my friend", as both sides will share another common enemy. Line three, the supporting details to the main theme, indicates this bought military will act as *the rear guard*. The use of color by Nostradamus, in this case *white*, is a reference to a religious belief. As such, *white territory* means the land of Christians.

People innumerable will show suddenly at Vicenza	*Peuple infini apparoistra à Vicence*
Without strength fire to consume there Basilica	*Sans force feu brusler la Basilique*
As it were touching to Islam-time defeated great of Much-worth,	*Pres de Lunage deffait grand de Valence,*
In that time which Venice through moorish will embrace pike.	*Lors que Venise par more prendra picque.*

Note: Originally listed as quatrain number 11 in Centurie VIII. In *Vicenza* there is the *Basilica Palladiana*, named after the architect Andrea Palladio (his first major work), which was begun in 1549 (during Nostradamus' time), and finished in 1617. The word *Valence* is correct Old French, although the definition refers one to look up the word meaning *Valliant*. It could be possible that *Valence* is a variation in Old French for "*Valenza,*" although the French now spell it the same as the Italians. *Valenza*, Italy is on the opposite end of the mainland, close to France, and is not close to *Vicenza* or *Venice*. The name *Valence* is the correct spelling for several French towns, with the one in Tarn-et-Garonne Department being in the prominent southwestern region of France; but that is twice as far away from the main theme focus, which is in northeast Italy.

Spring delays, escapes them more neighboring Roman,	*Flora fuis, fuis le plus proche Romain,*
In the lights-the-year will be battle given:	*Au fesulan sera conflict donné:*
Kindred scattered abroad them more substantial ones seized with public power,	*Sang espandu les plus grands prins à main,*

Chapter 22 - Spearheads to Submission

Church neither sex not will be forgiven.	*Temple ne sexe ne sera pardonné.*

Note: Originally listed as quatrain number 8 in Centurie VII. It may be tempting to see the name *Flora* as representative of the Italian city Florence. However, there is nothing indicating the city was rooted in that name, and the Italian name is *Firenze*; with the Latin name *Florentia* (meaning, "flourishing"). It seems that Fesulae was the name of the town now named *Fiesole*, Italy, 5 miles northeast of Florence. However, in the lower case, *fesulan* becomes a descriptive word, rather than a specific place name. As such, the Etruscans found *Fesulae* a place to train "augurs", or "diviners," such that *fesulan* (as *fues-l'an*) can mean something akin to, "in the star lights that year". In that case, Spring is following the initial invasion, and the new year predicts more battles.

Of Spring event to his death will be cause,	*De Flora issue de sa mort sera cause,*
One time before for youthful ones & old to drink	*Un temps devant par jeusne bueyre*
Through them three lily it will be causing such pause,	*Par les trois lys luy feront telle pause,*
For one's fruit saved much like unto flesh unripe to transform.	*Par son fruit sauve comme chair crue mueyre.*

Note: Originally listed as quatrain number 18 in Centurie VIII. This quatrain and quatrain VII-08 both have the capitalized word *Flora* in the main theme statement. Line one makes the most sense as a main theme statement when *Spring* is tied to the possessive pronoun *sa*. When seen as Jesus Christ and his Spring event, one sees the primary focus being on Easter, and the cause that is the reason behind Christianity. Line two is then showing the connection to Easter to pagan festivals and rites, such as the Easter Bunny, which is attractive to the young ones, but aligned with the pagan fertility rites of spring. The use of three has Trinity connotations, and if *bueyre* is indeed a form of to drink, it and flesh (*chair*) state the body and blood of the communion service. The verb saved (*sauve*) also has special purpose to Christians. I see this as a change coming, away from Christianity, which took place in Nazi Germany. With Flora being a word in German, this could be the focus of this quatrain.

A valiant aged man all full of life laid in grave,	*Le bon viellard tout vif ensevely,*
Near to the great river by violently burst distrust:	*Pres du grand fleuve par fausse souspecon:*
Them recent ancient with vast means made noble,	*Le nouveau vieux de richesse ennobly,*
Taken in journey everything the gold of there ransom.	*Prins au chemin tout l'or de la rançon.*

Note: Originally listed as quatrain number 72 in Centurie III. Nostradamus refers to a "*chef vieillard*" ("principal commander aged man") in the main theme of quatrain I-78, and to a "*viellart eschappé*" ("aged man escaped", same spelling as here) in line three of quatrain V-100. I see it as

The Epic Poem Prophesied by Nostradamus

a safe bet all are related as the same aged man.

Them exiled ones round about to there One's outstretched,	*Les exilez autour de la Soulongne,*
Trained ones of to hurt considering to proceed upon the Auxois,	*Conduis de nuit pour marcher à Lauxois,*
Two from Modena disposed to fight with Bologna,	*Deux de Modene truculent de Bolongne,*
Thrust into discovered ones by death from this Brown people year.	*Mis descouvers par feu de Burançoys.*

Note: Originally listed as quatrain number 13 in Centurie IX. *The Auxois* is a correct spelling for a breed of French horse, which is rare today, but was prevalent in the Middle Ages. That could mean a reference to the horses rode by Crusading knight. The word *descouvrir* means, "to discover," however, the past participle was *descouvert*, making *descouvers* only possible as *descouvert-s* (discovered ones). In the *Cote d'Or* department, which is where one finds the rare Auxois horses still bred, is a commune named *Bure-les-Templiers*, which translates as, "Brown the Templars", who were renowned Crusaders. The people of this commune are called *Burois*. The *Basilica of Saint Stephens*, in *Bologna*, Italy, is a Templar church, built in the 11th century. Still, Nostradamus occasionally referred to the commune *Auch* as *Aux*.

The army Celtic against them mountaineers,	*L'armée Celtique contre les montaignars,*
Who will be known ones & taken to there big bite:	*Qui seront sceuz & prins à la lipee:*
Countrymen fresh ones will be pushing quickly shipwrecks,	*Paysants fresz pouseront tost faugnars,*
Steep downfall all in the edge of the sword.	*Precipitez tous au fil de l'espee.*

Note: Originally listed as quatrain number 63 in Centurie IV.

One principal commander Celtic in a battle wounded,	*Un chef Celtique dans le conflict blessé,*
Next to cave seeing his own ones killed to ruin:	*Aupres de cave voyant siens mort abbatre:*
With kindred & hurts & from enemies constrained,	*De sang & playes & d'ennemis pressé,*
Both assisted ones by unknown ones of four.	*Et secourus par incogneus de quatre.*

Note: Originally listed as quatrain number 10 in Centurie V. The word *cave* can also translate as, "a vault, a hollow place in the ground, or a cellar."

Chapter 22 - Spearheads to Submission

The principal commander with the army camp in the middle to there thrust close together,	Le chef du camp au milieu de la presse,
From one stroke of shaft will be wounded in the thighs	D'un coup de fleche sera blessé aux cuisses
In that time which Geneva upon the offensive and defensive weapons & hard terms	Lors que Geneve en larmes & detresse,
Will be treacherously dealt with through Lausanne & ones of Switzerland.	Sera trahie par Lozan & Souysses.

Note: Originally listed as quatrain number 9 in Centurie IV. This quatrain appears to connect to quatrain V-10, due to the repeating of terms, "chef", "presse", and "blessé". With both this and quatrain V-10 being placed in the vicinity of northwest Italy, along the Po River source, near Turin, Lake Geneva and Switzerland is only 100 miles to the northwest.

Him arm hanging & there leg bound,	Le bras pendu & la jambe liée,
Aspect of a man pale with the spot on the face dagger hidden:	Visage pasle au seing poignard caché:
Three who will be ones that have taken oaths to there mixed,	Trois qui seront jurés de la meslee,
In the high of Tortured ones will be them weapon delivered.	Au grand de Gennes sera le fer lasché.

Note: Originally listed as quatrain number 28 in Centurie V. The word *liee* can equally mean, "combined or united with and holding or hanging together." One must be cognizant of an "*arm*" being a branch of a main body, such as a division of an army; and a "*leg*" can be a part of atrip. This quatrain links to quatrain X-78, where the liberators of Rome will find traitorous Italians (tortured into submission) holding weapons on other Italians being held prisoners, in torturous conditions.

Through hunger there spoil will cause greedy fellow prisoner,	Par faim la proye fera loup prisonnier,
Them setting on in that time at uttermost hard terms,	L'assaillant lors en extreme detresse.
A ship holding with them being bound unto the rear,	Le nay aiant au devant le dernier,
Him high not body of a column with them the midst of the crowd of people.	Le grand n'eschappe au milieu de la presse.

Note: Originally listed as quatrain number 82 in Centurie II. This quatrain is related to quatrain IV-09 by the repeat of terms, "*detresse*", "*milieu*", and "*presse*". The use of "wolf" ("*loup*") can be

215

The Epic Poem Prophesied by Nostradamus

seen as a symbolic reference to Rome, which is symbolized by Romulus and Remus being raised by a wolf. The word "*n'escappe*" is cleanly defined as "not escaped." The Old French word *escaper* (only one "p") directs one to look up *eschapper* (two "p"s). The English word "*escape*" is said to be rooted in Latin, as *excappare*. This means, "to take off one's cape," which is a way of stating, "*escape*." This would have a bearing on secondary translations.

Between two seas will govern promontory,	*Entre deux mers dressera promontoire,*
Which after will perish by reason of the stings from the cavalry:	*Que puis mourra par le mords du cheval:*
Them belonging to himself Neptune will fold the sail black,	*Le sien Neptune pliera voyle noire,*
On Gibraltar & fleet next to Rock-valley.	*Par Calpre & classe aupres de Rocheval.*

Note: Originally listed as quatrain number 77 in Centurie I. The word *dresser* can mean many things, such as, "to straighten, set right, make level, even; to raise, advance, erect, lift, set, hold or take up; to direct, instruct, train, govern, or order; to fashion, frame, build or make." In Greek mythology (from which Poseidon is the near equivalent of Neptune), a *black sail* symbolized, "mourning", and "perversity, the forces of darkness". Likewise, women in mourning also wear a "*black veil*". As a "*black ship*", the image of a stealth bomber comes to mind, where its *black veil* is designed to avoid detection. It must never be forgotten that the "color" *black* is Nostradamus' reference code for Muslims. The *valley* of Gibraltar is known as the Genal *Valley*, in Andalusia, which runs roughly from Ronda, south to Estepona, on the edge of the territory held by the Commonwealth of Great Britain – *Rock* of Gibraltar.

A child from the great not standing upright with his ancient inheritance,	*L'enfant du grand n'estant à sa naissance,*
Will bring unto subjection them high ones mountain ones Apennines:	*Subjuguera les haultz monts Apennis:*
Will cause to tremble everything, those to there balance	*Fera trembler tous, ceux de la balance*
Both of them mounts deaths until unto in mountain Old Man.	*Et des monts feux jusques à mont Senis.*

Note: Originally listed as quatrain number 61 in Centurie V. The use of balance, in line three, is a reference to the United States of America, whose Ascendant is Libra. The word *senis* is the genitive masculine singular form of the word *senex*, meaning, "old, aged," and specifically, "old man." Mont Cenis (a phonetic possibility) is in the Alps, in Savoy (France), where a tunnel exists connecting the Cottian and Gracian Alps (Switzerland, Italy, France).

Chapter 22 - Spearheads to Submission

The two forces at the ramparts not will be having strength to join	*Les deux copies aux murs ne pourront joindre*
Within this is instant to tremble Milan, Pavia:	*Dans cest instant trembler Milan, Ticin:*
Hunger, thirst, doubt if mighty them will arrive to sting,	*Faim, soif, doubtance si fort les viendra poindre,*
Flesh, bread, neither means not will be having one by itself not that valiant.	*Chair, pain, ne vivres n'auront vn seul boncin.*

Note: Originally listed as quatrain number 90 in Centurie IV. The Italian city Pavia was named Ticinum in ancient times, due to it being at the mouth of the Ticino River, where it reached the Po River. Pavia is 35 kilometers (just under 22 miles) south of Milan, with both in Lombardy.

Vercelli, Milan will give capacity,	*Verceil, Milan donra intelligence,*
Within Pavia will be achieved there contented,	*Dedans Tycin sera faite la paye,*
To make speed through Siena emotion, kindred, death at Florence.	*Courir par Siene eau, sang, feu par Florence.*
Entire to tumble down from high into lowest part of effecting pile of unshucked corn.	*Unique choir d'haut en bas faisant maye.*

Note: Originally listed as quatrain number 7 in Centurie VIII. *Vercelli* is in the Piedmont region of Italy, near where it borders the Lombard region. The capitol of the Lombard region is *Milan*, which is said to be a 50 minute train ride apart (less than 70 Km). *Pavia* is also in Lombardy, due south of *Milan* (approximately 30 Km) and just north of the Po River. *Florence* is further south, centrally located in the region of Tuscany.

Him army lodged more great from rout thrust into at flight,	*Le camp plus grand de route mis en fuite,*
Not long more pierced born will be eagerly pursued:	*Guaires plus oultre ne sera pourchassé:*
Army back encamped, & legion reduced,	*Ost recampé, & legion reducte,*
Moreover out of with the French ones of the whole sum will be put to flight.	*Puis hors des Gaules du tout sera chassé.*

Note: Originally listed as quatrain number 12 in Centurie IV. A *legion* is defined as 6830 soldiers. The word *Gaules* is French as the name for the people of Gaul, as *les Gaules*. The French name

217

The Epic Poem Prophesied by Nostradamus

for French people is *Gaulois*, which is similar, but not an exact match, since Roman Gaul included Belgium and parts of Germany, Switzerland. Old French cleanly used *gaule* to denote a "big rod, or pole", which indicates a form of tool used for punishing, or beating.

Because there support which the city will forge,	*Pour la faveur que la cité fera,*
With the great who suddenly will lose field of main battle.	*Au grand qui tost perdra champ de bataille.*
Escaped ones them range Ford Ticino will put out.	*Fuis le rang Pau Thesin versera.*
From blood, fires, deaths drowned ones with blow to shred.	*De sang, feux, mors noyes de coup de taille.*

Note: Originally listed as quatrain number 26 in Centurie II. It is possible that the phonetic of *Pau* is reference to the Po River. There is no evidence that *Pau* is French, which indicates the Po River (as some have claimed in the past). *Pau* is a French commune, where the origin of the name is guessed to mean a place to *Ford* the river, *Gave de Pau*. The word *pau* is also clean Old French, meaning, "stake." The *Ticino* River joins the *Po* River at Pavia (know to the Romans as Ticinum), which is due south of Milan. The word *taille* can equally mean, "a task or tax, imposition, or sliced, gashed, hacked, notched, engraved, indented, and taxed and assessed."

Him ruin themselves almost arrived at, death great blood poured out	*Le sac s'approche, feu grand sang espandu*
Po high tributaries, in them cow herd ones the adventure,	*Po grand fleuves, aux bouviers l'entreprinse,*
To Genoa, Nice, after long awaited,	*De Gennes, Nice, apres long attendu,*
Fossano, Turin, with Savigliano there captured.	*Foussan, Turin, à Savillan la prinse.*

Note: Originally listed as quatrain number 30 in Centurie VII. The *Po* River runs from west to east across northern Italy, from the Italian Alps to the Adriatic Sea. In the province of Piedmont in Italy, the "piedmontese" spell *Fossano* as *Fossan*. When the addition of a "*u*" is seen, it becomes possible to see the word as manufactured from the word "*fousser,*" meaning "to dig." The word *fousser* has a particular meaning, "to turn up a vineyard before the vines begin to bud." *Savillano* (I believe) is now known as Savigliano. It is less than 10 miles from *Fossano* (to the north-northwest), near Carmagnole, in the Piedmont region.

By reason of the tumor from Ebro Po, Tagus, Tiber & Rome,	*Par la tumeur de Heb. Po, Tag, Timbre & Rome,*
As well by the standing water Geneva & Arezzo:	*Et par l'estang Leman & Aretin:*
Them two great ones principal commanders & warned to appear ones to Garonne,	*Les deux grans chefs & cités de Garonne,*

Chapter 22 - Spearheads to Submission

Seized deaths drowned ones. To divide civil booty.	*Prins, mors noyés. Partir humain butin.*

Note: Originally listed as quatrain number 12 in Centurie III. There is nothing that supports a translation of Timbre (a clean French word) as a spelling for the Tiber River, in Italy. Some have made it appear the main theme list a river in Spain, a river in Italy, another river in Spain, and another river in Italy. Some even alter Rome to be "Rosne," which is possible to see in the typeset. This would create the Rhone River in France as another river being stated. However, the possibility is a main theme of important stages, with abbreviations used as representative of something other than rivers. The main theme can be read to say, "By there rising of Ebony (symbolic of Islam and in particular African Muslims) Po, Thievish, Bell & Rome." This removes Spain and France from the equation, as only Po and Rome are fully and properly spelled out. This makes the main theme be solely focused on Italy.

Nearby to the internal within from casks sealed ones,	*Pres de linterne dans de tonnes fermes,*
Places for lees of oil will act in defense of the eagle there directed,	*Chivaz fera pour l'aigle la menee,*
Them chosen broken with age his men unable ones,	*Leslu casse luy ses gens enfermez,*
Within Turin violent pulling away married brought in.	*Dedans Turin rapt espouse emmenee.*

Note: Originally listed as quatrain number 8 in Centurie VIII. The word *Chiva* is good Spanish, as the feminine form of *Chivo*, both of which means, "kid goat" (either male – *Chivo*, or female – *Chiva*). In Spanish provincial, Chivo is a, "pit, place for lees of oil," but it also represents, "fraud; plot, intrigue; smuggling; illegal trading; and contraband" in some Caribbean usage. According to InterTran translation, Chiva means, "tattletale, sneak". There is an Italian commune named "Chivasso," which is only 20 kilometers northeast of Turin. This has to be considered as a possibility, although there is also a Chiva, Spain, in the Valencian Community. The word *menée* can also mean, "conspiracy, plot, practice, shift and device."

The great ducked down ones folded not will show,	*Le grand tappis plié ne monstrera,*
Except which in half there majority of the chronicle:	*Fors qu'à demy la pluspart de l'histoire:*
Expelled out of to the government long way off harsh will be apparent,	*Chassé du regne loing aspre apparoistra,*
Who at the achievement of war all them will come to trust.	*Qu'au faict bellique chascun le viendra croire.*

Note: Originally listed as quatrain number 61 in Centurie VI. Line two, following the statement in line one, makes one think of the story (another translation for *histoire*) of the Trojan horse, with

The Epic Poem Prophesied by Nostradamus

the men concealed within. The word *croire* also means, "to have confidence in," and "to trust."

Them great grave of the people Aquitaine,	*Le grand sepulcre du peuple Aquitanique,*
Themselves will approach close to there Tuscany:	*S'aprochera aupres de la Toscane:*
When War will be near to the angle as relatives	*Quand Mars sera pres du coing germanique*
Both in the land with the people Mantua-born.	*Et au terroir de la gent Mantuane.*

Note: Originally listed as quatrain number 32 in Centurie III. When written in the lower case (as it clearly appears in the 1568 Lyon edition), the word *germanique* cannot be directly translated as "Germanic," which would directly state, "the German people." The Germans are not called such by the French, and the reason is Germany is a collection of places unified, coming from *the same stock*. In a secondary sense, however, an area close to nation of Germany, where blood descent is possible, the Germanic people live in places like Italy and France. This is how the word can be interpreted. *Mantua* is near Verona, in the Lombardy region, capital of the province Mantova. The French word *mantouane* means "one from Mantua," thus *Mantua-born*. That *land* is Italy.

Them three the furred ones from far off themselves will be fighting,	*Les trois pellices de loing s'entrebatron,*
There more great lesser will continue with the prying companion:	*La plus grand moindre demeurera à l'escoute,*
He great moon not in will be more defender,	*Le grand selyn n'en sera plus patron,*
Him will speak of death crescent-shaped wicker shield white rout.	*Le nommera feu, pelte, blanche route.*

Note: Latin: *pelta*, Greek: *plete* = *small shield; crescent-shaped wicker shield*. Originally listed as quatrain number 53 in Centurie X. The translation of *pellices* as "the furred ones" gives the connotation of people from northern climates, where fur is a normal wear. This name would go along with names like *Aquilonaires* (Northerners). The word *selin* could be a variation of the word "*selene*," meaning, "goddess of the moon," but the lower case makes it less likely to have the same meaning, as it would if capitalized.

There people French & nation foreign,	*La gent Gauloise & nation estrange,*
Beyond the mountains, death seized & lowered ones:	*Outre les monts, mors prins & profligés:*
In the month much disagreeing & near to grape harvest,	*Au moys contraire & proche de vendange,*

Chapter 22 - Spearheads to Submission

By them landlords into agreement ordered ones.	*Par les seigneurs en accord redigés.*

Note: Originally listed as quatrain number 38 in Centurie III. Both of the words *gent* and *nation* mean basically the same thing, becoming interchangeable. Line one, as presented, best shows a *nation* ruled by *foreign people*, making France a *nation foreign*. Still, as *There people French & nation foreign*, the *people* are *French* troops stationed in Italy.

At the bottom of the examiner of the dragged marriage,	*Soubz la colleur du tracte mariage,*
Deed of noble spirit by great Lord- one arm of the sea,	*Fait magnanime par grand Chyren selin,*
Saint-Quentin, Arras recovered ones with the voyage	*Quintin, Arras recouvrez au voyage*
With Spaniards act next after seat in the galley not guile.	*D'espaignolz fait second banc macelin.*

Note: Originally listed as quatrain number 54 in Centurie VIII. Both *Arras* and *Saint-Quentin* are close to the French border with the Netherlands, near the Strait of Dover, which separates England from France and Europe.

With vestments uncouth ones next unto fashioned there found,	*D'habits nouveaux apres faicte la treuve,*
Lewd device woven & crafty invention:	*Malice tramme & machination:*
Foremost will decay whom upon will do the experiment,	*Premier mourra qui en fera la preuve,*
Shadow white lead pigment in cosmetics practicing of wiles.	*Couleur venise insidiation.*

Note: Originally listed as quatrain number 6 in Centurie IV. When the capitalization of the preposition *De* is abbreviated and attached to a lower case *habits*, the affect is to make *Habits* (important, higher meaning habits) become the focus. The higher meaning is then of religious focus, with *Habits* being known as what the customary outfits of nuns are called. Therefore, the main theme statement is about a new fashion design that will be found forced upon nuns. This makes this quatrain focus on those serving the Catholic Church.

The Epic Poem Prophesied by Nostradamus

Before them folk race will be scattered abroad,	*Devant le peuple sang sera respandu,*
Which from the most glorious heaven born will come to keep aloof:	*Que du hault ciel ne viendra esloigner:*
Rather of one outstretched time not will be understood,	*Mais d'un long temps ne sera entendu,*
The spirit with one alone him will arrive to testify.	*L'esprit d'un seul le viendra tesmoigner.*

Note: Originally listed as quatrain number 49 in Centurie IV. The word *devant* is also the present participle of the verb "devoir," meaning, "having or owning." Line one could be referencing the Jews, as those *cast abroad*, but in the context of the story, and this quatrain, it could also be those of Palestine, or Iraq, or other Middle Eastern nations where war and unrest in their homelands have led them to become refugees. This problem is quite prevalent in Europe, and has been for a long time; but it is also comparable to the illegal immigration problem in the United States.

One not will uphold accord someone determined,	*On ne tiendra pache aucune arresté,*
Everything takings will be going by reason of delusion:	*Tous recevans iront par tromperie:*
With agreement & a limited cessation of war world & sea openly affirmed,	*De paix & trefue terre & mer proteste,*
For Barcelona order seized from endeavor.	*Par Barcelone classe prins d'industrie.*

Note: Originally listed as quatrain number 64 in Centurie VI. A false peace is indicated in line two, where mercenary warriors will run roughshod over their conquests, taking whatever they so desire as the spoils of war, by agreement.

Chapter 23

A World at War Again

France is Invaded

To an end of a time elderly will proceed judgment slow	*D'un chief vieillard naistra sens hebete*
Unlike one's ancestors through experience in & of weapons:	*Degenerant par savoir & par armes:*
The chief of French for its sister withdrawn,	*Le chef de France par sa sœur redoubté,*
Large subjects of discourse divided ones, conceded unto ones with the men of arms.	*Champ divisés, concedés aux gendarmes.*

Note: Originally listed as quatrain number 78 in Centurie I. France is to be considered the *sister* of the United States, due to both being the product of revolutions, with strong feelings about the rule of the people, as republics. In that sense they are *sister* nations. When the main theme is read with *chef* translating as "the end of a place, time, or business", one is able to see how the End Times becomes the focus, where the *elderly* nations will act as old men, *slow of wit*. It is then through this senility that France has *withdrawn* from her *sister*. The withdrawal will be over how one uses weaponry technology to keep the world subservient.

Bridge & mill ones in December poured out ones	*Pont & moulins en Decembre versez*
At so high rank will rise there Garonne:	*En si haut lieu montera la Garonne:*
Walls, building ones Toulouse overthrown ones,	*Murs, edifices Tholose renversez,*
That one not will conceive its reckoning as much born sage woman.	*Qu'on ne sçaura son lieu autant matronne.*

Note: Originally listed as quatrain number 37 in Centurie IX. In the Occitan language, *Toulouse* is named "*Tolosa*". A *mill* is basically defined as, "a machine designed to grind, crush, or press", but also to, "shape, cut, and polish". France has a number of windmills, which were built to grind grains, and are called *moulins*. The famous *Moulin* Rouge, notarized by Henri Toulouse-Lautrec, was of 19th nightlife. However, there is still a 14th century *Moulin* in Lautrec, France. Toulouse has a long history, with the Daurade *Bridge* a 12th century milestone. A 16th century *bridge*, the

The Epic Poem Prophesied by Nostradamus

Pont-Neuf, still exists in *Toulouse*, France. This *bridge* has survived despite many past floods of the *Garonne* River. Line four could be a reference to the history of the landing of the "Three Maries" at Saintes-Maries-de-la.Mer, France, in Provence, who split up and settled at various places. Toulouse was one of the sites of the Inquisition against the Cathars, who could have been descended from one of those "*motherly women*". Due to that eradication, *one will not conceive its reckoning*, for having lost that true direction for Christianity.

Them aged without wrinkles having a beard beneath the status austere,	*Le vieux plain barbe soubs le statut severe,*
Has lion forged above the Eagle Celtic:	*A lyon faict dessus l'Aigle Celtique:*
Him young privileged too much more maintained stoutly,	*Le petit grand trop outre perseveré,*
Loud sound of weapon in the sky: sea red Ligurian Italians.	*Bruit d'arme au ciel: mer rouge Lygustique.*

Note: Originally listed as quatrain number 85 in Centurie II. Line one gives the feel of young Muslim clerics, who appear older because of their *beards*. The *beard* demands a level of austerity, because of the status of holy men. Line three give the feel of Osama bin Laden, who was a young privileged Saudi, who chose to maintain himself more severely. Lines two and four are relative to the plan to lessen the United States, to the point that the British will have to step forward and defend a weakened Eagle. With the British in the lead, the French will also rise as their own *Eagle*. They will be sent into Italy, where line four predicts the war that will challenge the French.

Within Lyon twenty-five to one breathing,	*Dedans Lyon vingtcinq d'une alaine,*
Five citizens Near-kin ones bressans, Italian ones	*Cinq citoyens Germains bressans, Latins*
By reason of beneath ones noble will be managing wearisome conspiracy	*Par dessouz noble conduiront longue traine*
Both uncovered ones by barking noises of rude fellows.	*Et descouvers par abbois de mastins.*

Note: Originally listed as quatrain number 59 in Centurie X. The French name for Germany is "*Allemagne*", thus *Germain* is a generic term. The word *bressan* is the correct French spelling for a citizen of Bresse, an area of eastern France, not far from both Switzerland and Germany. The word is accurately used as an adjective, in the lower case (*bressan*). One of the current regions that once was part of Bresse is the Rhone-Alpes, where *Lyon* is the capital.

Chapter 23 - A World at War Again

First upon Western Europe, first into Romania,	*Premier en Gaule, premier en Romanie,*
Through sea & world to the deceitful Creditor & Paris	*Par mer & terre aux Angloys & Parys*
Strange forged ones by reason of house of servants mighty menial	*Merveilleux faitz par celle grand mesnie*
Violating monsters will lose them NOT BUT THE WITHERED ONES.	*Violant terax perdra le NORLARIS.*

Note: Originally listed as quatrain number 60 in Centurie VIII. In line two, it is possible to see *English & Paris* as a reference to a part of France that has historically been both under British and French rule. Such a place would be Aquitaine, the region of southwest France. The use of NORLARIS, if referring to GOLD, it would act in support of Angloys translating as a deceitful Creditor.

The igniter of one's fire overtaken,	*Le boutefeu par son feu attrapé,*
From the light to the sky at Carcassonne & Comminges:	*Du feu du ciel à Carcas & Cominge:*
Middle, With them, Mazères, secret old man delivered from,	*Foix, Aux, Mazeres, haut viellart eschappé,*
For those of Hesse, with the Saxons & Thuringia.	*Par ceux de Hasse, des Saxons & Turinge.*

Note: Originally listed as quatrain number 100 in Centurie V. The city of *Carcassonne* was named from the Celtic name of the hill it was built on, which was *Carsac*. As a minor anagram, where the "s" and the "c" are reversed, it becomes *Carcas*. The commune *Carcassonne* is in the Aude Department, in the Languedoc-Roussillon region, which is bordered by the Haute-Garonne and Ariège departments (among others). The Gascon name for *Comminges* was *Comenge*. The name of the people who were original *Saxons* were mostly from north-central West Germany. Those migrated to Italy, Gaul, and Britain. Today, Saxony is a term referring to the people of east Germany, particularly those of the southern East Germany, with their influences on other surrounding Slavic regions also being considered *Saxon*.

The first-born valiant from the lass to the King,	*L'aisné vaillant de la fille du Roy,*
Will be thrust back even as profound them French ones:	*Respousera si profond les Celtiques:*
That it will thrust into thunderbolts, how many upon such array,	*Qu'il mettra foudres, combien en tel arroy,*
Short & far off moreover deep into the Western ones.	*Peu & loing puis profond es Hesperiques.*

225

The Epic Poem Prophesied by Nostradamus

Note: Originally listed as quatrain number 99 in Centurie IV. The main theme statement places focus on the British royal family, when the time they have a *King* has come. As it stands now, that would be Prince Charles. With him *King*, the *first-born* would be Prince William, and he would be from the *lass* to Charles, who was Diana Spencer. Line two is then a statement of profound impacts on both England and France, as both are in general *Celtic*, although Roman Gaul included Celtica, which was what is now primarily France. Line two would also act in a secondary sense to refer to Diana Spencer's death, having been a planned action in France, where she was repulsed and thrust back in the limousine wreck. The primary focus is aeriel attacks on the far reaches of *Western* Europe, and its *Western* allies.

Expelled out of ones will be to cause wearisome battle,	*Chassés seront sans faire long combat,*
For a region being more powerful oppressed ones:	*Par le pays seront plus fort grevés:*
Places without defensive walls or ditches & summoned to appear will be having more great disagreement,	*Bourg & cité auront plus grand debat,*
Carcassonne Narbonne will be containing courage tried ones.	*Carcas. Narbonne auront cœurs eprouvés.*

Note: Originally listed as quatrain number 5 in Centurie I. The presence of *Carcas* in this quatrain shows it as abbreviated with a period mark. The name *Carcas* also appears (without a sign of abbreviation) in quatrain V-100 (line two). Both translate as *Carcassonne*, the commune in southwestern France. It must be noted that *Carcassonne* is not a *Bourg*, as it was (and still is) a fortress city, with a "*Narbonne* Gate", which leads to the road to *Narbonne*, also in the Aude Department.

In the places made holy ones beasts solemn promise with ones picked out from among others,	*Aux lieux sacrez animaux veu à trixe,*
Together with this one who not will dare them pleading place	*Avec celuy qui n'osera le jour*
In Carcassonne upon disgrace gentle	*A Carcassonne pour disgrace propice*
Will be seated considering more spacious residence.	*Sera posé pour plus ample sejour.*

Note: Originally listed as quatrain number 71 in Centurie IX. The main theme statement uses the word *animaux*, which is not too far from a real animal, rather than a figurative one, serving in a religious order.

Chapter 23 - A World at War Again

The fortress Nice not will cause battled,	*Le fort Nicene ne fera combatu,*
Overthrown will be by reason of shining metal	*Vaincu sera par rutilant metal*
Its action will be one extended opportunity disputed on,	*Son faict sera un long temps debatu,*
With the free men of the city harsh related to proving.	*Aux citadins estrange espouvental.*

Note: Originally listed as quatrain number 19 in Centurie VII. The word *Nicene* is properly spelled to represent the *Nicene* Creed, which originated from the Counsel of *Nicaea* (Turkey). The Latin name *Nicaea* equally applies to *Nice*, France and (now) *Iznik*, Turkey, with both being fortified cities. The translation of *Nice* is more in line with the theme of the storyline of *The Prophecies*, and the *Fort du Mont Alban* is a well-preserved fortress, built in the 19th century. The word *Nicene* can break into *Nice-ne*, translating optionally as, "*Nice-born.*" The words, "*shining metal*", could be hot, burning fragments, but it could also be a reference to gold or silver (i.e. money).

Disavowed going forth upon fame from the princely decrees harsh ones,	*Niee sortie sur nom des letres aspres,*
There lofty short cloak will make gift not belonging to him,	*La grande cappe fera present non sien,*
Neighboring with the three seen at the walls with green ones goats	*Proche de vultry aux murs de vertes capres*
After no bullets a gale at favorable swarm.	*Apres plombin le vent à bon essien.*

Note: Originally listed as quatrain number 26 in Centurie IX. IThe 1568 Lyon edition makes it difficult to read the first word as "Nice". The last two letters of the first word look exactly the same, as "e"s. Thus, the word in print is "*Niee*", which is Old French for "*Denied*". Most other editions prefer to represent this word as, "Nice." The name given to Nice came from the Greek settlers at Marseille, who gave a name related to the god Nike, meaning "victory." The word Nice in French means, "lazy", among other possibilities. It is difficult to overlook the modern usage of the word *sortie*, which is defined as, "an armed attack." Bishops and Popes wear a *Cappe* Magna during high ceremony, but the "magna" is a long trailing cloak. A simple *cappe* is for ordinary church wear.

Bourdeaux Poitiers at the sound of the bell,	*Bourdeaux Poitiers au son de la campane,*
With mighty fleet will journey until unto at the Point:	*A grande classe ira jusques à l'Angon:*
On the other side of France will be their coming from the north,	*Contre Gauloys sera leur tramontane,*

The Epic Poem Prophesied by Nostradamus

| When things made contrary to nature ghastly will be produced by near to Orgon. | *Quand monstres hydeux naistra pres de Orgon.* |

Note: Originally listed as quatrain number 90 in Centurie I. The city of *Bordeaux* is a port city at the mouth of the Garonne River, near the Atlantic Ocean. The town of *Poitiers* is north-northwest of Bordeaux approximately 100 miles, where the Aquitaine Basin meets the Paris Basin. In either case, the order of the words, and the lack of punctuation between them, is an indication of a line of importance. Generally, it shows a front line and command point. The word *campane* is translatable as, "an alembic or stillatory", which makes the distillation process of cognac come to light, as both *Bordeaux* and *Poitiers* are in the wine region that is known for making that wine. The word *l'Angon* is clean French for the *javelin* or *harpoon* that was particularly used by the Germanic tribe the *Anglii*. These people are who migrated to England and became (to the French) the *Anglais*. The small town of *Orgon* is north of Salon-de-Provence, and west of Saint Remy-de-Provence.

Base ones & Cavalry in there next after carefully attended	*Piedz & cheval à la seconde veille*
Will be causing first blow given will be preying upon everything by the sea,	*Feront entree vastient tout par la mer,*
Within a minute distance will have access unto from Marseille,	*Dedans le poil entrera de Marseille,*
Trickles, loud noises, & blood, at any time not one time so full of anguish.	*Pleurs, cris, & sang, onc nul tems si amer.*

Note: Originally listed as quatrain number 88 in Centurie X. When *Pieds & Chaval* surround an ampersand, one has to look at how the two words are both similar (system of ampersands), in particular with regard for both words being capitalized (system of capitalization). The element of military divisions then becomes the importance (greater than simply "*feet & horse*"), such that the *Foot ones* of a military is its ground troops, or *foot soldiers*, and the ground support for those troops is the modern mechanized *Cavalry* (a word from *Cheval*), which are tanks, helicopters, and the like. This makes the main theme be stating an important presence of military on the ground, establishing a major *foundation*.

The year that Saturn will be out of servitude,	*L'an que Saturne sera hors de servaige,*
In the free land will be from water overwhelmed:	*Au franc terroir sera d'eau inundé:*
To race Courageous determination will be its marriage,	*De sang Troyen sera son mariage,*
Both will be sure with Spaniards to envelope.	*Et sera seur d'Espaignolz circunder.*

Note: Originally listed as quatrain number 87 in Centurie V. Line one indicates, on a astronomical

Chapter 23 - A World at War Again

timing level, that *Saturn* will have had been in a sign representative of *servitude*, or *slavery*. This means either *Saturn* will have been in Pisces, the sign of submission, where the needs of others are paramount to self-need, or Virgo, the sign that naturally rules the house of Work, Service, and Health, and where servitude is a necessary means to an end. *Saturn* last left the sign of Virgo on July 10, 2010. It next enter the sign of Pisces in early March 2023, and will leave that sign in 2026 (twice). On a symbolic level, *Saturn* represents Hardship and Patience, of which *slavery* begets. Line three is making the statement that *Saturn* will be *wedded* to those of *Trojan* traits.

There guard foreign will betray fortress,	*La garde estrange trahira forteresse,*
Trust & pretense of more secret marriage:	*Espoir & umbre de plus hault mariage:*
Defense circumvented, powerful seizing within the crowd of people,	*Garde deceue, fort prinse dans la presse,*
Loire, His Rhone Gardon at death much violence.	*Loyre, Son Rosne Gar. à mort oultrage.*

Note: Originally listed as quatrain number 25 in Centurie II. Line four lists two major rivers of France, with another river abbreviated. The *Loire* flows north, through central France, before turning west and entering the Atlantic, at Nantes. It originates in the Massif Central mountain ranges, in the *Cevennes* mountains. The *Gardon* River (a.k.a. *Gard* River) originates in the same *Cevennes* mountains, but flows east to the *Rhone*. The *Saone* flows south in eastern France, joining the *Rhone* in Lyon. The *Rhone* flows south from Switzerland (from Lake Geneva), emptying into the Mediterranean Sea, at Marseille. The *Garonne* flows north from the Pyrenees Mountains and bends westward, entering the Atlantic, at Bordeaux.

With the mountain Adjusted awl over the anvil will be worthy concealed,	*Du mont Aymar sera noble obscurcie,*
Him evil will issue from at the seam from toll of the bell & no rose	*Le mal viendra au joint de sonne & rosne*
Inside timber hidden ones soldiers shadow to Light,	*Dans bois caichez soldats jour de Lucie,*
Whose not had been ever one so abominable throne.	*Qui ne fut onc un si horrible throsne.*

Note: Originally listed as quatrain number 68 in Centurie IX. The word *aymar* is a good anagram for the third person past simple form of the Old French verb *aimer*, as *aimra*. The verb aimer is defined as meaning (from only one reference), "to adjust an awl over an anvil." It seems to have some significance in pinning things together, as it is related to the verb *épingler*. The word *épinglere* means spinal cord, and it related to the word *moelle*, which means, marrow, pith, and cord. The Feast of Saint *Lucy* (aka *Lucia*) is held (in the West) on December 13, which is considered to be the longest night in the year. She is the patron saint of blindness. The name Lucia is spelled Lucie in French, and is derived from Latin, meaning, "bright, clear, and light."

The Epic Poem Prophesied by Nostradamus

By reason of there extreme wrath from one who will look for the water,	*Par la fureur d'un qui attendra l'eau,*
Through his great madness all the infantry urged forward:	*Par la grand raige tout l'exercite esmeu:*
Loaded with the gallant ones ten September boats,	*Chargé des nobles à dix sept bateulx,*
With them extended to the Rhone, long in coming messenger arrived.	*Au long du Rosne, tard messagier venu.*

Note: Originally listed as quatrain number 71 in Centurie V. The word *bateulx*, as the plural form of *batel*, is known specifically as a *bateau*, which is a narrow flat-bottomed boat with a pointed bow and stern. Still, it can mean any small boat. The word *Rosne* is a Provencal name for the *Rhone* River. As *Ros-ne* it can represent Christianity, as "*Rose-born*," but that appears to be secondary, as the greater meaning of the quatrain is telling about battle problems and logistical woes.

By reason of there discord negligence French,	*Par la discorde negligence Gauloise,*
Will be course to Muslim apparent:	*Sera passaige a Mahommet ouvert:*
From lineage steeped there soil & sea Themselves quarrel,	*De sang trempé la terre & mer Senoise*
A harbor for ships Marseille to them veiled & ships hidden.	*Le port Phocen de voiles & nefs couvert.*

Note: Originally listed as quatrain number 18 in Centurie I. In line four, *The port Phocen* is most likely a reference to Marseille, which was founded by the *Phocens*.

The course inevitable perpetual by no preachers,	*L'ordre fatal sempiternel par chaisne*
Will grow to make sour by order consequent:	*Viendra tourner par ordre consequent:*
To the harbor Marseille will be undone the chain,	*Du port Phocen sera rompue la chaisne,*
There city taken, the adversary regarding & that deliver into the hands.	*La cite prinse, l'ennemy quant & qnant.*

Note: Originally listed as quatrain number 79 in Centurie III. Just as in quatrain I – 18, when Nostradamus referred to "*le port Phocen*," "*Du port Phocen*" here has to be seen as a reference to the port city of *Marseille*, founded by the Phocees of Phocaea. The lore of *Marseille* is that a *chain* was placed around the harbor by Hercules, to secure it from invasion. When the word *corbel* is looked up, it is defined as, "small gabions." The word "gabion" is then defined as useful

Chapter 23 - A World at War Again

in hydraulic engineering, as, "An openwork frame, as of poles, filled with stones and sunk, to assist in forming a bar dyke, etc., as in harbor improvement." In Old French, the idiom, "*quant & quant*", translated as, "forthwith, incontinently, therewith, by and by." In French, *quant* is always accompanied by the preposition *à*, meaning, "with, to, in, at". The last word of line four, in the 1568 Lyon edition, is clearly spelled "*qnant*", making it appear to be a printer's error, where the "u" was set upside down. However, "*nant*" was a clean Old French form for *nantir*, and "*q*" was a standard typeset abbreviation for "*que.*"

There tower of the sea three time taken & taken back again,	*La tour marine trois fois prise & reprise,*
By Spaniards, Moors, Ligurians:	*Par Hespaignolz, Barbares, Ligurins:*
Marseille & Aix, Arles of the ones with Pisa,	*Marseille & Aix, Arles par ceux de Pise,*
Emptied, dead, weapons, robbed of all Avignon to them Thurins.	*Vast, feu, fer, pillé Avignon des Thurins.*

Note: Originally listed as quatrain number 71 in Centurie I. The number in line one (*three*) is explained in the secondary theme, as the *three* peoples: *Spanish*, *Moors*, and *Ligurians*. Those *three* are then associated with *three* cities, whose histories show occupation and influence from those three cultures. *Pisa* is like *Arles* in that it no longer is a seaport today, due to sediment and silt filling in what used to be their harbors. The commune of *Thurins* is north of Arles, in the Rhone department. Arles is in the Bouches-du-Rhone delartment (Mouths of the Rhone), such that line four is indicating how far norht the damage occurs, all along the Rhone.

Besides bottom not hand from within sea & forcible,	*Sans pied ne main dend ayguë & forte,*
Through globe with the strong of sea fish resembling a gurnard & the first ship:	*Par globe au fort de porc & lainé nay:*
Near to the portal treacherous transported,	*Pres du portail desloyal se transporte,*
Selene gave bright light, scarce great brought in.	*Silene luit, petit grand emmené.*

Note: Originally listed as quatrain number 58 in Centurie II. When one reads the main theme statement so that one sees an object that is *without hands* or *feet*, capable of going to the bottom of a sea, which has the important (ampersand) distinction of being powerful, one sees the main them is about submarines. When the word *porc* is translated to mean a gurnard, which can either be a *Sea Robin* or a *Flying Gurnard*, both are *fish* with strange pectoral fins and spiny "legs". It is also listed as the name of a U.S. N. attack submarine of the Sturgeon class.

The Epic Poem Prophesied by Nostradamus

Of the whole sum Marseille with the inhabiting in ones changed,	*Du tout Marseille des habitants changée,*
Incursion into an enemy's country & pursuit until at them near to Lyon:	*Course & poursuitte jusques au pres de Lyon:*
Narbonne Toulouse through Bordeaux outraged,	*Narbon. Tholoze par Bourdeaux oultragée:*
Killed ones lost liberty ones in a manner from one million.	*Tués captifz presque d'un milion.*

Note: Originally listed as quatrain number 72 in Centurie I. The information of this quatrain matches that of quatrain I-71, in the sense that line three in that quatrain told of *Marseille*, which is in the main theme of this quatrain. Line two's secondary theme mentions *Lyon*, whereas lays out a line between Avignon (less than 40 miles north-northwest of *Marseille*) and Thurins, which is less than 15 miles west of *Lyon*. The two main themes here tell of an invasion that is quickly as far north as *Lyon*, from *Marseille*, while almost as deep (to the west) as *Bordeaux*.

Within Toulouse not far off from Belvèze-du-Razès	*Dedans Tholoze non loin de Belvezer*
Effecting a hill long way off, house of parliament to spectacle	*Faisant un puys loing, palais despectacle*
Store of abundance obtained one every man will journey to torment,	*Tresor trouvé un chacun ira vexer,*
Both into two tatters everything & near to the downpours.	*Et en deux locz tout & pres del vasacle.*

Note: Originally listed as quatrain number 30 in Centurie VIII. The town of *Belvezè-du-Razès* (aka *Belvezè*) is in the Aude department, in the Languedoc-Roussillon region. *Razès* is a name common to several communes in the Aude Department. *Toulouse* is the capitol of the old Languedoc province, not far from *Belvezè*, about 40 miles to the west. Line two may be referencing Washington, D. C., since its *houses* of government are called "*the hill*". As well, it may be referencing London, following the comma separating the two segments, where the *palais* could be both the royal family, while also being the *House* of Parliament.

Chapter 23 - A World at War Again

Waste, run away ones to Toulouse them red ones	*Vuydez, fuyez de Tholose les rouges*
From the sacrifice to cause the act of coming to a close,	*Du sacrifice faire expiation,*
The general of them pained with course the cloak of widespread devastations	*Le chef du mal desour l'ombre des courges*
Death to smother edge making prediction.	*Mort estrangler carne omination.*

Note: Originally listed as quatrain number 46 in Centurie IX. The main theme statement is about a time when communists, or socialists, will hold control of *Toulouse*, but that time will result in a major (capitalization) *Waste*, or *Void*, creating *Wide empty spaces, Devoid of life*. The secondary theme them explains why the *red ones* would be running away from *Toulouse*. Others will be making *sacrifices* to bring the *red* rule to a close. In their retreat, the *reds* will have to cover up their atrocities. The word *omination* is defined through the action form of the word, *ominati*ng, which means, "to presage, to foreshow, to foretoken."

Chapter 24

The Unholiness of War

Rome is Attacked

There one great who owns planet for seven lights will be on fire,	*La grand' estoille par sept jours bruslera,*
Clouded will cause two sun to appear:	*Nuée fera deux soleil apparoir:*
A sad mastiff everything darkness will howl,	*Le gros mastin toute nuict hurlera,*
Seeing that great pontiff will change with country.	*Quand grand pontife changera de terroir.*

Note: Originally listed as quatrain number 41 in Centurie II. In line one, the word "*grand*" is followed by an apostrophe. The French only rarely use an apostrophe to show the possessive, while the English use it frequently. However, as this is the only sue use in *The Prophecies*, and seeing how each word has to be read individually, the use of a possessive apostrophe (implying an "s" to follow) makes the word *grand* different than the word *grandes* (which would be read as "great ones"). When this possessive is followed by the word *star*, or *planet*, ownership can only be said to be God's. In the 1568 Lyon edition, the word *soleil* is in the singular.

Upon them warned to appear where a wolf will have access into.	*En la cité ou le loup entrera.*
As it should be nearby to there the adversary ones being:	*Bien pres de là les ennemis seront:*
Troops unacquainted great country will disdain.	*Copie estrange grand pays gastera.*
To the walls & mountains them loving mates will be surmounting.	*Aux murs & alpes les amis passeront.*

Note: Originally listed as quatrain number 33 in Centurie III. Line one's use of *wolf* relates to quatrain II – 41, as a *mastiff* that *howls*. Rome is the city founded by Romulus and Remus, who were raised by a wolf.

Gray & dark brown, half without color war,	*Gris & bureau, demie ouverte guerre,*
To darkness will be assaulted ones & ravaged ones:	*De nuict seront assaillis & pillés:*

Chapter 24 - The Unholiness of War

The brown russet embraced will overrun through there thrust up together,	Le bureau prins passera par la serre,
Its temple large two in the mortar withered.	Son temple ouvert deux au plastre grillés.

Note: Originally listed as quatrain number 65 in Centurie VI. The color *Gray* is the result of mixing black with white. When religions are the essence of colors in *The Prophecies*, with black equating to Islam, and white equating to Christianity, *Gray* becomes an important place (capitalization) where Islam and Christianity mix. The United States certainly is to be considered *Gray*, to some extent. The use of "*gray*" as the blurring of law, between the black and white of the letter of the law, can also play a role in interpretation. The color *brown* is representative of non-Muslim, non-Christian Africans, who primarily practice tribal religion. The meaning of *ouverte*, as "*without color*", means, by definition, "white." The color "white" is actually defined as, "the absence of color." However, "*without color*" also means "transparency." Still, the last half of the main theme statement is about half-Christians, who become openly for war.

In barrels without smears of oil & fat,	Dedans tonneaux hors oingz d'huille & gresse,
Will be twenty one owing the customs paid for freight enclosed ones:	Seront vingt un devant le port fermés:
To the assistant in the duel observation of death will be forging dutifulness:	Au second guet par mort feront prouesse:
To achieve them ways to enter & with the careful spying stricken down ones.	Gaigner les portes & du guet assommés.

Note: Originally listed as quatrain number 40 in Centurie VII. Line one's statement of "*Barrels*" of "*oil*," where the capitalization states a significant number of *Barrels*, rather than simply a few, becomes evidence of a oil tanker, whose load is measured in *Barrels*. These carriers will have some smaller containers that will not have any product or mineral cargo. Instead, they will be empty, except for *twenty* being filled with watchers, or spies.

One Braga male with the language twisted	Un Braga mas avec la langue torte
Will issue from the gods a shelter from danger,	Viendra des dieux la sainctuaire,
With the heretics he will disclose there way to enter	Aux heretiques il ouvrira la porte
At raising up the church soldier-like.	En suscitant l'eglise militaire.

Note: Originally listed as quatrain number 78 in Centurie VIII. *Braga* is a city in northern Portugal, close to the Atlantic coast.

The Epic Poem Prophesied by Nostradamus

By reason of arcs fires pitch & for dead ones driven back ones,	*Par arcs feux poix & par feux repoussés,*
Loud noises howling ones above there midnight heard ones:	*Cris hurlements sur la minuit ouys:*
Inwardly are thrust into through the walls of fortresses broken with age ones,	*Dedans sont mis par les ramparts cassés,*
Through underground passages them tradition ones flee.	*Par cunicules les traditeurs fuis.*

Note: Originally listed as quatrain number 77 in Centurie II. The term *traditeur* is said to be related to "ecclesiastic history", where it is defined as, "name of those who, with the persecution, will be giving the sacred books to the pagans (or heathens)." It is different form a "traitor" (in French *traiteur*), and in more in line with preserving traditions.

Good Lord! huge to me Rome your destruction itself drawing near unto,	*O vaste Romme ta ruyne s'approche,*
Not of your walls of your blood & substance	*Non de tes murs de ton sang & soubstance*
The rough handling by reason of them to be will make so horrible spell,	*L'aspre par letres fera si horrible coche,*
Weapon sharp at the point thrust into all until at the handle.	*Fer poinctu mis a tous jusqu'au manche.*

Note: Originally listed as quatrain number 65 in Centurie X. The word *coche* also meant, "a woman grown fat by ease and laziness," as well as "a young sow," plus "notch, snip and knock." It can also represent "coach" or "stagecoach."

Younger King causes his father will put to death,	*Puisnay Roy fait son pere mettre à mort,*
Following bickering of murdered most dishonest:	*Apres conflit de mort tres inhonneste:*
Piece of evidence obtained jealousy will deliver up left behind,	*Escrit trouve soubson donra remort,*
At what time greedy fellow expelled out of the bed of ease.	*Quand loup chassé pose sur la couchette.*

Note: Originally listed as quatrain number 8 in Centurie IX. The word *escrit* meant *written*, but allowed for the same translations as the word "*escript*," which meant: manuscript, a writing, and piece of evidence.

Chapter 24 - The Unholiness of War

Them fortified ones you batter in the sky wearisome time,	*Les armes battre au ciel longue saison,*
The tree at the center of there warned to appear tumbled into:	*L'arbre au millieu de la cite tombé:*
Sacred branch, circumcised, lance upon face firebrand,	*Verbine, rongne, glaive en face tyson,*
In that time an absolute prince from Adriatic Sea overcome.	*Lors le monarque d'Hadrie succombé.*

Note: Originally listed as quatrain number 11 in Centurie III. The word *firebrand* is defined as, "A person with a penchant for militancy in speech and/or action," but it is also definitive of "burning wood". This definition makes the "*Tree*", "*Branch*" theme of wood stay consistent.

The divine word will be from the sky blasted as with lightning,	*Le divin verbe sera du ciel frappé,*
Who neither will have strength to keep on course more forward:	*Qui ne pourra proceder plus avant:*
To them revealing the hidden matter shut up,	*Du reserant le secret estoupé,*
That one will tread on above & owing.	*Qu'on marchera par dessus & devant.*

Note: Originally listed as quatrain number 27 in Centurie II.

There great summoned to appear from assault ready at hand & unlooked for,	*La grand cité d'assaut prompt & repentin,*
Taken napping from night, defenses interrupted ones:	*Surprins de nuict, gardes interrompus:*
Them keeping watch ones & vigils sanctified Quintin,	*Les excubies & veilles saint Quintin,*
Massacred ones guards & the portals torn asunder ones.	*Trucidés gardes & les pourtails rompus.*

Note: Originally listed as quatrain number 8 in Centurie IV. The feast day for Saint *Quintin* is October 31st, which was the date of his martyred death, in A.D. 287. For the USA that date is Halloween, or All Hallows Eve. There is a commune named *Quintin*, which is in the *Cotes-d'Armor* department, in the *Bretagne* region.

The Epic Poem Prophesied by Nostradamus

That into inwardly fish, weapon & command enclosed,	Qu'en dans poisson, fer & lettre enfermée,
Out of will come forth that which hillocks will cause there warfare:	Hors sortira qui puis fera la guerre:
Will have by sea its fleet thoroughly thicket,	Aura par mer sa classe bien ramée,
Suddenly showing as it were touching the place belonging to Latin language land.	Apparoissant pres de latine terre.

Note: Originally listed as quatrain number 5 in Centurie II. From the statement of "*fish*", a comma separates that individual word thought from a following individual word thought, which is "*weapon*". This is then clarifying the *fish* as one that is a *weapon*, which a submarine classifies as. The use of *puis*, can also be read as the Old French *puy-s*. The word *puy* must be understood, in the singular, to mean, "hillock, or high clot of earth". In the plural, it becomes *hills*. Rome is known as the city of seven *hills*, and the supporting evidence in line four states that, from the use of *latine*.

Seat at city is from darkness assaulted,	Siege en cité est de nuict assaillie,
Nobody got safe away: not much off to sea battle:	Peu eschapés: non loing de mer conflict:
Woman of joy, returns son failed,	Femme de joye, retours filz defaillie,
Poison & commands secret ones within him weave.	Poison & lettres cachées dans le plic.

Note: Originally listed as quatrain number 41 in Centurie I. The "*Woman of joy*" is the Virgin Mary, most celebrated by the Roman Catholic Church. The word *plique* is rooted in the verb *pliquer*, which is a malady of the hair, beard, and other body hairs, such that they stick together. In Latin, the word *plecto*, from which the infinitive is *plico*, means, "braid, weave, plait," as well as, "twist, bend, and turn."

Good will festive not long way off placed them siege,	Amour alegre non loing pose le siege,
In the religious barbarity will be the preparations,	Au saint barbar seront les garnisons,
Bear-like ones Adriatic Sea because French will be making by the seaside	Ursins Hadrie pour Gaulois feront plaige
Upon terror yielded unto ones to the army at the Gray with age ones.	Pour peur rendus de larmée aux Grisons.

Note: Originally listed as quatrain number 38 in Centurie X. *Barbar* is the name of an ancient city in Bahrain, the tiny island nation in the Persian Gulf. The word "*barbare*" means, "*barbarous*,"

Chapter 24 - The Unholiness of War

in French, but "*barbaria*" means, "foreign country." This was opposite the culture of Greece or Rome, thus the word is further defined as, "want of culture, rudeness, savagery." The capitalized word *Grisons* is correct French for the largest and most eastern Canton of Switzerland. In English, it is recognized by its German name, "*Graubünden*", which translates as, "Gray Leagues". This Canton borders northern Italy; and would be a point of flight that would be the result of preparations against them. Still, the males of the French commune (small) Grisy-sur-Seine are called *Grisons*.

Will be given over him fire quick, death concealed,	*Sera laissé le feu vif, mort caché,*
Within them globe ones most ugly frightful	*Dedans les globes horrible espouventable*
From darkness with fleet city into dust delivered,	*De nuict à classe cité en poudre lasché,*
There warned to appear to light, the enemy favorable.	*La cité à feu l'ennemy favorable.*

Note: Originally listed as quatrain number 8 in Centurie V. When one reads, "*death hidden*," one has to see how the effects of radiation on a body, such that internal tissues and organs begin to break down, on a path to eventual *death*, but these hidden failures are not outwardly expressed as a *dead* body, another translation possibility of *feu*.

By reason of battle head man of a party, government will leave at random,	*Par conflit roy, regne abandonnera,*
A more lofty principal commander will end with the necessity:	*Le plus grand chef faillira au besoing:*
Cause of destruction nearly finished ones nobody upon will regenerate,	*Mors profligés peu en rechapera,*
Everything chopped to pieces ones, one into will be witness.	*Tous destranchés, un en sera tesmoing.*

Note: Originally listed as quatrain number 45 in Centurie IV. Line one, due to the comma in the middle, is not primarily focusing on a leader abandoning his lead, although that is expected to be a secondary element. The words, "*regne abandonnera*", must be seen as anarchy, due to *conflict* blamed on the *chief*. In this case, all *rule* of law *will be abandoned*.

By reason of them physics the high King left without,	*Par les phisiques le grand Roy delaissé,*
Through casualty not guile of the Hebrew is upon whole age:	*Par sort non art de l'Ebrieu est en vie:*
He & his kind in the kingdom high turned,	*Luy & son genre au regne hault poulsé,*

The Epic Poem Prophesied by Nostradamus

Reckoning presented with race whom Christ longing after.	Grace donnée à gent qui Christ envie.

Note: Originally listed as quatrain number 18 in Centurie VI. The main theme statement (line one) points out that when the natural laws of the material realm have more appeal to the people, as superseding the Laws of God, then man will have turned it back to God, leaving the *without* the *Grace* of the true *King*. The use of *lot* is because casting *lots* was an *art* only skillfully read by temple priests. The casting of *lots* was a form of divination forbidden to the regular people. Nostradamus identifies *l'Ebrieu* as *Christ*, such that Jesus was *the Jew* of a *whole age*. Line three's *Him* is Jesus and *his kind* are the followers called Christians. The word *poulsé* also means: pushed, enforced and driven, making it show getting to Heaven become a stressful goal. Being Christian is then seen as *favor*able, thus cause for lusting and desiring the right to say Heaven is assured them.

Until one will come them mighty king to make appeasement offerings	Quand on viendra le grand roy parenter
Deeply in that he should have all the soul restored:	Avant qu'il ait du tout l'ame rendue:
This one which least them will grow to complain pitifully,	Celuy qui moins le viendra lamenter,
By reason of lions, with eagles, cross, crown sold.	Par lyons, d'aigles, croix, couronne vendue.

Note: Originally listed as quatrain number 71 in Centurie VI. Line one is making the main theme statement about the guardianship of souls while Jesus has resurrected, *Until* he *will come* again. That guardian is the pope of Rome. The present subjunctive is used, with the word "*ait*," which is the ultimate purpose of what the pope should *have* happen to *all souls*. They should be *restored* to God. Line three, the direct support of the main theme, tells of the corruption of the pope. The use of *l'aigles*, as "*the eagle ones*", can include the Americans, French and ancient Romans, as all had periods when an *eagle* was their emblem or symbolic standard. Line four states these are the defenders of Christianity, but through wealth gained serving the pope, wearing the shields of a *cross*, the guardian's reputation will succumb to desires for wealth and material gains.

Paul broad-o-mind will die three leagues to the not rose	Pol mensolée mourra trois lieües du rosne
Escape them two next ones monster way between two hills:	Fuis les deux prochains tarasc destrois:
Because Mars will cause them more hideous itself throne	Car Mars fera le plus horrible trosne
With cock & to eagle from France brothers three.	De coq & d'aigle de France freres trois.

Note: Originally listed as quatrain number 46 in Centurie VIII. The word *mensolée* is manufactured, and the translation is open for debate. It depends on understanding lines two and three for making an accurate translation. Line two's word *tarasc*, which is completely spelled *trasque*, is the root of the town Tarascon, in southwestern France. Tarascon has the lore of this amphibious *monster*,

Chapter 24 - The Unholiness of War

whose demise is attributed to the holy presence of Saint Martha. When the word *destrois* is seen as *destroict-s*, it becomes definable as, "way between two hills". This connects to *leagues*, as a short distance of only *two miles*, such that the *hills* of Rome become the focus. Vatican Hill is approximately *two miles* from the center of Rome. In the space *between* Vatican Hill and Capitoline Hill is the Field of *Mars* (Campus Martius).

Him captive potentate with the Italians vanquished	*Le captif prince aux Italles vaincu*
Will hold on course Torture ones by sea until with Dedicated to war,	*Passera Gennes par mer jusqu'à Marselle,*
Through great striving with the full force with the bore holes toward subdued	*Par grand effort des forens survaincu*
Leap blow from fire barrel liquor of bee.	*Saut coup de feu barril liqueur d'abelle.*

Note: Originally listed as quatrain number 24 in Centurie X. The 1568 Lyon edition does not include an "i" in the name "*Marselle*", meaning it does not spell the name of the city Marseille. Marseille is in France, not Italy, and while it is along the same general Mediterranean coast as is Genoa, the Latin meaning of the name *Marselle* bears greater importance. Still, in the Catalan language Marseille is spelled *Marsella*. The word in line four, *d'abelle*, also is missing an "i" to make it what it appears to be, *d'abeille*. However, in the Catalan language, the feminine form of *abeille* is *abella*.

Through mighty ones to be in the powers of them captive escaped,	*Par grans dangiers le captif eschapé,*
Nobody from time great there luck changed:	*Peu de temps grand la fortune changée:*
Inwardly the palace him people east entrapped,	*Dans le palais le peuple est attrapé,*
Through favorable prophecy the city is besieged:	*Par bon augure la cité est assiegée:*

Note: Originally listed as quatrain number 66 in Centurie II. The 1568 Lyon edition shows line four ending with a colon, indicating another quatrain will follow this one, adding information that will clarify line four, or the whole quatrain. Other editions show a period mark. However, if a colon is the intention, it becomes evidence of the quatrains linking together to tell stories in segments.

The Epic Poem Prophesied by Nostradamus

Him principal commander of fleet through cheating shift in war,	*Le chef de classe par fraude stratageme,*
Will cause cowardly ones to come forth with theirs Mediterranean warships,	*Fera timides sortir de leurs galleres,*
Fitted with ones crushed ones end of time ones yielding rent from cream skimmed off the top,	*Sortis meurtris chefs renteux de cresme,*
Moreover by the waylaying he will be paying back them hired ones.	*Puis par l'embusche luy rendront les salarés.*

Note: Originally listed as quatrain number 79 in Centurie IX.

Prelate princely his bowing downward too much forced upon,	*Prelat royal son baissant trop tire,*
Substantial flood of blood will come forth for the head,	*Grand fleux de sang sortira par la boche,*
The kingdom England-that by government paused,	*Le regne Anglieque par regne respiré,*
Extended opportunity dead living in Tunis much as direct line of pedigree.	*Long temps mort vif en Tunys comme soche.*

Note: Originally listed as quatrain number 56 in Centurie X. The spelling *Anglieque* can be an anagram for *Angelique*, but *Anglie* is Czech for *England*. This would make *Anglie-que* become "England-that." This would support the use of "*royal*" in line one.

By reason of great disagreement there tempest will tremble	*Par grand discord la trombe tremblera*
Agreement broken advancing the headiness in the heaven:	*Accord rompu dressant la teste au ciel:*
Overture into saturated with blood in him lineage will swim,	*Bouche sanglante dans le sang nagera,*
At the ground there face anointed with milk & honey.	*Au sol sa face ointe de laict & miel.*

Note: Originally listed as quatrain number 57 in Centurie I. The word *trombe* is used in French today to state "whirlwind" or "waterspout," both of which are tornado-type circular winds (over land and over water). However, in the 1611 Old French Dictionary it is described as: a round and hollow ball of wood, having a peak like a casting-top, and making a loud noise when it is cast like a top.

Chapter 24 - The Unholiness of War

Informer & pushed will make a beginning for the front	*Index & poulse parfondera le front*
With Synod-gallic him Count in one's son particular	*De Senegalia le Conte à son filz propre*
There Myrmidon furnished with weapons by large number with highest brow	*La Myr. armée par plusieurs de prinfront*
Three within September courts wounded ones cause of destruction.	*Trois dans sept jours blesses & mors.*

Note: Originally listed as quatrain number 8 in Centurie X. The classical Latin name for Senegal was *Gaetulia*, which were generally the people of the northwest of Africa. The capital city, Dakar, was established in the 15th century, and was primarily a slave trading population. Islam had arrived in the Senegal region in the 11th century. It is perhaps better to see *Senegalia* as "*Sene-galia*," which translates as Old French-English, "*Synod-gaul*." The capitalized *Conte* means, "Count," as a title of royalty, but also, "*Counted*," as adding numbers, and, "*Story, Tale*," as an account. The capitalization of the abbreviation "*Myr.*" makes this relative to the use of *Myrmidon* in quatrain IX-35, which mentions Ferdinand and Macedon as well.

One with another two small boat ones foundation ones & public powers tied ones,	*Entre deux cimbes piedz & mains estachés,*
From sweetness figure anointed & with him possessed maintained:	*De miel face oingt & de l'aict substanté:*
Wasps & informers, within bounds love angered ones,	*Guespes & mouchez, fitine amour faschés,*
This cupbearer to dip, Communion cup tampered with.	*Poccilateur saulcer, Cyphe tempté.*

Note: Originally listed as quatrain number 89 in Centurie VI. The word *pie* (non-accented) means, "pious, religious, godly and devout." A separate definition shows it with a variety of meanings, such as, "drink, liquor, a goose, a certain cooked beef," the "monstrous appetite of maids and big-bellied women" and "coals, ashes, paper" and other such unnatural meats." As to the word *mouche*, one unaccented (as was written) form of the word means, "ship-boy or sailor." The other unaccented form means *fly*; but, this form is also spelled "*mousche*," which equally means, "spy, informer, eavesdropper and promoter." The accented form of *mouché* means, "wiped, snuffed, mocked and curtailed," as well as being the length of a vine branch that becomes supported by under propping elements.

The Epic Poem Prophesied by Nostradamus

Upon navigating captive taken noble prelate,	*En navigant captif prins grand pontife,*
Great preparation to disappoint them church persons seditious:	*Grand apretz faillir les clercz tumultuez:*
Next after elected missing its with good reason looking ill,	*Second esleu absent son bien debife,*
His minion base born to death massacred.	*Son favory bastard à mort tue.*

Note: Originally listed as quatrain number 15 in Centurie V. Both *bifé* and *biffé* have the same definition, meaning it is okay to see *debifé* as a variation of *debiffé*.

The year that Mercury, Mars, Venus, retrograde,	*L'an que Mercure, Mars, Venus, retrograde,*
From the high Absolute ruler there degree of kindred not to end:	*Du grand Monarque la ligne ne faillir:*
Chosen of the people them inuring near Paniful-gag,	*Esleu du peuple l'usitant pres de Gagdole,*
That upon peace & kingdom will arrive mighty to grow old in years.	*Qu'en paix & regne viendra fort envieillir.*

Note: Originally listed as quatrain number 97 in Centurie IV. Line one is stating a specific order of planets moving into retrograde. Mercury goes retrograde three times a year, for approximately 13-14 days each time. Mars goes retrograde approximately every 22-23 months (almost 2 years), for about 55-59 days. Venus goes retrograde approximately every year and one half, for about 41-43 days. Therefore that specific order, when each will go retrograde, is repeatable, but relatively limited. One example will occur in 2018. Between March 23 and April 14, Mercury will be retrograde. Between June 26 and August 27, Mars will be retrograde. Between October 5 and November 15, Venus will be retrograde; and, Mercury will make its final retrograde for 2018 just over one day after Venus goes direct, on November 17.

The election to forge in Frankfort,	*L'eslection faicte dans Frankfort,*
Not will occupy frivolous seat Milan itself will protest against:	*N'aura nul lieu Milan s'opposera:*
Them his own more neighboring will make show of as mighty fortress	*Le sien plus proche semblera si grand fort*
Who beyond the Rhine are marshal ones will reject.	*Que outre le Ryn es mareschz chassera.*

Note: Originally listed as quatrain number 87 in Centurie VI. From Wikipedia, "From 855 the German kings and emperors were elected in Frankfurt and crowned in Aachen. From 1562 the kings/emperors were also crowned in Frankfurt, Maximilian II being the first. This tradition ended

Chapter 24 - The Unholiness of War

in 1792, when Franz II was elected." The *Rhine* River formed (along with the Danube River) a northern border for the Holy Roman Empire.

Seven month without more will obtain office of prelate	*Sept moys sans plus obtiendra prelature*
Through its death substantial schism will cause to be produced:	*Par son deces grand scisme fera naistre:*
September month will judge one other there office of magistrate	*Sept moys tiendra un autre la preture*
Near to Venice peace united one to be born reborn.	*Pres de Venise paix union renaistre.*

Note: Originally listed as quatrain number 93 in Centurie VIII. The use of "*moys*" can be read as "*moy-s*," where the personal pronoun usage makes it state, "my ones." This could be some indication of people who interpret Nostradamus' quatrains.

For hood ones red ones quarrels & unheard of before ones divisions in the church,	*Par chapeaux rouges querelles & nouveaux scismes*
In regard of one will have elected him Sabine ones:	*Quant on aura esleu le Sabinois:*
One will furnish with lecheries contrary to his noble ones raising trivial objections,	*On produira contre luy grans sophismes,*
Likewise will be Rome injured by Albanians.	*Et sera Rome lesee par Albanois.*

Note: Originally listed as quatrain number 46 in Centurie V. In the 1611 Old French Dictionary, under the listing of *chapeau*, this specific example is given, "*chapeau à l'Albanoise*, meaning a high crowned hat; a hat with a crown like a sugar-loaf; or, of the Spanish block." In general, it means, "hat," but it also is the term used to state a "mass of solid grapes on the surface during the fermentation of wine."

245

Chapter 25

France Tries Not to Surrender

The French Campaign

Armor cutting inwardly the torches small boat ones	*Harnois trenchant dans les flambeaux caichez*
In Lyon a day to the Sacrament,	*Dedans Lyon le jour du Sacrement,*
Those of Vienne will be all sliced ones	*Ceux de Vienne seront trestous hachez*
For them road intersections Roman ones Mâcon not lies.	*Par les cantons Latins Mascon ne ment.*

Note: Originally listed as quatrain number 70 in Centurie IX. The commune *Vienne* is 30 kilometers south of *Lyon*, on the Rhone River, in the Isère department. *Mâcon* is approximately 60 kilometers north of *Lyon*, on the Saône River, which joins the Rhone in Lyon. *Mâcon* is in the Saône et Loire department.

Peace abundantly extended while place will praise:	*Paix uberté long temps lieu louera:*
For all its realm abandoned of humanity there bloom of lily:	*Par tout son regne desert la fleur de lis:*
Corpse killed ones with water, land the many will arrive near the shore,	*Corps morts d'eau, terre la lon aportera,*
Hoping for ones in vain luck of to be there laid in graves.	*Sperants vain heur d'estre la ensevelis.*

Note: Originally listed as quatrain number 20 in Centurie IV.

Among French he uttermost dishonored,	*Entre Gaulois le dernier honnoré,*
With vassal enemy will be victorious:	*D'homme ennemy sera victorieux:*
Might & ground upon importance looked far into,	*Force & terroir en moment exploré,*

Chapter 25 - France Tries Not to Surrender

With one stroke of dart at what time will perish the repining.	D'un coup de traict quand mourra l'envieux.

Note: Originally listed as quatrain number 100 in Centurie III. In line two, the use of *homme*, which means, "tenant, vassal, subject", more than it means, "man", is referencing a group of people, who have become the *enemy*, as *vassals*, or *tenants*. These are also *of France*, which describes those who seek their own autonomy, like the Catalans and Basque peoples.

All ones those of Lerida will be within there Moselle,	Tous ceux de Ilerde seront dedans Mosselle,
Sending ones to death everything the ones to Loire & Seine:	Mettans à mort tous ceux de Loire & Seine:
Him course of the sea will arrive as it were touching from high wishes,	Le cours marin viendra pres d'haute velle,
Notwithstanding Spanish ones will open whole full of veins.	Quand Hespagnolz ouvrira toute veine.

Note: Originally listed as quatrain number 89 in Centurie I. The city *Ilerda* (Latin spelling) is now called *Lerida* and is in eastern Spain, on the border with France at the Mediterranean Sea, in northwestern part of the region of Catalonia. Both *Moselle* the department and river are in the northeast corner of France, with the *Moselle* River basin being in Luxembourg and France, with it being a feeder to the Rhine River in Germany.

Of Arras & Bourges, from Cloaks of leather great ones insignias,	D'Arras & Bourges, de Brodes grans enseignes
A more substantial band of soldiers with ones of Basque heritage to batter as foundation,	Un plus grand nombre de Gascons batre à pied,
Those extended to the Rhone will be bleeding them Spanish ones:	Ceux long du Rosne saigneront les Espaignes:
Close unto from the mountain where Sagunto settles.	Proche du mont ou Sagonte s'assied.

Note: Originally listed as quatrain number 3 in Centurie IV. The commune of *Arras* (aka *Atrecht*) is in northern France, near the English Channel coast city Calais, in the Pad-de-Calais department. The first settlement in what is now *Arras* France was on the "hill of *Baudimont*." The commune of *Bourges* is in central France, on the Yèvre River, in the department of Cher. The name of the place now known as *Bourges* is rooted in the meaning of the word meaning, "hill/village." As such, the primary focus could be *Arras*, with *Bourges* being an importance of *Arras* being a Hill village, since the place *Bourges* is only 200 kilometers south of the place *Arras*. The Old French word *brode* (singular) has four separate definitions, with one being, "broth, pottage, brew;" another being, "a black, swarthy or sun burnt wench; [a form of language] a loose, laskey, squattering, scurvy; also an effeminate manner of speech." Its last meaning is, "embroidered. " Still, the word "*brodes*" (with an "s") meant, "a cloak, or mantle, of leather."

The Epic Poem Prophesied by Nostradamus

Will remove from one place to another into there high Germany,	*Translatera en la grand Germanie,*
Brabant & Flanders, Ghent, Bruges, Boulogne-sur-Mer:	*Brabant & Flandres, Gand, Bruges, Bolongne:*
The truce devised them substantial military governor from Armenia,	*La trefve faincte le grand duc d'Armenie,*
Will assail Vienna & there Cologne.	*Assaillira Vienne & la Coloigne.*

Note: Originally listed as quatrain number 94 in Centurie V. *Flanders* was a region that now overlaps France, Belgium and the Netherlands. The cities *Ghent, Bruges* and *Boulogne* represent Belgium and France. The commune *Boulogne* was the site of a treaty (or truce) between England and Scotland, in 1550 (Peace of *Boulogne*), which was only 5 years before Nostradamus wrote *The Prophecies*. The present nation of *Armenia* is just north of Iran, but it used to stretch from the Caspian Sea to eastern Turkey. *Armenia* represents Middle Eastern Christians. The cities of *Vienna* and *Cologne* are in Austria and *Germany*.

To overrun Guyenne, Languedoc & them Rhone,	*Passer Guienne, Languedoc & le Rosne,*
With Agen holding from Marmande & there Round plate of armor used in defense,	*D'Agen tenens de Marmande & la Roolle,*
Of to open on middle for chief Marseille will occupy its command position	*D'ovrir par foy par roy Phocen tiendra son trosne*
Battle close religious Paul to Mausoleum.	*Conflict aupres de saint Paul Mauseole.*

Note: Originally listed as quatrain number 85 in Centurie IX. *Guienne* and *Languedoc* are ancient provinces or regions of southwest-southern France, stretching from the Atlantic Ocean to the Mediterranean Sea, where the Rhone River empties, north of Marseille. Both *Marmande* and *Agen* are in the Lot-et-Garonne department, with *Marmande* approximately 35 kilometers northwest of *Agen*. La Roéole is a commune closer to Bordeaux than *Marmande*, with a bridge over the Garonne River. The name *Phocen* probably relates to the city of Marseille, which was settled by Phoenicians and has a connection to the name *Phocéen* now (soccer team name?). *Saint Paul de Mausole* is a monastery of importance near the ancient Roman ruin of Glanum, 1 kilometer from Nostradamus' birth town, Saint Remy. It is in southern France, near the Rhone River.

Bazas, them Stored, Condom, Auch, people of Agenais,	*Bazaz, Lestore, Condon, Ausch, Agine,*
Provoked ones by courses of justice, action against & monopoly:	*Esmeus par lois querelle & monopole:*
Considering that Bordeaux Toulouse Bayonne will thrust into desolation	*Car Bourd. Toulouze Bay. mettra en ruine*

Chapter 25 - France Tries Not to Surrender

Them to reintegrate proposing their hunting bull.	*Renouveller voulant leur tauropole.*

Note: Originally listed as quatrain number 79 in Centurie I. *Bazas* is in the department of Gironde, south of Bordeaux. *Lectoure* is in the Gers department, north of Auch, southeast of Condom. The Occitan spelling for Auch is *Aush*. The city *Agen* is in the Lot-et-Garonne department, close to the other places listed. However, the spelling of *agine* makes it less probable that *Agen* is primarily intended. The word *tauropole* is obviously Greek, associated with the goddess Artemis, as Artemis *Tauropole* meant Artemis the bull killer. The people of Spain are known for enjoying bull fighting.

The people of Agen for those of Drodogne,	*Les Nictobriges par ceux de Perigort,*
Will be afflicted ones holding until at the Rhone:	*Seront vexez tenant jusques au Rosne:*
Them associated to people of Gascony & One-eyed,	*Lassocie de Gascons & Begorn,*
To betray a church, him priest resting in the lying down.	*Trahir le temple, le prebstre estant au prosne.*

Note: Originally listed as quatrain number 76 in Centurie IV. *Nitiobroges* were people in ancient Gaul, who lived on both sides of the Garonne River, in both Guyenne and *Gascony*, southeast of Bordeaux. Their capital is the place now known as Agen. Quatrain IX-85 and I-79 refer to those places. Their leader was known as Teutomatos, and he was the son of their king Ollovico, of which Caesar wrote, in his accounts of the conquests of the tribes of Gaul. *Perigord* was an unofficial region of Aquitaine, now roughly named the department of Dordogne, which is east of Bordeaux. I could find no indication that either Bèarn or Bigorre was spelled as *Begorn*. Still, both are ancient fiefdoms of Aquitaine, and may be implied.

Blood Holy had slipped away, Monheurt, Manly, Aiguillon,	*Sang Royal fuis, Monthurt, Mas, Eguillon,*
Fully supplied ones being to people of Bordeaux them wild uncultivated plains,	*Remplis feront de Bourdelois les landes,*
Navarre, Bigorre sharpened at the point ones & provocations,	*Navarre, Bygorre poinctes & eguillons,*
Secret ones of much appetite to swallow up with one's own glands.	*Profonds de faim vorer de liege glandes.*

Note: Originally listed as quatrain number 79 in Centurie IV. It must be noted that the first two word, both capitalized, say in French *Sang Royal*, which are the root words in *Sangrael*, from the theme of Arthur, as *Holy Blood*, Holy Grail. The commune of *Monheurt* is on the Garonne River in the Lot-et-Garonne department. The word *Mas* is the traditional term for house or farmhouse in Provence, thus Le *Mas* can be found everywhere. There is evidence of a *Bourdelois* near Perigord,

The Epic Poem Prophesied by Nostradamus

in the department of Dordogne. There is a department in southwest France, formerly of the Guyenne and Gascony provinces, named *Landes*. It borders the Atlantic – Bay of Biscay, bordering Lot-et-Garonne. The *Landes* Forest or *Landes* Natural area, covers a large are of land in southwest France, in particular that between the Garonne River at *Bordeaux*, and the Atlantic.

Them Atom knowing ones of Agen & them Built,	Les Artoniques par Agen & l'Estore,
With holy Blessed will be making their reasoning:	A sainct Felix feront leur parlement:
Those to Bazas will be arriving at there in an evil hour,	Ceulx de Basas viendront à la mal'heure,
To seize Condom & Marsan quickly.	Saisir Condon & Marsan promptement.

Note: Originally listed as quatrain number 72 in Centurie IV. Line one of quatrain I-79 lists *Agen, Lestore, Condon*, and *Bazaz*, all of which are listed in this quatrain. It is possible to see *Lestore* as Lectoure, phonetically, but not *l'Estore*. The word "*estoré*," from "estorer," means, "built, made, erected, edified; also furnished, stored, garnished with, and provided of." The ampersand indicates the importance of a building for the "*Atom knowing ones*," which would be a nuclear reactor. Between *Agen* (18.6 miles downstream on the Garonne) and Toulouse is the Golfech Nuclear Power Plant. There are several communes in southwest France that have the prefix to the name being *Saint-Felix* (ex. *Lauragais*, in the Haute Garonne department; *de-Foncuade*, in the Gironde department; and *de-l'Heras*, in the Herault department) in southwest France. The commune of *Bazas* is in the Gironde department and in Occitan it is spelled *Basats*. The commune of Mont-de-Marsan is the capitol of the Landes department, south of Bordeaux (Gironde department). *Condom* is east of *Marsan*, in the Gers department.

Everything close to Auch, from The built & Watch tower,	Tout aupres d'Aux, de Lectore & Mirande
Great fire from the sky upon three nights will fall:	Grand feu du ciel en troys nuicts tumbera:
Matter will fall out quite astonished by force & extraordinary to see,	Cause aviendra bien stupende & mirande:
Aptly almost nobody after there ground will tremble.	Bien peu apres la terre tremblera.

Note: Originally listed as quatrain number 46 in Centurie I. In French the word *aux* is a combination preposition-article, such as "at the" or "with the." To list it with a preceding preposition, as *d'Aux*, the capitalization makes this most probably a form of the city *Auch*, in Aquitaine. The commune of *Lectoure* is 32 kilometers north of *Auch*. *Mirande* is approximately 32 kilometers southwest of *Auch*. The name *Mirmande* comes from the Latin word *mirari*, and a *mirande* is a Catalan-style *watch tower*. Similar examples of this architecture are found in Marmande, Mirmande, and Mirande, France. They were originally *built* for defensive purposes.

Chapter 25 - France Tries Not to Surrender

Sacrifice & Auch & goshawk to Watch tower	Condon & Aux & autour de Mirande
I see from the sky death which them surrounded,	Je voy du ciel feu qui les environne,
Ground War united with the Lion then house to overlook the Garonne River	Sol Mars conjoint au Lyon puis marmande
Thunderbolt, great hail, wall fallen in Garonne.	Fouldre, grand gresle, mur tombe dans Garonne.

Note: Originally listed as quatrain number 2 in Centurie VIII. In Latin, the word "condono" means: to give away, present, give up and sacrifice; but also to overlook and to forgive (especially in debt). As the first word in line one, also followed immediately by an ampersand, making it a stand-alone statement, the city of *Condom* (misspelled from original) may actually be a secondary consideration, as the place "*sacrificed.*" This would then be followed by the sacrifice of *Auch*, where *aux* means "with them." Along with *Mirande*, all three places are in the department of Gers; but *autour de Mirande* can indicate a aircraft flying above as aerial surveilance, with the translation being *goshawk to Watch tower*. The commune of *Marmande* is in the department of Lot-et-Garonne, north of *Condom*, but the lower case takes the meaning of the name, which is also to be a *watch tower along the Garonne*. Obviously, *Sol* and *Mars* are astrological orbs, with *Lion* being the sign of Leo. As a secondary meaning this times the quatrain when both Sun and Mars will be in Leo (Aug. 2015 & 2017). However, *Sol* primarily means, "*Ground, Soil*". The word *tombe* can also have the secondary meaning of "tomb" or "gravestone," as the *fallen wall* will represent the death of defensive lines.

Deeply in battle him substantial will tumble down:	Avant conflict le grand tumbera,
Them mighty at death, killed mightily unlooked for & bewailed:	Le grand à mort, mort trop subite & plainte:
Not hold half accomplished: there more country will float,	Nay miparfaict: la plus part nagera:
Close to the stream of blood the earth stained.	Aupres du fleuve de sang la terre tainte.

Note: Originally listed as quatrain number 57 in Centurie II. The 1611 Randle Cotgrave dictionary does not show the word "*imparfaict,*" but in modern French, the word means, "imperfect, incomplete." Still, the 1568 Lyon edition clearly shows "*miparfaict,*" which separates to *mi-parfaict*, meaning, "*half-perfected*, or *half-accomplished.*" The combination of words, *plus part*, can also be written as "*plupart,*" meaning "majority."

The Epic Poem Prophesied by Nostradamus

With leaf of metal upon marble will be them walls conducted home again ones	De brique en marbre seront les murs reduits
September & fifty years of crops quiet ones,	Sept & cinquante annees pacifiques,
Joy in them humane ones restored The drawn water,	Joie aux humains renové Laqueduict,
Health, noble ones return rejoicing & time mellifluous.	Sante, grandz fruict joye & temps mellifique.

Note: Originally listed as quatrain number 89 in Centurie X. France is the main theme reference (sort to the fall of the wall on the river Garonne), which would mean that (given the war beginning in 2012) 50 years back would be 1962. This would mean France would have had to be in a war no later than that year. France fought the French-Indochina was until 1954, when it then fought the Algerians in their war for independence, which was granted upon the 1962 withdrawal of the French troops in Algeria. P.S. *Aquaduct* = *aqua+doctor* = water-guide. Nostradamus did not write that word.

Upon the Sheltered ones at Devouring & Dungeon,	En Arbissel à Veront & Carcari,
From night trench of stone ones for not Savona to overtake,	De nuict conduitz par Savonne atraper,
Them quick ones of Gascony Uproar & there Themselves answered loudly to a loud demand	Le vifz Gascon Turbi & la Scerry
Anew to stretch out in stiffness wall ancient in years & fresh palace to seize.	Derrier mur vieux & neuf palais gripper.

Note: Originally listed as quatrain number 39 in Centurie IX. This quatrain ranks as one of the most enigmatic to solve, in all of The Prophecies. This is because of the capitalization of words (7), where only two are cleanly spelled (*Gascon* and *Carcari*). There is a small commune named "*Arbrissel,*" (in *Bretagne,* France) which has one too many "r"s to be *Arbissel*. The word *Turbi* is an allowable version of the Latin word "*Turba,*" and possibly "*Turbo*". The word *Derrier* is not correctly spelled, for it to be the French word, "*derrière*", but it is close to the French word "*dernier*", which has the same meaning as "*derrière*." Obviously, this quatrain is still open for interpretation, due to the translation difficulties. The place *Carcari* is at the foot of Rome's Capitoline Hill and was an ancient prison, where Rome's prisoners were sent to usually die of starvation or strangulation. *Gascony* is in the most southwest part of France, bordering Spain and the Atlantic Ocean. It could be possible that *Turby* is reference to "Tarbes," a city in *Gascony*.

Chapter 25 - France Tries Not to Surrender

In them the midst to there forest Mayenne,	*Dans le millieu de la forest Mayenne,*
Bottom of a place with the lion the thunderbolt will light upon,	*Sol au lyon la fouldre tombera,*
A noble son of the people not rightly bred of the mighty from the Maine,	*Le grand bastard yssue du grand du Maine,*
This light people of the ferns edge upon kindred will enter.	*Ce jour fougeres pointe en sang entrera.*

Note: Originally listed as quatrain number 19 in Centurie IX. *Mayenne* is a department if the Pays-de-la-Loire region in northern France, west of Paris and just east of the Brittany peninsula. *Maine* is a former province and country that covers most of what is now the Pays-de-la-Loire. There is a *"Forest of Mayenne"*, but it now is only a small forest. *Fougères* is a commune on the edge of Brittany, bordering Normandy and *Maine*. The *blood* of reference would be Norman, or British.

Lamentations & weeping ones shrieks & great ones howling ones	*Plainctes & pleurs crys & grands urlemens*
Near to Narbonne with Bayonne & upon Times,	*Pres de Narbon à Bayonne & en Foix,*
My Lord! what most ugly misfortune ones conversions,	*O quel horrible calamitz changemens,*
Having that Mars turned wholly some ones faiths.	*Avant que Mars revolu quelques foys.*

Note: Originally listed as quatrain number 63 in Centurie IX. The city of *Narbonne* (Occitan – *Norbona*, or commonly *Narbo*) is near the Mediterranean coast (Gulf of Lyon), in the department of Aude. The commune of *Bayonne* is in the department of Pyrenees-Atlantic, on the coast near the border with Spain. The city of *Foix* (formerly the country of *Foix*) is central between Narbonne and Bayonne, south of Toulouse, in the department of Haute-Garonne. The idiom *"quelque fois"* means, "sometimes, one time or another."

Begun in Bayonne & devout John to Light of life	*Entre Bayonne & saint Jean de Lux*
Will be placed from War there promontory	*Sera posé de Mars la promontoire*
With the followers of Ba'al from Year which not Joyous will remove hope,	*Aux Hanix d'Aquin Nanar ostera lux,*
Moreover this smothered in the bed without assistant.	*Puis suffocque au lict sans adjutoire.*

Note: Originally listed as quatrain number 85 in Centurie VIII. Fort Socoa is a fortress on a

The Epic Poem Prophesied by Nostradamus

promontory, on the extreme northwest side of bay of *St. Jean de Luz*. This string of words must be seen as a secondary interpretation, representing a place very close to *Bayonne*. If *Hanix* is a follower of Ba'al, this is then representative of Syrian Arabs.

This one who in that time will bring forth the unheard of before ones,	*Celui qui lors portera les nouvelles,*
After a little he will grow to breathe.	*Apres un peu il viendra respirer.*
Fish ponds, Altered one, Mountain arming & Plunder them,	*Viviers, Tournon, Montferrant & Pradelles,*
Hailed on & overthrown by a tempest ones them will make to sigh.	*Gresle & tempestes les fera souspirer.*

Note: Originally listed as quatrain number 66 in Centurie I. In French, the word *vivier* means "fish pond," such that *Viviers* is a place of important *Fish Ponds*. There is a *Viviers* in the department of *Ardéche*, which is also the name of a feeder river to the Rhone, northwest of Avignon. However, there is a *Viviers*-les-Montagnes in the Tarn department, where Castres and Albi are located. The word *tourney* means "turned." The commune *Tournon*-sur-Rhone is in the department of Drôme, just north of Valence, but several communes contain Tournon in their name. Tournon, France is in the Savoy department, of the Rhone-Alps region. *Montferrant*, in Latin, can mean "Mountain you see iron (weapons)". Montferrant, in French, can mean "Mountain Ferrier" (as a Blacksmith), or a "Mountain with an Iron Mine." There is a place known as Clermont-*Ferrant*, in central France, but that is not close to the first two places. There are wines known as from *Montferrand* in the Languedoc-Roussillon region, which borders Spain and the Mediterranean Sea (plus Angora). Interestingly there are the "caves of *Montferrand*" in the Cataluna region of Spain, bordering the Languedoc-Roussillon region of France. Still, with *fer* the root word of *ferrant*, and *fer* being a way of stating "weapon", *Montferrant* may be a place where *weapons* are stored inside a *mountain*. The Latin word *"praedelasso"* means "to weary beforehand." The small commune of *Pradelles*-Cabardés is in the department of Aude, in the Langudoc-Roussillon region, just north of Perpignan. These definitions can play secondary purpose for the cities listed in line three.

This that will live & not having any judgment,	*Ce que vivra & n'ayant aucun sens,*
Will arrive to wound with death its skill:	*Viendra leser à mort son artifice:*
Oneself Autun, Chalon-et-Saone, Langres & them two Sens,	*Austun, Chalon, Langres & les deux Sens,*
There hailed on & hardened will cause great offence.	*La gresle & glace fera grand malefice.*

Note: Originally listed as quatrain number 22 in Centurie I. The combination *"Ce que"* can be read simply as "What" in conversational French. Unfortunately, *The Prophecies* cannot be read as typical conversation. The commune of *Autun* is in the department of Saône-et-Loire, northwest of *Chalon*-sur-Saône, which is south of Dijon and north of Mâcon. *Langres* is a small commune in the Haute-Marne department, north-northeast of Dijon. The commune of *Sens* is in the department of Yonne, north of the capitol Auxerre, which is between Paris and Dijon.

Chapter 25 - France Tries Not to Surrender

Army lodged close to Meadowdam will hold on course marsh of Goussauville,	*Camp pres de Noudam passera Goussanville,*
Likewise with Ancestors will set aside its insignia,	*Et à Maiores laissera son enseigne,*
Will transform in instant more of thousand,	*Convertira en instant plus de mille,*
Seeking them two to revive in chain & bequeathed.	*Cherchant les deux remettre en chaine & legne.*

Note: Originally listed as quatrain number 56 in Centurie IX. The 1568 Lyon edition is very difficult to read, making it impossible to determine the actual spelling of many words. The 1566 Lyon edition, which is very clearly printed but personally seen as one of the most flawed editions taking liberties to change the text, shows "*Majotes*" as the third word in line two. While this is a clean name for an African town, and "*Mayotte*" is an Indian Ocean island, neither translations make any sense for interpretation. However, when the difficulties in distinguishing an "r" from a "t" are realized, "*Maiotes*" can become, "*Maiores*," which is clean Latin, a form of the word "*magus*".

From light heavenly in the Royal house ready built,	*De feu celeste au Royal edifice,*
In regard there clearness of War will languish:	*Quant la lumiere de Mars defaillira:*
Seven month substantial war, dead nation to ill act,	*Sept mois grand guerre, mort gent de malefice,*
Red horse, Blessed with the King not will disappoint.	*Rouen, Eureux au Roy ne faillira.*

Note: Originally listed as quatrain number 100 in Centurie IV. This quatrain links to quatrain IX-56, in the sense that *Incheville* (where the *Marsh of Goussauville* is near) is also in the Haute-Seine department of Normandy. That location is south of the major port city *Dieppe*, which is a ferry point to Newhaven, England, on the English Channel. Those locations are north of *Rouen*, and *Evreux*. Still, the use of *Rouen* and *Eureux* can mean a *Red horse* and *Blessed*, allowing this quatrain to focus entirely on the *Royal house built*, which is England, and not France. The capitalization of *Roan horse* gives it biblical implications, as that of the second rider in *The Revelation of John*.

Him assistant principal commander to the government born Denmark,	*Le second chef du regne Dannemarc,*
Through the ones of Friesland & the island born of Britannia,	*Par ceulx de Frise & l'isle Britannique,*
Will act to lay out upon more to a hundred a thousand feeble,	*Fera despendre plus de cent mille marc,*
Forceless to put in execution journey into land of Italic languages.	*Vain exploicter voyage en Italique.*

255

The Epic Poem Prophesied by Nostradamus

Note: Originally listed as quatrain number 41 in Centurie VI. *Friesland* is the largest province of the Netherlands, with the island string off the North Sea coast being the East *Frisian* and West *Frisian* Islands. The North *Friesian* Islands are off the North Sea coast of German, at their border with Denmark.

Thirty from London secret will be joining in a private confederacy,	*Trente de Londres secret conjureront,*
On the other side of their King concerning them bridge the encroachment upon:	*Contre leur Roy sur le pont l'entreprise:*
It, fatalities there death will be dropping down by little and little.	*Luy, fatalites la mort degousteront.*
A Head man of a party elected blonde, descended from Friesland.	*Un Roy esleu blonde, natif de Frize.*

Note: Originally listed as quatrain number 89 in Centurie IV.

There freedom born will be this again obtained,	*La liberté ne sera recovréce,*
Them will possess black proud slave unequal:	*L'occupera noir fier vilain inique:*
In regard of the cause for to the sea will be traveled,	*Quant la matiere du pont sera ouvrée,*
From Lower Danube, Venice vexed there commonwealth.	*D'Hister, Venise faschee la republique.*

Note: Originally listed as quatrain number 29 in Centurie V.

Bridge one will act quickly with small longboats,	*Pont on fera promptement de nacelles,*
To transport the army to the great chief Belgium:	*Passer l'armee du grand prince Belgique:*
In favor of melted ones & not far from Brussels,	*Dans profondréz & non loing de Brucelles,*
Opened transported ones, chopped into pieces ones seven with this pinched.	*Outre passés, detrenchés sept à picque.*

Note: Originally listed as quatrain number 81 in Centurie IV. The capitol city of Belgium is Brussels, which is spelled "*Bruxcelles*" in French. It is phonetically identifying that city; and while this is certainly an intended reference in this quatrain, the spelling *brucelles* is the correct spelling

Chapter 25 - France Tries Not to Surrender

for the word *tweezers*, or *pincers*. Brussels is centrally located in Belgium, such that being *not far off* could be anywhere in the country. The word *picque* is also spelled *pique* and can also mean, "spade or pickax or pike." This makes Pincer have more impact, especially when the last word, *picque*, is seen as *c'piqué*, meaning, "*this pinched.*"

Montauban, Nimes, Avignon, & Coffins for dead corpses,	*Montauban, Nismes, Avignon, & Besier,*
Pestilence, thunder & pock marked at cunning of War:	*Peste tonnerre & gresle à fin de Mars:*
To Paris bridge, Lyon wall Montpellier,	*De Paris pont, Lyon mur Montpellier,*
From six hundred a hundred ones & September twenty three side.	*Depuis six cent & sept vingt trois pars.*

Note: Originally listed as quatrain number 56 in Centurie III. *Montauban* is in the Tarn-et-Garonne department, 31 miles north of Toulouse, and roughly 125 miles west-southwest of *Nîmes*. *Nîmes* is the capitol of the Gard department, east of *Montauban*, near (west of) *Avignon* and Arles. *Avignon* is the capitol of the Vaucluse department and the former seat of the papacy during a schism in the 14th century. *Béziers* is a town in Languedoc, in the Hérault department, southwest of *Nîmes*, with *Montpellier* between the two. However, when the lack of a "z" and an "s" at the ends (pl.), the three before the ampersand (importance) is summed up as, *Bieres*, meaning, "*Coffins for dead corpses.*" *Lyon* is northeast of *Avignon*, and southeast of *Paris*. *Lyon* can be read as, "*Lion,*" indicating the British. *Paris* can be read as *Pari-s* (plural past participle), becoming, "*Bet-ones.*" With the exceptions of *Montauban*, *Paris*, *Lyon*, and *Avignon*, the other communes are in the Languedoc-Roussillon region. Only *Paris* is in the northern half of France.

With lance there defense blast of wind enclosed round sea will be,	*De bois la garde vent cloz rond pont sera,*
Noble them taken of will strike him the eldest son of France,	*Hault le reçeu frappera le Daulphin,*
Him old this clipped head of a deer united ones will pass forth,	*Le vieux teccon bois unis passera,*
Going more forwards with the provincial governor them reasonable neighbor.	*Passant plus oultre du duc le droit confin.*

Note: Originally listed as quatrain number 27 in Centurie IX. The *Dauphine* was a former province of France, the area between Lyon and Grenoble, along the Italian border. The word *duc* is similar to the Italian word duce, and it originates from Latin. It is possible that "teccon" is referring to someone from the commune in the Tarn department (Midi-Pyrenees region) named *Técon*, which dates back to the 13th Century and the *Albigeous* people. This is the only place *teccon* is found in the quatrains.

The Epic Poem Prophesied by Nostradamus

Him great battle that one prepared at Nancy,	*Le grand conflit qu'on appreste à Nancy,*
The Arabian king will tell all you subdued ones,	*L'æmatien dira tout je submetz,*
The isle British by reason of wine, salt upon this ground,	*L'isle Britanne par vin, sel en solcy,*
Hemisphere half two Physics long time born will hold Metz.	*Hem. mi deux Phi. long temps ne tiendra Metz.*

Note: Originally listed as quatrain number 7 in Centurie X. The commune of *Nancy* is in the Lorraine region, in the *Meurthe-et-Moselle* department of eastern France. An *Emathian* is either one from Macedonia, Samothrace, Ethiopia, Aethopia, or Troy (modern Turkey), somewhere in the ancient world around Greece. The actual nation now named Macedonia is next to Kosovo, Serbia, Bulgaria, Greece, and Albania. However, *L'œmation* was found in quatrain IX-64, and that was an indication of *an Arabian king* (from Greek mythology). It is an identifier for Osama bin Laden. That makes this use probably fall under the same guideline, as *an Arabian king*. Metz is the capital of the Lorraine region, in the department of Moselle, at the confluence of the Moselle and Seille rivers.

Them lily of Ave-et-Auffois will bring forth within Nancy	*Le lys Dauffois portera dans Nansy*
Until upon Flanders elector with the empire,	*Jusques en Flandres electeur de l'empire,*
Uncouth filled in with the noble Montmorency,	*Neufve obturee au grand Montmorency,*
Out of places prows delivered in cleric pain.	*Hors lieux delivre à clerc peyne.*

Note: Originally listed as quatrain number 18 in Centurie IX. The use of *lily* is a reference to French people, or of French descent-influence. The people of *Ave-et-Auffe* are listed as being referred to as, "*Ave-et-Auffois*", at least for the males (add an "e" for the feminine). Rochefort, Belgium (where *Ave-et-Auffe* is located), is 50 miles (through Luxembourg) from the French border, where the Moselle River becomes the Luxembourg-Germany border. The closest "*empire*" to Belgium is the one called the British Empire. The commune *Montmorency* is less than 10 miles from the center of Paris, and is historically known as where nobility lived. It is at the heart of the wealthy of Paris.

With the aqueduct from Utican, Gardon,	*De laqueduct d'Uticense, Gardoing,*
Through there large wooded wilderness & mountain inaccessible:	*Par la forest & mont inaccessible:*
Upon half to the bridge will be tasked from the fist,	*En my du pont sera tasché au poing,*

Chapter 25 - France Tries Not to Surrender

Him general Not absent oneself who so many will be most fearful.	*Le chef Nemans qui tant sera terrible.*

Note: Originally listed as quatrain number 58 in Centurie V. The name *Uticense* originated as a final name for Cato the Younger, who committed suicide in *Utica* (Tunisia – near Carthage), rather than accept clemency from Caesar. The people of *Utica* then buried Cato the Younger as a hero and erected a statue in his honor. The department of *Gard* is in southern France in the Languedoc-Roussillon region, where the *Gard*on River flows, between Nimes and Arles, to the Mediterranean. Mont Aigoual is the highest point in the department and it is located in the Cévennes National Park. The Celtic god *Nemausus* was whom the city *Nimes* was named. *Nimes* is the capital of the Gard department. However, the *Neman* River flows through Eastern Europe, rising in Belarus, flowing through Lithuania before emptying into the Baltic Sea. As such, *Nemans* could be Eastern Europeans, or former Soviets. As *N'emans*, the focus is placed the presence of someone feared through his past lore and history.

With them enclosed capitulation out of there hold,	*Au conclud pache hors la forteresse,*
Not will depart out of the one upon desperation thrust into:	*Ne sortira celuy en desespoir mis:*
In regard for those to Arbois, with Langres, towards Bresse,	*Quant ceux d'Arbois, de Langres, contre Bresse,*
Will be occupying mountains them Dole, mountaineer from enemies.	*Auront monts Dolle, bouscade d'ennemis.*

Note: Originally listed as quatrain number 82 in Centurie V. *Langres* is roughly 60 miles due north of *Arbois*. *Bresse* is generally eastern France, surrounding its Swiss borders, in which fell *Langres* and *Arbois*. *Dole* is between Dijon, France and Lausanne, Switzerland, in the Franche-Comte region, Jura department. It is about 15 miles northwest of *Arbois*, and about 35 miles southwest of *Langres*. There is evidence that the word *boucade* is related to *capra* and *chevre* (both meaning "she-goat"), as *bouc* means "goat." The French use the -ade ending to indicate the feminine form of action, as the one performing said action. Thus, a *boucade* would be one acting like a goat. The "s" is often deleted from Old French, but could act as an anagram, creating the prefix of "*se*" to *boucade*. In the context of mountains, a *boucade* could be a mountain goat, or symbolic of a mountaineer.

Through there forest with the Dense one made a glade,	*Par la forest du Touphon essartee,*
For hermitage will be placed them temple,	*Par hermitaige sera posé le temple,*
Him military governor of Printings by his stratagem devised,	*Le duc d'Estampes par sa ruse inventee,*
From the mountain The hour prelate will bestow precedent to follow.	*Du mont Lehori prelat donra exemple.*

Note: Originally listed as quatrain number 87 in Centurie IX. A "*glade*" is an open space in a

The Epic Poem Prophesied by Nostradamus

forest. The word "*hermitage*" can mean a "rich, full-bodied, usually red win of southeast France", but in the context here it means, "A habitation for a hermit or group of hermits, or a place where one can live in seclusion, as an abbey or monastery."

Him military commander of Langres besieged within the Dole,	*Le duc de Langres assiegé dedans Dolle,*
Consorted with the Army one & the region of land up to Lyon:	*Accompagné d'Ostun & Lyonnois:*
Geneva, Augsburg, joining those to the Watch tower,	*Geneve, Auspourg, joinct ceux de Mirandole,*
To convey them mountains against them Ancône ones.	*Passer les monts contre les Anconnois.*

Note: Originally listed as quatrain number 4 in Centurie VII. *Langres* is roughly 75 miles northeast of *Dole*. Some have translated *d'Ostun* as being the commune *Autun*, which Nostradamus mentions in quatrain I-22, also along with *Langres*. I see this as an intentional misdirection, where *Autun* has a secondary purpose. The term *Lyonnaise* is correctly spelled *Lyonnois* and means, "in the manner of Lyon." The region controlled by *Lyon* is then the region of *Lyonnois*, which is named the Rhône-Alpes. *Augsburg* is about 160 miles northeast of *Geneva*. *Mirande* is rooted in the Latin word *mariari*, meaning "to watch intensely." *Ancône* is a commune in the Drôme department of the Rhône-Alpes region. It is due south of Lyon. The "mountains" would be the French Alps, including the Jura.

To change at Beaune, Nuits-Saint-Georges, Chalon-sur-Saône & Dijon,	*Changer à Beaune, Nuy, Chalons & Dijon,*
The military commander proposing to send away there Latticed	*Le duc voulant amander la Barrée*
Marching near river, fish, beak of diving bird,	*Marchant pres fleuve, poisson, bec de plongeon,*
Will observe there tailed: entrance will be closed.	*Verra la queue: porte sera serrée.*

Note: Originally listed as quatrain number 17 in Centurie IV. Probably only 25 miles separate all of the places in line one, if they are as listed, in the Burgundy region. The ancient region of what is today east-central France contained Autun, Lyon, and Geneva, and included parts of northwestern Italy, as well as much of western Switzerland, and some southwestern Germany. *Dijon* is roughly 100 miles north of Lyon, and is the capital of the Côtes-d'Or department, and the Burgundy region.

Ruined with them people of South France from terror so forcible most fearful ones,	*Ruyné aux Volsques de peur si fort terribles,*
Their great warned to appear stained, deed infectious:	*Leur grand cité taincte, faict pestilent:*

Chapter 25 - France Tries Not to Surrender

To ravage Bottom place, Muslim & to violate their churches:	*Piller Sol, Lune & violer leurs temples:*
Likewise the two flows of water to grow red with kindred flowing along.	*Et les deux fleuves rougir de sang coulant.*

Note: Originally listed as quatrain number 98 in Centurie VI. The *Volques* included the "*Volcae Arecomici*" (around Narbonne and Nimes), and the "*Volcae Tectosages*" (in Aquitaine, around Toulouse). *Volcae* were also a force in parts of Moravia (Czech Republic), the Danube regions, Spain (the Ebro), and Turkey. The use of *Lune r*epresents Islam and Muslims.

In that time which one will observe to cleanse by sacrifice the religious church.	*Lors qu'on verra expiler le saint temple.*
More great of them born rose theirs sacred ones to violate	*Plus grand du rosne leurs sacrez prophaner*
By reason of they will be born of plague so encompassing,	*Par eux naistra pestilence si ample,*
Pope flees unreasonable not will act to condemn.	*Roy fuit injuste ne fera condamner.*

Note: Originally listed as quatrain number 62 in Centurie VIII. The Rhone River is called "*Rôno*" in Arpitan (the equivalent of "*Rosno*"), and "*Ròse*" in Occitan, such that "*Rosne*" is accepted to be a reference to the Rhone. However, when this is spelled in the lower case, the same cannot be said, at least as far as the main meaning to find. Rhone River is therefore plays an intentional secondary role. The translation of "*born rose*" has religious intentions, which follows the main theme lead of "*sacred church*". Jesus is that *rose*, and Christianity is the religion that builds houses in his honor. In line four, the capitalized *King* has to be seen as a human being of true Royal stature, such that in a religious context only the *Pope* can be interpreted from that title. Still, as Jesus the *King*, he will have slipped away from the *Pope*, due to the *Pope* having run away from being a true religious leader, connected to God.

By reason of pestilence hatred of Rome like the Volsci,	*Par pestilente inimitié Volsicque,*
Dissembled will drive away the violent governor:	*Dissimulee chassera le tyran:*
At the bridge to Sorgues oneself will act there trade,	*Au pont de Sorgues se fera la traffique,*
From to thrust into to death him & his accessory.	*De mettre à mort luy & son adherant.*

Note: Originally listed as quatrain number 21 in Centurie VII. Quatrain VI-98 referred to *Volsques* in the main theme, while mentioning "*pestilent*" in line two. Both words (in similarity) appear in this quatrain. This quatrain makes it possible to the *Volsci* as a parallel group of ancient tribe, of

261

The Epic Poem Prophesied by Nostradamus

which the Romans had to force under their dominion. On a religious level of thought, a comparison could be made to those of the Reformation, who were under the umbrella of Christianity, headed in Rome (as allies), who were the strongest enemies of Rome (having been forced into submission). The city of *Sorgues* is in the department of Vaucluse, in Provence, to the north of Avignon. The *Sorgue* River flows into the Ouvèze River, which is a tributary to the Rhone Rover. Along the path of the *Sorgue* is a place known as the *L'Isle-sur-Sorgues*, which is known as the Venice of Provence. The word "*traffic*" is thought to be rooted in the Catalan "*trafegar*," meaning, "to decant."

Traveling along them bridges to them arrive near to arbors of roses,	*Passant les pontz venir pres des rosiers,*
Long in coming come unto sooner than he will have thought,	*Tard arrivé plustost qu'il cuydera,*
Will be growing them tied on ones Spanish (knots) in Beziers,	*Viendront les noues espaignolz à Besiers,*
Whom the same man inquiring after enterprise will cancel.	*Qui icelle chasse emprinse cassera.*

Note: Originally listed as quatrain number 25 in Centurie IX. In the main theme statement, the focus leads us to find *roses*. In the world of Islamic terrorism symbolism, as reported by "Terrorism Expert", Dr. Maria Alvanou, *roses* are all symbolic of some form of martyrdom, specifically related to the color of the rose. There is an Old French word *nouër*, which means, "to knit, to tie, to bind, to fasten with knots". In carpet making, there is a technique used, called a *Spanish knot*. There are also techniques used in sailing and outdoors use, which use the name *Spanish*, such as the *Spanish Windlass Knot*, and *Spanish Bowtie Knot*. While the word is capitalized to show the name of a people, the lower case would apply to a *knot* simply attributed to an origin in Spain. *Beziers* is in Languedoc, in the department of Hérault, between Perpignan and Montpellier.

By reason of War overt Arles not will give battle,	*Par Mars ouvert Arles ne donra guerre,*
Of night will be them soldiers astonished ones:	*De nuict seront les soldats estonnés:*
Black, white with them light blue dissembled ones in country,	*Noir, blanc à l'inde dissimuléz en terre,*
At the bottom of ones there pretense for traitors surely ones & rang the alarm ones.	*Soubz la faincte umbre traistres verez & sonnés.*

Note: Originally listed as quatrain number 2 in Centurie VII. The colors of Nostradamus are found used in line three. *Black* means Muslims (Brown is Dark Africans), while *white* represents Christians, particularly those of *white* Europe. The *light blue pretenders* are the troops who are uniformed under the United Nations banner and colors (particularly their azure helmets). Since *soldartz* is an anagram primarily, it has a secondary translation as *sol-dartz*, which is "*ground-darts*", or the landing of missiles on the ground, with their exploding being the cause of *astonishment*.

Chapter 25 - France Tries Not to Surrender

Two sad from Without doubt, to Rodez & Milhau,	*Deux gros de Mende, de Roudés & Milhau,*
Cahors, Limoges, Castres to prefer, increasingly to flow	*Cahours, Limoges, Castres malo sepmano*
From white-haired them to hand over, with Bordeaux one flint stone,	*De nuech l'intrado, de Bourdeaux uncailhau,*
Through Perigord in the derangement of there yearly field produce.	*Par Perigort au toc de la campano.*

Note: Originally listed as quatrain number 44 in Centurie IV. With *Two* the capitalized first word, seeing three communes following it makes sense that *Mende* is the odd commune out, particularly since it has meaning to the name. The city of *Millau* (or *Milhau* in Occitan) is on the Tarn River, where the Dourbie River meets, also in the Aveyron department. The *Millau* viaduct is a recent attraction as the world's tallest cable-stayed road bridge. This can play a role in the quatrains that tell of a bridge. *Cahors* is located west-northwest of *Rodez* in the Lot department, on the Lot River. The commune of *Limoges* is east of *Bordeaux* and north of *Cahors*. The commune of *Castres* is east of Toulouse, south of Albi. Phonetically, if *neuch* is pronounced as *neuk*, a new view of line three comes into play, from "nukes" to "flint stones". There is a city gate in *Bordeaux* that is called *Porte Cailhau*, with *Cailhau* being the name of a commune in the Aude department, in the Languedoc-Roussillon region. The region once known as *Perigord* is east of the Gironde department and *Bordeaux*.

Tours, Orleans, Blois, Angers, Reims, & Nantes,	*Tours, Orleans, Bloys, Angiers, Reims, & Nantes,*
Warned to appear ones vexed ones by sudden transforming:	*Cités vexées par subit changement:*
Through speeches unaccustomed to ones being cast up again ones provoked ones,	*Par langues estranges seront rendues tentes,*
Rivers, darts people of Rennes, land & sea trembling.	*Fleuves, dards Renes, terre & mer tremblement.*

Note: Originally listed as quatrain number 20 in Centurie I. The commune of *Tours* is in the Indre-et-Loire department, the largest city in Centre region of France, between *Orleans* and the Atlantic. *Orleans* is the capital of the Loiret department, in the Centre region, east of *Tours*. The commune of *Blois* is the capital of the Loir-et-Cher department, on the banks of the lower Loire River, between *Orleans* and *Tours*. The commune of *Angiers* is on the banks of the Maine River, in the Maine-et-Loire department, 191 miles southwest of Paris. *Reims* is 89 miles east-northeast of Paris, in northeastern France, in the Champagne-Ardenne region, in the Marne department. It is the largest city in that region. These cities draw a line through northern France; and, that line indicates surrender. *Rennes* is a city in northwestern France, east of Brittany, capital of the Bretagne region, in the Ille-et-Vilaine department.

The Epic Poem Prophesied by Nostradamus

By reason of insatiable thirst after things, through force & violence	*Par avarice, par force & violence*
Will grow to extremely grieve them its own chief ones of Orléans,	*Viendra vexer les siens chiefz d'Orleans,*
Nearby holy Myself watched assault & resistance.	*Pres saint Memire assault & resistance.*
Dead inwardly one's hanging tapestry will be telling that it became a vagabond in that place.	*Mort dans sa tante diront qu'il dort leans.*

Note: Originally listed as quatrain number 42 in Centurie VIII.

Paris conspired against one high murder to commit.	*Paris conjure un grand meurtre commettre.*
Blois them will cause to deliver out of upon smooth success of a thing:	*Bloys le fera sortir en plain effect:*
Those of Orléans will be desiring their general to pardon	*Ceulx d'Orleans voudront leur chef remettre*
Angers, Troyes, Langres, theirs will be acting an offence.	*Angiers, Troye, Langres, leur feront un meffait.*

Note: Originally listed as quatrain number 51 in Centurie III. *Blois* is between *Orléans* and Tours, about 100 miles southwest of *Paris*. The French *Troyes* was an important Roman settlement, and the name is the root of the number "three" (*trois*). *Troyes* is a commune in the NE Aube department, on the Seine River, 93 miles SE of Paris.

In the church high with Blois consecration of a prelate Selene,	*Au temple hault de Bloys sacre Salonne,*
Darkness bridge to Loire, prelate head man ruining	*Nuict pont de Loyre, prelat roy pernicant*
Messenger subduing with the fishing lines from there many	*Curseur victoire aux maresets de la lone*
From where prelateship of whites to born brayed one.	*Dou prelature de blancs à bormeant.*

Note: Originally listed as quatrain number 21 in Centurie IX. The word *Salonne* is the singular form of the word that names the place *Salonnes*. However, *Salonnes* is in the far east of France, while *Blois* is in the north central. The national monument of France, known as the *Blois* Cathedral, is said to have been originally the collegiate church of Saint *Solenne*, dating to the 12th century. It is now named the Cathedrale Saint-Louis de *Blois*. Saint *Solenne* is probably the reference in *Salonne*, as an anagram to *Solenna*. *Solenne* is a variation of *Selene/Selena*. *Selene* is the goddess of the moon, and would represent a Muslim.

Chapter 25 - France Tries Not to Surrender

Them the aged in years frustrated, & deprived of one's dignity,	*Le vieux mocqué, & privé de sa place,*
By reason of the foreigner who him will deprave into lewdness:	*Par l'estrangier qui le subornera:*
Public power ones to his son fed on ones before its outward appearance,	*Mains de son filz mangées devant sa face,*
The friar with Public records, Orleans Red horse will deal treacherously with.	*Le frere à Chartres, Orl. Rouan trahyra.*

Note: Originally listed as quatrain number 61 in Centurie IV. The word *suborn* is defined as, "to induce one to do acts of evil or wrongdoing." The place *Chartres* is 60 miles SW of Paris, and the home of the "finest gothic cathedral in France", in the Cathedrale Notre-Dame de *Chartres*. *Orleans* is 81 miles SW of Paris, with *Rouen* northwest of Paris, due north of *Orleans*. In Occitan, *Rouen* is spelled *Roan*. However, the word *Rouan* is a good spelling for *Roan*, a *Red horse*, while also being an adjective describing a mixture of white, gray, and reddish-brown hair, particularly on a horse. A *Red horse* is symbolic of the second rider of *The Revelation of John*.

Interred not dead one who has apoplexy,	*Ensevely non mort apopletique,*
Will be contrived to contain them public authorities fed on ones:	*Sera trouvé avoir les mains mangées:*
At what time there summoned to appear will sentence to death the heretic,	*Quand la cité damnera l'heretique,*
Who uses theirs justice proceedings itself their own appears converted ones.	*Qu'avoit leurs loix se leur sembloit changées.*

Note: Originally listed as quatrain number 36 in Centurie III. The word *apoplexy* is defined as, "a sudden impairment of neurological functions; stroke." The word *avoit* is the Old French 3rd person Imperfect for the verb "*avoir*," now spelled "*avait*". Likewise, the word *sembloit* can be seen as the 3rd person Imperfect form of "*sembler*," now spelled "*semblait*."

A high magistrate of Orleans placed with dead,	*Le grand baillif d'Orleans mis à mort,*
Will be by reason of one from kindred acting out revenge:	*Sera par un de sang vindicatif:*
To death deserved not will die, nor for hazard,	*De mort merite ne mourra, ne par sort,*
From base ones & public power ones wrong them acts servile.	*Des piedz & mains mal le faisoit captif.*

The Epic Poem Prophesied by Nostradamus

Note: Originally listed as quatrain number 66 in Centurie III. Randle Cotgrave explained the term "*bailiff*" as, "of much more authority than [and English] bailiff: To which he takes notice of treasons committed, false money coined, robberies and murders done, rebellions or seditions raised, unlawful assemblies made, arms born or soldiers levied without warrant, protections or sanctuaries [legal] violated, pardons and charters [legal] abused, fairs, markets, and freedoms otherwise usurped." He furthered to inform that in ancient times there were four "Bailiffs of France," who had supreme authority to appoint other, lesser judges, and they convened court in "Vermendois (Picardy), Sens (Bourgogne), Mâcon (Bourgogne), and Saint-Pierre de Moustier (Provence-Alpes-Cote d'Azur)."

As it should be protected them acted for principal goodness,	*Bien defendu le faict par excellence,*
Defense you Tower ones from your near destruction:	*Garde toy Tours de ta proche ruine:*
London & Nantes through Reims will make fortification	*Londres & Nantes par Reims fera defense*
Not time past opened at the opportunity to there blasted with mist.	*Ne passé outre au temps de la bruine.*

Note: Originally listed as quatrain number 46 in Centurie IV. The Old French word "*tour*" translates as, "*tower*," but also means, "turn, circle, compass, wheeling, revolution, and a course [as the *Tour* de France]." There is a city named *Tours*, but *Towers* makes *London & Nantes* become symbolic of the *Towering* nations *England & France*. *Tours* is the largest city in the Centre region of France. *Nantes* was once the most important city in the province of Brittany, which had historic ties to Britain.

Him King full of tricks will have intelligence of his ambushes	*Le Roy rusé entendra ses embusches,*
From three regions enemies to set upon,	*De trois quartiers ennemis assaillir,*
A multitude foreign the weapons of diseases	*Un nombre estrange larmes de coqueluges*
Will arrive The hard-press with the translator to misunderstand.	*Viendra Lemprin du traducteur faillir.*

Note: Originally listed as quatrain number 81 in Centurie IX. The line one last word, "*embusches*", is not an exact match, as a rhyme, with "*coqueluges*", unless the sound the same, such that the "g" gets a "ch" pronunciation. As spelled, "*coqueluges*" is not a word, but "*coqueluches*" is. This could be a printer's error; unless the Latin combined form makes more sense. As a disease, Randle Cotgrave stated about *coqueloche* (in Old English, *coqueluchoe*), it "troubled the French about 1510, and 1557; and us but a while ago." It is now known as whooping cough, a very contagious bacterial respiratory infection.

Chapter 25 - France Tries Not to Surrender

After there rain milked as much as needs somewhat long,	*Apres la pluye laict assés longuette,*
Upon a vast number degrees of Reims them sky stricken:	*En plusieurs lieux de Reims le ciel touché:*
My Lord! what battle with kindred nearby as it were touching to water themselves prepared for,	*O quel conflict de sang pres d'eux s'apreste,*
Fathers & boys chiefs neither will be having the heart to approach.	*Peres & filz roys n'oseront approcher.*

Note: Originally listed as quatrain number 18 in Centurie III. The 1568 Lyon edition is not clear to read, due to opposite page bleed-over. That condition it makes it appear the word, "*assés*" is accented in line one. This accent is confirmed in the 1557 Utrecht edition. However, there is no word that corresponds to either "*assé*" or "*assés*". This makes the Latin the best bet, if the accent is the way to read the word.

Before Red horse to Insubres thrust into the rear,	*Devant Rouan d'Insubres mis le siege,*
By reason of country & sea shut ones them straits:	*Par terre & mer enfermés les passages:*
From Hainaut, & Flanders, with Ghent & those of Liege,	*D'Haynault, & Flandres, de Gand & ceux de Liege,*
Through bribes the brazened ones will be taking away forcibly the coasts.	*Par dons lænées raviront les rivages.*

Note: Originally listed as quatrain number 19 in Centurie IV. It should be noted that the Arpitan spelling of *Roanne* (France, in the east-central area) is "*Rouana.*" *Roanne* is not supported by the listing of Belgium in line three. *Rouan* is clean French for *Roan*, a *Red horse*. This is symbolic of the second rider of *The Revelation of John*. The *Insubres* people were the founders of Milan, Italy, but they were descended from Gaulish tribes (people from France); and their history shows them having supported Hannibal against the Roman troops. *Hainaut* (also spelled *Hainault*) is the western-most province of Wallonia, Belgium. It borders both East and West *Flanders*. The city of *Ghent* is in *Flanders*. All places are in Belgium. *Liege* is the easternmost province in the Wallonia region; as such, *Hainaut, Flanders,* and *Liege* consist of the total of the Wallonia region. The Picardy region of France borders Belgium (this region), with *Rouen* being in the next region to the west, on the Seine River, north of Paris.

Through the show of supposed holiness,	*Par l'apparence de faincte saincteté,*
Will be dealt treacherously with the enemy ones the seat of justice:	*Sera trahy aux ennemis le siege:*
Darkness that one believes to sleep in security,	*Nuict qu'on cuidoit dormir en seureté,*

The Epic Poem Prophesied by Nostradamus

Near to Brabant will be marching those from Liège.	*Pres de Braban marcheront ceux du Liege.*

Note: Originally listed as quatrain number 30 in Centurie VI. The word cuidoit is translated as Old French spelling for *cuidait*, the third person singular indicative imperfect form of the verb *cuider*. One source states that *cudoit* is Old French for "forethought," making it based on *cuider*. The combination of *Brabant* and *Liege* together, as provinces, represents a center "wedge" into Belgium, from the German border, into the middle of Belgium. The United Nations International Court of *Justice* is located in The Hague, The Netherlands, northeast of Belgium.

At what time those of Hainault with Ghent & to Marsh-home,	*Quand ceux d'Hainault de Gand & de Brucelle,*
Will be observing at Langres a seat of justice before thrust into:	*Verront à Langres le siege devant mis:*
Rear their ones flanks will be strife ones bloodthirsty ones	*Derrier leurs flancz seront guerres cruelles*
There wound ancient will be worse than adversaries.	*La plaie antique sera pis qu'ennemis.*

Note: Originally listed as quatrain number 50 in Centurie II. Since both the 1557 Utrecht edition and the 1568 Lyon edition show *Brucelle* without an "s" at the end, while both editions show the line three rhyming word, *"cruelles"*, having one, the lack of an "s" was intentional. This shows, along with the misspelling [not *Bruxcelles* – missing two letters], that something other than Brussels is the primary intention, although the line's references to the two halves of Belgium [Hainaut and Ghent] would include the centrally placed Brussels on a secondary level. The word for the city Brussels means, *"marsh home."*

Of to wage battle born will be given sign,	*De batailler ne sera donné signe,*
From the enclosed grove of trees will be drawn tight with to come forth out of,	*Du parc seront constraint de sortir hors,*
To Ghent them on all sides will be known the distinguishing mark,	*De Gand l'entour sera cogneu lensigne,*
Which will act to put to all them his own desires.	*Qui fera mettre de tous les siens amors.*

Note: Originally listed as quatrain number 83 in Centurie X. The last line appears, in the 1568 Lyon edition, to end with one word, *"amors."* The 1557 Utrecht edition shows this as *"à morts."* However, most instances where Nostradamus placed the preposition *à*, he had the accent mark placed (unless it was the capitalized first letter of a line). Since there is no "t" present in the 1568 Lyon edition, there are only two options, *"a mors"* or *"amors."*

Chapter 25 - France Tries Not to Surrender

Them games new ones upon France made amends ones,	*Les jeux nouveaux en Gaule redressés,*
Following getting an upper hand on the enemy to the people of Milan in armory:	*Apres victoire de l'Insubre champaigne:*
Mountains of Italy, the substantial ones united ones, itself pared ones:	*Monts d'Esperie, les grands liés, troussés:*
From fear to tremble there Roman & the whole of the Spanish peninsula.	*De peur trembler la Romaigne & l'Espaigne.*

Note: Originally listed as quatrain number 36 in Centurie IV. In Old French (Randle Cotgrave's version), *Gaule* is not defined as "France", although "*Gaulois*" is defined as a "Frenchman." France made a bid for the 2012 Olympics, finishing second to London, England. Line one's use of *redressed* makes an Olympic hosted in France after 2012 *The new games* they sought but failed to get in 2012. The definitions of "*redress*" are, "to set right, remedy, rectify; to make amends to and for; and, satisfaction for wrong or injury." Line two states these Olympics will come *After* these Olympics will come there will be a military move towards northern Italy, the region of Cisalpine Gaul (France / Italy). Seeing the word *toussés* as an anagram (oneself pared ones) means the campaign to Italy will leave oneself vulnerable. The word *lie* means both united and "bound."

Chapter 26

Paris Burning

The Fall of Paris

The bird royal over the city belonging to the sun,	*L'oiseau royal sur la cité solaire,*
September month before will form in the night time conjecture of things to come by use of birds:	*Sept moys devant fera nocturne augure:*
Wall from Asia Minor will tumble down thunder, enlightened,	*Mur d'Orient cherra tonnerre, esclaire,*
Seven days with them carried ones the enemies at the hour.	*Sept jours aux portes les ennemis à l'heure.*

Note: Originally listed as quatrain number 81 in Centurie V. Tommaso Campanella wrote a book entitled, *City of the Sun* (1602, published 1623), after Nostradamus' death (1566), but well after Thomas Moore wrote *Utopia* (1516). *City of the Sun* was a view of a utopian Italy, which incorporated the values of Christian doctrines, along with the ever-increasing scientific enlightenments of the Renaissance. In essence, it was a treatise against Rome, since Campanella had just been sentenced to life in prison for sedition and heresy. As such, the *city solar* would stand as Rome, in the overall sense. However, Nostradamus referenced the *Sun* as Christianity, and/or Jesus Christ.

In the month third themselves raising him Gold,	*Au moys troisiesme se levant le Soleil,*
Wild Boar, Leopard, to the camp Weapon in defense of to battle:	*Sanglier, Liepard, au champ Mars pour combatre:*
Lion laid apart, with the heaven stretch out one's eye,	*Liepard laisse, au ciel extend son œil,*
An Eagle round about to the Sun to view themselves to sport.	*Un Aigle autour du Soleil voir s'esbatre.*

Note: Originally listed as quatrain number 23 in Centurie I. Line one is reference to the "games" of quatrain IV-36. In ancient Persia (now Iran), the *Wild Boar* was a symbol of fierce and brave creatures. A Wikipedia article on "*Wild Boar*" states, "The famous Sassanid spahbod, Shahrbaraz, who conquered Egypt and the *Levant*, had his name derived Shahr(city) + Baraz(*boar* like/brave) meaning "*Boar* of the City". A *libbard* is the same thing as a *leopard*. In the Middle Ages, a *leopard* was seen as a *lion*, as a mix between a *lion* and a *panther*. Britain used the black lion,

Chapter 26 - Paris Burning

or *leopard*, as its symbol in many of its early colonial expansions. In Old French, the contraction *s'esbatre* was defined without the word *se* stated, such that it simply meant, "to sport, to play, to dally, to jest; to pass away the time in mirth, and recreation."

There city seized through craft & cheating,	*La cité prinse par tromperie & fraude*
By an endeavor from a handsome youth entrapped:	*Par le moyen d'un beau jeune attrapé:*
Assailing delivered up Canal de la Robine as it were touching to THE AUDE.	*Assault donné Roubine pres de L'AUDE.*
He & everything dead ones in defense of means quite circumvented	*Luy & tous morts pour avoir bien trompé*

Note: Originally listed as quatrain number 85 in Centurie III. The *Aude* department is along the Mediterranean coast, one department north of the Spanish border. A canal, called a *roubine*, is common in the Rhone delta region known as *La Carmague*, to the east of *Aude*. The word "*roubine/robine*" is defined as, a "canal of communication [to get through] between one pond and the sea." *Aude* has similar canals. The *Canal du Midi* begins at the Mediterranean, at *Sète*, and ends at Toulouse, where it joins the *Canal du Garonne*, and goes to the Atlantic. The *Canal de la Robine* (Robine is a variation of Roubine) connects the Mediterranean to *THE AUDE RIVER*.

How many of time seized city belonging to the sun,	*Combien de foys prinse cité solaire,*
Will be ones, converting them justice proceedings barbarous ones & full of veins ones:	*Seras, changeant les loys barbares & veines:*
Your evil themselves drawing near to: More bars tribute paying,	*Ton mal s'approche: Plus seras tributaire,*
There mighty Adriatic will disclose anew your without purpose ones.	*La grand Hadrie reovrira tes vaines.*

Note: Originally listed as quatrain number 8 in Centurie I. The combination of words, "*cité solaire*" is repeated in the main theme of quatrain V-81. The Italian commune *Adria* is at the mouth of the Po and Adige rivers.

Near to Coarse lawn condemns there forest flowered ones,	*Pres de Quintin damns la forest bourlis,*
Within the abbey will be Priests hoarse ones,	*Dans l'abbaye seront Flamens ranches,*
Them two puny ones from blows half without spirit ones	*Les deux puisnais de coups my estourdis*

The Epic Poem Prophesied by Nostradamus

Prosecution weighed down & defense all torches.	*Suitte oppressee & garde tous aches.*

Note: Originally listed as quatrain number 40 in Centurie IX. The French commune of *Saint-Quentin-sur-Sioule* is located in the *Puy-de-Dôme* department, in central France. There is also a *Saint-Quentin* (spelled with an "e") in the *Aisne* department, which is named such because it was the place where the Roman citizen *Quintinus* (spelled without an "e") was martyred in Gaul. That commune is in the Picardy region of northeastern France (also an historical province), almost bordering Flemish Belgium (and thus Flanders), while touching the Walloon region of Belgium, at one small point. The *Abbey of Arrouaise* was originally a hermitage that provided a service to the travelers in the great *Forest* of Arrouaise, in Artois (Belgium / Flanders). This *forest* extended westward to the *Forest* of the Ardennes, to the east of St. *Quentin*. Nostradamus also mentions *Quintin* in quatrains IV-08, VIII-54, and IX-29. The 1568 Lyon edition shows the word "*dans*," but with a printer's abbreviation mark over the "a," indicating that an "m" or "n" should be placed in the word next. That makes the intended word become "*damns*." The French use the word "*damner*," but "*damns*" is English.

Him great Empire will be quickly abandoned of all comfort,	*Le grand Empire sera tost desolé,*
Also removed from one place to another near to high forest:	*Et translaté pres d'arduenne silve:*
Them two sons of the people by reason of the eldest him unglued,	*Les deux bastardz par l'aisné decollé,*
Both will have sovereign authority over Upper armor, sense of vulture.	*Et regnera Aenodarb, nez de milve.*

Note: Originally listed as quatrain number 45 in Centurie V. The word "*embase*" means, "to bring down or lower; to debase; to degrade; to deteriorate." The *Ardennes* Forest of Belgium (*Ardenne* in Belgian), is etymologically rooted in the Roman name, "*Arduenne Silva*," meaning, "*Forest of Ardienna*", with Ardienna being a Celtic goddess who rode the back of a wild boar. In lower case meaning, the words mean, "*height woods*." While that is certainly a secondary intention, the lack of capitalization, and the words being separate, means other translations act as the primary interpretation. In quatrain IX-40, line three begins by stating, "*Les deux puisnais*" (The two younger ones), which is consistent with "*Les deux bastardz*" (Them two sons of the people) found here, also in line three.

At what time in him government will come forward in the world it limping,	*Quand dans le regne parviendra le boiteux,*
Fellow suitor will contain adjoining son of the people:	*Competiteur aura proche bastard:*
He & the rule will be growing even as powerful not arrogant ones,	*Luy & le regne viendront si fort rogneux,*

Chapter 26 - Paris Burning

Which before whom it healed one's feat will be good turn tardy.	*Qu'ains qu'il guerisse son faict sera bien tard.*

Note: Originally listed as quatrain number 73 in Centurie III. Some may think the word "*rognuex*" comes from the French verb *rogner*, which means, "to pare, clip, shear, and cut." I have found nothing that indicates the past participle is anything other than "*rogné*," meaning the "u" is unexplained. Still, in a secondary sense, this may be intended to be seen.

By reason of them determined to two matters sufficing ones	*Par le decide de deux choses bastars*
Nephew of the blood will possess him realm	*Nepveu du sang occupera le regne*
Within chosen will be them power with projectiles	*Dedans lectoyre seront les cops de darts*
Son of a brother through fright will bow the argument of something.	*Nepveu par peur pleira l'enseigne.*

Note: Originally listed as quatrain number 43 in Centurie VIII. It is interesting to note the rhyming words of lines one and three. The 1568 Lyon edition clearly shows *bastars* ending line one, without a "d", which most want to insert. Then, in line three the word *darts* is correctly spelled with a "t", instead of a "d" at the end (*darts* rather than *dards*). To lead one to think of "*bastards*" is intentional, as it relates to the "*two sons of the people*" in quatrains quatrain V-45, and the singular "*bastard*" in quatrain III-73 (along with others). Those two are the British royal sons, thus they are implied. However, the primary word to interpret is the Catalan "*bastar*," meaning "sufficing." As for the use of "*dart*", that is the English spelling for a word originated from Old French. The use of English is to confirm the *bastards*" are British. The "*Nephew of the blood*" is a relative come to power in Belgium.

Guardian you chief Frenchman from your nephew	*Garde toy roy Gaulois de ton nepveu*
Who will act as worthy that belonging to you only threads.	*Qui fera tant que ton unique filz.*
Will be bleak with beating at Arrived ones forging religious promise,	*Sera meurtry à Venus faisant vœu,*
Accompanied with darkness who three & half a dozen.	*Accompaigné de nuict que trois & six.*

Note: Originally listed as quatrain number 32 in Centurie VIII.

The Epic Poem Prophesied by Nostradamus

This which ravished will be from young Vulture,	Ce que ravy sera de jeune Milve,
For them people of Normandy to France & Picardy:	Par les Normans de France & Picardie:
The obscure ones with the temple from the rank of Moor forest	Les noirs du temple du lieu de Negresilve
Will be making the lodging place & light from Lombardy.	Feront aulberge & feu de Lombardie.

Note: Originally listed as quatrain number 16 in Centurie VI. Quatrain V-45 uses the rhyming words (in lines two and four), "*silve*" and "*milve*", which are repeated here. The name for the Black Forest of Germany, in Catalan, is *Silva Negra*. The name *Normans* came from "Northman" and "Norseman", and they were of Frankish, Gallo-Roman stock. *Normandy* and *Picardie* make up the majority of the northern France coastal land along the English Channel. The region of *Lombardy* is in north central Italy. Randle Cotgrave defined *Lombardie* as the "hithermost part of Italy." The word "hithermost" can be defined as "nearest."

From darkness will arrive at there forest of Queens,	De nuit viendra par la forest de Reines,
Two direction valley the twisted Herniated there stone white	Deux pars vaultorte Herne la pierre blanche
The monk black into whitish within Lean and dry lands	Le moine noir en gris dedans Varennes
Chosen hooded cause light, lineage cut off.	Esleu cap. cause tempeste feu, sang tranche.

Note: Originally listed as quatrain number 20 in Centurie IX. There is a forest de la Reine in the Meurthe-et-Moselle department, approximately 12 miles northeast of Nancy, France. There is a city in northern France, named *Vautorte*, whose name came from the Romans because it was at a winding valley. It is in the Mayenne department of northwestern France, where Brittany and Normandy meet. The city of *Herne* is in Belgium, in the Flemish Brabant section of Flanders. There are eight (8) communes in France named *Varennes*, all over the map, but mostly to the east-northeast. There are another 19 communes with *Varennes* being part of their name (17 *Varennes*-, 2 -*Varennes*). One of these communes of *Varennes* is in the *Meuse* department and known for being where Louis XVI was caught trying to escape to Austria.

Them converting will be extremely painful,	Le changement sera fort difficile:
Warned to appear, place subdued militarily in the exchange advantage will forge:	Cité, province au change gain fera:
Opinion lofty, prudent thrust into, hunted after it powerful,	Cœur haut, prudent mis, chassé luy habile,

Chapter 26 - Paris Burning

Sea, world, people one's state will change.	Mer, terre, peuple son estat changera.

Note: Originally listed as quatrain number 21 in Centurie IV. France is now a series of departments and regions. However, prior to the reorganization that took place beginning in 1790, due to the French Revolution, the departments replaced the old *provinces*. Wikipedia states the definition of a French *province* evolved as such: "The existence of *provinces* came from the *droit coutumier* ("customary law") and was merely certified by the *state*. A *province*, also known as *état* ("*state*"), was characterized by the laws that belonged to it. A *province* itself could encompass several other *provinces*. For example, Burgundy was a *province* but Bresse — another *province* — was nevertheless a part of Burgundy."

By reason of betraying ones turned ones in death beaten,	Par trahysons de verges à mort battu,
Embraced overcome will be through its confusion:	Prins surmonté sera par son desordre:
Assembly of counselors vain with the great taken prisoner by war neglected,	Conseil frivole au grand captif sentu,
Sense for extreme wrath in regard this Bey will arrive to sting.	Nez par fureur quant Begich viendra mordre.

Note: Originally listed as quatrain number 32 in Centurie VI. The only sensible anagram that I could find in *Begich* is *c'Beigh*. The title (thus worthy of capitalization) *Bey* is also spelled as *Beigh*, *Bey*, or *Beg*. It was originally a title below a Sultan, although it was a distinction of royalty in Tunis. However, its use over the years (by the 19th century) made it become diminished in value, becoming more common, as "sir" is used in English today. Nostradamus would have recognized it as a title of "leader."

There helmet blue will forge the self-willingness whitish,	La teste blue fera la teste blanche,
So much from harm that France with action their benefit.	Autant de mal que France a faict leur bien.
Death to them born sooner great hanging above there to bank,	Mort à l'anthene grand pendu sus la brance,
At what time caught to them his own ones the Pope will say how much.	Quand prins des siens le Roy dira combien.

Note: Originally listed as quatrain number 2 in Centurie II. By writing *blue* (the English spelling) instead of *bleu*, Nostradamus gave an indication that there is a link to the English people in the color *blue*. The use of color is always significant, and *blue* is the color of the United Nations flag, and their "peacekeeping troops" wear light *blue* helmets. The letters *anthene* can create a variation of *athenien*, or "one of Athens." Since line one's rhyming word is *blanche*, line three's rhyming word makes a match as *branche*, although *brance* meant, "bearded red wheat." It makes more

275

The Epic Poem Prophesied by Nostradamus

sense as an anagram, where "*banc*" is also spelled "*banque*." The "r" can then be either a prefix abbreviation ("re-"), or the suffix ("-er"). The root word, "*banc*," is Italian, which supports the use of "*Roy*" as "*Pope*."

Head cut off of the valiant captain.	*Teste tranchee du vaillant capitaine.*
Will be hurled before its adversary:	*Sera gettee devant son adversaire:*
His body hanging from one's rank in the mast,	*Son corps pendu de sa classe à l'antenne,*
Disordered will flee on rowed ones with wind adverse.	*Confus fuira par rames à vent contraire.*

Note: Originally listed as quatrain number 92 in Centurie IV. The word capitaine can also mean, "ring-leader." Line three's use of l'antenne makes it seem connected to quatrain II-02, where Nostradamus wrote, "*l'anthene*." Both quatrains also have "*teste*" in the main theme.

THE ARCH of the treasure for Major weakness disappointed,	*L'ARC du thresor par Achilles deceu,*
In them engendered ones understood there four-cornered:	*Aux procrees sceu la quadrangulaire:*
With the act Royal the explanation will be knowledge of,	*Au faict Royal le comment sera sceu,*
Total bulk of in respect of hanged at the solemn promise to the common people.	*Corps veu pendu au veu du populaire.*

Note: Originally listed as quatrain number 1 in Centurie VII. Line one's all-caps *L'ARC*, when followed by *treasure*, sound like the meaning is the pot of gold at the end of *THE RAINBOW*. With *L'ARC* meaning *THE IRIS*, one has to recall that Nostradamus mentioned the goddess *Iris* (capitalized) in quatrains VI-44 and I-77. With the capitalized *Royal*, in line three, being a reference to a true royal lineage, this supports a main theme that is British (the only true *Royal* line of any consequence now). This means *Achilles* is related to Great Britain. In that regard, Ireland has been called the British *Achilles*. Still, the term is forever linked to the Greek mythology tale of the hero *Achilles*, whose only "weak link" was his heel. Therefore, *Achilles* means a major weakness.

A course Lorraine will forge dignity with Vendôme,	*Le ranc Lorrain fera place à Vendosme,*
Him noble placed humble & them base put at most glorious,	*Le hault mis bas & le bas mis en hault,*
The sons of Riches will be culled within Rome,	*Le filz d'Mamon sera esleu dans Rome,*
Also he two great ones being thrust into need of judgment.	*Et les deux grands seront mis en deffault.*

Chapter 26 - Paris Burning

Note: Originally listed as quatrain number 18 in Centurie X. As spelled, the word *Lorrain* is correct for the *language* spoken in the *Lorraine* region of France and also the Gaume part of Belgium, which has some German influence. It is recognized as both a regional language of France and Wallonia (Belgium). The commune of *Vendôme* is in north-central France, in the Loir-et-Cher department, on the Loir River. It is 40 minutes from Paris by rapid train. The current Dauphin of France is from that house. The name *Mamon* is correctly spelled, but can also be written as *Mammon*. Jesus stated, "Ye can not serve God and *Mammon*" (Matthew 6:24). *Paradise Lost* was originally a 10-part poetic series published a hundred years after Nostradamus published his 10-Centurie epic poem, and 200 years before Goethe's *Faust*.

Hill Aventine to consume with fire darkness will be regarded,	*Mont Aventine brusler nuict sera veu,*
Them heaven hard to understand all at one cast of the dice in Flanders:	*Le ciel obscur tout à un coup en Flandres:*
At what time the singular ruler will hunt after its son of a sister,	*Quand le monarque chassera son nepveu,*
Theirs people from Congregations of Christians will be giving over them slander ones.	*Leurs gens d'Eglise commetront les esclandres.*

Note: Originally listed as quatrain number 17 in Centurie III. Aventine Hill is one of the Seven Hills of Rome. The word *slander* is defined legally as, "Oral communication of false statements injurious to a person's reputation", and typically as, "A false and malicious statement or report about someone." Line four is supporting the secondary theme of a happening in Belgium. Line three is supporting the main theme, while the spelling of "*nepveu*" links this quatrain to quatrains II-92, IV-73, VI-22, VI-82, VII-43, and X-30.

Them two sons of a sister at differing places brought up to ones:	*Les deux nepveus en divers lieux nourris:*
Navy of ships fought, country fathers tumbled down ones:	*Navale pugne, terre peres tombés:*
Will be growing so most glorious elevated ones into again healed ones,	*Viendront si hault eslevés enguerris,*
To revenge the offence done enemies overcome ones.	*Venger l'injure ennemis succombés.*

Note: Originally listed as quatrain number 29 in Centurie III. The French verb *guérir* means, "to cure, heal, and recover", and the past participle of this verb is *guéri*, meaning, "cured, healed, and recovered." The extra "r", "s", and "en" become a prefix ("r" = re-), suffix ("s" = -s), and separate word (*en*), such that "*enguerris*" becomes, "*en r'guéri-s*. This translates as, "*into again recovered ones*". On a secondary level, the word enquérir, meaning, "to inquire, ask, make search, demand, or inquisition after", is a perfect anagram ("enquérris") for what appears to be "*inquiries*". Unfortunately, that is not the case (spelling and letters not correct), but it does intend one to see renewed health seeking to begin a new inquisition after those who will have persecuted innocent civilians in Europe.

Chapter 27

A Greater Holocaust

Italy is Punished

Naples, Palermo, & all there the Time,	*Naples, Palerme, & toute là Secille,*
By power of authority barbarous will decide habitation,	*Par main barbare fera inhabitee,*
Of Corsica that, Salerno & to Sardinia an island,	*Corsicque, Salerne & de Sardeigne l'isle,*
Extreme desire for pestilence, war urged an issue from evil ones not provoked.	*Faim peste, guerre fin de maulx intemptee.*

Note: Originally listed as quatrain number 6 in Centurie VII. It is easy to mistake *Secille* as meant to be "Sicily", which in French is spelled, "*Sicilie*." Because of the extra "l", it would have to become an anagram to make believe "*l'Secile*" means, "the Sicily." Certainly, Sicily is an intended mistake, meaning it plays a secondary role in interpretation. However, because *Naples* is mainland peninsula, and *Palermo* is on the island of Sicily, more is being stated by seeing the primary intention of the word presented being *the Time*. The main theme is of na important *Time* when all prisoners taken in Italy will be placed on an island prison. It is also important to note that Nostradamus spelled either *Secille*, *Secile*, or *Sicile* (several also along with Palerne and/or Naples) in 10 other quatrains. The French spell Corsica, as "*Corse*." The Italians and Corsicans spell it "*Corsica*". In Catalan and Occitan is its "*Corsega*."

Of lineage & dearth more substantial misery,	*De sang & faim plus grande calamité*
September times oneself prepared for in there marine arm of the sea without haven:	*Sept fois s'apreste à la marine plage:*
Admonish of extreme desire, state seized, captivity,	*Monech de faim, lieu pris, captivité,*
Them lofty directed in an instant into hard cage.	*Le grand mené croc en ferrée caige.*

Note: Originally listed as quatrain number 10 in Centurie III. Most have seen *Monech* as a spelling for *Monaco*, which is similar to the Occitan spelling of *Moneque*. It probably is, but I also see a change from the original Greek form, to one more Latin. If the primary intention is to use

Chapter 27 - A Greater Holocaust

the Latin word *moneo*, with an ending that means, "*of moneo*," the primary intention is to point to "reminding, advising, warning, admonishing, foretelling, and presaging." If it is rooted in the word "*moneta*," the intention is to show a coast that is of high value.

Since Admonish until with them near to Time,	*Depuis Monech jusques au pres de Secile,*
Everything there by the seaside will remain desolated:	*Toute la plage demourra desolée:*
It neither will hold suburb city nor enclosed town,	*Il ny aura fauxbourg cité ne ville,*
That by reason of Barbarous ones pillaged may be & them fled.	*Que par Barbares pillée soit & vollée.*

Note: Originally listed as quatrain number 4 in Centurie II. This quatrain mirrors quatrain III-10 in the use of *Monech* and *plage*. The same question about the meaning of *Monech* is stated in that quatrain's explanation. Both *Monech* and *Secile* have the intent of misleading to see Monaco and Sicily, when neither is what it appears to be. This is why Nostradamus warned about jumping to conclusions about his "places."

There commonwealth with the noble city,	*La republique de la grande cité,*
With lofty strictness not will intend to approve of:	*A grand rigueur ne voudra consentir:*
Pope to deliver out of by reason of trumpeter alleged,	*Roy sortir hors par trompette cité,*
The ladder at the wall, there warned to appear to repent something done.	*L'eschelle au mur, la cité repentir.*

Note: Originally listed as quatrain number 50 in Centurie III. The capitalization of *Roy* in line three means a true monarch of Royalty. Since line one is supported by line three, where Nostradamus states "*La republique*", the *Roy* cannot be a British King. The reason is England has not had a *republic* since Oliver Cromwell. Italy, however, has a *republic*, and a *King*, in the sense that a *Pope* has that same recognition, as the *King* of the Vatican.

To a name which never not had been with the King of France,	*Du nom qui onques ne fut au Roy Gaulois,*
Never neither had been one thunder-bolt so dreading:	*Jamais ne fut un fouldre si craintif:*
Shaking an Italy, a Spain & them English,	*Tremblant l'Italie, l'Espaigne & les Anglois,*
From female foreigners extremely vigilant.	*De femme estrangiers grandement attentif.*

The Epic Poem Prophesied by Nostradamus

Note: Originally listed as quatrain number 54 in Centurie IV. As far as the *name* of *Kings of France* goes, the most frequently used are Louis, Charles, Philip, Henry, and Robert. The use of *one day born*, rather tna "never" (from the combination *onques ne*) means a title that has always been associated with a French King. This does not mean line one is referring to France. Line three ends, following the ampersand, with *them English*, making that a supporting importance of line one. The name Henry has represented both France and England.

In substantial sorrow will be there nation of France,	*En grand regret sera la gent Gauloise,*
Courage void, of small weight, will believe foolhardiness:	*Cœur vain, legier, croira temerité:*
Loaf of bread, salt, nor wine, water: poison not brewed with grain and herbs,	*Pain, sel, ne vin, eaue: venin ne cervoise,*
More mighty captured, extreme need of food, frigid, tremendous pressure.	*Plus grand captif, faim, froit, necessité.*

Note: Originally listed as quatrain number 34 in Centurie VII. This is reminiscent of the conditions found in the Nazi concentration camps, by the Allied forces. The main theme states the *people of France* will be the ones described in this horrid quatrain, but it is difficult to see these conditions if allowed to live off the land. Line four gives the clue that the people are indeed locked up, as only those of strong will and determination are free. Those are *captured* when they too are without *necessities*.

There commonwealth disastrous barren,	*La republique miserable infelice,*
Will be devastated from the uncouth governor:	*Sera vastée du nouveau magistrat:*
Their substantial large number to them exile offence,	*Leur grand amas de l'exil malefice,*
Will cause Suebi to take away forcibly their own mighty covenant.	*Fera Sueve ravir leur grand contract.*

Note: Originally listed as quatrain number 61 in Centurie I. The use of *republique* is a link to quatrain III-50, where it was determined to be a reference to Italy. The word is repeated in line one, and the word *infelice* (rather than the Latin *infelix*) is Italian, with the same meanings (unhappy, unfortunate, bad, poor), such that the use of an Italian word confirms that the unhappy republic is Italy. The French spelling of *Sueve* is correct for identifying the *Suebi* (or *Suevi*), who were ancient Germanic tribes, first mentioned by Julius Caesar. They later migrated and established holdings on the northern Iberian Peninsula (Spain – Portugal), called Galicia. The name *Andalusia* is commemorative of their name (Vandalitia). The Goths ousted them to North Africa, where they established a colony after conquering Carthage. They returned to sack Rome in 455 AD.

Chapter 27 - A Greater Holocaust

A great Celtic will begin to put himself within Rome,	*Le grand Celtique entrera dedans Rome,*
Leading huge number of relegated ones & confiscated ones:	*Menant amas d'exilés & bannis:*
Him lofty pastor of a flock will thrust into to death every subject,	*Le grand pasteur mettra à mort tout homme,*
Whom in respect of him cock being at the Alps joined together ones.	*Qui pour le coq estoient aux Alpes unys.*

Note: Originally listed as quatrain number 28 in Centurie VI. The same combination of *amas* and *de l'exil* is found in quatrain I-61, as line two states, "*amas d'exilés.*" The use of *Celtique* appears here, as one of 15 quatrains stating this word (including two plural "*Celtiques*"), but closely linked to quatrain VI-53, which speaks of the "*Prelat Celtique.*"

Them Albanians will be carrying over within Rome,	*Les Albanois passeront dedans Rome,*
Being the means for Langres half-for them clothed ones,	*Moyennant Langres demipar les affublés:*
Prince appointed governor & Military commander neither to release a debt with subject,	*Marquis & Duc ne pardonner à homme,*
Death, blood smallpox subtlety to water, to offend them well ones.	*Feu, sang, morbilles point d'eau, faillir les bledz.*

Note: Originally listed as quatrain number 98 in Centurie IV. The *Albanois* were Papal Guards, which would make them from *Alba* Longa, the oldest Latin town and legendary birthplace of Romulus and Remus, the founders of Rome. However, that makes little sense; and, when the word *Albanaise* is seen to represent the people of *Albania* (originally the *Albanoi*), one sees the connection to *Albania*, which is on the Adriatic coast, neighboring Serbia (province of Kosovo), Macedonia, Greece and Montenegro. The commune of *Langres* is correctly spelled and in eastern France, in the Haute-Marne department. The word *blé* meant both corn and wheat, such that it stood for grains. The 1568 Lyon edition shows a "*p*" at the end of "*demi*", with a "*p*" being a printer's abbreviation for "*par*". As combined with *demi-*, it can represent "*-part*. The word *bled* meant *corn* in OF, but modern French defines it as "*hole.*" That becomes indicative of water wells.

A mighty military commander of White themselves will grow to rebel from,	*Le grand duc d'Albe se viendra rebeller,*
With its lofty ones priests will make the betraying:	*A ses grans peres fera le tradiment:*
Him high from False appearance them will come to overcome by war,	*Le grand de Guise le viendra debeller,*

The Epic Poem Prophesied by Nostradamus

Taken prisoner in war moved & erected tomb.	*Captif mené & dressé monument.*

Note: Originally listed as quatrain number 29 in Centurie VII. The French write *Alba Longa* as *Albe-la-Longue*. *Guise* is a commune in the northeastern part of France, in the *Aisne* department, on the *Aisne* River (near Belgium). The House of *Guise*, of which there were two *Dukes* of *Guise*, was in the region of France bordering Germany. This house was created to become a factor in what would become the French Wars of Religion. Line four could relate to quatrain III-36, where the main theme statement begins, *"Buried not dead."*

There people foreign will sort the parcels spoils taken,	*La gent estrange divisera butins,*
Hardship in War one's view frantic:	*Saturne en Mars son regard furieux:*
Hideous unacquainted with the Tuscans & peoples surrounding Rome,	*Horrible estrange aux Tosquans & Latins,*
Greeks who will be in to strike more careful than need be.	*Grecs qui seront à frapper curieux.*

Note: Originally listed as quatrain number 83 in Centurie I. The planet *Mars* has a much faster trip through the zodiac than does *Saturn*. This means that basically every two (or so) years [a *Mars* revolution through all 12 signs], it is bound to conjunct [an astrological aspect] *Saturn*. This will next occur (as of this writing) on August 15, 2012, followed by August 25, 2014, then August 24, 2016, and April 2, 2018. Such a short time span (roughly 7-10 days within orb aspect) would make the astrological aspect element secondary. It would support a timing for when to see the symbolisms become more prevalent, such that line two's use of *furieux,* translated to mean *impatient*, is a symbolism of that aspect.

From stock slave metrical poems, discourses in rhyme & petitions,	*De gent esclave chansons, chantz & requestes,*
Servile ones by Princes & Master with the prisons:	*Captifs par Princes & Seigneur aux prisons:*
In them to come to pass by reason of people with no proper rule within the commonwealth besides self-willingness ones,	*A l'avenir par idiotz sans testes,*
Will be received of ones for coming from God communications.	*Seront receus par divins oraisons.*

Note: Originally listed as quatrain number 14 in Centurie I. In the modern French language, *l'avenir* means, "future." This can be read into the OF form, as *"them to happen,"* such that it is speaking about something not yet having had happened. From an American perspective, the main theme certainly is descriptive of the roots to "soul music" or "the blues." Line two is a perfect match for the *slave owners*, and the royal figures that allowed *slave* trading to exist. Line three certainly describes those leaders as foolish to think that was a right thing to do. However, lines

Chapter 27 - A Greater Holocaust

three and four, particularly in the modern setting, of supposedly religious men preaching "liberation theology", or "Nation of Islam" hatred of the oppressor, it becomes easy to see how the shoe fits the feet of many. This quatrain shows how easily the oppressed can be led to follow anyone who tells the masses what they so strongly want to hear. On an international perspective, the same may be said of Eastern Europeans.

The charcoal white to the black will be expelled out of,	*Le charbon blanc du noir sera chassé,*
Prisoner action guided with the cart carrying the condemned:	*Prisonnier faict mené au tombereau:*
Moor Camel south bases entangled ones with others,	*More Chameau sur piedz entrelassez,*
In that time the younger him will twist the bird of prey.	*Lors le puisné fillera l'aubereau.*

Note: Originally listed as quatrain number 85 in Centurie IV. In Old French the combination of words, *charbon blanc* meant, "a kind of coal made from the wood of the Crimson cedar (also prickly cedar)," and "*le charbon*" was reference to an artists first sketches with charcoal on a blank piece of canvas-paper. Further, the word *charbon* was used to tell of "plague sores," due to the blackish color on the skin. Separately, *charbon blanc* means *black* and *white*, but together they can indicate Christians of non-*white* lineage. One definition of *tumbrel* is, "a crude cart used to carry condemned prisoners to their place of execution, as during the French Revolution." The word *aubereau* also means all types of falconry birds, including eagles, falcons and hawks.

Pope & his court in the place of speech white,	*Roy & sa court au lieu de langue halbe,*
Inwardly him church face has look of a palace,	*Dedans le temple vis a vis du palais,*
In the garden provincial governor from one god of Hell & with priestly Alb,	*Dans le jardin duc de Mantor & d'Albe,*
Alba Longa & Mantis-like one dagger tongue & government house.	*Albe & Mantor poignard langue & palais.*

Note: Originally listed as quatrain number 22 in Centurie IX. The French idiom, "*vis à vis*" means, "*face to face; directly opposite; or right over-against*," but the *a* is not accented, indicating it should be read as the third person form of "*avoir*." The spelling of *Mantor* is still questionable. It could be derived from the French *Mantoue*, which is *Mantua* (the Italian spelling is *Mantova*). If one representing a *Mante* (Praying *Mantis*), it gives the impression of being religious, while only being a predator.

The Epic Poem Prophesied by Nostradamus

France, shameless persons, & cats to kindred will be fed ones,	*Coq, chiens, & chats de sang seront repeus,*
As well from there wounded from the violent governor devised murdered.	*Et de la plaie du tyran trouvé mort.*
In the lair of stone to one other legs & ropes for a sail undone ones,	*Au lict d'un autre jambes & bras rompus,*
That which not has fear to perish from unmerciful death.	*Qui n'avoit peur mourir de cruel mort.*

Note: Originally listed as quatrain number 42 in Centurie II. The word *chien* was also used as a derogatory word, meaning, "a base, filthy or shameless fellow." It could be possible that a *cat of blood* represents a predatory cat, such as a lion, tiger, bobcat, wildcat, etc.

There sect tyrannous in robe continual,	*La faction cruelle à robbe longue,*
Will come to conceal under the pointed ones daggers with slender blades	*Viendra cacher souz ses pointus poignars*
To seize Florence a provincial governor & place of long faith	*Saisir Florence le duc & lieu diphlonque*
His discovery by reason of walled-in ones & side-guards.	*Sa descouverte par immeurs & flanguards.*

Note: Originally listed as quatrain number 33 in Centurie X. The main theme pointing to a *robbe longue* makes this quatrain describe the garment worn by priests, called an "alb." In this sense, this quatrain may link to quatrain IX-22, where Nostradamus capitalized twice "*Albe.*" He also used "*duc*" in that quatrain, and "*poignard*", matching those found here. Both the spelling and translation of *flanguards* is still questionable.

Younger playing with the fresh ones below the cask,	*Puisnay jouant au fresch dessouz la tonne,*
Him noble to the crowned middle before there remnant,	*Le hault du roict du milieu sur la reste,*
The father head man of the company in the church holy Solenne,	*Le pere roy au temple saint Salonne,*
Offering sacrifice will consecrate smoke of festival day.	*Sacrifiant sacrera fum de feste.*

Note: Originally listed as quatrain number 23 in Centurie IX. Quatrain IX-21 also mentions "*sacre Salonne*" and "*temple hault*". That quatrain mentions *Blois*, which is in France, and is the site of Cathedral of Saint Louis, which was originally founded in the 12th century by *saint Solenne*. There is reference for *Salonne* being near "Castle Salt marshes (Moselle)," with *Salonne* being said

Chapter 27 - A Greater Holocaust

to be a convent. According to the 1568 Lyon edition, line two appears to spell the words, "*roict*", and "*reste*". However, other editions (including the 1566 Lyon edition) show these words as "*toict*" (roof, cover of a house) and "*teste*" (head).

There public power shoulder belt & the leg bound with bands,	*La main écharpe & la jambe bendee,*
Outstretched furthermore ship to Calais will support	*Long puis nay de Calais portera*
With the word from the careful spying there death will be stayed,	*Au mot du guet la mort fera tardee,*
Pit within the church at Passover will let blood.	*Puis dans le temple à Paques saignera.*

Note: Originally listed as quatrain number 45 in Centurie VIII. The commune of *Calais* is the largest town in the department Pas-de-*Calais*, in northern France, on the coast of the English Channel, close to Belgium. *Calais* is on the Strait of Dover portion of the English Channel, representing its narrowest point of crossing.

At what time principal commander Perugia not will be bold enough to act its coat of armor,	*Quand chef Perouse n'osera sa tunique,*
Knowledge in the hidden everything bare themselves to deprive of:	*Sens au couvert tout nud s'expolier:*
Being embraced September feat Aristocratic,	*Seront prins sept faict Aristocratique,*
Him father & son cause of death by first violent brunt of things in the collar	*Le pere & filz mors par poincte au colier*

Note: Originally listed as quatrain number 67 in Centurie V. The 1568 Lyon edition clearly does not place a period at the end of line four. According to the systems, this would be an indication of this quatrain's focus being continued into the main theme of another quatrain.

Trap Trasimene will support evidence,	*Lac Thrasmien portera tesmoignage,*
Of the conspired against ones will be ones within Perugia,	*Des conjurez sarez dedans Perouse,*
One of them polar ones will imitate him discrete	*Du despolle contrefera le sage*
Killing Torch-like ones to spread & cut ones to pieces.	*Tuant Tedesque desterne & minuse.*

The Epic Poem Prophesied by Nostradamus

Note: Originally listed as quatrain number 47 in Centurie VIII. *Lake Trasimene* was the site of a battle between the Carthaginians, led by Hannibal, and Romans, led by Flaminius. It was won by Hannibal's troops, and is still considered to be one of history's greatest military ambush success stories. Thus, *Trasimene* was a great (capitalization) *Snare*, or *Trap*. It represents North Africa against Italy. *Perugia* is also listed in quatrain V-67, VI-36, and VII-05.

Them September youths into hostage abandoned ones,	Les sept enfans en hostaige laissés,
A third will issue from one's child to slaughter:	Le tiers viendra son enfant trucider:
Two by reason of his sons will be from rapier pierced ones,	Deux par son filz seront d'estoc perces,
Genoa, Florence, in that time will come upon those to flourish with waves.	Gennes, Florence, lors viendra encunder.

Note: Originally listed as quatrain number 60 in Centurie IV. Line one's main theme could be focusing on the prisoners being held at Guantanamo Bay, as "enemy combatants." The secondary theme statement (line two) can be viewed from a perspective of "suicide bombers." The letter "u" is interchangeable with the letter "o" in the word "*unde*", such that it refers to "*onde*" for its translation. The manufacturing of a word that breaks into "*en-c'onder*" or "*c'en-onder*" is then not far from words that seem relative to "*encunder*" (not a word), such as "encounter" and "encumber". Both words play secondary roles in furthering the interpretation, which begins from a word fashioned to tell of a naval invasion.

A ship formless through horror smothered,	Le nay difforme par horreur suffoqué,
Inwardly there summoned to appear to the noble Pope inhabitable:	Dans la cité du grand Roy habitable:
An edict grave, with the captive ones countermanded,	L'edict severe, des captifs revoqué,
Hail & thunder, Sacrifice immeasurable.	Gresle & tonnerre, Condon inestimable.

Note: Originally listed as quatrain number 97 in Centurie V. The secondary theme statement presents a capitalized version of "*Roy*", which identifies a place "*suitable to live in*" for a Royal figure. This is theme limited to the British Royal family (England) or the *Pope* (Rome – Vatican City). Line four, where the supporting details emerge for line two, uses a capitalized Latin word "*Condono*" to identify the place as Italy. The use of *Condon* as representative of *Condom*, France, becomes secondary, as an indication that simultaneous attacks will begin there at the time of this quatrain's event.

Chapter 27 - A Greater Holocaust

Within risen Bologna will propose to cleanse its transgressions,	*Dedans Bologne voudra laver ses fautes,*
It not will have the power in the church of the sun,	*Il ne pourra au temple du soleil,*
She will take flight making cases as high ones	*Il volera faisant choses si haultes*
At sacred principality not into had been never one equal with.	*En hierarchie n'en fut oncq un pareil.*

Note: Originally listed as quatrain number 53 in Centurie VIII. The town of *Bologna* is in north-central Italy in the Emilia-Romagna region, between the Po River and the Apennines. As an Italian town, the main focus is upon Italy. Line two is then the Roman Catholic church. The capitalization of "*Il*," in both lines two and three, means one has to be either "*He*," "*She*," or "*It*." Since the Roman Catholic Church is the one most adoring of the Virgin Mary, the use of *She* in line three yields more interpretive meaning. The use of "*sun*" is a reference to Christianity. The *sacred principality* is Vatican City, which had been ruled by a holy government, with the Pope its "President."

The provincial governor will propose them those belonging to him to exterminate,	*Le duc vouldra les siens exterminer,*
Will direct unto the more defended camps places unacquainted ones,	*Envoiera les plus fortz lieux estranges,*
Through violent government Pisa & Lucca to ruin,	*Par tyrannie Pize & Luc ruiner,*
Moreover the ignorant ones out of wine will be doing grape gatherings.	*Puy les barbares sans vin feront vendanges.*

Note: Originally listed as quatrain number 80 in Centurie IX.

Him sum you trade with the great Lion changed,	*Le gros traftic du grand Lion changé,*
There more share given in exchange upon accustomed waste	*La plus part tourne en pristine ruine*
Booty to the soldiers by reason of ravaged grape harvest:	*Proye aux souldars par pille vendenge:*
For will swear mountain & Suebi hot mist that burns plants.	*Par jura mont & Sueve bruine.*

Note: Originally listed as quatrain number 83 in Centurie II. During the Roman rule of Julius Caesar, when *Lyon* was known as *Lugdunum*, Gaul was seen as divided into three parts. One part was called the *De Bello Gallico*, which was land occupied by one of the *Suebi* tribes. Wikipedia states: "The *Suebi* of Julius Caesar's *De Bello Gallico* live in 100 cantons of arable land, of which

287

The Epic Poem Prophesied by Nostradamus

each canton retains ownership, parceling farm lots to individuals to use for up to one year. They wear animal skins, bathe in rivers, and prohibit wine. They allow trade only to dispose of their *booty* and otherwise have no goods to export." The *Jura Mountains* (as secondary reading of the lower case *jura*) form the border of France, Switzerland, and Germany, which is where the *Suebi* people lived.

Following victory from the Lion with them Lyon	Apres victoire du Lyon au Lyon
Above there mountain from WILL SWEAR Cut atom to enrich	Sus la montaigne de JURA Secatombe
Coming from calamity & brown ones seventh million	Delues & brodes septiesme million
Lyon, Elm at Mausoleum dead & tomb.	Lyon, Ulme à Mausol mort & tombe.

Note: Originally listed as quatrain number 34 in Centurie VIII. The southern Mediterranean coast of France is called the Golfed du Lion, rather than being spelled *Lyon*. This would make the second *Lyon* in line two more probable to be the city of *Lyon*, although a British victory in France would be more likely naval than ground. The city of *Lyon* is near the *Jura* Mountains. The word *secatombe* cannot yield the word *tombe* because that word is clearly stated in line four. In addition, the French word "*seccer*" is the verb meaning, "*to divide*." This leaves "*atombe*" to represent "*atom.*" with the German word "*atombombe*" meaning "*nuclear bomb*." The city of *Ulm* is surrounded by the forests and hills of the "*Swabian Alb*", which is also known as the *Swabian Jura*. The name "*Swabian*" is founded in *Suebi*, and the words "*Suebi, jura, mountain,* and *Lyon*" are found in quatrain II-83, linking this quatrain to that one.

Him black high tower where sea signal at what time will have tried	Le noir farouohe quand aura essayé
His public power bloody through death, weapon, arcs made towards ones:	Sa main sanguine par feu, fer, arcs tendus:
Most all them people will be so much afraid,	Trestout le peuple sera tant effraié:
To behold the more mighty ones by neck & foot ones hanged.	Voyr les plus grans par col & pieds pendus.

Note: Originally listed as quatrain number 47 in Centurie IV. The word "*farouohe*" is clearly spelled, in the 1568 Lyon edition, with two "*o*"s, and no "c." The tendency is to make it become "*farouche*," which might have an intentional secondary meaning. However, the word cleanly breaks into French words, "*Far-ou-ohé* ," which represents a *tower* designed to get one's attention. A "*Far*" is defined as a "high tower, or beacon at the mouth of a harbor, wherein continual lights are kept anights for the direction of sea-faring people; a lantern on a watchtower by the seaside."

Chapter 27 - A Greater Holocaust

Sun fervent within them larynx to close up surely,	*Soleil ardant dans le gosier coller,*
From kindred humane to sprinkle ground Tuscany:	*De sang humain arrouser terre Etrusque:*
End of a time pail of water, to persuade its sons to extend in length,	*Chef seille d'eaue, mener son filz filer,*
Lost liberty lady training country Turkic.	*Captive dame conduicte terre turque.*

Note: Originally listed as quatrain number 58 in Centurie IV. The word *"turque"* means *"Turkic* language," which is spoken by many nations around the Black Sea and the Caspian Sea, including Turkey, as well as Eastern Europe. In Old French, it meant simply, *"Turk."* Still, a reference to *"Turk"* is commonly accepted to be a reference to the warriors of the Ottoman Empire, who were under Turkish rule.

Those within them islands to tedious times besieged ones	*Ceulx dans les isles de long temps assiegés*
Will be receiving vigor violence against adversary ones:	*Prendront vigueur force contre ennemis:*
That they by reason of on the outside of a corpse from need of food debased ones,	*Ceux par dehors mors de faim profliges,*
Upon more substantial famine than ever will be thrust into.	*En plus grand faim que jamais seront mis.*

Note: Originally listed as quatrain number 71 in Centurie III. In present day French, the word *"ceux"* is the masculine-plural spelling of the word *"celui,"* with the feminine singular and plura being, *"celle, celles."* In Old French, the masculine plural was spelled *"ceulx,"* and the singular masculine spelled *"celuy."* This means that the first word of the quatrain is placing focus on the Old French spelling, which means the dropping of the "l" was not then correct. This means that the first word of line three, "Ceux", is not intended to be seen on a primary level as it appears (as if the new spelling was also acceptable). The spelling of *"Ceux"* is then best viewed as *"C'eux"*, meaning *"This them"* or *"That they."*

Principal commander to people of Fosse will hold gorge cut,	*Chef de Fossan aura gorge copee,*
By reason of him leader from the bloodhound & greyhound:	*Par le ducteur du limier & levrier:*
Them acted shepherded by those with the mountain Tarpean,	*Le faict patré par ceulx du mont Tarpee,*
Hardship upon Lion 13th of February.	*Saturne en Leo 13. de Fevrier.*

The Epic Poem Prophesied by Nostradamus

Note: Originally listed as quatrain number 96 in Centurie III. The idiom, "*coupe-gorge*" means whenever a military position is so poor the troops occupying it must either surrender, or be cut to pieces. Randle Cotgrave lists "*Cope gorgée*", and states, "instead of *Gorge coupée*." This use of words in this order means that meaning is important to realize, although secondary to the individual words written. *Tarpeia* was a Vestal Virgin thrown from the Capitoline hill rock by the Sabines. The *Tarpian* rock was where a temple to *Saturn* was built, and it represents a place of execution by being thrown off a steep cliff. Pope *Leo* XIII ruled until July 20, 1903, leading the Church into the 20th Century. He was elected pope on the 20th of *February*, 1878. However, the word "*leo*" is Latin, meaning "*lion*." The planet *Saturn* was last in the sign of *Leo* in September 2007. It will next go into that sign in late August 2034. This makes the symbolism play a more important role in interpretation.

Chapter 28

A Flase Pope

The End of the Papacy

One who them gods to Hannibal lower ones,	*Un qui les dieux d'Annibal infernaulx,*
Will act to begin again, terrorist to the humane ones:	*Fera renaistre, effrayeur des humains:*
Never more with loathing bred additional to tell records.	*Oncq' plus d'horreur ne plus dire journaulx.*
Whom set in the way will come through Babel to them Romans.	*Qu'avint viendra par Babel aux Romains.*

Note: Originally listed as quatrain number 30 in Centurie II. The contraction *qu'avint* is stating the third person plural (present indicative or subjunctive) for the verb *avier*, meaning, "to set in the way." The verb avier refers one to also see the word aviver, meaning, "to quicken, make living, put breath into, and give spirit unto. The name Babel is Biblical, and represents modern Iraq.

With the orator one will be relinquished him a realm,	*A logmyon sera laissé le regne,*
To the mighty Moon-goddess that which more will be from deed:	*Du grand Selin qui plus sera de faict:*
Through them Italians will stretch forth his mark,	*Par les Italies estendra son enseigne,*
Commanded will be by cunning counterfeit.	*Regisera par prudent contrefaict.*

Note: Originally listed as quatrain number 42 in Centurie VI. The Gaulish deity *Ogmios* has been used as a metaphor by some scholars to depict eloquence in the use of bardic practices (related to the poetic-historian Bards of Ireland and Scotland in particular), and thus simplified as an orator. The deity *Ogmios* was shown as a bald old man leading a group of men by chains connected from the tongue of *Ogmios* to the ears of the followers. As personified by capitalization, *Selin* is most likely a form of the word "Selene," meaning "Moon," from the goddess of the Moon's name. As such, *Selin* represents Islam.

The Epic Poem Prophesied by Nostradamus

Him produced in-bred condition to silver-tongued one,	*Le procree naturel dogmion,*
With September in unheard of before of the way to alienate from	*De sept à neuf du chemin destourner*
Has chief from loin & dear companion with the half man,	*A roy de longue & amy aumi hom,*
Owes to Navarre fortress to PAU to strike down.	*Doit à Navarre fort de PAU prosterner.*

Note: Originally listed as quatrain number 44 in Centurie VIII. Nostradamus also used the word "*ogmion*" (as "*l'ogmion*") in quatrain VI-42. As such, the mention here, to one "*from ogmios one*" (as "*d'ogmion*") can be a reference to an offspring to that orator. *Navarre* is autonomous region in Spain. The commune of *PAU* is 50 kilometers from Spain, and 100 kilometers from the Atlantic Ocean.

There great city will be thoroughly abandoned of all comfort,	*La grand cité sera bien desoleé,*
Of the inhabiting ones only one not will persevere:	*Des habitants un seul ny demoura:*
Defense kind, church, & virgin violated,	*Mur sexe, temple, & vierge violee,*
By weapon, fire, plague, canon of the law people will decease.	*Par fer, feu, peste, canon peuple mourra.*

Note: Originally listed as quatrain number 84 in Centurie III. The first three words, "*La grand cité*" is proof again that syntax is not to be read into *The Prophecies*, as the gender is not consistent (i.e.: should be *grande*). The word *canon* also meant the military weapon called a canon. This, however, would be secondary, as the word *fer* would include all types of weapons. While one can see *virgin* girls, or young women being *violated*, since the word *virgin* follows an ampersand (important *virgin*), which followed "*church*", the primary meaning is the *Virgin Mary*.

Will be manifest church glittering adorned,	*Apparoistra temple luisant orné,*
There full of lamps & big wax candle used in religious rites End & Port Armament.	*La lamp' & cierge à Borne & Bretueil.*
Considering the lamp him road intersection altered from,	*Pour la lucerne le canton destourné,*
At what time one will behold them substantial cock in the coffin.	*Quand on verra le grand coq au Cercueil.*

Note: Originally listed as quatrain number 5 in Centurie VIII. The word *coq* is said to also mean, "Saint Peter's fish." The term, "Saint Peter's fish", comes from the New Testament story

Chapter 28 - A False Pope

of Peter catching a fish with a coin in its mouth. This has been seen as a moniker for Tilapia fish. Line four can denote a Christian funeral, where the saint of the Vatican (Saint Peter's Square) has symbolically died, with Christians being the pall-bearers, *"at the coffin."*

To the faultless ones a kindred from widower them & virgin:	*Des innocens le sang de vefve & vierge:*
So much from hurtful ones acts for occasion themselves noble Requested	*Tant de maux fait par moyen se grand Roge*
Sacred ones likenesses household wines at burning big wax candle	*Saintz simulachres trempez en ardant cierge*
With terror doubt of not will perceive not any that fished.	*De frayeur crainte ne verra nul que boge.*

Note: Originally listed as quatrain number 80 in Centurie VIII. The main theme (line one) is a statement about Christianity, as a *kindred from* a *widower* (Joseph, who had other marriages, and other children), and his young pregnant wife-to-be, the *virgin* Mary.

To the people from congregation of Christians kindred will be largely extended,	*Des gens d'eglise sang sera espandu,*
As much as with the water even as substantial abundance:	*Comme de l'eau en si grand abondance:*
Likewise of one outstretched opportunity not will be quenched again	*Et d'un long temps ne sera restanché*
Or perhaps to the educated cleric ruined & moaning.	*Ve ve au clerc ruine & doleance.*

Note: Originally listed as quatrain number 98 in Centurie VIII. The main theme (line one) is pointing to the wide spread of Christianity, well beyond its European center in 1555. Line two is stating Christianity will spread as far as the earth's oceans will sail a ship. Line three is saying that the spread of a message of one man (Jesus) will never be repeated by another, as that opportunity has come, and he will only be outstretched on a cross one time. Line four ends with the word *"lamentation"*, which is the way Jeremiah saw the woes of the children of Israel and Judah, after they had let their educated clerics lead the people away from Yahweh. It is the Jews who do not believe in Jesus as the Messiah, and it will be they who will cast doubt to the world that Jesus was the only Savior. That will be the ruin that will repeat before Jesus returns.

The Epic Poem Prophesied by Nostradamus

By reason of stock unaccustomed, & Romans much removed,	*Par gent estrange, & de Romains loingtaine,*
Their noble city next unto water fortress put in turmoil:	*Leur grand cité apres eaue fort troublée:*
Daughter without, excess unlike an honor,	*Fille sans, trop different domaine,*
Seized principal, fittings of iron not to have remained roamed armed to do harm.	*Prins chief, ferreure n'avoir esté riblée.*

Note: Originally listed as quatrain number 54 in Centurie II. Line one is referencing the Holy *Roman* Empire, which had its more devout and strongest alliances in Eastern Europe ("*people foreign*"). Still, due to the Slavic breed of European being much different than that of the finery of Rome, the two worlds were much removed from one another.

With the head man of a party an Augur above him general there hand to thrust into	*Au roy l'Augur sus le chef la main mettre*
Will arrive to implore in regard of the accord Italian:	*Viendra prier pour la paix Italique:*
In there public power sinister will come to change a monarchy	*A la main gauche viendra changer le sceptre*
From Pope will grow Emperor quiet.	*De Roy viendra Empereur pacifique.*

Note: Originally listed as quatrain number 6 in Centurie V. The spelling Augur is Latin (French is Augure), making it elevated (along with the capitalization) to a holy level, one relative to Rome (the center of the latin language). The word "*augur*" means, "*augur*, soothsayer, seer," and is making the elevated statement of Biblical prophecy. The main theme is thus making a statement about a national leader (*president*, *prime minister*, etc.) will act as a prophet acted in the Bible, one prophesied to come again. This will lead *him* to command his *military leader* to move troops. The secondary theme identifies the place these troops will be moved as *Italy*.

By reason of there authority from three chiefs ones of the temple,	*Par la puissance des trois rois temporelz,*
Into another place will be placed him sacred seat,	*En autre lieu sera mis le sainct siege:*
Where there matter of the inclination bodily.	*Ou la substance de l'esprit corporel.*
Will be careless & in defense of true throne.	*Sera remys & receu pour vray siege.*

Note: Originally listed as quatrain number 99 in Centurie VIII. The main theme is placing focus on *three leaders of nations*, all of which are elected for a *temporary* number of years. These leaders

Chapter 28 - A False Pope

will have an impact in Italy, where the pope is *him* on the *holy see*.

From humane bundle nine will be placed in fenced ground.	*D'humain troupeau neuf seront mis à parc.*
To sentence & court separated ones:	*De jugement & conseil separés:*
Their fate will be devised by design at departure,	*Leur sort sera divisé en depart,*
Twenty, Death, Place at back of the skull cause of death proclaimed ones digressed ones.	*Kappa, Thita, Lambda mors bannis esgarés.*

Note: Originally listed as quatrain number 81 in Centurie I. The letter *Kappa* is the tenth letter of the Greek alphabet, and has a numerical value of twenty. The symbol for *Theta* was used by the Greeks to represent "*death*." The lowercase symbol for the Greek letter *lambda* is used to represent the radioactive half-life of isotopes in physics. It is the symbol for the radioactive decay constant. The word *Lambda* is also used to name the point at the back of the skull, along which the two parietal bones join with the occipital bone.

Brothers & sisters into diverse places captive ones,	*Freres & seurs en divers lieux captifz,*
Themselves will be lighting upon to transport as it were touching to the monarch:	*Se trouveront passer pres du monarque:*
Them to view with much earnestness his branches vehemently set upon ones,	*Les contempler ses rameaux ententifz,*
Troublesome to behold chin, front part of a thing, disgrace, the arrests.	*Desplaisant voir menton, front, nez, les marques.*

Note: Originally listed as quatrain number 20 in Centurie II. With the quatrain beginning with "*Brothers & sisters*", and seeing how that is clearly a statement of those serving the church (*Priests & nuns*), line two's use of "*monarch*" is then possible to identify as the Pope.

In writ will be a returning sacrificers,	*En bref seront de retour sacrifices,*
Resisting ones being thrust into with extreme torment:	*Contrevenants seront mys à martire:*
More not will be monks, abbots, nor those newly entered into a religious order ones,	*Plus ne seront moines, abbés, ne novices,*
The honey will be very much more dear than the comb of wax from the hive.	*Le miel sera beaucoup plus cher que cire.*

The Epic Poem Prophesied by Nostradamus

Note: Originally listed as quatrain number 44 in Centurie I. Line three is supporting the main theme of *"sacrificed ones,"* by naming *"monks"* and *"abbots"*, and those in *"religious orders."* This is an indication of Christian elements, but most related to those serving the Roman Catholic Church.

Them two grudge-bearing ones to Revenge united with,	Les deux malins de Scorpion conjoinct,
A high lord murdered within his hall:	Le grand seigneur meurtry dedans sa salle:
One who ruins others in the Church through him uncouth chief joining,	Peste à l'Eglise par le nouveau roy joint,
Them Europe low ground & the seven stars of the Great Bear.	L'Europe basse & Septentrionale

Note: Originally listed as quatrain number 52 in Centurie I. In traditional astrology there are *two malefics* (meaning: evil or malicious – same basic meaning as *maling*), which were the Greater Malefic (Saturn) and the Lesser Malefic (Mars). As for Mars, it rules the sign of *Scorpio*, with modern astrology assigning the planet Pluto to this association with Scorpio. It too could have this distinction as *maling*. Line one, as an astrological aspect, being an apparent *conjunction* between Saturn and Mars, can time the events of this quatrain. In that regard, Saturn will next enter *Scorpio* in October 2012, and Mars will conjoin Saturn in late August of the year 2014 (at 17 degrees Scorpio). Still, the main theme is primarily focused on *two evil* elements who have *joined* forced. With *The Revelation of John* telling of the coming of *scorpions*, this would be the stings from the soldiers of these *two evil* leaders.

From night in bed the highest person strangled,	De nuict dans lict le supresme estrangle,
Against more than needs to occupy just before battled, blonde elected,	Pour trop avoir subtourné, blond esleu:
By reason of three them sovereignty substituted carried to the end,	Par troys l'empire subroge exancle,
At death will place piece of paper, packet not perused.	A mort mettra carte, pacquet ne leu.

Note: Originally listed as quatrain number 39 in Centurie I. The use of *supresme*, where the *-esme* ending indicates a superlative (*-ist*), refers to a human being of the highest rank or dignity. It is one of a *bed*, who would be *strangled*, which is a theme seen in the murder of Pope John Paul I. The person of the main theme is either a King or a Pope, known by the use of *l'empire* in line three. Line two clarifies that it is a Pope, because they are *elected*, unlike Kings. As far as the story of *The Prophecies* is concerned, only one *blonde* Pope will occupy that position, being of Germanic roots. That is Pope John Paul II, which means line one is about the *strangling* of his predecessor, Pope John Paul I. Line four indicates that either of these popes will have left a note explaining the murder; but as line four is the supporting details of line two, it can be deduced that Pope John Paul II wrote something of an admission of complicity, which was not thoroughly read through, after his death.

Chapter 28 - A False Pope

Him heavy cruel person from city expelled,	*Le gros mastin de cité dechassé,*
Will be wearied with an alien league of friendship,	*Sera fasché de l'estrange alliance:*
After in the open pieces of ground to use him stag hunted after,	*Apres aux champs avoir le cerf chassé,*
The wolf & The Bear itself will be giving defiance.	*Le loup & L'Ours se donront defiance.*

Note: Originally listed as quatrain number 4 in Centurie V. The use of animal symbolism has to focus on the capitalization of *The Bear* being Russia, with *The wolf* representing Rome. This becomes a strange alliance between Christianity and Atheism.

People without principal commander of Spain & to Italy,	*Peuple sans chef d'Espaigne & d'Italie,*
Cause of destruction, ruined ones within the Peninsula:	*Mors, profligés dedans le Cherrennosse:*
Their spoken treacherously dealt with through quick folly.	*Leur dict trahy par legiere folie.*
The race to float for everything in there across.	*Le sang nager par tout à la traverse.*

Note: Originally listed as quatrain number 68 in Centurie III. It is easy to mistake the use of *Cherrenosse* as the Greek spelling, "*Chersonesos*", which many would take as a reference to an ancient Greek colony with that name, near what today is Sevastopol, Crimea. This would be wrong, as would one thinking it meant Gallipoli, Thrace, the *peninsula* at the Dardanelles. The Greek word means, "dry land island", or "island of dry land." In short, the word means a major (capitalized) *Peninsula*. This would then describe *Italy*, which is stated in line one, following an ampersand (significator of importance to follow).

Before city with them towards to overthrow country,	*Devant cité de l'insubre contree,*
September year ones will act a siege being bound unto placed:	*Sept ans fera le siege devant mis:*
Him very-lofty Pope there unto will cause his entrance,	*Le tresgrand Roy y fera son entree,*
Warned to appear, then free out of from its enemies.	*Cité, puis libre hors de ses ennemis.*

Note: Originally listed as quatrain number 15 in Centurie VII. The use of a lower case *insubre* makes it difficult not to translate it into the upper case, as the ancient place "*Insubria*." This area is synonymous with Lombardy, and Milan, Italy, and was originally settled by tribes from French Gaul. They did not name themselves "*Insubrians*," the Romans did, because they were a threat to

The Epic Poem Prophesied by Nostradamus

Rome's control of Italy. Thus, the lower case forces one to understand the root of the name, as those with the potential to overthrow one; and the *Insubrians* helped Hannibal do that, when the Carthaginians invaded Italy by crossing the Alps. On a secondary level, it also points to the place of interest (to be overthrown) as Italy, with places greatly effected being in the Lombardy region.

Will be evident to them as it were touching with Brescia	*Apparoistra au pres de Buffalorre*
Him of importance & tall one with another within Milan	*L'hault & procere entre dedans Milan*
An abbot of Time together with those to sanctified mouth with pronounced lips	*L'abbe de Foix avec ceux de saint morre*
Will be forging there cunning trick the able ones in villa.	*Feront la forbe abillez en vilan.*

Note: Originally listed as quatrain number 12 in Centurie VIII. The name *Buffalora* is both relative to a Swiss Alp, in the Italian-speaking region, near the Italian border, while it is also the name of a pass to travel between the countries. *Foix* is a commune in southern France, which was once its own autonomous principality, near the border with Spain and Andorra. Saint Christopher was called a Greek name that means, "dog-faced." There is also a French saint, name Guinefort, who was a dog that saved a baby's life, only to be killed wrongfully, by the father of the baby thinking the dog had killed the baby.

Abundance from tribunals wealth from the sales of booty & divisions of military personnel	*Renfort de sieges manubis & maniples*
Converted ones them received into religious order & occurrences past over a notice given by a priest to the parishioners,	*Changez le sacre & passe sur le prosne,*
Seized & lost liberty ones not resolved them near ones tripled ones	*Prins & captifs n'arreste les prez triples*
More through bottom ones put elevated, set at the throne.	*Plus par fonds mis eslevé, mis au trosne.*

Note: Originally listed as quatrain number 73 in Centurie VII. Source for the Old French is the 1605 Lyon edition, based on the 1568 edition, but including additional Centuries (XI & XII), along with some Presages. At the end of Century VII, the publisher introduces four additional quatrains as, "*OTHER QUATRAINS drawn from 12 under the Centurie seventh: of which upon had been rejected 8 which themselves are found are Centuries previous.*" This identification of four, being with eight confirmed to be from Nostradamus, acts to confirm these as legitimate for being considered also from Nostradamus. In some other editions, the word *preztriples* appears in line three. The 1605 edition shows this as two words, "*prez triples,*" which would translate as "*near ones triples.*"

Chapter 28 - A False Pope

Pope will obtain this that he had longings for so much,	*Roy trouvera ce qu'il desiroit tant,*
In as much as him Prelate will be rebuked with displeasure:	*Quant le Prelat fera reprins à tort:*
Again rubbed to the militarycommander them will restore evil satisfied,	*Responce au duc le rendra mal content,*
Who within Milan will put many to death.	*Qui dans Milan mettra plusieurs à mort.*

Note: Originally listed as quatrain number 31 in Centurie VI. In French, the combination, "*à tort*", as appears in line two, has its own reading, as "wrongfully, unjustly, and unworthily". Nostradamus used the word spelled as "*responce*" in two other quatrains (I-37 and I-38), with the use in I-38 also capitalized as the first word in a line (line two). The word is rooted in the word "*poncer,*" meaning "to rub, or polish with pumice." As one word [English, from Old French], *malcontent* means, "someone dissatisfied with existing conditions."

For them desert ones to place, at liberty, & savage,	*Par les desers de lieu, libre, & farouche,*
Will come to offend through nephew of the great Pontiff:	*Viendra errer nepveu du grand Pontife:*
Felled in September together with that ones descendants of,	*Assommé à sept avecques lourde souche,*
Through those who following will be seizing him cup.	*Par ceux qu'apres occuperont le cyphe.*

Note: Originally listed as quatrain number 82 in Centurie VI. To make *nepueu* become *nephew*, one has to pretend that the first "u" is really an "h." I struggle with this, since "nephew" was spelled either "*neveu*" or "*nepheu*." The simple anagram explanation is to create "*p-neveu*," where "*p*" acts as the abbreviated form of "*par*."

Land of Rome who interprets presage,	*Terroir Romain qu'interpretoit augure,*
For nation of France by reason of too much will be put in turmoil:	*Par gent Gauloyse par trop sera vexée:*
More people Celtic will fear the clock,	*Mais nation Celtique craindra l'heure,*
North Wind, fleet mightily long way off him to use themselves placed.	*Boreas, classe trop loing l'avoir possée.*

Note: Originally listed as quatrain number 99 in Centurie II. The main theme is referencing Italy, and in particular *Rome*. In a modern sense, one who interprets presage, or divination, could be one who interprets the prophecies of the *Holy Bible*, through the signs that match those stated to

The Epic Poem Prophesied by Nostradamus

modern times. The lean on the usage is away from holy means, and more towards pagan forms of prediction. Line two is adding to the main theme of problems in Italy, by stating that *France* too would suffer on its own, and (from knowing the story line of The Prophecies) in Italy too. Line three is placing the majority of the focus on Great Britain, which has historic connections with France. They too will have their future told in these stories. Finally, the *North Wind* is Russia. The comma separates them from a prediction of turmoil, but places them as the root cause. They will sell *fleets* to one far off, and let them do their work towards revenge.

The business of long continuance themselves will make an absolute end of,	*L'œuvre ancienne se paracheuera,*
With them house itself will tumble down a lofty hurtfully overthrown:	*Du toict cherra sur le grand mal ruyne:*
Innocent acted dead one will charge with a crime:	*Innocent faict mort on accusera:*
Wicked put on ship, underbrush in there blasted with the hot mist.	*Nocent caiché, taillis à la bruyne.*

Note: Originally listed as quatrain number 37 in Centurie VI. The word, "*Oeuvre*", is further explained as a place in a church, as being "where the parish church wardens sit together on festival days." There have been 13 popes going by the name of *Innocent*. In the 1611 French-English Dictionary by Randle Cotgrave, the listing for "*Caiche*" states, "As the Italian, "*Catzo*"; membre viril." The idiom, "*membre viril*" means "male organ", where "*viril*" means, "manly". In Italian, the word "*cazzo*" (pronounced "*catzo*") is [at best] slang, where "prick" is the least vulgar translation possible. However, *caiche* (unaccented) is a varriant of *quaiche*, which is a small boat.

An evil Roman Emperor youthful inwardly them three chimney ones	*Le Neron jeune dans les trois cheminees*
Will act to young servants sparkling ones in regard of to desire fervently to push forth,	*Fera de paiges vifz pour ardoir getter,*
Blessed who long way off will be from such ones induced ones,	*Heureux qui loing sera de telz meneez,*
Three of its lineage them being death to lie in wait for.	*Trois de son sang le seront mal guetter.*

Note: Originally listed as quatrain number 53 in Centurie IX. The main theme's use of a *Roman Emperor*, followed by the word *cheminees*, connects the two to a series of popes, whose elections are announced through smoke from a *chimney*. With the number *Three* being repeated and capitalized, the *trinity* is certainly implied, while physically indicating *three* popes, who will oversee the end of the Roman Catholic Church. The first of these is Pope John Paul II, who was *young* when Pope John Paul I was murdered.

Chapter 28 - A False Pope

Hunch-backed will be elected by him body of counsel,	*Bossu sera esleu par le conseil,*
More hideous deformed creature on earth not perceived,	*Plus hideux monstre en terre n'apperceu,*
Him fling meaning will break to pieces the sight,	*Le coup voulant crevera l'œil,*
A wicked fellow with the Pope in regard of the religious accepted of.	*Le traistre au Roy pour fidele receu.*

Note: Originally listed as quatrain number 41 in Centurie III. The main theme statement is of a Pope being *elected* by the Papal conclave, due to the use of *Roy* in line four. This pope selected will be severely *deformed*, including having a seriously *Hunched* back. Line two's use of *monster* will be supported by other quatrains and their similar verbiage.

From darkness Christianity will be meditating of to hold solemn promise,	*De nuict soleil penseront avoir veu,*
At what time him swine to some degree man one will regard:	*Quand le pourceau demy homme on verra:*
Sounded very harshly, sung in meter hung with a clapper, year heaven to beat at received:	*Bruict, chant bataille, au ciel battre aperceu:*
Both beasts ones without feeling or reason in speech many will implore.	*Et bestes brutes a parler l'on orra.*

Note: Originally listed as quatrain number 64 in Centurie I. The word "*chante*" can mean a "*roundelay*." A "*roundelay*" is a song with a regularly repeating refrain.

Great army of men conduit for youth,	*Grand exercite conduict par jouvenceau,*
Themselves will grow to cause to pass at the hands of the enemies:	*Se viendra rendre aux mains des ennemis:*
More an aged man not possess with the half swine,	*Mais le viellard n'ay au demi pourceau,*
Will make Fishnet & himself Mason to be friends.	*Fera Chalon & Mascon estre amis.*

Note: Originally listed as quatrain number 69 in Centurie III. It is important to realize that the alternative translations for the word *conduict* are "gutter" or "trench of stone, whereby water or the course of a river is turned." Line one's main theme is about *youth* finding a way to "channel" their energies towards future successes, through military experience. Line three seems to be referencing both Jews and Muslims, who stay away from eating "unclean meat", or *pork*. This theme makes the

The Epic Poem Prophesied by Nostradamus

two "places" of line four be better translated as the meanings the words carry.

At what time an animal with a man domestic,	*Quand l'animal à l'homme domestique,*
Following noble ones punishments & leaps will grow to converse,	*Apres grans peines & saults viendra parler:*
A thunderbolt in virgin will be as evil doing,	*Le foudre à vierge sera si maleficque,*
To country taken, & held in suspense on species of a thing.	*De terre prinse & suspendue en l'air.*

Note: Originally listed as quatrain number 44 in Centurie III. The main theme of this quatrain is focusing on the "*domestication*" of *animal with man*, through being "familiar" and "private" with one another. The word *domestic* means, "of or involving the home or family."

Third part owes from the bottom with the best will resemble,	*Tiers doit du pied au premier semblera,*
Has one uncouth singular ruler of humble importance	*A un nouveau Monarque de bas haut,*
That which Pisa & Lucca Tyrant will usurp by force	*Qui Pyse & Luques Tyran occupera,*
With the preceding to set right an offence.	*Du precedant corriger le deffaut.*

Note: Originally listed as quatrain number 5 in Centurie IX. The city of *Pisa* is in the Tuscany region of Italy, on the Ligurian Sea – Mediterranean coast. The town of *Lucca* is less than 10 miles from *Pisa*.

Elected of Pope, with chosen will be this mocked,	*Esleu en Pape d'esleu sera mocque,*
Unlooked for quick moved nimble & timorous,	*Subit soudain esmeu prompt & timide,*
For excess virtuous pleasing in to die this incensed	*Par trop bon doulx à mourir provocqué*
Fear abolished there night to its altar death guided.	*Crainte estainte la nuit de sa mort guide.*

Note: Originally listed as quatrain number 12 in Centurie X. This is again related to the *Hunchedback Pope elected*, as seen in the main theme statement of quatrain III-41. He will be *mocked* for his deformity.

Chapter 28 - A False Pope

Inwardly almost nothing will relate to no purpose without feeling or reason easily broken,	Dans peu dira faulce brute fragile,
To lowest part of into haughty raised quickly at hand:	De bas en hault eslevé promptement:
Moreover at moment treacherous & subject unto falling.	Puis en instant desloyale & labile.
That which born Verona will enjoy power.	Qui de Veronne aura gouvernement.

Note: Originally listed as quatrain number 12 in Centurie I. Due to Old French publications often using a "*u*" to denote a "*v*" in a text, the word written in line two, "*esleué*", is translated as, "*eslevé*". However, the "*u*" is present in the word "*esleuë*," meaning, "elected, chosen, culled, or picked out." The use of the accented "*é*" is how one knows "*eslevé*" it written. Still, in a secondary sense, the "*elevated*" comes by having been "picked out". *Verona* is in the Venito region, 75 miles west of Venice. This makes the statement that the one elected is in Italy, which means a pope.

At what time to them crusaders one found from understanding sedition	Quand des croisez un trouvé de sens trouble
Upon seat of the holy will observe one bull having horned	En lieu du sacre verra un bœuf cornu
Through virgin swine one's place then will be accomplished,	Par vierge porc son lieu lors sera comble,
By reason of chief more continuation not will be supported.	Par roy plus ordre ne sera soustenu.

Note: Originally listed as quatrain number 90 in Centurie VIII. From the book, *The Two Babylons* (Rev. Alexander Hislop), a comparison is made showing how the Vatican seems to be a model of an ancient Assyrian form of worship, under King Nimrod and his wife. In his book he makes reference to Cronus (Saturn) being "the horned one," and comparable to Nimrod. In this argument the author stated that "* Hence the *"Horned bull"* signified *"The Mighty Prince."* The "mighty prince" is reference to a god. This comparison was showing Rome as the second Babylon, of which *The Revelation* wrote.

Four year ones them seat of justice some few rightly will hold,	Quatre an le siege quelque peu bien tiendra,
One will occur suddenly libidinous of life:	Un surviendra libidineux de vie:
Ravenna & Pisa, neither Verona will be bearing up,	Ravenne & Pyse, Veronne soustiendront,
Because to raise there sign of the cross to Pope spited.	Pour eslever la croix de Pape envie.

The Epic Poem Prophesied by Nostradamus

Note: Originally listed as quatrain number 26 in Centurie VI. When one realizes that elected officials, like the President of the United States (and other nations as well), are chosen to serve *four-year* terms, them become *"four year ones"*. However, with each word seen separately first, the main theme begins talking about *four* who will serve for *years*. There is a French commune named *"Veronne,"* but that would bear little weight in understanding line three. The use of *"Veronne"* in quatrain I-12 links this quatrain to that series.

There sanctity too much supposed & leading aside,	*La saincteté trop faincte & seductiue,*
Having the company of one tongue well spoken:	*Accompagné d'une langue diserte:*
The warned to appear ancient & Parma mightily soon coming,	*La cité vieille, & Parme trop hastive,*
Florence & Siena will be giving back more abandoned of all people ones.	*Florence & Sienne rendront plus desertes.*

Note: Originally listed as quatrain number 48 in Centurie VI. The place (*There*) where *sanctity* is a certainty is a "holy *city*." For Christians, outside of Jerusalem, that would be Rome, or the Vatican. In the story of Nostradamus, the Vatican is *"too much forged"*, along that line since the murder of Pope John Paul I. Line two then becomes relative to *"Ogmios"*, which means someone proposing to send French troops into Italy. The *city* of *Parma* was founded in the Bronze Age, making it one of the *oldest* settlements in Italy. *Florence & Siena* are both in the Tuscany region, on the Tyrrhenian Sea coast, south of Parma.

Beyond the Alps great army will transport,	*Dela les Alpes grande armée passera,*
A few owing to be born monster by reason of void:	*Un peu devant naistre monstre vapin:*
Monstrous & unlooked for will alter,	*Prodigieux & subit tournera,*
Them great Tuscany in its place more a match as a result.	*Le grand Tosquan à son lieu plus propin.*

Note: Originally listed as quatrain number 20 in Centurie V. The questions of this quatrain are the two words with "p"s generated via solving mystery words as simple anagrams. which seem to work as anagrams, where the "*p*" equals "*par*", both in French and Latin. The *monster* could be a nuclear weapon being used, since *army* (in line one) is a military term.

After him King to them this stretch to inquire after ones talking,	*Apres le Roy du soucq querres parlant,*
The island Amorica them will hold in disesteem,	*Lisle Harmorique le tiendra à mespris,*

Chapter 28 - A False Pope

Some ones years principal parts of a matter eating away at one & depriving	Quelques ans bons rongeant un & pillant
By reason of lordly cruelty to the island changing respect for things.	Par tyrannie a lisle changeant pris.

Note: Originally listed as quatrain number 36 in Centurie X. The word *soucq* can be read as *c'souque*, where it states "this pig ear that". This is because the word *sou* is a correct spelling for *souse*, which is a pig's ear. In that case, the "*c*" may be seen as accented to phonetically sound like an "s." This would create *sous-que*, or pig ear that. *The island* would appear to be Great Britain, but the *pig* reference can make it also related to Sicily or one of the prison *islands*. The French word *harmonique* is only one letter off, meaning "harmonious." It therefore is read as *Armorique*, which is *Amorica*. That is the northwest area of ancient Gaul, now known as Brittany. However, it is tantalizingly close to phonetically being representative of America. The Gaulish origin of the name is said to mean that "Aremorica (*Armorica*) is not a 'country name', but a word that describes a type of geographic region that is by the sea."

Beneath pretense for a matter feigned to seven heads shaven ones	Soubz couleur fainte de sept testes rasees
Will be spread abroad ones wayward spies:	Serons semés divers explorateurs:
Pit & wells with poisons sprinkled ones,	Puys & fontaines de poysons arrousées,
To the mighty of Genoa mild ones ones to seize upon.	Au fort de Gennes humains devorateurs.

Note: Originally listed as quatrain number 66 in Centurie IV.

Within a well being devised ones them bones,	Dedans le puys seront trouvés les oz,
Will be an incest delegated through the stepmother:	Sera l'incest commis par la maratre:
The condition of things converted one will send for this talk of the people & agreements,	L'estat changé on querra bruit & loz,
Both will have Mars attending in regard of one's fate.	Et aura Mars attendant pour son astre.

Note: Originally listed as quatrain number 50 in Centurie VI. The use of the word, "*bruict*", is repeated in quatrain I-64, where it begins line three, as a capitalized word.

The Epic Poem Prophesied by Nostradamus

By head shaving will arrive quite unseemly to pick out,	*Par teste rase viendra bien mal eslire,*
More than his accusation assaulted an enemy born upheld will pass forth:	*Plus que sa charge ne porte passera:*
Even as mighty extreme wrath & fury will cause to speak,	*Si grande fureur & rage fera dire,*
Who has fire & race all kind will carve.	*Qu'a feu & sang tout sexe trenchera.*

Note: Originally listed as quatrain number 60 in Centurie V. Quatrain IV-66 states, "*testes rasees*", in the main theme (line one), with line one here stating "*teste rase*". Line three's supporting details to this quatrain's main theme of one with a *shaved head*, says he is *mighty*, and his *extreme wrath* will have been displayed in the (line two) *accusation* that he masterminded an *assault* on *an enemy*. This then identifies Osama bin Laden, and then states that *fury* will be generated whenever he sends in a new tape-recorded message, where he is moved *to speak*.

There widow sanctified conceiving them new ones,	*La vefve saincte entendant les nouvelles,*
With her branches put pestered in spirit & disquieted:	*De ses rameaux mis en perplex & trouble:*
Which will be this used to quiet the debates,	*Qui sera duict appaiser les querelles,*
For one's eager pursuit from the shearing ones will make heaped full of.	*Par son pourchas de razes fera comble.*

Note: Originally listed as quatrain number 29 in Centurie VI. This is certainly a quatrain about troubles that the branches of Christianity will face in the future. Line four brings to mind the nursery rhyme, "Bah bah black sheep, have you any wool? Yes sir, yes sir, three bags full." This then shows the *troubles* to be on the sheep of the flocks, with their *shearing ones* being the cause for pestered spirits.

Him great brought taken in war to foreign country,	*Le grand mené captif d'estrange terre,*
From gold chained to the Pope THIS BEATER offered:	*D'or enchainé au roy CHYREN offert:*
That which in Ausonia, Milan will lose there war,	*Qui dans Ausone, Milan perdra la guerre,*
As well all its army put to fire & with weapon.	*Et tout son ost mis à feu & à fer.*

Note: Originally listed as quatrain number 34 in Centurie IV. The all-caps name CHYREN is

Chapter 28 - A False Pope

certainly open for debate, as to how the letters can be arranged to find meaning.

Chapter 29

Converting Christians to Islam

France is Punished

Government French you will be thoroughly transformed,	*Regne Gauloys tu seras bien changé,*
Into state unaccustomed east wind removed from one place unto another them jurisdiction:	*En lieu estrange est translaté l'empire:*
Upon another ones customs & laws will be ones ordered,	*En autres mœurs & loix seras rangé,*
Roan, & Public records involving country you will be forging fully to the worse.	*Roan, & Chartres te feront bien du pire.*

Note: Originally listed as quatrain number 49 in Centurie III. The word Roan is English, either for a sheepskin-type leather, or a bay horse with gray and white. The root of the word is linked to the Spainish word *roano*. If this is the case, then the *foreign place translated* would be identified as Spain. Ironically, the French word for *roan* is rouen, which many want to replace in the test, making it become representative of either the French cities Roanne or Rouen. The French city *Chartres* would be closer to Roanne, France.

In the kingdom great with the dominion domineering,	*Au regne grand du regne regnant,*
Through force of arms them mighty ones gates of brass	*Par force d'armes les grands portes darain*
Will cause to betray the head man of a party & provisional governor putting together,	*Fera ouvrir le roy & duc joignant,*
Harbor demolished ship at depth day calm.	*Port demoly nef à fons jour serain.*

Note: Originally listed as quatrain number 80 in Centurie X. Line two's use of portes d'arain, or "gates of brass," comes from Psalm 107:16, cross-referenced with Isaiah 45:2, where both state, "For he has shattered gates of bronze (or brass) and cut bars of iron asunder." The Psalm goes on to talk about sinking and drowning, which matches the *Harbor demolished* with a *ship at depth* verbiage of line four.

Chapter 29 - Converting Christians to Islam

Him great This Rammer himself to take possession of Avignon,	Le grand Chyren soy saisir d'Avignon,
From my Rome them to be in sweetness full of extreme despitefulness	De Romme letres en miel plein d'amertume
Writing ambassador to depart from to no-Chain,	Letre ambassade partir de Chanignon,
Carpentras reward for provincial governor black red fleeced.	Carpentras pris par duc noir rouge plume.

Note: Originally listed as quatrain number 41 in Centurie IX. Nostradamus used the word, "*Chyren*", on six occasions, including here (quatrains II-79, IV-34, VI-27, VI-70, and VIII-54, being the other five). The word is always capitalized, with two uses in all-caps, and it appears with the word "*Selin*" twice. The commune of *Avignon* is where the French papal castle was built, to house several popes in the 14th century. If the word *Chanignon* is an anagram meaning, "*no Chain*," this would denote Marseille, France, who's protective *chain* (myth) will have been broken, or found to be *non*-existent. *Carpentras* is in the Vaucluse department, north of Marseille and close to *Avignon*, only a few miles to the west-northwest.

A year that Saturn upon water will be united,	L'an que Saturne en eau sera conjoinct,
With that Foundation, him Chief mighty & forcible:	Avecques Sol, le Roy fort & puissant:
In Will have replaced & Mineral springs will be admitted of & smeared,	A Reims & Aix sera receu & oingt,
After conquests will crush faultless ones.	Apres conquestes meurtrira innocens.

Note: Originally listed as quatrain number 86 in Centurie IV. *Saturn* will next enter a *water* sign (Scorpio) on October 6, 2012. *Saturn* will leave Scorpio on September 15, 2018, meaning it will be in a water sign for almost six *years*. An alternate translation of line one is, "*The year that Lead on water will be conjoined*". This would match the astrological aspect, as a naval attack. The word *Aix* in the name of French communes (there are several) is said to come from the Latin word "*aquae*," meaning "*waters*." The word *Aix* denotes the presence of "mineral springs." This usages supports the main theme's use of "*water*." However, perhaps the most prominent commune of such is *Aix-en-Provence*, which is best known simply as *Aix*. It is in the Bouches-du-Rhone department, which includes Marseille. Marseille is not far due south of *Aix*. *Reims* is in northeastern France, in the Champagne region, in the Marne department. This would make *Reims* far from *Aix*, and make little continuity appear. However, it *Reims* is seen as an anagram, *Remis*, it states, "*Will have replaced*," which becomes a reference to a powerful action, while also representing a change of *Foundation*, as well as (when Sol is seen as representative of *Christianity*) a religious change.

The Epic Poem Prophesied by Nostradamus

Will be commissioner account to anoint in duchy	*Sera commis contre oingdre aduché*
Of Salter & made holy White & Beggar business	*De Saulne & sainct Aulbin & Beli' œuvre*
To pave with marble from towers far off plucked	*Paver de marbre de tours loing espluché*
Not Blockhead branch to resist & end of a time to workmanship.	*Non Bleteram resister & chef d'oeuvre.*

Note: Originally listed as quatrain number 36 in Centurie VIII. The accented version of *"conté"* means, "the region assigned to an Earl, or an Earldom." A *duchy* is a territory ruled by an appointed governor, known as a duke. Seeing *Saulne* as *l'Saune*, or *the Salter* makes line two begin with a reference from Jesus, that believers were the "salt of the earth." This implies Jesus is *the Salter* who keeps "taste" in believers. There are two communes in France named *Aubin*, one in Aveyron, and the other in Pyrenees-Atlantic (both are departments). *Saint Aubin* was a monk in France, later becoming the Bishop of Angers (northwest France), and who also playing an important role in the Counsel of Orleans (529 AD). The word Bleteram is phonetically English for *Bleat ram*. This would symbolize a male sheep calling the flock to be warned.

The Easterner will deliver out of his seat of justice.	*L'Oriental sortira de son siege.*
To hold on course the mountains Apennines to behold there France:	*Passer les monts Apennins voir la Gaule:*
To strike through from the sky them waters & snow,	*Transpercera du ciel les eaux & neige:*
Both each will smite with one's big rod.	*Et chascun frappera de sa gaule.*

Note: Originally listed as quatrain number 29 in Centurie II. This quatrain links to quatrain V-54 as both quatrains present a capitalized *Transpercera*, along with two uses of *"gaule."* The main theme of quatrain V-54 states two *Eastern* places; and that quatrain is telling of Osama bin Laden. Thus, he is *The Easterner* of this quatrain. In the lower case, "oriental" also can mean, "bright and clear." The Roman area designated as *"Gaul"* (Gallia) included what is now *France*, Belgium, and parts of The Netherlands, northern Italy, Switzerland, and Germany. Thus, *Gaul* is Western Europe, but mainly associated with *France*. The use of *"ciel les eaux,"* can be seen as a reference to timing, where the Sun is in a period of time in a *water* sign, meaning, *"heaven of the waters"*. This would match the main theme of quatrain IV-86, where *"Saturn upon water"* means, "during a time when Saturn is in Scorpio" (as the next example of when Saturn goes into *water* - Oct. 6, 2012). The use of the lower case *gaule* is a biblical reference to prophecy, where it has been said the God will smash to pieces evildoers, like a *"rod* unto a potter's vase." *Rods* that *strike through the air* are now called rockets and missiles.

Chapter 29 - Converting Christians to Islam

A King with the Horns of a deer in Avignon to reign	*Le Roy de Bloys dans Avignon regner*
One different from the former faith ones him people the monopoly,	*Une autre foys le peuple emonopolle,*
Within the Rose-born through walls will act to moisten	*Dedans le Rosne par murs fera baigner*
Until at five the later in rank nearby to Refusing.	*Jusques à cinq le dernier pres de Nolle.*

Note: Originally listed as quatrain number 38 in Centurie VIII. The commune of *Blois* is on the Loire River, between Orleans and Tours. The city of *Avignon* is known for its *Palace du Pape*, or the "Palace of the *Pope*," where a French papal center thrived in the 13th century. The transforming of *Blois* into *l'Bois*, and thus "*the Horns of a deer*", makes this quatrain link to quatrain VIII-90, where a religious rite is performed by one with *horns*. This same theme threads to quatrain IX-21, where *Blois* is also found. Line three is some form of "baptism" gone wrong, where line four indicates a major individual or group "*Refusing*" to allow this act *to moisten* be performed on them.

In a year that one eye upon France will hold sovereign authority over,	*En l'an qu'un œil en France regnera,*
There low will be at a thoroughly offensive molestation:	*La court sera à un bien facheux trouble:*
Him lofty with the Horns of a deer ones paramour will massacre,	*Le grand de Bloys son amy tuera,*
The realm thrust into evil & reverent awe of twice as much.	*Le regne mis en mal & doute double.*

Note: Originally listed as quatrain number 55 in Centurie III. The use of "*qu'un œil*" in line one is not a reference to someone with "one eye." It is a reference to the "*all-seeing eye*," which is the *eye* of God. It means that God will see the *offensive* actions going on in *France*.

In place of the great who will be condemned,	*En lieu du grand qui sera condemné,*
To prison without his lover in her place:	*De prison hors son amy en sa place:*
The hope Trojan upon six month joined, death ship,	*L'espoir Troyen en six moys joinct, mort nay,*
Him Foundation at the crematory urn will be taken flows of water into ice.	*Le Sol à l'urne seront prins fluves en glace.*

Note: Originally listed as quatrain number 52 in Centurie VI. The *month* that represents the number *six*, in the Roman calendar, is August. The first month is the month spring begins, in March.

The Epic Poem Prophesied by Nostradamus

A chief with the Horns of a deer in Avignon to govern,	*Le roy de Bloys dans Avignon regner,*
To Amboise & spread abroad will arrive them outstretched with the Indre	*Damboise & seme viendra le long de Lyndre*
Talon in Poitiers holy women flying ones to destroy	*Ongle à Poytiers sainctes aisles ruiner*
Being bound unto brave men.	*Devant boni.*

Note: Originally listed as quatrain number 52 in Centurie VIII. This quatrain is said to be missing part of line 4, as if censored. If so, it was published in that condition, as it appears in the 1568 Lyon edition with a period mark following "*boni.*" Certainly, because "*Lyndre*" does not rhyme with "*boni,*" it is the only quatrain without a complete ABAB rhyme scheme. Line one of this quatrain is the same as line one in quatrain VIII – 38, with the one exception being the lower case presentation of "*roy*" here. The commune of *Amboise* is in the department of *Indre*-et-Loire, on the banks of the Loire River. It is about 20 miles southwest of *Blois*. The town of *Poitiers* is on the Clain River in west central France, in the department of Vienne, northeast of Bordeaux. The *boni* was a political faction of the late Roman Empire. Since a period follows *boni*, making line four become a short and abrupt statement, the possibility of *boni* being an abbreviation (due to the period mark) must also be considered.

Within Avignon everything an end of time to them most supreme power,	*Dans Avignon tout le chef de l'empire,*
Will act final judgment of a court in defense of Paris abandoned of all comfort:	*Fera arrest pour Paris desolé:*
Three darts cast will hold him Hannibal-like wrath	*Tricast tiendra l'Annibalique ire*
Lyon through conversion will be ill comforted.	*Lyon par change sera mal consolé.*

Note: Originally listed as quatrain number 93 in Centurie III. The use of "*chef*" and "*Avignon*" in the main theme matches the use of *Avignon* and some other word representative of a "*chef*" in the main themes of quatrains VIII-38, VIII-52, and IX-41. The word *Lyon* can mean the city of *Lyon* or be representative of the British *Lion*.

There city ancient from past year prayed unto made,	*La cité antique d'antenoree forge,*
More born enabling him violent governor to support:	*Plus ne pouvant le tyran supporter:*
Them again a flat large furnace devised at the temple to slit throat,	*Le manche fainct au temple couper gorge,*

Chapter 29 - Converting Christians to Islam

Them his own owns a people in death will grow anew budded.	*Les siens le peuple à mort viendra bouter.*

Note: Originally listed as quatrain number 76 in Centurie VI. Line one appears to state it is about a "*city old*" with an "*antenna made.*" This would be Paris, and its Eiffel Tower. Unfortunately, the word "*d'antenoree*" is not a word meaning, "antenna." Still, Paris can be seen on a secondary level of interpretation.

From the main ones of city rebelled from,	*Des principaux de cité rebellée,*
Who will be keeping fortress in defense of liberty to have again:	*Qui tiendront fort pour liberté ravoir:*
To chop to pieces males unfruitful put among,	*Detrencher masles infelice meslee,*
Shrieks howling ones in Nantes miserable to see.	*Crys hurlemens à Nantes piteux voir.*

Note: Originally listed as quatrain number 33 in Centurie V. *Nantes* is in western France, near the Atlantic Ocean, on the banks of the Loire River. This city is listed in four quatrains (the other three are: I-20, IV-46, and VI44), with all making statements of impending doom and destruction, particularly by surprise involving activities at sea.

Chapter 30

Moors Coming Home

Spain is Converted

No person or thing of them Spain anymore to an ancient France	*Nul de l'Espaigne mais de l'antique France*
Neither will be chosen because a quaking small boat,	*Ne sera esleu pour le tremblant nacelle,*
With the enemy will be forged trust,	*A l'ennemy sera faicte fiance,*
That which inwardly one's realm will be one that ruins others unmercifully.	*Qui dans son regne sera peste cruelle.*

Note: Originally listed as quatrain number 49 in Centurie V. The main theme is addressing the areas of southern *France*, which have always been French, but have historically been aligned with *Spanish* kingdoms (such as the Kingdom of Navarre, and Andorra), along the Pyrenees border.

Then true large blaze will engulf there lady,	*La vraye flamme engloutira la dame,*
Who will propose to thrust into them Faultless ones to death:	*Qui voudra mettre les Innocens à feu:*
As it were touching from an assault the army of men themselves inflamed,	*Pres de l'assault l'exercite s'enflamme,*
In regard of in Seville monster upon bull will be seen.	*Quant dans Seville monstre en bœuf sera veu.*

Note: Originally listed as quatrain number 19 in Centurie VI. The use of *lady* in the main theme seems like "*Lady* Liberty" on Ellis Island, New York, where her lamp lights the way to immigrants. The main theme is about an attack that will *engulf* New York City, and the nation that was the source of the attack will not be who fired the missiles, as that nation will be *them Innocent ones*. This nation is then identified in line four as Spain, who will have been invaded by ground troops, who will be *inflaming* the Spanish differently that New York.

By reason of Rebel to discover from born-Bursting to pieces travel,	*Par Nebro ouvrir de Brisanne passage,*

Chapter 30 - Moors Coming Home

Thoroughly driven far away ones the area Tagus lighthouse survey,	Bien eslongnes el tago fara muestra,
In Peligros will be committed an offence an abuse	Dans Pelirgouxe sera commis l'otraige
To there great lady fixed before the theater stage.	De la grand dame assise sur l'orchestra.

Note: Originally listed as quatrain number 25 in Centurie X. The name *Nebro* is said to be found identified in the Gospel of Judas as an angel of Heaven said to rule of chaos and the underworld. The name *Nebro* is also Hebrew meaning, "*Rebel.*" With the presence of Spanish in line two, as well as the word "tago," as a reference to the river Tagus, the word Nebro could become North Ebro, or its source in the Cantibria region of Spain. The word "*Brisanne*" could be a form of the French word "*Brisans,*" which means, "the foamy breaking of the sea against the rocks or banks of sand." The French word briser means, "to burst, break; bray; beat in pieces; rend; crush or bruise extremely, as well as interrupt, break off, and violate." The Spanish in line two is debatable, but, "*el tago fara moestra*" is an indication of Spain being the focus. The word *peligros* in Spanish means, "pitfalls."

From sister he priest by reason of private hatred hypocrisy,	De sœur le frere par simulte faintise,
Will grow to mingle dew of heaven into mineral:	Viendra mesler rosee en myneral:
Upon there flat-cake delivered up at eve of holy day long in coming,	Sur la placente donne à veille tardifve,
Dies, him gaining experience will be uncompounded & agricultural.	Meurt, le goustant sera simple & rural.

Note: Originally listed as quatrain number 36 in Centurie V. The main theme statement sounds like the descendants of Adam, such that Eve was his "*sister*", from which the lineage of *priests* for the One God would spring. Line one is then stating that Adam and Eve were created for this purpose, because the original "Man" (human life forms on earth) was flawed, with "*private hatred,*" which was not openly displayed, causing evil to multiply. The word *placenta* is rooted in Greek, and the Latin thereof, with the original literal translation being "*flat cake.*" With this following the secondary theme, where *dew of heaven* is placed upon *mineral*, a form of *flat cake* is then reminiscent of "manna from Heaven," which fed the children of Israel while in the wilderness.

Them undertaken to fight against infidels brother by affection without government	Le croisé frere par amour effrenee
Will act for Judge Bellerophon to die,	Fera par Praytus Bellerophon mourir,
Order with thousand years there woman furious	Classe à mil ans la femme forcenee
Soaked in them drink all two following to come to ruin.	Beu le breuvage tous deux apres perir.

The Epic Poem Prophesied by Nostradamus

Note: Originally listed as quatrain number 13 in Centurie VIII. *Bellephoron* is correctly spelled *Bellerophon*, which makes a simple anagram generate the correct spelling. The mythology of *Bellerophon* is he was a Greek hero, who tamed Pegasus, then went to Corinth to slay the Chimera. He did so by placing a block of lead on the end of a spear, which he caused to lodge in the Chimera's throat. It fiery breath melted the lead, suffocating it. The idiom, "*tous deux*" is typically condensed to say, "both."

Chapter 31

The Onset of War in the West, Outside of Europe

The Effects on England

Him supported born will be fully acquainted with one's absolute rule,	Le sublevé ne cognoistra son ceptre,
The children lusty ones to the more noble ones will dishonor,	Les enfans jeunes des plus grands honnira,
Never not had been one more loathsome to behold unmerciful being,	Oncques ne fut un plus ord cruel estre,
Because them marital partners to murder dark will seize.	Pour leur espouses à mort noir bannira.

Note: Latin: *sublevo = to raise, lift, encourage*. Originally listed as quatrain number 57 in Centurie X. Charles becomes king.

By reason of the spite of the King tolerating inferior to,	Par le despit du Roy soustenant moindre,
Will be murdered her representing them low-what,	Sera meurdry luy presentant les baques,
Him father with the sons intending nobility to peep out	Le pere au filz voulant noblesse poindre
Feat much as in Persia of old caused the Magi.	Fait comme à Perse jadis feirent les Magues.

Note: Originally listed as quatrain number 21 in Centurie X. The use of *Roy* in the main theme is translated as *King*, due to line three mentioning *Him father with the sons*. Popes are celibate and without children (at least by rule). The word *Magus* (from Old Persian – *maguš*) is the singular form, with *magi* the plural. It is clearly a Persian title of a magician, but in the *Holy Bible* we see the *Magi* as the Wise Men.

The Epic Poem Prophesied by Nostradamus

Two with poison seized ones, new arrived ones,	Deux de poison saisiz, nouueaux venuz,
Within the kitchen of the great Sovereign to pour out:	Dans la cuisine du grand Prince verser:
By the kitchen boy everything both in the deed noted ones,	Par le souillard tous deux au fait cogneuz,
Seized who would think murder with the eldest to trouble.	Prins qui cuidoit mort à l'aisné vexer.

Note: Originally listed as quatrain number 42 in Centurie VII. This would seem like a perfect explanation of the murder of Pope John Paul I, but there were more than two involved in that murder. The repeating of two, especially where the capitalized Two shows an important pair, appears to connect to quatrain X-16. This is due to the use of cuisine, or kitchen, with quatrain linked to Charles and Diana by the repeating of the word heureux, with one capitalized. Heureux is the way the quatrain telling of Charles and Diana's wedding began. The two are then the two sons between those two, with the eldest being Prince William. This, of course, is in the future, at a time when Charles will be King, as stated in quatrain X-16's line four.

Fire color of gold from the sky on world beheld.	Feu couleur d'or du ciel en terre veu.
Blasted as with lightning from the deep ship, action account strange:	Frappé du hault nay, fait cas merveilleux:
Mighty homicide human: undertaken with the noble him nephew,	Grand meurtre humain: prins du grand le nepveu,
Killed ones to outside displays escaped the stately.	Morts d'expectacles eschappé l'orguilleux.

Note: Originally listed as quatrain number 92 in Centurie II. The use of *gold* in the main theme may have implications relative to the Sun representing that metal alchemically. Thus, the *Fire* is the *color* (red, blue, yellow), with *to gold of the sky* meaning the Sun. The main theme's meaning is then focused on a major *Fire coloring* the *sky*, as brightly as the Sun. In other quatrains that mention *fire in the sky*, it is reference to a missile having been fired from some distance away.

In that time which one will regard them two unicorns,	Lors qu'on verra les deux licornes,
Him one yawning, the other bowing downward,	L'une baislant, l'autre baissant,
Large numbers of people in the middle, to bend to the limits	Monde au milieu, plier aux bornes
Oneself will get packing as fast as possible a nephew laughing.	S'enfuira le neveu riant.

Note: Originally listed as quatrain number 43 in Centurie VII. Source used is the 1627 Lyon

Chapter 31 - The Onset of War in the West, Outside of Europe

edition. The word *licorne* also refers specifically to the "*horn*" of a *unicorn*. The *unicorn* is said to symbolize, "strength, courage, and virtue." The *horn* was believed to have been an antidote to poison. In the middle ages, it was lore that only a pure maiden could catch a *unicorn*, by frequenting the place where one was known to visit. This story was recognized as an allegory of the return of Christ, with the maiden the Virgin Mother.

Beneath ones him land to the round globe of the moon,	*Soubz le terroir du rond globe lunaire,*
In that time that will be master Mercury:	*Lors que sera dominateur Mercure:*
The Island with Scotland will forge one candle,	*L'Isle d'Escosse fera un luminaire,*
Which them English will place at equal sharing of bankrupt goods among creditors.	*Qui les Anglois mettra à desconfiture.*

Note: Originally listed as quatrain number 93 in Centurie V. The secondary theme adds to the concept in the main theme of Project *Mercury*, which was the first human spaceflight program in the United States. What has to be seen is how little the third and fourth lines play into that possibility. When *Mercury* is understood to be the *Messenger* of the gods, line two can be an indication of a communication satellite in a sub-*lunar* orbit around the Earth. This would be one nation's *superiority* militarily, to be able to know the movements of all potential enemies before they could act as a threat. Line three indicates this surveillance equipment has been placed into orbit by Great Britain. Line four then indicates economic problems may limit the effectiveness of that program. If it is a first defense system, a lack of funds may yield it unable to live up to its billing.

Him lineage of the rightful in London will make transgression,	*Le sang du juste à Londres fera faute,*
Enflamed by lightning strikes from twenty three them six:	*Brusle par fouldres de vint trois les six:*
There dame old will tumble down from dignity noble,	*La dame antique cherra de place haute,*
To self same faction a vast sort will be slaughtered.	*De mesme secte plusieurs seront occis.*

Note: Originally listed as quatrain number 51 in Centurie II. While not in the series associated with quatrain III-97, line one of this quatrain links perfectly with line one of III-97, whereas the "*transgression made*" will be the "*unrightful*" theft of Palestine, on their watch, by the Jews. Line two's main theme is stating some form of aerial bombardment, where *thunderbolts* indicates rapidly striking targets, rather than lazily dropped bombs (à la WWII). The important *Enflamed* ones are the results sent by those stolen from, to set the British ablaze. The numbers then total *twenty*, hitting all *three* segments of the Island of *London*, Wales, Scotland, and England. The indication is then that *London* will be struck by *six*. That leads to line three, where "*La dame*" is the Queen of England and Great Britain. Line four indicates that the Queen, along with many nobles she will be with, will die in these attacks.

The Epic Poem Prophesied by Nostradamus

There fortress close to the Thames	*La forteresse aupres de la Tamise,*
Will tumble down then him King inwardly restrained:	*Cherra par lors le Roy dedans serré:*
Compared with the sea will be desire in smock	*Aupres du pont sera veu en chemise*
One before murdered, pit within the fort bolted.	*Un devant mort, puis dans le fort barré.*

Note: Originally listed as quatrain number 37 in Centurie VIII. This appears to be telling of an attack on London, where the royal fortress is leveled by a blast. The *King* (Charles?) will be be safe in a secured dungeon of some sorts, but when found some awful secret will be exposed.

September times to transform will view people British,	*Sept fois changer verrez gens Britannique,*
Stains on lineage upon two hundred no sooner than year:	*Taintz en sang en deux cens nonante an:*
At liberty not moment by reason of buttress Germanic,	*Franche non point par appuy Germanique,*
Withered ones mistrust its end of an axis one of the lower Danube.	*Aries doubte son pole Bastarnan.*

Note: Originally listed as quatrain number 57 in Centurie III. The Latin word, "*cento*", also has a "war" meaning, "coverings to ward off missiles or extinguish fires." The *Bastarnae* people lived in the lower Danube River region, which today is generally Eastern Europe and the Ukraine.

A head man of a party French for the Celtic skillful,	*Le roy Gaulois par la Celtique dextre,*
Perceiving disagreement from there great Kingdom:	*Voiant discorde de la grand Monarchie:*
Upon them three shares will act to blossom his sovereignty in chief,	*Sus les trois pars fera florir son sceptre,*
In opposition to the cape of the high Sacred Principality.	*Contre la cappe de la grand Hierarchie.*

Note: Originally listed as quatrain number 69 in Centurie II. The *Celtic* portion of France is Brittany, which is the western peninsula that helps form the English Channel. The Romans called this area *Amorica*. The combination of words, "*grand Monarchie*", gives the feel of "Great Britain." Line one's use of the lower-case "*roy*," when compared to line two's upper-case "*Kingdom*," shows two different places are being the point of reference for disagreement. The main British Island has *three parts*, England, Wales, and Scotland, all of which share *Celtic* heritage.

Chapter 31 - The Onset of War in the West, Outside of Europe

Has to support there noble cape in turmoil,	*A soubstenir la grande cappe troublee,*
In defense of them to explain the red ones will be marching	*Pour l'esclaircir les rouges marcheront*
From death house will be in a manner utterly ruined.	*De mort famille sera presque acablee.*
Them vermillion ones blood-red ones him red will be overbearing with blows.	*Les rouges rouges le rouge assomeront.*

Note: Originally listed as quatrain number 19 in Centurie VIII. With all three translations of "*rouge*" used in line four, the line states (in essence), "Those Cardinals (known for *vermillion capes*) with blood on their hands, the Communist (*him red*) will be overbearing with blows."

Them outstretched ones hairs of heads to there France Celtic,	*Les longs cheveulx de la Gaule Celtique,*
Associated ones to foreign nations:	*Accompaignés d'estranges nations:*
Will be putting servile the people of Aquitainia,	*Mettront captif la gent Aquitanique,*
In regard of to yield with no ruins.	*Pour succomber à internitions.*

Note: Originally listed as quatrain number 83 in Centurie III. In Roman times the province of *Gallia Aqitania* originally comprised the region of *Gaul* between the Pyrenees Mountains and the Garonne River. However, Julius Caesar added the land north to the Loire River to it.

BEFORE a coming of destruction Celtic,	*AVANT venue de ruine Celtique,*
Within the church two will be discoursing with:	*Dedans le temple deux parlamenteront:*
Dagger mind, from one ascended in the messenger & this grudge,	*Poignard cœur, d'un monté au coursier & picque,*
Without to cause rumbling them mighty will be hiding in the earth.	*Sans faire bruit le grand enterreront.*

Note: Originally listed as quatrain number 1 in Centurie V.

321

The Epic Poem Prophesied by Nostradamus

From the kingdom English an unworthy expelled,	Du regne Anglois l'indigne deschassé,
Him to admonish through rage thrust into with death:	Le conseillier par ire mis à feu:
One's accessories will be going in sort lowest part of to follow,	Ses adherans iront si bas tracer,
That them not rightly bred will be half accepted of.	Que le bastard sera demy receu.

Note: Originally listed as quatrain number 80 in Centurie III.

With the state either SECULAR & with Crime themselves marrying,	Au lieu ou LAYE & Scelde se marient,
Will be them nuptials from continual times managed ones	Seront les nopces de long temps maniees
In the house of Antwerp in what place there low seat going too far.	Au lieu Danvers ou la crappe charient.
Youth themselves rude partnered undefiled ones.	Jeune viellesse consorte intaminee.

Note: Originally listed as quatrain number 52 in Centurie X. The Latin word *scaena* also means, "scene, theater, natural background, and publicity." Belgium became the second country in the world to legalize Gay Marriage (in 2003), with The Netherlands being the first. The English word "crap" is said to be rooted in the Old French word "*crappe*", with that from Latin "*crappa*," implying a use meaning "excrement." A bedfellow is defined as, "a bed mate", and a "yokefellow" is defined as, "a mate, especially, a partner in marriage." The prefix *infect-* is Latin, meaning "to stain."

Ghent & them Barbarous will be marching against an Inside	Gand & Bruceles marcheront contre Envers
Counsel of citizens to London will be putting to death their head man of a party	Senat de Londres mettront à mort leur roi
Him noble & wine he being with him in the presence of,	Le sel & vin luy seront à lenvers,
For they to hold the government in confusion.	Pour eux avoir le regne en desarroy.

Note: Originally listed as quatrain number 49 in Centurie IX. As a form of the name of the city of *Brussels*, Belgium, the etymology of that name states it comes from the Old Dutch word "*Broucsella*" or "*Brucsella*" or "*Broekzele*", meaning "*marsh [brouc/bruc/broec] home [sella]*," or better, "*home consisting of one room in the marsh.*" However, while intended on a secondary level, the word *Bruceles* is missing an "l', and cannot become an accurate spelling for *Brussels* or

Chapter 31 - The Onset of War in the West, Outside of Europe

French word "*Brucelles*," meaning "Tweezers." The 1568 Lyon edition clearly shows a capitalized, "*Envers*", at the end of the main theme (line one). The 1566 Lyon edition shows this as, "Anvers", which is the French spelling for Antwerp. That, again, is to be seen on a secondary level of interpretation, with "*Envers*" the primary word to interpret.

The West not subject unto them Island ones Britannic ones	*L'Occident libre les Isles Britanniques*
Him acknowledged to surpass the humble, moreover most glorious	*Le recogneu passer le bas, puis haut*
Not pleased with what one has discontented one to Revolt constitution of the body ones like Shoots off the tree	*Ne content triste Rebel corss. Escotiques*
After to rise up against one's sovereign for more & through night cared for.	*Puis rebeller par plus & par nuit chaut.*

Note: Originally listed as quatrain number 80 in Centurie VII. Source of the Old French is the 1605 Lyone edition of *The Prophecies*.

To them more of much capacity from the west English,	*Du plus profond de l'occident Anglois,*
Whereas east him chief to the island British:	*Ou est le chef de l'isle Britannique:*
Will enter fleet within Gironde for Blois.	*Entrera classe dans Gyronde par Blois.*
By reason of wine & salt, deaths kept secret ones with them barricaded ones.	*Par vin & sel, feuz cachés aux barriques.*

Note: Originally listed as quatrain number 34 in Centurie V. The *English* of the *west* are primarily the United States and Canada, or North America. *Gironde* is the French department where Bordeaux is a major seaport in Aquitaine. *Blois* is northeast of *Gironde* in the Loir-et-Cher department, on the Loire River, between Orleans and Tours.

Applause, Madness placed, Gironde & there Rock-wide,	*Euge, Tamins, Gironde & la Rochele,*
Good Lord blood Trojan Death at the port from the shaft:	*O sang Troien Mort au port de la flesche:*
Behind a river to the fort placed them squadron of soldiers,	*Derrier le fleuve au fort mise l'eschele,*
Instant ones fire great homicide upon there breached.	*Pointes feu grand meurtre sus la bresche.*

The Epic Poem Prophesied by Nostradamus

Note: Originally listed as quatrain number 61 in Centurie II. *Tamins* is a town in the district of Imboden in the Swiss canton of Graubunden. The city of *La Rochelle* is a major seaport in France, on the Bay of Biscay, north of Bordeaux, which is in the *Gironde* department, at the Garonne River. The French word *eschelle* also means, "ladder and scale."

Child besides public authority never beheld even as mighty thunder-bolt,	*Enfant sans mains jamais veu si grand foudre,*
An infant princely at a game of service wounded:	*L'enfant royal au jeu d'œsteuf blessé:*
With the hillock beaten in pieces ones flashed ones traveling to pound into pieces,	*Au puy brises fulgures alant mouldre,*
Three at the bottom of the chains by reason of them the middle of cast away ones.	*Trois soubz les chaines par le millieu troussés.*

Note: Originally listed as quatrain number 65 in Centurie I. The word *esteuf* is defined as, "tennis ball." However, several examples of its use in statements show how it has a contextual meaning of "foolishness, straining after uncertainties, serving others while waiting one's turn, and going after that which is impossible to achieve, while letting go of what one had." Following the word "*jeu*," meaning, "game, sport, play, recreation, and pasttime," while also being tennis-specific, as "the upper end of a tennis court (next to the house) ... within the streak of chalk drawn around the court," (Center Court?) the indication is that *d'esteuf* means a young prince is at a function where he pretends to be of service to others. This could be attending a tennis match at Wimbledon, which is a subburb of London. The event is known for Royal patronage, and it begins each year in the month of June (between the 20th and 26th).

One sons of the King so many of languages has embraced,	*Un fils du Roy tant de langues aprins,*
To his eldest with the kingdom controversy:	*A son aisné au regne different:*
His father beautiful in him more noble male child comprised,	*Son pere beau au plus grand filz comprins*
Will cause to come to ruin sovereign accessory.	*Fera perir principal adherant.*

Note: Originally listed as quatrain number 87 in Centurie IV.

Two princely ones brothers in sort powerful will be fighting,	*Deux royalz freres si fort guerroyeront,*
Which entered they will be there warfare so deadly:	*Qu'entre eux sera la guerre si mortelle:*

Chapter 31 - The Onset of War in the West, Outside of Europe

That one each placed ones strengths will be usurping by force,	*Qu'un chacun places fortes occuperont,*
With kingdom & living will be their noble difference.	*De regne & vie sera leur grand querelle.*

Note : Originally listed as quatrain number 98 in Centurie III.

Descended upon this world through copulated when capable of producing fruit,	*Nee en ce monde par concubit fertive,*
With two noble thrust into by reason of them sorrowful ones fresh ones,	*A deux hault mise par les tristes nouvelles,*
Gone into enemy ones will be seizing imprisoned by war,	*Entre ennemys sera prinse captive,*
Both fetched unto with Grudge-bearing ones & Tweezers.	*Et amené à Malings & Brucelles.*

Note: Originally listed as quatrain number 54 in Centurie X. The word *Bruscelles* is clean French, meaning, "*Tweezers.*" The city Brussels, Belgium, in French is spelled *Bruxelles*. The name of the city means, "one room house in the marsh," which may or may not apply in this quatrain. Brussels is the capital of Belgium, with both Dutch and French spoken by the inhabitants.

Gone into two mountains them both mighty ones assembled ones	*Entre deux monts les deux grans assemblés*
Will be leaving their private hatred concealed:	*Delaisseront leur simulte secrette:*
Marsh home & the Treachery by reason of Langres overthrown ones,	*Brucelle & Dolle par Langres acablés,*
In defense of with Grudge-bearing ones to execute their pestilence.	*Pour à Malignes executer leur peste.*

Note: Originally listed as quatrain number 47 in Centurie VI. The commune of *Dôle* France was named *Dolla* by the Romans, but in Old French, it was "*Dol.*" It is in eastern France, in the *Jura* department of the *Franche-Comté* region. *Langres* is also in eastern France, north of the *Franche-Comté* region, in the *Haute-Marne* department. This quatrain links to quatrain X-54 due to both containing the word "*two,*" along with *Malignes* and *Brucelles*.

The Epic Poem Prophesied by Nostradamus

To the most glorious of them mount ones with them on all sides Coast along a country	*Du hault des montz à lentour de Lizere,*
Harbor to there rock Strong patch-work assembled ones	*Port à la roche Valen. cent assemblez*
Of castle strange stone lathe into with eleven shaven,	*De chasteau neuf pierre late en donzere,*
On the other side him sprung forth Romans confidence flocked ones.	*Contre le crest Romans foy assemblez.*

Note: Originally listed as quatrain number 67 in Centurie IX. *The Isère* is both a department and a river, in the Rhone-Alpes region of eastern France, where Grenoble is the capital of *Isère* and Lyon is the capital of the Rhone-Alpes region (and the Rhone department). The commune of *Valence* France was known in Roman times as *Valentia Julia*; and, it is 65 miles south of Lyon. *La Rochelle* is on the Atlantic coast of France, north of Bordeaux. The *Chateauneuf*-du-Pape is in the Vaucluse department in southeast France, bordered by the Rhone River to the west and the Durance River to the south.

Kingdom at process against with the brothers divided,	*Regne en querelle aux freres divisé,*
To receive them armed ones & the reputation of Britain	*Prendre les armes & le nom Britannique,*
Name of England will be long in coming warned,	*Tiltre Anglican sera tard advisé,*
Taken napping with night to lead to the favor of men French.	*Surprins de nuict mener à l'air Gallique.*

Note: Originally listed as quatrain number 58 in Centurie VIII.

Through there Guyenne endlessness of English	*Par la Guyenne infinité d'Anglois*
Will be usurping by force of name with corner of Aquitaine	*Occuperont par nom d'anglaquitaine*
To them Languedoc for Islam people of Bordeaux.	*Du Languedoc lspalme Bourdeloys.*
Which they will be terming next unto Barbarous-Occitania.	*Qu'ilz nommeront apres Barboxitaine.*

Note: Originally listed as quatrain number 6 in Centurie IX. The language known as Occitan is the root of the word *Languedoc*, as "language Occitan" is written, "*Lenga d'òc*." The term "*Oc country*" refers to the territory where Occitan is spoken, which is *Occitania*. The spelling "*Occ*" is abbreviated by the accent in "*òc*". For Nostradamus to use an "*x*" in his spelling, this is an indication of a "double c" sound, just as the plural of a French word typically ending in "s" becomes

Chapter 31 - The Onset of War in the West, Outside of Europe

"x" (whereas English would be "s' ").

Under ones to chain Guyenne from the sky blasted like lightning,	*Dessoubz de chaine Guien du ciel frappe,*
Not far off of there east concealed the accumulation for future use:	*Non loing de la est caché le tresor:*
That which for tedious ones centuries has assembled,	*Qui par longs siecles auoit este grappé,*
Found will decay, the eye torn apart with itself issue again.	*Trouvé moura, l'œil crevé de ressort.*

Note: Originally listed as quatrain number 27 in Centurie I. The capitalized name in line one, *Guien*, means Guienne, the ancient province of southwestern France, which included Bordeaux and much of Aquitaine. Line four can be viewed as a 16th century explanation for nuclear physics, where a device uses radioactive materials, which are in a constant state of *decay*, being initially *split apart*, creating a chain reaction, whereby itself will *issue again* this effect of splitting. The effect of a blast will render one sightless, from the blinding flash.

With Languedoc, & Guyenne more to ten,	*De Languedoc, & Guienne plus de dix,*
Thousand will be proposing the Alps to pass over again:	*Mille voudront les Alpes repasser:*
Mighty ones Allobroges to march against Brundisium	*Grans Allobroges marcher contre Brundis*
Aquino & Bresse them will be arriving to discharge again.	*Aquin & Bresse les viendront recasser.*

Note: Originally listed as quatrain number 31 in Centurie VII. The area known as *Languedoc* was also known as the country of Toulouse; and, it was the home of the Cathar religious movement. The ancient province of *Guienne* was later named the region of Aquitaine and was the Atlantic coast compliment to the Mediterranean coast *Languedoc*. The *Allobroges* were ancient peoples of Gaul, who were Celtic warlike tribes. They lived between the Rhone River and Lake Geneva. The commune of *Bresse* is in southeastern Alpine France. The name *Aquin* is the same some used to name Thomas Aquinas (meaning Thomas of Aquin). That city is *Aquino*, in Latinum, near Rome.

One prince of England Acts with one's courage from heaven,	*Un prince Anglois Mars à son cœur de ciel,*
Will intend to earnestly proceed in his destiny favorably:	*Voudra poursuivre sa fortune prospere:*
Of the two fighting ones the one will transfix a resentment,	*Des deux duelles l'un percera le fiel,*
Hated to him, thoroughly loved from her mother.	*Hay de luy, bien aymé de sa mere.*

The Epic Poem Prophesied by Nostradamus

Note: Originally listed as quatrain number 16 in Centurie III. In Greek mythology *Mars* was the god of war, thus *Mars* symbolically stands for *War*. However, in its basic sense, "*Mars*" means "*Action*." In line four, the pronoun "*him*" is the counter-balance to "*mother*", such that "*him*" is the father to whom *Hated* applies. The two prepositions, "*de*", become interchangeable as "*to*" and "*from*," such that Prince Charles could show *hatred*, as Harry is not being from royal stock, or not acting royal. That *hatred* is then returned, back to the father.

Him lion young him aged in years will surmount,	*Le lyon jeune le vieux surmontera,*
On field of war through extraordinary fighting:	*En champ bellique par singulier duelle:*
Within cage with gold them sights it will burst,	*Dans caige d'or les yeulx luy crevera,*
Two armed forces one, after to decay, death unmerciful.	*Deux classes une, puis mourir, mort cruelle.*

Note: Originally listed as quatrain number 35 in Centurie I. The use of "*lion*", in line one, has to be seen symbolically as England. With the system allowing for the transfer of importance from a first word article (*Le*), to the following noun (*lion*), the result is *Lion*, which fits the higher level meaning of the British *Lion*.

Them young not have with the realm British	*Le jeune nay au regne Britannique,*
Who will hold a father dying again jointly appointed,	*Qu'aura le pere mourant recomande,*
This one murdered THE ONE WITH HIM will deliver up logical and probable arguments,	*Iceluy mort LONOLE donra topique,*
Both with its sons the kingdom demanded.	*Et à son filz le regne demande.*

Note: Originally listed as quatrain number 40 in Centurie X. The word ending line two, "*recomandé*", is misspelled, missing an "*m*" (according to the 1568 Lyon edition). When that possibility of "again jointly appointed" comes up, it becomes reminiscent of the time England was co-ruled, under William & Mary. In this case, it would become William & Harry. The single letter *O* is stated to be used instead of the word "*avec*," which means *with*, as in the phrase, "*Venez O moy* (hunts with me) or *I m'en vay O vous* (Here me in sight with you)."

In the house of OAK ONES a King will be at rest,	*Au lieu de DRUX un Roy repousera,*
As well will search after the course of justice transforming from Excommunicated,	*Et cherchera loy changeant d'Anatheme,*

Chapter 31 - The Onset of War in the West, Outside of Europe

Hanging him heaven in sort most mighty will thunder,	*Pendant le ciel si tres fort tonnera,*
This Entryway new Chief will kill himself the same.	*Portce neufve Roy tuera soy mesme.*

Note: Originally listed as quatrain number 57 in Centurie IX. The symbol of an *OAK* tree, which represents, "strength and endurance," has been chosen as the national tree of England. Line two is a secondary theme of the legal aftermath of the execution of a *King* (the main theme). Line four is an indication of a suicide committed by one close to the executed *King*, due to his knowledge of prior crimes, as well as being an accessory.

The indignation raging from the conflict frantic,	*L'ire insensée du combat furieux,*
Will act with domain of land for brothers a weapon to be bright:	*Fera à table par freres le fer luire:*
Them to divide, ulcerated, heedful,	*Les despartir, blessé, curieux,*
The unmerciful war will grow into France to hurt.	*Le fier duelle viendra en France nuire.*

Note: Originally listed as quatrain number 34 in Centurie II. The spelling of duelle is Middle English, although rooted in the same Latin words, with the meaning being, "duel."

Of France which decayed through war will usurp by force	*Gauloys qu'empire par guerre occupera*
For its proper brother minor proposition in a syllogism will be treacherously dealt with,	*Par son beau frere mineur sera trahy,*
In regard for mechanized armor barbarous managing in narrow circles will practice,	*Pour cheval rude voltigeant traynera,*
To them argument in pleading the priest continual opportunity will be hated.	*Du fait le frere long temps sera hay.*

Note: Originally listed as quatrain number 34 in Centurie X. The word *syllogism* means (from Greek), "conclusion, inference." As such, syllogism is a logical form of argument, which draws from minor propositions to gain a major conclusion. For understanding this possibility in interpretation, it acts out the following premise. If it is fair for the French to have Mandate over Syria and Lebanon, leaving them to govern themselves; AND it is fair for France's brother in Mandate (Great Britain) to have Mandate over Palestine, but then allow Palestine to be fairly stolen by foreign citizens; THEN it is fair for foreign citizens to seize France and force it to be theirs.

The Epic Poem Prophesied by Nostradamus

Him eldest Princely toward trained swift charger managing in a narrow circle,	*L'aisné Royal sur coursier voltigeant,*
To pierce will approach, so harshly to make hostile incursions upon:	*Picquer viendra si durement courir:*
Throat, empowered, base within the tight press ensuring	*Gueule, lipee, pied dans l'estrein pleignant,*
Trailed, forced from, hideously to perish.	*Trainé, tiré, horriblement mourir.*

Note: Originally listed as quatrain number 38 in Centurie VII. A *courser* is defined as, "a swift horse, a charger." A tilting horse was used in jousting, where a lance was used. In modern terms, this would be literally impractical in warfare. However, as symbolic of mechanized armor, it becomes a swift charger able to follow a course of obstacles. This would be some form of tank, which matches quatrain I-35, where line three states, "*In cage of gold*". The word "*lipee*" is defined from the defined word, "*liperquam*," which states, "*faire de liper*," and defines this as meaning, "To show his authority, to let the world see his power; to bear himself as one who can do all in all; to take exceeding much upon him."

For not to fall between hands of her uncle,	*Pour ne tumber entre mains de son oncle,*
Who their children by reason of to reign destroyed ones,	*Qui ses enfans par regner trucidez,*
Speaking with the people laying foundation towards Not to banish	*Orant au peuple mettant pied sur Peloncle*
Murdered & themselves conspiracy one with another coach horses trapped ones.	*Mort & traisne entre chevaulx bardez.*

Note: Originally listed as quatrain number 89 in Centurie VIII. The word "*barde*" meant "armor or decoration for horses", during ancient times when horses rode into battle. This appears to be about Diana, her children, and the divorce. As an anagram, "*Peloncle*", changes to become the way Diana did nothing to anger the royal family, due to her having the princes. The "*uncle*" is then a reference to Prince Andrew, publicly the *uncle* to the children, while in reality being the father, of "*their children*"

Chapter 32

War into the Far West

The Effects on the United States of America

War & the kingdom itself will meet with combined,	*Mars & le sceptre se trouvera conjoinct,*
Beneath ones South most unfortunate strife:	*Dessoubz Cancer calamiteuse guerre:*
One almost nothing next unto will be new King anointed,	*Un peu apres sera nouveau Roy oingt,*
Who for wearisome opportunity will appease there world.	*Qui par long temps pacifiera la terre.*

Note: Originally listed as quatrain number 24 in Centurie VI. The word *sceptre* meant, "a (Royal) scepter; also, a monarchy, kingdom, absolute rule, and sovereignty in chief." In astrology, the glyph for Jupiter is said to resemble a scepter (♃). As such, Jupiter has the astrological qualities of a sovereign or *King*, which is representative of the largest sphere in the Solar System. Jupiter next will be in Cancer between June 2013 and July 2014. Mars will move into Cancer on July 14, 2013, and it will conjunct Jupiter, in Cancer, on July 22, 2013.

An exploit radiant with nine old in years chosen	*Le fait luysant de neuf vieux esleve*
Will be in sort high ones by midday northern,	*Seront si grand par midi aquilon,*
From his faithful one's own substantial allied ones elevated,	*De sa seur propre grande aliesleve,*
Delaying of to develop in the thicket with in the company of him many.	*Fuyant murdry au buysson d'ambellon.*

Note: Originally listed as quatrain number 69 in Centurie X. The word "*alié*" can also be spelled as "*allié*", which is more in line with those in alliance.

The Epic Poem Prophesied by Nostradamus

Through the fraud government, forces to deprive of,	*Par fraulde regne, forces expolier,*
There fleet besieged, grazing cattle ones with them closely observed:	*La classe obsesse, paissaiges à l'espie:*
Two false ones friends themselves will be coming to reassemble,	*Deux faincts amys se viendront rallier,*
To stir up hatred from long time quieted.	*Esueillier hayne de long temps assoupie.*

Note: Originally listed as quatrain number 33 in Centurie VII. The 1568 Lyon edition clearly shows ten letters in the line two word shown as *paissiages*, with (minimally) two of the letters "i"s. The double "s" is most questionable, but because the previous word also contains a double "s" (as well as one in line four) it appears the way presented is correct. There is a possibility that the *cattle* reference of this quatrain has something to do with the *ruminating animals* of quatrain X-13.

Light east one great fire some will see,	*Soleil levant un grand feu lon verra,*
Loud sound & brightness before Eagle one drawing near unto:	*Bruit & clarté vers Aquilon tendant:*
Within them free murdered & shrieks they will implore,	*Dedans le rond mort & cris lon orra,*
By missile, death, extreme desire of things, killed weary expecting ones.	*Par glaive, feu, faim, mort las attendants.*

Note: Originally listed as quatrain number 91 in Centurie II. In Latin, the word "*aquila*" means, "an eagle," with "*aquil*" being simply "eagle." In French, the word for "of an eagle" is "*aquilin*". If the word *Aquilon* is read as "*Aquil-on*," the Northern place of reference is an "*Eagle one*." This then identifies the United States, here and in all quatrains where Nostradamus wrote *Aquilon*. The use of "*orra*", which can mean, "will pray," is an indication of how a nation, which had lost its link to God, will react in "*shrieks.*" The use of "will pray" connects to line four's "*attending ones,*" where "*expecting ones*" is a better fit. Those who will have expected a painless "Rapture" will find their expectations somewhat off, having lived lives lusting in "*extreme desires for things.*" Those pious people will be amid those killed, because of their lack of acting to avoid this destruction. Instead of ease and comfort in Heaven, they will wearily be over-toiled by the affects of death.

An eye by subject of the sight will act much like in a knob,	*L'oeil par object fera telle excroissance,*
In such manner & burning which will tumble down there snow,	*Tant & ardante que tumbera la neige,*
Land sprinkled will arrive upon declining state,	*Champ arrousé viendra en descroissance,*

Chapter 32 - War into the Far West

That them metropolitan will surrender with Directed.	*Que le primat succumbera à Rege.*

Note: Originally listed as quatrain number 70 in Centurie X. There is a Latin saying: Pro Fide, Lege et Rege, which translates as, "For Faith, Law and *King*." It is also interesting to note the French usage of "*decrossiance radioactive*," which means "radioactive *decay*." Realizing this, it is interesting that the word "*excroissance*," meaning "*like a knob*," becomes descriptive of a mushroom cloud, with the *burning tumbling snow* radioactive fallout.

In two a house with night them fire will embrace,	*Dans deux logis de nuict le feu prendra,*
Many within suffocated ones & roasted ones:	*Plusieurs dedans estoufées & rostis:*
Near to both rivers in regard of alone it will happen,	*Pres de deux fleuves pour seul il aviendra,*
Bottom of a place, the Arch, & Capricorn whole sum will be extinguished ones.	*Sol, l'Arq, & Caper tous seront amortis.*

Note: Originally listed as quatrain number 35 in Centurie II. The astrological sign symbolized by *the Archer* is Sagittarius (November 22 to December 21), which is the sign the *Sun* moves through each year before it moves through the sign of *Capricorn* (December 22 to January 19). However, the capitalization of "*l'Arq*" makes it quite capable of representing "*the Ark*," which was the instrument of amazing power built at the directions of God, by the children of Israel. The capitalized *Caper*, in French, means, "*To cloak*," which means to wrap in a sleeveless covering (like is a cigar). In war technology, "*To cloak*" means to use stealth technology. The French word *Sol* primarily means, "Ground, Soil, Bottom of something, Foundation," although it can also mean *Sun*, from its Latin root.

At the bottom of them in opposition with portion of the world Mesopotamian,	*Soubz l'opposite climat Babylonique,*
Substantial will be from race pouring out:	*Grande sera de sang effusion:*
That world & sea, air, firmament will be unrighteous,	*Que terre & mer, air, ciel sera inique,*
Factions, extreme desire for things, governments, pestilent people who ruin others, complete disorder.	*Sectes, faim, regnes, pestes, confusion.*

Note: Originally listed as quatrain number 55 in Centurie I. Line three is making a statement for the scope of mankind. It will have covered the whole *world*, which during Nostradamus' time was still much unknown (South America, Western North America, Pacific Islands, etc.). In that

The Epic Poem Prophesied by Nostradamus

endeavor of expansion, it had mastered the *sea, air,* and outer space, which is the *heavens,* or the *firmament.* That is a timing factor for the 20th century, and beyond. That timing will then be representative of a *world unrighteous* or unequal in religious beliefs.

From death proposing there shifting stratagem,	*De feu voulant la machination,*
Will grow to turmoil with the great chief besieged ones:	*Viendra troubler au grand chef assiegés:*
Within will be such sedition,	*Dedans sera telle sedition,*
Which upon desperation will be them nearly finished ones.	*Qu'en desespoir seront les profligés.*

Note: Originally listed as quatrain number 34 in Centurie VI. The word *machination* meant, "frame, contrivement; a subtle plot or conspiracy; a crafty invention or circumventing trick." The word *sedition* is defined as, "conduct or language inciting rebellion against the authority of the state; or, insurrection, rebellion." Line two sounds as if it could mean the "*shifting stratagem*" of line one becomes the creation of inner *turmoil*, by having gained access in the realm, or government of the *great chief*. The separation of the word "*chef*" then places emphasis on the office of President, who begins an end of a time of Constitutional rule, with the populace becoming the *beleaguered ones*. One's own government becoming oppressive would lead to the act, in line three, of *sedition*.

Rumor worries, bodies of counsel lamentations, cowardly,	*Vent chaut, conseil pleurs, timidité,*
Of night to the lair of stone in a building besides them fortified ones:	*De nuit au lit assailly sans les armes:*
From overcharging great calamity,	*D'oppression grande calamité,*
A wedding song changed weeping ones & tears.	*L'epithalame converty pleurs et larmes.*

Note: Originally listed as quatrain number 83 in Centurie VII. The source of this quatrain is the 1630 Lyon edition of The Prophecies, with the 1605 Lyon edition too faint at places to make out some of the punctuation marks. However, the 1605 clearly shows a colon at the end of line two, whereas the 1630 edition clearly shows a comma. In line two where Nostradamus wrote *sans les armes*, the word *armes* means both offensive and defensive *weapons*. In this sense it states that one who will have boasted of defensives *arms* will be let down by their ineffectiveness. The word *oppression* also means, "overcharging, overlaying; an unreasonable surcharge; a grievous burden, taxation or exaction; or, the imposing of any of the above."

That one which woman ones & weapon with them achieved warlike,	*Celuy qu'en luitte & fer au faict bellique,*
Will enjoy endured more mighty than him them honor gotten:	*Aura porté plus grand que luy le pris:*

Chapter 32 - War into the Far West

Of night in the bed six he will be causing there thrust into,	*De nuict au lict six luy seront la pique,*
Naked without armor sudden will be too high a price.	*Nud sans harnois subit sera surpris.*

Note: Originally listed as quatrain number 30 in Centurie III. I see this as telling of a new president elect, who is worried about authorizing the use of certain weapons against an enemy. Line two shows his (*luy*) popularity with the people and those in power. His country is cast into war by surprise attack, with a lack of proper defense allowing his people to be easily victimized. It may be important to link the six of this quatrain to the six stated in line two of quatrain I-51.

There mighty forces which will be themselves chased away,	*La grand copie qui sera deschassée,*
In one consequence will make much use of with the Pope,	*Dans un moment fera besoing au Roy:*
The faithfulness vowed from long way off will be breach,	*La foy promise de loing sera faulcée,*
Discovered itself will look in distressful confusion.	*Nud se verra en piteux desarroy.*

Note: Originally listed as quatrain number 22 in Centurie IV. In Old French, the word "*faucefoy*" is defined as, "A faith breaker, a treacherous companion." Line three begins with "*The faith*" (*La foy*) and ends with "*breach*". In this sense, the word "*faulcée*" works well as an anagram, as "*l'faucée*", stating *The faith will be "them broken."*

There compassion great will be without long way off to delay,	*La pitié grande sera sans loing tarder,*
Those who had yielded will be ones forced against one's will of to embrace.	*Ceux qui donoient seront contrains de prendre.*
Discovered ones famished ones with chill, thirst, it to tie with strings,	*Nudz affames de froid, soif, soy bander,*
Them mountains to hold on course committing an offence might a slaughter.	*Les monts passer commettant grand esclandre.*

Note: Originally listed as quatrain number 69 in Centurie VI.

The Epic Poem Prophesied by Nostradamus

With them nearby to the gates & in two cities,	*Au pres des portes & dedans deux cités,*
Will be both judgments of God & never neither noted one like:	*Seront deux fleaux & onques n'aperceu un tel:*
Supposed ones within pestilent people who ruin others, of weapon out of nations stricken ones,	*Fains dedans peste, de fer hors gens boutés,*
To denounce by proclamation help to the to the great God eternal.	*Crier secours au grand Dieu immortel.*

Note: Originally listed as quatrain number 6 in Centurie II. The capitalized first word of line three, according to the 1568 Lyon edition, is clearly spelled as, "*Fains*". This is not a word in either French or Latin, although it is in English. It has been seen as an abbreviation for a word ending with "t" or "ct." This would be the explanation for seeing "*Fains*" as "*Fainct-s*." Other editions show this word as "*Faim*", including the 1557 Utrecht edition, but there is no doubt this was due to an attempt to make a word that was not a word into a known word.

Them thoroughly at ease ones not thought of being humbled	*Les bien aisez subit seront desmis,*
By reason of the three brothers a vast number of people thrust into turmoil:	*Par les trois freres le monde mis en trouble:*
Warned to appear from the sea will be taking possession of enemies,	*Cité marine saisiroit ennemis,*
Extreme desire for things, death, race, pestilent people who ruin others, & to everything evils them doubled.	*Faim, feu, sang, peste, & de to* maux le double.*

Note: Originally listed as quatrain number 17 in Centurie VIII. The 1568 Lyon edition shows a large black dot above and immediately following "*to*", in line four, following the ampersand. The 1566 Lyon edition shows this as the word, "*tous*", which is the plural form of "*tout*", matching the plural "*maux*", which follows. A typical printer's abbreviation would be placed over a letter, usually when either an "m" or "n" was to follow.

Earth-quaked fire to the very middle of the country,	*Ennosigée feu du centre de la terre,*
Will cause to tremble in the tower with city new:	*Fera trembler au tour de cité neufve:*
Two mighty ones rocky ones extended opportunity will be forging there war,	*Deux grands rochiers long temps feront la guerre,*

Chapter 32 - War into the Far West

Then Fountain will grow red unheard of before stream.	Puis Arethusa rougira nouveau fleuve.

Note: Originally listed as quatrain number 87 in Centurie I. *Arethusa* is the name of a nymph who was chased by the river *Alpheus* under the sea to Sicily.

There great city to Atlantic Ocean of the seacoast,	La grand cité d'Occean maritime,
Surrounded with marshes into ice:	Environnees de maretz en cristal:
Within the solstice done in winter & the first hour of the day,	Dans le solstice hyemal & la prime,
Will be worried from blast of wind them filled with horror.	Sera temptee de vent espouvental.

Note: Originally listed as quatrain number 48 in Centurie IX. The word *maritime* is defined as being adjacent to the sea and involved in marine shipping and navigation. The Winter Solstice is around December 22nd. The word "*prime*" has a specific seasonal definition, which states, "the first hour of the day (in summer at four o'clock, in winter at eight)." This would then make line three indicate 8:00 PM, on December 22. The word *espouventer* is Old French, referring one to look up *espoventer*. However, the word "*espouvanter*" is the modern spelling, which meets the need as an anagram. As a modern spelled word, the quatrain is associated with modern time.

Of more great loss unknown before ones reported ones,	De plus grand perte nouvelles raportées,
A delivery of a tale feat the army lodged itself will astonish:	Le raport fait le camp s'estonnera:
Companies of soldiers joined together ones shock of the enemy rebelled ones,	Bandes unies encontre revoltées,
Twice as much battalion of soldiers mighty will leave at random.	Double phalange grand abandonnera.

Note: Originally listed as quatrain number 13 in Centurie IV. The word *phalange* is defined as being a battalion of soldiers (between 8,000 and 18,000 strong), ranked so that they may encounter the enemy in any way. This is attributed to Phillip II of Macedonia, who first devised this method of staging troops.

There themselves expelled with the government will convert,	La deschassee au regne tournera,
One's enemies: devised ones from them conspired against ones:	Ses ennemis: trouvés des conjuréz:
More than never its opportunity will triumph,	Plus que jamais son temps triomphera,

The Epic Poem Prophesied by Nostradamus

Three & September before in death more than needs assured ones.	*Trois & septante à mort trop asseuréz.*

Note: Originally listed as quatrain number 74 in Centurie VI. The 1568 Lyon edition appears to show a colon after the second word of line two (*ennemis*). It is possible it is bleed from the facing page.

Placed abundance church citizens Westerner lands	*Mys tresor temple, citadins Hesperiques*
Inwardly this one harbored at secret dwelling place,	*Dans iceluy retiré en secret lieu,*
Him temple to discover them shackles the kept long fasting ones	*Le temple ouvrir les liens fameliquesl*
Recapture forcibly carried away ones prey horrible in the midst.	*Reprens ravis proye horrible au milieu.*

Note: Originally listed as quatrain number 81 in Centurie X. It could be possible that the apparent "l", at the end of line three (1568 Lyon edition), was a typeset colon ":", where the base imprinted, obliterating the colon. If so, that would make line four the clarification of line three. In ancient times, Italy and Spain were considered to be the *Western lands*.

The falseness messenger for election seeming other than it is	*Le faux messiage par election fainte*
To overrun through city here, undone condition agreed upon decreed,	*Courir par urben, rompue pache arreste,*
Voice through procured by money ones with race little church colored.	*Voix acheptees de sang chapelle tainte.*
And in one different from the former him diminished covenant.	*Et à un autre l'empire contraicte.*

Note: Originally listed as quatrain number 20 in Centurie VIII. The word "*urben*" is still debatable. On the surface, it could be read as "urban," which is rooted in Latin, and meaning, "city". As such, it could be a French combination, as "Urban-into."

The great counsel of citizens will distinguish one thing from another there ostentation,	*Le grand senat disernera la pompe,*
With them one who next unto will be convinced by reason pursued,	*A l'un qu'apres sera vaincu chassé,*
One's adhering ones being in his from shout of an elephant,	*Ses adherans seront à son de trompe,*

Chapter 32 - War into the Far West

Riches made common ones enemies himself ejected ones.	*Biens publiez ennemys dechassez.*

Note: Originally listed as quatrain number 76 in Centurie X. The definition of *pomp* states, "dignified or magnificent display; splendor; while also, vain or ostentatious display." The Latin word *pompa* meant, "pomp and procession". All could fit in line one's interpretation of meaning.

Him next to last with the surname of the prophet,	*Le penultiesme du surnom du prophete,*
Will embrace Diana in defense of her day & rest:	*Prendra Diane pour son jour & repos:*
Long way off will move from place to place through out of one's mind headiness.	*Loing vaguera par frenetique teste.*
Also giving over unto from a great people to not in control.	*Et delivrant un grand peuple d'impos.*

Note: Originally listed as quatrain number 28 in Centurie II. The name *Diane* prompts one to seek information for the Greek goddess Artemis, who was also known as Selene, and depicted with a crescent moon over her head. Artemis was also the twin sister of Apollo, the sun god, making her a moon goddess in that sense. As representative of the moon, her day is then Monday (as Moon day). Still, as Diana, line one could represent one of the royal princes, sons of the late Diana Spencer. That would make her day either her birthday, or death day. Nostradamus only used the word Diane on one other occasion (quatrain IX-12). The Latin word "*impos*" (gen), when combined with the words "*animi*" or "*mentis*" makes it read as "out of control of mind", or "dementia". While the combination is absent, line three states that "*frantic head.*"

Chapter 33

War into the Near East

The Inevitable War with Israel

By reason of them two head ones & three arm of the body divided ones,	*Par les deux testes, & trois bras separés,*
There city high through leaks will be disquieted:	*La cité grande par eaux sera vexee:*
With the mighty ones from one with another they for exile wandered from ones,	*Des grans d'entre eux par exil esgarés,*
Of self-willfulness piercing a vessel Istanbul powerful constrained.	*Par teste perse Bisance fort pressee.*

Note: Originally listed as quatrain number 86 in Centurie V. The main theme statement (line one) is about the *two* mandated Protectorates in the Middle East, France and Great Britain. The second half states there would be *three* parts *divided*, which were initially Syria, Palestine, and Mesopotamia. These three, which were under the *arm* of the Ottoman Empire, were then further divided to create Transjordan and Lebanon. Line two's secondary theme is then about Jerusalem, "*The city*" wanted by Zionists.

Within the land from the great temple divine,	*Dedans la terre du grand temple celique,*
By Nephew in London for agreement forged murdered:	*Nepveu à Londres par paix faincte meurtry:*
The bark at that time will grow disunited,	*La barque alors deviendra scismatique,*
Ample choice feigned will be with the horn & proclamation.	*Liberté faincte sera au corn & cry.*

Note: Originally listed as quatrain number 22 in Centurie VI. In recent times, the Episcopalian Church, or the Anglican Communion, has had divisions due to the ordination of a gay bishop. Others have had problems over the ordination of women. In other words, we have already entered the times of *schism*.

Chapter 33 - War into the Near East

Them besieged ones will be making pretenses their own ones atonements,	Les assiegés couloureront leur paches,
September day ones after will be causing cruel toll	Sept jours apres seront cruelle issue
Inwardly foiled ones, death, race. Seven put to a torch	Dans repoulsés feu, sang. Sept mis à l'hache
Lady lost liberty who has there accord woven.	Dame captive qu'avoit la paix tissue.

Note: Originally listed as quatrain number 18 in Centurie VII.

There city bountiful from liberty achievement serves,	La cité franche de liberté fait serve,
To them overthrown ones & weak-minded ones exploited place of freedom:	Des profligés & resveurs faict asyle:
The head man of a party transformed in them not so proud:	Le roy changé à eulx non si proterve:
From patchwork will be become ones more to a thousand.	De cent seront devenus plus de mille.

Note: Originally listed as quatrain number 16 in Centurie IV. A *fop* is defined as, "a man who is preoccupied with and often vain about his clothes and manners; a dandy."

To this substantial number who they will cast out,	De ce grand nombre que lon envoyera,
In regard of to help within a fortress besieged ones:	Pour secourir dans le fort assiegés:
Infection & extreme need for food everything them will devour.	Peste & famine tous les devorera.
Out of laid seventy who will be overcome ones.	Hors mis septante qui seront profligés.

Note: Originally listed as quatrain number 37 in Centurie II.

The Epic Poem Prophesied by Nostradamus

Hardship into South, Growth together with War	*Saturne en Cancer, Jupiter avec Mars*
In February with a Weapon to be safe world,	*Dedans Fevrier Chaldondon salvaterre,*
Uneven many them Chaste assailed from three quarters,	*Sault Castallon assailly de trois pars,*
As it were touching to who He that was born of the word conflict deadly warfare.	*Pres de Verbiesque conflit mortelle guerre.*

Note: Originally listed as quatrain number 48 in Centurie VIII. Certainly, this quatrain is filled with enigmatic capitalized words that may or may not be as they appear. It is important to know that *Saturn* was in the sign of *Cancer* between June 22, 1944 and August 2, 1946. *Jupiter* and *Mars* were together in Libra and then Scorpio, between August 10, and November 6, 1946. When *Chaldondon* is split into *Chaldon - don*, giving the impression of "*Chaldean gift.*" Although a person from Chaldée is a Chaldéen (in French), if *Chald-on* is allowed to be seen as "*one*" of "*Chaldée,*" then line two may be referring to the February 1947 announcement that Great Britain was leaving Palestine, with their military occupation of Mesopotamia (Chaldea) lifted in the same year. As "*safe land,*" the *land*, which would become Iraq, would have been seen as no longer threatening to British interests. This *safe land* would also include no worry over Iraq going to war to keep the Jews from winning a war against the Palestinians, where that *land* was also vacated by the British. Line three's use of "*three parts*" or "*three factions*" could be the "Big Three," Stalin, Truman, and Attlee, who did nothing to end the fighting in Palestine; or they could be the Arab League, the Palestinians, and the Zionists. The word *Castallon* can be seen as an anagram, such as "*l'Casta-l'on,*" where *the Chaste* one can mean Holy Land, to both Jews and Arabs. In any case, this quatrain appears to be focused on Israel, and the Arab conflict with the Jews.

In temples enclosed the thunderbolt there will enter,	*Dans temples clos le foudre y entrera,*
Them citizens within their own ones mighty ones grieved ones:	*Les citadins dedans leurs forts grevés:*
Mechanized armors, cattle, liegemen, the streaked like waves wall will blast,	*Chevaux, bœufz, hommes, londe mur touchera,*
By reason of extreme desire for things, drought, at the bottom of the more feeble ones provided with weapons ones.	*Par faim, soif, soubz les plus foibles armez.*

Note: Originally listed as quatrain number 6 in Centurie III. It must be noted that line one uses no verbiage that indicates a harmful strike from a *thunderbolt*, nor any indication of something occurring with *lightning* quickness. This is then a main theme about one procuring a weapon that has *thunderbolt* capabilities. The word "*temples*" is an either indication of a Christian nation (churches) or Israel (temple ones). Then this weapon is *enclosed* or *shut up*, so as not to be detected. It is also a weapon that *blasts* with *waves*. Without the accent mark, the word "*greve*" meant, "the place of execution in Paris."

Chapter 33 - War into the Near East

Two beleaguered ones into greedy hastiness,	Deux assiegés en ardente ferveur,
From desire to drink lost ones in regard of both spacious pieces of level land heaped ones:	De soif estainctz pour deux plaines tasses:
Them powerful looked askew at, & one old man dreaming fop,	Le fort limé, & un viellart resveur,
With the people of Geneva to Neither will depart will demonstrate path.	Aux Genevois de Nira monstra trasse.

Note: Originally listed as quatrain number 59 in Centurie IV. The *Two beleaguered ones* could be France and Britain, following World War I and through World War II, during which time both had Protectorate Mandate from the League of Nations over lands of the Middle East. Line two would then be stating the *desire to drink* from the Jordan River again, after the Jews will have experienced centuries of of drought, away from the *plains* that made up Israel and Judah (the Promised Land).

Into city held hostage in them walls liegemen & wives,	En cité obsesse aux murs hommes & femmes
Enemy ones without him principal commander provided ones with oneself to give back:	Ennemis hors le chef prestz à soy rendre:
Blast of wind will be powerful shock of enemies them people of arms,	Vent sera fort encontre les gensdarmes,
Driven away ones being by reason of lime, thick dust & cinders.	Chassés seront par chaux, poussiere & cendre.

Note: Originally listed as quatrain number 52 in Centurie IV. The word *beset* is defined as, "to attack from all sides." Quatrain IV-59 uses the word, "*limé*," which is the English translation of "*chaux*," while meaning, "filed, polished." In modern French, the mineral "*lime*" can be seen in the French word, "*lime*," meaning "*limé*" could mean, "*limed*." That is the effect stated in line four. Quatrain IV-59 also uses the word "*assiegés*," which has the same meaning as the use of "*obsesse*" in this quatrain.

Into following five flock not will put out of one	En apres cinq troupeau ne mettra hors un
Full of evasions for the Travailed one will Pasture,	Fuytif pour Penelon Paschera,
Falseness to rumble help to arrive by reason of in that time,	Faulx murmurer secours venir par lors,
The chief him tribunal in that season will abandon.	Le chef le siege lors habandonnera.

Note: Originally listed as quatrain number 3 in Centurie X. Line one's use of "*five*" links it

The Epic Poem Prophesied by Nostradamus

to quatrain IX-34, where line three leads with that word. Line one is about the Mandate over *five* Middle Eastern nations (1918), of which *one will not be put out* as an independent nation (1948). This quatrain ends with the Palestinian representative at the United Nations leaving without furthering discussions over the theft of Palestine.

Wind North will cause to remove from them siege of a town,	*Vent Aquilon fera partir le siege,*
On wall to cast themselves ashes lime & thick dust	*Par murs geter cendres chaus & pousiere*
By reason of rain following that which their own will make good snare,	*Par pluye apres qui leur fera bien piege,*
Last relief just on the other side their frontier.	*Dernier secours encontre leur frontiere.*

Note: Originally listed as quatrain number 99 in Centurie IX. This quatrain is linked to quatrain IV-52, through the use of the words, "*murs, vent, cendre, chaux, poussiere,* and *encontre.*"

After them scraped even ones burnt ones them without air ones,	*Apres les limes bruslez le asiniers,*
Forced ones will be to change uniforms diverse:	*Contrainctz seront changer habitz divers:*
The Bitter ones inflamed ones by reason of them of the mills,	*Les Saturnins bruslez par les meusniers,*
Without there majority who not will be to cower over ones.	*Hors la pluspart qui ne sera couvers.*

Note: Originally listed as quatrain number 17 in Centurie VI. Nostradamus spelled the word "*Saturnins*" without an "e" (which etymology proves correct), but that spelling allows the word to be translated as *Saturn-in-s*. This becomes *Saturn in ones*. This would make the following possibly pertinent: Israel is said by some to be *Is(is) + Ra + El* (dating to their roots in Egypt), meaning the Moon goddess *Isis*, the Sun god *Ra* and the Hebrew name for Saturn, *El*. The first two are Egyptian and the last is Jewish. When the astrological symbolisms are seen as Emotion, Ego and Patience, they also represent Holy Spirit, Son and Father.

Within a battle him high who little almost nothing surrounding with a wall,	*Dans le conflict le grand qui peu valloit,*
To his last will cause thing strange:	*A son dernier fera cas merveilleux:*
Dangling which Adria will see this that he erred,	*Pendant qu'Hadrie verra ce qu'il failloit,*
In them feast pierced the proud.	*Dans le banquet pongnale l'orguilleux.*

Chapter 33 - War into the Near East

Note: Originally listed as quatrain number 55 in Centurie II. In Old French, the word *pongneor* refers one to lookup the word "*piqueur*," which means *pricker*. However, it also means, "a rider, especially one who pursues a fox with the dogs, at full speed." This seems to connect to quatrain II-02, only later in the story line of this quatrain's central character. The spelling of "*orguilleux*" refers one to look up the word "*orgeol*," which is described as, "A long wart resembling a Barlie corn, and growing on the edge or corner of an eyelid." Still, it appears the spelling can be the equivalent to "*orgueilleux*," as that word and translation follows "*orguilleux*, which follows "*orgueil*."

Six days them setting upon being due warned to appear dated:	*Six jours l'assaut devant cité donné:*
Delivery of something given will be powerful & vehement fight between two armies:	*Livree sera forte & aspre bataille:*
Three there will be bringing to pass & to forgiven,	*Trois la rendront & à pardonné,*
Them remnant in fire & parentage pruned lattice frame.	*Le reste à feu & sang tranche traille.*

Note: Originally listed as quatrain number 22 in Centurie III. The main theme statement (line one) begins with the capitalized word "*Six*", followed by the word "*days*". Together, "*Six days*" has importance as the length of the 1973 war between Israel and united Arab nations.

September rent of assist taken prisoner in war ones tied ones uncivilly,	*Sept cens captifz estachéz rudement,*
Because there half-part to crush, presented a chance:	*Pour la moitie meurtrir, donné le sort:*
Them neighboring confidence will issue from even as at hand,	*Le proche espoir viendra si promptement,*
But not as swiftly than one fifteenth killed.	*Mais non si tost qu'une quinzieme mort.*

Note: Originally listed as quatrain number 48 in Centurie III. The British mandate over Palestine (and Transjordan), and the French mandate over Syria (and Lebanon), became officially effective on *September* 29, 1923. These are supporters of the plan to attack the United States, most effectively on *September* 11, 2001. In 1st Kings 12:33, it states, "On the fifteenth day of the eighth month, a month of his own choosing, he offered sacrifices on the altar he had built at Bethel." This could then be a reference to the return of religious festivals in the Jewish lands. Over 8,200 (soldiers and civilians, both sides) are estimated to have died in the 1948 Arab-Israeli War.

The Epic Poem Prophesied by Nostradamus

There synagogue barren besides of no value fruit	*La synagogue sterile sans nul fruit*
Will be received of one with another them faithless ones	*Sera receu entre les infideles*
With Babylon there daughter to the benefited	*De Babylon la fille du porsuit*
Wretchedness & sad he will cut off them winged ones.	*Misere & triste luy trenchera les aesles.*

Note: Originally listed as quatrain number 96 in Centurie VIII. Line one is focused on the "branch that bears *no fruit*" without the "vine." This is representative of a Jewish religion that has not accepted Jesus as their Messiah. (John 15:5, "I am the vine, you are the branches.")

Hearkened beneath world sacred lady report seeming other than it is,	*Ouy soubs terre saincte dame voix fainte,*
Humane flame in regard of coming from God to perceive to give light:	*Humaine flamme pour divine voyr luire:*
Will act to them alone ones from their own kindred earth colored,	*Fera des seulz de leur sang terre tainte,*
Likewise them holy ones temple ones in defense of the dishonest ones to subvert.	*Et les saints temples pour les impurs destruire.*

Note: Originally listed as quatrain number 24 in Centurie IV.

Fresh ones arrived ones place made without safeguard,	*Nouveaux venus lieu basty sans defence,*
To occupy there place by in that time deserted:	*Occuper la place par lors inhabitable:*
Meadows, houses, fields towns to take with rejoicing,	*Prez, maisons, champs villes, prendre à plaisance,*
Famine, Plague, war, acre of land wearisome able to be worked.	*Faim, Peste, guerre, arpen long labourable.*

Note: Originally listed as quatrain number 19 in Centurie II. The interesting thing about this quatrain is it states a series of events that will be mimicked in the future, following the pattern of the past. It is about the future time when the Palestinian people will rejoice at having their land back. Just as the Jews had been allowed in *without safeguard* in place by the British, their deaths will recreate the same lack of security. The difference is found in line four, where the end of the world will have begun, making the gains for the Palestinians everyone's losses.

Chapter 34

War Along the Fringes of Europe

The State of Greece

Him one with a gifted tongue to enslave others substantial dusky condition will summon to appear by process,	*Logmion grande bisance approchera,*
Cast off will be there uncultivated branch of pedigree:	*Chassé sera la barbarique ligne:*
To them two jurisdictions the one an east partial them will set the teeth on edge,	*Des deux lois l'une l'estinique lachera,*
Barbarous & free at continual underhanded laboring for trust.	*Barbare & franche en perpetuelle brigue.*

Note: Originally listed as quatrain number 80 in Centurie V. The name *Ogmios* (*Ogmius* in Latin) comes from Celtic mythology, and was the diety depicted as an old, balding man, who had golden chains coming from his tongue, connected to the necks of his followers. He was the "middle aged" equivalent of the Greek hero Hercules. Some believe he is related to the Celt god *Ogma*. The implication, due to the information in the quatrain, is that *Him Ogmion* is associated with the legal wrangling of the United Nations, particularly about Zionism. Without capitalization, the word *bisance* may be *bis-ance*, which would be *"the state of brown,"* as the word *bis* meant, "brown, dusky and blackish." Capitalized (spelled *Byzance*), it was the name of the capital of the Byzantine Empire, later to be named Constantinople, then Istanbul.

In them around, upon in the upper air & stronghold,	*Dans les cyclades, en perinthe & larisse,*
Within Sparta all them the Peloponnese ones:	*Dedans Sparte tout le Pelloponnesse:*
Surely substantial famine, contagion, by reason of false known ones,	*Si grand famine, peste, par faux connisse,*
Unknown before month will hinder & everything costly breaking all the joins of a wheel themselves.	*Neuf moys tiendra & tout le cherrouesse.*

Note: Originally listed as quatrain number 90 in Centurie V. In line one there are three Greek locations that are correctly spelled, but not capitalized. The Greek meaning for the islands known

The Epic Poem Prophesied by Nostradamus

as the Cyclades is simply the islands that "*surround*", or "*encircle*" the sacred island of Dilos. The Greek word *larissa* means "stronghold" in English. As such, line one can be making the statement, "*Within them encircled, in thus near & stronghold.* Line two would then be naming Greece as the place of line one. The Cheronesus peninsula is now known as Gallipoli. However, since Chersonesus is not what Nostradamus wrote, it most probably is *cher-roues-se*, which means, "*very costly – breaking all the joints of the wheels – themselves.*"

War & Communication & them gentlemen with coats of arms joined one against the other,	*Mars & Mercure & l'argent joint ensemble,*
Towards the south extreme drought:	*Vers le midi extreme siccité:*
At the depth of Asia one will report world trembled,	*Au fond d'Asie on dira terre tremble,*
Corinth, Ephesus then in perplexity.	*Corinthe, Ephese lors en perplexité.*

Note: Originally listed as quatrain number 3 in Centurie III.

There substantial general hunger that I understanding to summon to appear by process,	*La grande famine que je sens approcher,*
Many times to round, moreover to be belonging to all:	*Souvent tourner, puis estre universelle:*
Surely mighty & continual which one will grow to draw up by the root,	*Si grande & longue qu'on viendra arracher,*
With the lance cause of the matter, & the child from nipple.	*Du bois racine, & l'enfant de mammelle.*

Note: Originally listed as quatrain number 67 in Centurie I. The first half of line four is stating nuclear warheads on missiles (*lances*, or *spears*) will be the cause of *famine*, and what will have been used Many times, such that a toxic cloud will have formed, which will make round the world, until it effects everyone. Once the child has been taken from the *breast*, or from its *pap*, it dies without nourishment. Without children, humanity will have no way of replenishing its population.

Changes In Northern Europe

By then that one King will be against them those belonging to him,	*Par lors qu'un Roy sera contre les siens,*
Native to Blois will bring to subjection Ligurians,	*Natif de Bloys subjuguera Ligures,*
The Breast, Cordoba & them Dalmatians,	*Mammel, Cordube & les Dalmatiens,*

Chapter 34 - War Along the Fringes of Europe

With them September after the pretense for head man of a party not handselled ones & them here many.	*Des sept puis lombre à roy estrennes & lem tres.*

Note: Originally listed as quatrain number 44 in Centurie X. The city of *Cordoba* is in southern Spain in the province of Andalusia. The modern meaning for the word *estrennes* is "New Year's Present, Christmas Box, or Christmas Bonus." As *handselled*, the definition implies a "first" nature, but, in Old French the word could also mean, "beaten, cudgeled, swinged (punished with blows, thrash) or corrected." The 1568 Lyon edition shows the last (two) words as "lem tres." The rhyme scheme would better fit the word "lemurs," as some editions show. However, there is a clear space between the "m" and the "t." The word *lemures* is known in Roman Mythology (aka *larvae*) to mean, "spirits of the dead, or ghosts."

One poisonous snake heeded near with the bed regal,	*Un serpent veu proche du lict royal,*
Will be for lady, darkness shameless fellows not will be loudly railing on:	*Sera par dame, nuict chiens n'abayeront:*
In that time to be rise at France a chief so much majestic,	*Lors naistre en France un prince tant royal,*
From the heaven arrived everything them Potentates will be observing.	*Du ciel venu tous les Princes verront.*

Note: Originally listed as quatrain number 93 in Centurie IV. In Old French, the "combined word", or idiom, "*chien-lict*", meant, "shiteabed; shitten fellow, beastly companion, filthy scoundrel, stinking jack, scurvy mate." This helps one realize "*chiens*" has less chance of being about actually four-legged dogs.

River which hazarded them rare ship to Celtic,	*Fleuve qu'esprove le nouveau nay Celtique,*
Will be upon high with the Empire dominion mutinous:	*Sera en grande de l'Empire discorde:*
Him young potentate through people of the Christian clergy,	*Le jeune prince par gent ecclesiastique,*
Will expel from the kingdom belonging to a crown from agreement.	*Ostera le sceptre coronal de concorde.*

Note: Originally listed as quatrain number 3 in Centurie VI.

The Epic Poem Prophesied by Nostradamus

More than needs long in coming all to them, the bloom ones will be past hope of recovery ones,	*Trop tard tous deux, les fleurs seront perdues,*
Contrary to there course of justice poisonous snake not will want to act:	*Contre la loy serpent ne voudra faire:*
To the members of a league powers by reason of people of Brittany mingled together,	*Des ligueurs forces par gallotz confondues,*
Savona, Albenga for many great death suffered for the truth.	*Savone, Albingne par monech grand martyre.*

Note: Originally listed as quatrain number 62 in Centurie VI. The lower case word, "*gallotz*," is also equivalent of the French words "*gallec*" and "*gallo*." They become capitalized in English translation, as Gallic, or Gaulish, as an indication of non-Breton French. *Savona* is an Italian city on the Ligurian coast, near France. *Alba* is in the Piedmont region of Italy, north of *Savona*.

Whole sum them degrees of worship cleric of a Christian church,	*Tous les degrez d'honneur ecclesiastique,*
Will be converted ones into logical civil government of Italy:	*Seront changez en dial. quirinal:*
Upon Martial of or related to Quirinus like of the office of flamen,	*En Martial quirinal flaminique,*
After one Chief to France him will restore festival to Vulcan.	*Un roy de France le rendre vulcanal.*

Note: Originally listed as quatrain number 77 in Centurie V. The word *Quirinal* is directly related to one of the Seven Hills of Rome, specifically one related to the Sabine founders of Rome and their worship of *Quirinus*, their god of war. The Romans deified Romulus as their god of war and thus compared him to *Quirinus*. On this hill the *Quirinal* Palace was built, which later became the center for the Italian civil government in Rome, separate from the rule of the Vatican. In ancient Rome, a priest was known as a *flamen*. The word *vulcanal* is also correctly spelled volcanal and is defined as a "Temple to Vulcan." It has that specific definition because one specific altar to Vulcan, along with a *Lapis Niger* (the Black Stone), in Rome in 1899, well after Nostradamus wrote of it here.

Fate to snow & Eastern European, & the island British,	*Norneigre & Dace, & l'isle Britannique,*
Through them united ones brothers will be afflicted ones:	*Par les unis freres seront vexées:*
The principal commander of Rome issued from stock Gallic,	*Le chef Romain issu de sang Gallique,*

Chapter 34 - War Along the Fringes of Europe

Likewise the troops in them forests thrust back ones.	*Et les copies aux forestz repoulsées.*

Note: Originally listed as quatrain number 7 in Centurie VI. The word "*Norns*" is the English form of the French "*Nornes*." It is representative of Norse gods that are equivalent to the Greek *Fates*. Both have three entities which govern aspects of unchangeable *fates* in gods and humans. The word "*neiger*" clearly means, "*to snow*," making that a simple anagram. The use of "*to snow*" is symbolic of nuclear fallout. The ancient area known as *Dacia* is now Eastern Europe, around the Danube River, in northern Bulgaria and southern Romania, leading to the Black Sea coast. There the *Daci* people represented the frontier, of the hinterlands of Europe to the Greeks. This location makes the word *Nor* possibly be an abbreviation for the ancient land *Nor*icum, which was the land between the Alps and the Danube, roughly what is now Austria and southern Germany. The Roman Empire had hold of Europe as the *Gallic* Empire between 260 – 273 AD. This consisted of the *three brothers* (in service to Christianity), France, Spain and Britain.

There people from Eastern Europe, with England & Pole year	*La gent de Dace, d'Angleterre & Palonne*
Likewise from Bohemia will be forging new confederacy:	*Et de Boesme feront nouvelle ligue:*
In defense of to transport beyond to Hercules the estate of,	*Pour passer outre d'Hercules la colonne,*
Barcin ones, Tyrrhenian ones will advance tyrannous underhandedly laboring for.	*Barcins, Tyrrens dresser cruelle brigue.*

Note: Originally listed as quatrain number 51 in Centurie V. *Polonne* is in western Ukraine, around 100 km east of the Polish border. In French, the name for Poland is *Pologne*, which could be a secondary translation. *Bohemia* is most of the Czech Republic and Moravia, in central Europe. *Barcin* is a town in north-central Poland. Line three is stating the Rock of Gibraltar, which in French is written *Colonnes d'Hercule*.

The enemy ones to the fortress thoroughly driven off ones	*Les ennemys du fort bien esloignez*
By tank ones cannon him projecting part of a fortification,	*Par chariotz conduict le bastion,*
By reason of above them walls of Middle Class people born themselves grumbling ones,	*Par sur les murs de Bourges esgrongnez*
As for Hercules trumpeted ones an Arabian king.	*Quant Hercules barriz lhœmathion.*

Note: Originally listed as quatrain number 93 in Centurie IX. The modern French word, "*élongé*" (OF "*eslongé*) is synonymous with the French word "*alongé*." The word "*chariotz*" can be read as a military "*tank*," with the "*conduict*" being the cannon placed in its turret. One could even see how the turret of a *tank* could be seen by 16th century eyes as a "*bastion*," with the *tank* itself a

The Epic Poem Prophesied by Nostradamus

fortress. The 1568 Lyon edition is so difficult to read (due to print bleed from the opposing page), the word "*barriz*" is used. The word "*bastera*" is shown in the 1566 Lyon edition. The 1568 Lyon edition provides no evidence of seven letters having been placed in print. Instead, the bleed makes it appear only five letters, but closer inspection shows six letters are there. Only "*bar*" or "*bat*" can be discerned. The Greek mythological figure, *Emathion*, was the brother of the Ethiopian [not the African version] king Memnon.

This one who will possess so much from reputation & cheering ones,	*Celuy qu'aura tant d'honneurs & caresses,*
Has his means to come in to there Beaten down with a pole Belgium:	*A son entree de la Gaule Belgique:*
A time following will be in sort from rudeness ones,	*Un temps apres sera tant de rudesses,*
Both will be in opposition unto at the blossom so many of war.	*Et sera contre à la fleur tant bellique.*

Note: Originally listed as quatrain number 83 in Centurie VI.

By reason of mighty anger him Pope of Rome Belgium,	*Par grand fureur le Roy Romain Belgique,*
To trouble will propose for battalion of soldiers uncivil:	*Vexer vouldra par phalange barbare:*
Rage crashing will drive away stock light-skinned North Africans.	*Fureur grinsseant chassera gent libique.*
Oneself from Yugoslavia until Hercules there penned.	*Despuis Pannons jusques Hercules la hare.*

Note: Originally listed as quatrain number 13 in Centurie V. The Roman name for Belgium was *Gaule belgique*, which appears in quatrain VI-83. (See previous quatrain) *Pannons* are basically Hungarians, around the Danube. *Hercules* is the Pillar of *Hercules*, or Gibraltar. The French word *Libyan* also indicates the alphabet used in Libya, which is the *Tifinay* (the Berber Latin alphabet).

Them old in years ways will be all so stolen ones,	*Les vieux chemyns seront tous embelys,*
Many will fade at Memphis his first blow given,	*Lon passera à Memphis son entree,*
The great Messenger of Hercules bloom with purity	*Le grand Mercure d'Hercules fleurde lys*
Causing to tremble world, sea & country.	*Faisant trembler terre, mer & contree.*

Note: Originally listed as quatrain number 79 in Centurie X. The god *Mercury* (Hermes to the

Chapter 34 - War Along the Fringes of Europe

Greeks) was the holder of the Rod of Asclepius (the symbol of medicine / alchemy). *Hercules* has been seen as short for Gibraltar, which represents the British presence in the Mediterranean. The *fleur de lis* is not only a symbol of France, but also a symbol of purity, while often being seen placed in the hands of the dead.

Chapter 35

The Effects of War on the World

Changed Views of Christianity and Religion

From the seven the Christian branches to three being little strongholds	*Des sept rameaulx à trois seront reduictz*
Them more eldest ones will be found in the deed doing by death,	*Les plus aisnés seront surprins par mort,*
To murder one's own brother the two being seduced ones,	*Fratricider les deux seront seduictz,*
Them conspired against ones in sleeping will be murdered ones.	*Les conjurés en dormans seront morts.*

Note: Originally listed as quatrain number 11 in Centurie VI. In relationship to Christian *branches*, the number *seven* plays an important role in the Book of The Revelations of John. They are the *seven* churches: Ephesus, Smyrna, Pergamum, Thyatira, Sardis, Philadelphia, and Laodicea. These *seven* are then not to be seen as those *seven* specific places in and around Turkey, but expanded to represent the *seven* religions (via the Reformation) to come, where all have sinned against God and Jesus. The use of *three* is then confirming the Christianity focus, representative of the Trinity: God, Jesus, and the Holy Spirit. The Old French idiom, "*en dormant*," meant, "in his sleep, while he took his rest," or, "as he slumbered."

Being bound unto monastery devised child twin-like,	*Devant monstier trouvé enfant besson,*
From substantial kindred to monk & oneself clothed-like ones:	*D'heroic sang de moine & vestutisque:*
His public voice through sect form of speech & sway one's,	*Son bruit par secte langue & puissance son,*
Whose one will command mighty elevated them belonging to you thrust into.	*Qu'on dira fort elevé le vopisque.*

Note: Originally listed as quatrain number 95 in Centurie I. The word "*heroic*" is seen as "*heroique*," where a "*c*" was often used as an abbreviation of "*que*." Still, as the word means the same, as "*heroic*," in English, the use of a word of English can be designed to look towards Britain, as where the *twin* is to be found. The main theme sounds like an excuse used to dissuade someone from recognizing another, through the argument, "That was my twin brother. Not me. I am not that one you think I look like."

Chapter 35 - The Effects of War on the World

Who by reason of weapon priest will cast away ship from Convent,	*Qui par fer pere perdra nay de Nonnaire,*
To Dreadful female creature toward there will be lineage bringing to an end	*De Gorgon sur la sera sang perferant*
Upon land alien will cause in sort all from to keep quiet,	*En terre estrange fera si tout de taire,*
That which will burn him self & her fastening in.	*Qui bruslera luy mesme & son entant.*

Note: Originally listed as quatrain number 79 in Centurie VIII.

Monk religious of child death exposed,	*Moyne moynesse d'enfant mort exposé,*
To perish for rid out of the way & forcibly carried away through glazer,	*Mourir par ourse & ravy par verrier,*
By Time & Pamiers the camp will be placed	*Par Fois & Pamyes le camp sera posé*
The other side of Toulouse Severe to train up to make inroads.	*Contre Tholose Carcas dresser forrier.*

Note: Originally listed as quatrain number 10 in Centurie IX. A *moinesse* is said to be synonymous with *nun*, but also the word "*moniale*," which is defined as, "of or belonging to a monk." The French communes of *Toulouse* and *Carcassonne* are roughly 50 miles apart in southwest France. Unfortunately, *Carcas* does not complete the spelling of Carcasonne. The word *fois*, which means "*time*," can also be spelled "*foix*," which is the name of a city in SW France, near all the other cities named. *Foix* and *Pamiers* are both in the Ariege department. The word *furrier* is at the root of the English word "foray," and said to also be spelled *fourrier*. This in turn leads to the word, "*forreour*," meaning, "raider, plunderer." The Old French dictionary specifically lists *fourrier* as a harbinger, giving an example of a sign in the moon's appearance is a *harbinger* to a mature (menstruating) woman.

In city substantial one monk & handi-crafts man,	*En cite grande un moyne & artisan,*
Nearby to there entrance lodged ones & at them walls:	*Pres de la porte logés & aux murailles:*
On the other side of Modena secret, cave far removed,	*Contre Modene secret, caue disant,*
Treacherously dealt with ones in regard of at the bottom of pretense of marriages.	*Trahis pour faire soubz couleur d'espousailles.*

The Epic Poem Prophesied by Nostradamus

Note: Originally listed as quatrain number 73 in Centurie VI. The city of *Modena* (*Modène* in French) is in north-central Italy, in the Emilia-Romagna region. In Latin the word *caveo* means, "to be on one's guard, take care, beware." Still, in French *cave* means, "cave, cellar, vault or hollow place in the ground."

One scarce of time the temples to them colors	*Un peu de temps les temples des couleurs*
From white & black with the two intermingled:	*De blanc & noyr des deux entremeslée:*
Red ones & yellow ones their own will be stealing away them theirs,	*Rouges & jaunes leur embleront les leurs,*
Lineage, land, perilous persons who ruin others, extreme desire for things, death, to emotions spoiled.	*Sang, terre, peste, faim, feu, d'eau affollée.*

Note: Originally listed as quatrain number 10 in Centurie VI. Colors equate to religious significance: *white* = Judeo-Christian; *black* = Islamic; *red* = atheistic; *yellow* = polytheistic. Note: all are "pastured" from the same source, with Jesus directly related "*To white*," and of the "*black from them*," which are the "*two*" religions born from the children of Abraham, making the tribes "*between mixed.*"

From there departed to Hesitate lofty Pope,	*De la partie de Mammer grand Pontife,*
Will tame them neighbor ones of the Danube:	*Subjuguera les confins du Dannube:*
To follow after the cross for weapon rabble born rift,	*Chasser la croix par fer raffe ne riffe,*
Captive ones, now, prize rings for jousters more with hundred thousand reddened ones.	*Captifz, or, bagues plus de cent mille rubes.*

Note: Originally listed as quatrain number 49 in Centurie VI. The name *Mamers* in Latin meant the Oscan name of Mars, and the Mamertini were then mercenary soldiers, as assumed by certain groups. The use of *rube* as slang, meaning a backwards rustic and unsophisticated country fellow, and when combined with the Latin form *to be red*, becomes a perfect word to describe the Slavic roots of Eastern Europeans, who became red under Soviet domination. The *raffe ne riffe* in line three is opposite the saying *rif ny raf*, which is the root of the word "riffraff," meaning, "people regarded as worthless and disreputable."

Chapter 35 - The Effects of War on the World

World Economy

A substantial faith to gold, with silver them plenty	*Le grand credit d'or, d'argent l'abondance,*
Will act to blind through lust him praise	*Fera aveugler par libide l'honneur*
Will be understood from adultery the harm,	*Sera cogneu d'adultere l'offence,*
Who will come forward in the world to its high disgrace.	*Qui parviendra à son grand deshonneur.*

Note: Originally listed as quatrain number 14 in Centurie VIII. The word *credit* also meant, "reputation; renown; esteem; favor, good opinion of the world; trust; belief; faith; loyalty; credit given; debt entrusted." Line one perfectly describes the change from *gold* backed paper money to *silver* certificates. The word *aveugler* also meant, "ignorant or in error." With John F. Kennedy dead the USA quickly changed from silver certificates to Federal Reserve Notes. Line three could be alluding to the Marilyn Monroe affair, as the *adulterer*. Still, the Latin word *adultero* means, "to defile, falsify and corrupt." Line four states the hidden affair *will come forward* after Kennedy's death, to *discredit* his legacy for the *great* people of the USA.

By war continual all the trained army exhausted,	*Par guerre longue tout l'exercité expuise,*
That as soldiers not will be finding money:	*Que pour souldartz ne trouveront pecune:*
Credit from gold, to silver, leather one will issue this to use,	*Lieu d'or d'argent, cuir on viendra cuser,*
French brass, token (or note) crescent of Moon.	*Gaulois ærain, signe croissant de Lune.*

Note: Originally listed as quatrain number 25 in Centurie VII. In Latin, the word *exercitus* meant, "training, a trained body of soldiers, or army, especially the infantry." In line one the word shown in print, *expuise*, is translated as a misprint for *expulse*. The Old French word *aerein*, or *airain* or *arain*, all meant "brass," which would be of lesser value than copper, and may actually be the intention. Still, those Old French words equally meant "air," such that nothing is the value of currency; but, quality "air" (free of pestilence and radiation) is of greatest importance. The word *cuir* can also mean, "the skin, pelt or hide of an animal," but, from a cow it becomes *leather*.

Them representations of gold & with silver inflated ones,	*Les simulacres d'or & d'argent enfles,*
Which after the taking away to the great pool were thrown ones	*Qu'apres le rapt au lac feirent gettez*
With them evident spent all & seditions.	*Au descouvert estainct tous & troubles.*

The Epic Poem Prophesied by Nostradamus

In the marble written limited ones set between ones.	*Au marbre escript prescriptz intergetez.*

Note: Originally listed as quatrain number 28 in Centurie VIII.

Plight on Nature

Large open piece of level ground risen Ausones fertile, ample,	*Planure Ausonne fertile, spacieuse,*
Will yield gadflies if so be that as well grasshoppers:	*Produira taons si tant de sauterelles:*
Brightness belonging to the sun will become overcast.	*Clarté solaire deviendra nubileuse.*
To eat away them everything, mighty infection to come from them.	*Ronger le tout, grand peste venir d'elles.*

Note: Originally listed as quatrain number 48 in Centurie IV.

By reason of them Suebi ones & states lying close unto ones,	*Par les Sueves & lieux circonuoisins,*
Being in debate in defense of legal matter with them overcast ones:	*Seront en guerre pour cause des nuees:*
Field marine ones locusts & midges,	*Camp marins locustes & cousins,*
From the Geneva transgressions will be quite clean without ones.	*Du Leman fautes seront bien desnuees.*

Note: Originally listed as quatrain number 85 in Centurie V. The *Suebi* are mentioned in quatrain I-61 and II-83. Quatrain II-83 is focused on the border between France-Switzerland-Germany, as a known *Suebi* tribe was in that area. However, they settled throughout Europe, and in particular in the extreme SW of France, close to the Basque people.

Above a hill with Circuit judge & there Bresle	*Sur le mont de Bailly & la Bresle*
Being miserable ones of Grenoble them courageous ones,	*Seront chichez de Grenoble les fiers,*
Beyond Lyon, Vienne them in sort substantial hailed on,	*Outre Lyon, Vien. eulx si grand gresle,*
The grasshopper upon land born in will be more than enough one third.	*Langoust en terre n'en restera un tiers.*

Chapter 35 - The Effects of War on the World

Note: Originally listed as quatrain number 69 in Centurie IX. The word *bailly* (also spelled *bailli*) means *bailiff*, but also any provincial magistrate. *La Bresle* is a river in the Normandy region. Vienne is a commune 30 kilometers south of *Lyon*, in the department of Isère.

Wearisome times in the sky will be seen ash-colored hawk,	*Long temps au ciel sera veu gris oiseau,*
Next from Suffered pain & with Tuscany of earth:	*Aupres de Dole & de Touscane terre:*
Holding in the beak one flourishing branch,	*Tenant au bec un verdoyant rameau,*
Will decay quickly mighty & will end the war.	*Mourra tost grand & finera la guerre.*

Note: Originally listed as quatrain number 100 in Centurie I. *Dole* is in eastern France, in the Jura department, near Switzerland. However, in ancient Rome "the *dole*" was a minimum amount of grain provided for every citizen, particularly the poor. It was initially provided at a low rate, but later given for free. In Switzerland, *La Dôle* is the name of a mountain peak in the Jura Mountain range. It overlooks Geneva. *Tuscany* is in the northwest peninsula coast, north of Rome. The word *bec* also meant the point of land where two rivers (*branches*) meet.

There word listened unto from an unusual hawk,	*La voix ouye de l'insolit oyseau,*
Over them cannon of him them rested place of abiding,	*Sur le canon du respiral estaige:*
In sort noble will grow to the wheat the bushel,	*Si hault viendra du froment le boisseau,*
That a subject with man will be Cannibal-race.	*Que l'homme d'homme sera Antropophage.*

Note: Originally listed as quatrain number 75 in Centurie II. An "*uncommon bird*" could be Nostradamus' way of terming an airplane, or a nuclear cloud. In Greek, the word *anthropos* meant "human being." The 1568 Lyon edition shows "*Antrophopage*," with only one "h." This is then read as the Italian spelling, which becomes an indication where Cannibalism will set in.

In sort substantial general hunger by wave deadly.	*Si grand famine par unde pestifere,*
Through rain outstretched a length to them the pole northern:	*Par pluye longue le long du polle arctique:*
Itself bitter small substance patch-work states of an hemisphere,	*Samarobryn cent lieux de l'hemisphere,*
Will be where food is generated without law freed from him political.	*Vivront sans loy, exempt de pollitique.*

The Epic Poem Prophesied by Nostradamus

Note: Originally listed as quatrain number 5 in Centurie VI. The word *unde* is referred to *onde*, meaning *wave*. However, as *wave* refers to oceans and seas of water, the word *ondée* means: a great and sudden fall of rain. So, *onde* could be the *wave* track of a cloud generating a pestilent rain. The word *arctique* can also be read as *arctic*. Also, *cent lieux* can mean *100%* of the *places*. The break up the name *Samarorbyn* is as "S*e-amarus-obruo-in*," meaning, "[Se] *Itself*, Themselves, Himself; [amarus] bitter, pungent, disagreeable, unpleasant, irritable, *biting*, acrimonious; [obruo] *to fall*, collapse; to cover, bury, swamp, drown; to overwhelm, destroy, obliterate; [in] into, *on to*, towards, against." This becomes a proper name for a nuclear cloud, which is named as "Itself unpleasant to cover against."

Them judgments of God transported over ones lessened a large number of people,	*Les fleaux passés diminue le monde,*
Extended opportunity there peace grounds inhabited ones:	*Long temps la paix terres inhabitées:*
Out of danger will march for heaven, earth sea, & wave:	*Seur marchera par ciel, terre mer, & onde:*
After to fresh them warfare ones awakened ones.	*Puis de nouveau les guerres suscitées.*

Note: Originally listed as quatrain number 63 in Centurie I. The word *fleau* primarily means, "the beam of a great Balance; or, the tendril or young shoot of a vine, whereby it catches hold of what is next to it." However, the word is also used in metaphor to show:,"a scourge, plague or *judgment of God*." The word *inhabitee* means both inhabited and *uninhabited*.

Chapter 36

Unity for A Counter-Offensive

The Hibernating Bear Awakes

From the northern wind them efforts will be mighty ones.	*De l'aquilon les effors seront grands.*
Over the Atlantic Ocean will be there entrance evident:	*Sus l'Ocean sera la porte ouverte:*
The government in the island will be to again being integral,	*Le regne en lisle sera reintegrand,*
Will tremble London through them veiled detected.	*Tremblera Londres par voille descouverte.*

Note: Originally listed as quatrain number 68 in Centurie II. The name *Aquilon* (capitalized) is correctly spelled Old French for the *North Wind*. However, it is written in the lower-case. If that spelling is broken down into *aquil-on*, where the word *aquila* is Latin for "eagle" (*aquilin* in Old French), this repeated name could be stating "the eagle one," with implications of being the eagle of the north. This could be the United States, or France.

From where will provide for to cause to approach general hunger,	*D'ou pensera faire venir famine,*
To there will grow them state of being satiated:	*De la viendra le ressasiement:*
Them look to the sea by reason of insatiably thirsting after something dog-like	*L'oeil de la mer par auare canine*
Because with the one him another anew will yield up anointed, wheat.	*Pour de l'vn l'autre donnra huyle, froment.*

Note: Originally listed as quatrain number 15 in Centurie IV. The modern use of the word *ressaisir* is "to rally" (auto sports) and with "se" to gain "self-control." The same word in Old French is said to mean, "to fill, glut, sate, satiate and *satisfy*."

The Epic Poem Prophesied by Nostradamus

All For One and One For All

One dubious ones born will come long way off from the realm,	Un dubieux ne viendra loing du regne,
There more great portion them will wish to sustain.	La plus grand part le voudra soustenir.
A capitol neither will want by no means that it governed,	Un capitole ne voudra point qu'il regne,
His lofty commission not will have power to bear out.	Sa grande charge ne pourra maintenir.

Note: Originally listed as quatrain number 13 in Centurie VI. In Latin the word *capitolium* meant Rome, in particular the temple of Jupiter there. The word *Capitole* refers to *Capitoline* Hill in Rome; and that is the source of the English word *capitol*. The rumors and doubts about Barack Obama's citizenship seem to fit this quatrain.

A lineage royal will be in sort very mingled,	Le sang royal sera si tresmeslé,
Forced on against one's will being French with the Western land:	Constraint seront Gaulois de l'Hesperie:
One will look for that time evening slipped gently along,	On attendra que terme soit coulé,
Likewise what remembrance from there word might be lost.	Et que memoire de la voix soit perie.

Note: Originally listed as quatrain number 40 in Centurie V. The Latin name "*Hesperia*" also represented "Spain, or Italy."

To govern forces to increase with the Empire,	Dresser copies pour monter à l'Empire,
Of the Vatican him lineage Royal will maintain:	Du Vatican le sang Royal tiendra:
Flamingos, of England, Spain together with Aspired unto,	Flamans, Anglois, Espaigne avec Aspire,
Towards them Italy & France will contend.	Contre l'Italie & France contiendra.

Note: Originally listed as quatrain number 12 in Centurie VI. The French word *flaman* means *flamingo*, many of which are red or pink in hue. Sounds like the Noble Guard at the Vatican, originally model after the Spanish Nobel Guard, but forbid by Napoleon. This guard is now held by Swiss volunteers. The word could be seen (if a missing letter at the end is omitted in abbreviation) as *Flamand-s*, which translates as "*Flemish ones*," meaning "those who speak Flemish."

Chapter 36 - Unity for a Counter-Offensive

With North Wind mighty ones striving for a matter with whole strength through warlike woman	*Vers Aquilon grands efforts par homasse*
In a manner a Europe & the whole world to afflict,	*Presque l'Europe & l'uniuers vexer,*
Them two defecting ones will thrust into such violent expression,	*Les deux eclypses mettra en telle chasse,*
Likewise with them Hungarians whole time & death to strengthen again.	*Et aux Pannons vie & mort renforcer.*

Note: Originally listed as quatrain number 15 in Centurie VIII. The name *Aquilon* can mean the "Eagle One." The word *homasse* is said to be representative of a woman acting like a man, as would be the case in the changes allowing women to serve in the military. In this regard, Germany is led by Angela Merkle, who was raised in East Germany, in a family where the father was a Lutheran minister. She would fit the description of a man-like woman, as the leader of a strong European nation, where half was once a strong Soviet ally. Today, the region known as *Pannonia* is western Hungary, and parts of Austria, Slovenia, Croatia, Slovakia, Serbia, and Bosnia-Herzegovina.

As for those of the pole northern united ones together,	*Quant ceulx du polleartiq unis ensemble,*
In East great terrorist & dreaded:	*En Orient grand effraieur & crainte:*
Elected new upheld the high temple,	*Esleu nouveau soustenu le grand temple,*
Wandered ones, Istanbul with race Barbarous stained.	*Rodes, Bisance de sang Barbare taincte.*

Note: Originally listed as quatrain number 21 in Centurie VI. The word *effrayeur* is one who frightens, which is now commonly called a "terrorist." *Rhodes* is part of coastal the islands of Greece, but only 11 miles from the coast of Turkey. As *Rodé-s*, or *Wandered ones*, a more significant peoples are stated, who would be the returning Jews of modern Israel.

As it were touching long way off defection of two high lights,	*Pres loing defaut de deux grand luminaires,*
Which will happen one with another an April & War:	*Qui surviendra entre l'Avril & Mars:*
O what scarcity! more both noble ones courteous ones,	*O quel cherté! mais deux grans debonaires,*
Through country & sea will be assisting all function.	*Par terre & mer secourront toutes pars.*

Note: Originally listed as quatrain number 5 in Centurie III. The word *Mars* does mean the month *March*; however, the French do not capitalize the words representing months. As spelled, with the

363

capital letter, *Mars* would better represent the planet or the Roman god of the same name. While this would match line one's astrology statement (*luminaries* are either the Sun or the Moon, as they generate light – sourced or reflected), but a planet would not correctly fit surrounding an ampersand with *April*. Between *April* and *March* are eleven months.

Another Invasion to Liberate France

Like one griffin will come them head man of a party to Europe	*Comme un gryphon viendra le roy d'Europe*
Accompanied with those of the Northern Wind,	*Accompaigné de ceux d'Aquilon,*
From red ones & whitish ones will lead mighty through a turn	*De rouges & blancz conduira grand troppe*
Both will be marching in opposition to him chief of Babylon.	*Et yront contre le roy de Babilon.*

Note: Originally listed as quatrain number 86 in Centurie X. The spelling of *gryphon* is acceptable for *griffin*. It had the body of a lion, with head and wings of an eagle, representing two kings of two kingdoms (animals & birds) together. It was symbolic of being the guardian of the divine, with divine power. The combination of a lion and eagle is certainly the two "united ones" (Unis), the United States [eagle] and the United Kingdom [lion]. The name *Aquilon* can also mean "Eagle-one."

From sea through forces upon three region divided ones,	*De mer coppies en trois parts divisees,*
Has there another them been living ones will be ending,	*A la seconde les vivres failleront,*
Without hope ones searching fields the Lightning struck ones,	*Desesperez cherchant champs lHelisees,*
Foremost ones into breach between ones victory will be having.	*Premiers en breche entrez victoire auront.*

Note: Originally listed as quatrain number 97 in Centurie IX. The 1568 Lyon edition has some difficulties with being clear, due to opposite page ink bleed. The word "*divisees*" is determined due to the letter count matching, and the 1566 Lyon edition showing the word as "*divisée.*" The word that is determined to be "*entrez*" (line four) is entirely based on the 1566 Lyon edition. The *Elysian Fields* were where Greek Heroes went after falling in battle. In French, the English term "*Elysium*" is "*champs Élysées.*"

Chapter 36 - Unity for a Counter-Offensive

By reason of them noble prince them bordering upon to the Watch-tower,	*Par le grand prince l'imitrophe du Mans,*
Faithful & courageous general of the mighty army of men:	*Preux & vaillant chef du grand exercite:*
Through sea & land to you Brittany ones & Normandy ones,	*Par mer & terre de Gallotz & Normans,*
Them biting to pass Barcelona pillaged island.	*Caspre passer Barcelone pillé isle.*

Note: Originally listed as quatrain number 10 in Centurie VII. The commune of *Le Mans* is in northwest France, in the department of Sarthe, on the banks of the Sarthe River. In Roman times the city was called simply *Mans*. The *Gallotz* were the people who spoke the *Gallo* Language in the region bordering on *Normandy*, with its heart being in *Le Mans*. The *Normans* were the people of northern France, of eastern Brittany and western Flanders, who spoke the *Gallo*-Romance language. The Muslims were forced out of Spain, between 1200 and 1600 AD. However, the Caliphate of Cordoba, which ruled over Iberian Moors, with acceptance of both Christians and Jews, collapsed in 1031. This led to Islamic rule without tolerance then.

An army from sea being bound unto warned to appear will keep,	*L'armée de mer devant cité tiendra,*
After will divide besides to act extended journeyed,	*Puis partira sans faire longue allee,*
Citizen ones substantial spoil upon country will seize,	*Citoyens grande proye en terre prendra,*
To come back armed forces to restore great stolen.	*Retourner classe reprendre grande emblee.*

Note: Originally listed as quatrain number 68 in Centurie X. The *army before city* is very close to the siege placed in the series about Israel. Line four's statement about the *stolen* land taken by the *great* would be the Arab view of Israel and the land of Palestine. However, the story of the invasion of Western Europe will be another example of stolen lands, using the philosophy that "if might makes it right for you to steal Palestine for Israel, then here's might giving us the right to steal your lands of Europe and treat your people the same as the Israelis have treated Arabs."

Inwardly the means into a place of Garonne & Baïse	*Dedans l'entree de Garonne & Bayse*
Both there forest not far off to Damazan	*Et la forest non loing de Damazan*
With the marsh willows congealed ones, after hailed on & north wind	*Du marsaues gelees, puis gresle & bize*

The Epic Poem Prophesied by Nostradamus

Of ordained ones them frozen cold by reason of oversight from altar.	Dordonnois gelle par erreur de mesan.

Note: Originally listed as quatrain number 35 in Centurie VIII. There is a place identified as Valance-sur-*Baïse*, said to be just 8 kilometers south of Condom, 40 kilometers southwest of Agen and 30 kilometers northwest of Auch. This is in the department of Gers, in the Midi-Pyrenees region. The *Garonne* River flows through Agen, just east of where the Gers River joins it. The Gers River flows to the north, east of *Baïse*. The *Baïse* River is sourced near the base of the Pyrenees, and flows into the *Garonne* near the commune Aiguillon. This is in the department of Lot-et-*Garonne* department, in the Aquitaine region. The commune of *Damazan* is west of Aiguillon, by three miles. The commune of *Damazan* is northwest of Agen, in the Lot-et-*Garonne* department, which is where the Lot River joins the *Garonne* River. There is an area known as the Landes *forest*, which is also known as "*les Landes des Gascogne*," or "the Moors of Gascony." It covers a large triangle of land along the Atlantic coast, north to near the *Garonne* River, west of Agen, and follows the *Garonne* (to its west), until it reaches the coast. The *Dardanelles* takes its name from the city Dardania, which is not Anatolia. Line four is then most likely referring to the people of Anatolia, as *Dardonnois*.

IN THE PRESENCE OF Aquitaine by reason of assaults British ones,	VERS Aquitaine par insults Britanniques,
With for them very same ones mighty ones invasion ones	De par eux mesmes grandes incursions
Rains frozen ones will be causing grounds partial ones,	Pluyes gelées feront terrois iniques,
Port Islam fashions will forge incursions.	Port Selyn sortes fera invasions.

Note: Originally listed as quatrain number 1 in Centurie II. There is a city named *Vers* in the Lot Department, in the Langudoc region, near *Aquitaine*. There are two other communes with the name *Vers* in France, each further away. In French, the word *vers* translates as "towards." As the first quatrain in Century two, as with all first quatrains in a "chapter," all of the letters of the first word are capitalized. However, this cannot be seen as unintentional, as nothing in *The Prophecies* is to be viewed as unintentional. The word *incursion* is defined as, "an aggressive entrance into a foreign territory; a raid, invasion." The *Port* is most likely referring to Bordeaux, since line one states the area as *Aquitaine*.

In the fields full of herbs from Wind & to them Var born snow,	Aux champs herbeux d'Alein & du Varneigne,
Of the mountain Him dark of color close unto with the Durance,	Du mont Lebron proche de la Durance,
Army lodged from two regions battle will be so biting,	Camp de deux parts conflict sera si aigre,
Land between two rivers will wax feeble in there France.	Mesopotamie defaillira en la France.

Chapter 36 - Unity for a Counter-Offensive

Note: Originally listed as quatrain number 99 in Centurie III. It is possible the place appearing as *d'Alein* is the same as what is now known as *Alleins*. *Alleins* is between Salon-de-Provence and Lubéron.

Calais, Arras assistance in Thérouanne,	*Calais, Arras secours à Theroanne,*
Accord & seeming will pretend a thing is so a spy,	*Paix & semblant simulera lescoutte,*
Consolidated in them rings to descend on Roanne	*Soulde d'Alabrox descendre par Roane*
From Tornay people who will hand over there rout.	*Destornay peuple qui deffera la routte.*

Note: Originally listed as quatrain number 88 in Centurie IX. The French commune of *Calais* is on the English Channel coast, near Belgium. The commune of *Arras* (Dutch: Atrecht) is just south of *Calais*, in the same department – Pas-de-*Calais*. The commune of *Roanne* (Arpitan: Rouana) is in mid-eastern France, 90 kilometers northwest of Lyon, in the Loire department. *Tornay* is in the same department as Langres, to the southwest about 25 miles, near the Franche-Comté region border.

STAKE, SHIP, WHIP ONE more fire which in blood will be,	*PAV, NAY, LORON plus feu qu'a sang sera,*
Them Aude to swim, to flee mighty with them on the upper face of a plain,	*Laude nager, fuir grand aux surres,*
Them will provoke ones first entrance will repel,	*Les agassas entree refusera,*
One of Pamplona, Durance them will keep restrained ones.	*Pamplon, Durance les tiendra enserres.*

Note: Originally listed as quatrain number 1 in Centurie VIII. The first two names in line one (*PAU* and *NAY*) are of communes of SW France, in Aquitaine. Both are in what was the former province of Béarn. The river *Oloron* is named after the commune *Oloron*-Saint-Marie. All three names are then found related to the present Pyrenees-Atlantic department. *The Aude* refers to the river that flows through the department *Aude*, on the Mediterranean coast at the Pyrenees border with Spain, often referred to as "Cathar Country." The *Durance* flows from the southwest Alps, through four departments and into the Rhone near Avignon.

The Epic Poem Prophesied by Nostradamus

In Interchangeable course of things, Gien, defended will be eyes piercing into ones,	A Tours, Gien, garde seront yeulx penetrans,
Will be detecting from long way off the mighty bright:	Descouvriront de loing la grand sereine:
It & its uninterrupted course of things to the harbor for ships being entering ones,	Elle & sa suitte au port seront entrans,
Combat, violently put on ones, army of men excellent.	Combat, poulsés, puissance souveraine.

Note: Originally listed as quatrain number 14 in Centurie II. There is a major city in central France named *Tours*, in the Indre-et-Loire department. It is midway between Orleans and the Atlantic coast, on the Loire River. However, the word *tours* can mean, "turns, rounds, circles, compasses, revolutions; bouts, prowls; courses, ranks, places, orders; pranks, tricks, shifts, and devices." It is also a word used to denote a "rook" piece on a chess board, such that it means, "tower." The French commune *Gien* is in the Loriet department in north-central France, 50 miles east of Orleans, on the Loire River. Both *Tours* and *Gien* are in the Center Region, at opposite ends, *Tours* west and *Gien* east.

Bordeaux, Roan horse, & there La Rochelle joined ones,	Bourdeaux, Rouan, & la Rochele joints,
Will be holding at the tower there great sea ocean (Atlantic),	Tiendront autour la grand mer oceane,
English, Bretons & them Flemish ones conjoined,	Anglois, Bretons & les Flamans conjoints,
Them will be chasing until close to Roanne.	Les chasseront jusques aupres de Rouane.

Note: Originally listed as quatrain number 9 in Centurie III. There is a commune named *Bourdeaux* near Valence, south of Lyon. It is not on the Atlantic coast, where *Bordeaux* is located. The spelling should be seen as relative to *Bordeaux* due to its proximity to *La Rochelle*. *Rouen*, the city in France (the capital of Normandy), is near the northern coast, not far from Belgium. Those logistics makes little sense of the main theme statement. However, the use of *Roan horse* takes the focus to the biblical prophecy of *The Revelation*, and the second horseman, implying war. *La Rochelle* is a port city north of *Bordeaux*, on the Bay of Biscay (part of the Atlantic *Ocean*). *Flaman* is French for *flamingo*; but, it is also Latin for "priest of a god." Still, the Dutch spelling of *Flemish* is "*Vlamingen*." With V equaling F, it becomes *Flamings*, or *Flamants*. The commune of *Roanne* is in mid-eastern France, 90 kilometers northwest of Lyon.

There tower to Mouth will fear small galley Barbarous,	La tour de Bouq craindra fuste Barbare,
A time, continual opportunity after bark western:	Un temps, long temps apres barque hesperique:

Beastly, race, moving ones whole sum two will be forging assured loss of merchandise,	*Bestail, gens, meubles tous deux feront grant tare,*
Bull & Scales what deadly grudge?	*Taurus & Libra quelle mortelle picque?*

Note: Originally listed as quatrain number 28 in Centurie I. The Port du *Bouc* is where a fort was built around the 13th Century, with a lighthouse marking the grand mouth of the Rhone into the Mediterranean Sea. The lighthouse is known as the *Tour de Bouc*.

Islamic Persecution of the Gold Standard

There mighty casting of a fish net will grow to blame, to howl	*La grande pesche viendra plaindre, plorer*
From to occupy chosen, cheated ones being upon the days:	*D'avoir esleu, trompés seront en l'aage:*
Not long with them risen will intend to abide,	*Guiere avec eulx ne vouldra demourer,*
Betrayed will be through those from its language.	*Deceu sera par ceulx de son langaige.*

Note: Originally listed as quatrain number 35 in Centurie VII. The word *plaindre* means, "to bewail, bemoan, or moan for; to blame, accuse, expostulate, find fault with, and complain of; to grudge." This main theme does not mean the Children of Israel are complaining, due to the "*casting of a fish net*" being a Jesus reference; but the main theme is focused on Israel. The translation of "*l'aage*" as, "*the days*," is to convey the time of "*the days of reckoning*."

Him prince without to his territory Celtic.	*Le prince hors de son terroir Celtique.*
Will be dealt treacherously with, deceived by translator:	*Sera trahy, deceu par interprete:*
Roan horse, La Rochelle, by reason of those from an Amorica	*Rouan, Rochelle, par ceulx de l'Armorique*
At the port with Blaye deceived ones by monk & priest.	*Au port de Blaue deceuz par moyne & prebstre.*

Note: Originally listed as quatrain number 60 in Centurie VI. The commune of *Rouen* is in northern France and said to be the capital of Normandy. *La Rochelle* is a port city on the Bay of Biscay (part of the Atlantic Ocean), north of Bordeaux. Both "*Rouen*" and "*Rochelle*" also appear in quatrain III-09. The word *Rouen* makes more sense as "*Roan horse*," making it be a statement of the second Horseman of the Apocalypse. The name *Amorica* was used to denote in ancient times the part of Gaul that includes Brittany and the territory between the Seine and Loire rivers in France. In ancient times, the commune of *Blaye* was known as *Blavia*. It is on the Gironde estuary,

The Epic Poem Prophesied by Nostradamus

56 kilometers north of Bordeaux.

Beneath there gravestone will be found him singular ruler,	*Dessonbz la tombe sera trouvé le prince,*
Who will have them apprehended by on high Nuremberg:	*Qu'aura le pris par dessus Nuremberg:*
The Spanish Head man of a party into Capricorn thin,	*L'Espaignol Roy en Capricorne mince,*
Deed & dealt treacherously with by them substantial Wittenberg.	*Fainct & trahy par le grand Vvitemberg.*

Note: Originally listed as quatrain number 15 in Centurie VI. The German city of *Nuremberg* was the unofficial capital of the Holy Roman Empire. It was one of the largest trade centers between Italy and northern Europe, while also known for it Iron Maiden, the massacre of many Jews; and, the first acceptor of the Reformation. The German city of *Wittenberg* was the home of Martin Luther, and the University of Wittenberg (U-vitemberg) provided him with his outlet for the reformation (begun in 1502, Martin Luther was bestowed Doctor of Theology designation there, in 1508).

Them kindred of the Reasonable by reason of the Tryol people there fair,	*Le sang du Juste par Taurer la daurade,*
In defense of themselves to take revenge against them Bitter ones	*Pour se venger contre les Saturnins*
At the rare trap will be ducking the public authority in to,	*Au nouveau lac plongeront la maynade,*
Then will be marching against them Albanians.	*Puis marcheront contre les Albanins.*

Note: Originally listed as quatrain number 40 in Centurie VIII. The Greeks named the land *Taurica* or *Tauris* because of the *Tauri* people that lived in what is now called Crimea, which is a peninsula in the Black Sea, extending off the Ukraine. The highest mountain in the Austrian Alps is "Hohe Tauren", and the people of this area are historically known as Taurer people. The word *daurade* refers to the word *dorée*, which means, "guild over; also, of gold; also, fair, beautiful and brightly shining."

Being bound unto them snare where more esteemed your fire cast	*Devant le lac ou plus cher feut getté*
From September month, & his army defeated	*De sept mois, & son host desconfit*
Being ones of Spain through Albanians destroyed ones	*Seront Hyspans par Albannois gastez*
By reason of pause damage upon giving a conflict.	*Par delay perte en donnant le conflict.*

Chapter 36 - Unity for a Counter-Offensive

Note: Originally listed as quatrain number 94 in Centurie VIII.

The Russian Naval Assault on the Gibraltar Blockade

When the more mighty will bear the price,	Quand le plus grand emportera le pris,
To Nuremberg, from In the purge ones & those of Lowest part of them	De Nuremberg, d'Auspourg, & ceux de Basle
By reason of Cologne principal commander Frankfort recovered:	Par Agrippine chef Frankfort repris:
Will be piercing through for Flemish until upon Helmet.	Transverseront par Flamant jusques en Gale.

Note: Originally listed as quatrain number 53 in Centurie III. Both *Nuremberg* and *Augsburg* are in the German area of Bavaria, the most southern region of Germany. The town of *Basel* (also spelled *Basle*) is in northwestern Switzerland and is split by the flow of the Rhine River, which also marks the border of France and Germany, making *Basle* also border both France and Germany. The Roman figure *Agrippina* was the younger daughter of Germanicus (Emperor Claudius) and *Agrippina*, and she was born in the area where Cologne Germany now sits. She was the sister of Caligula and the mother of Nero and said to have canine teeth. Symbolically she would represent a diabolical female *leader*.

With the captain to the war naval,	Du conducteur de la guerre navale,
Red without government, rough horrible taken violently,	Rouge effrené severe horrible grippe,
Captive escaped from the eldest in there humble them:	Captif eschappé de l'aisné dans la basle:
In as much as he will take beginning of the great one son Agrippa.	Quant il naistra du grand un filz Agrippe.

Note: Originally listed as quatrain number 91 in Centurie VI. The word *effrené* also means, "rash, heady, resolute, unruly, disordered and without government." *Agrippa* was a Greek philosopher, the one who argued five grounds for skepticism. In French, the word *agrippé* means, "grabbed."

Chapter 37

When the Going Gets Tough, Use A Nuke

The Big Mistake

Them fortress ones of besieged ones thrust up together ones,	Les forteresses des assieges serrés,
By reason of dust with fire deepened ones into bottomless pit:	Par poudre à feu profondés en abysme:
The traitors being everything ones full of life ones closed ones	Les prodideurs seront touts vifs serrés
Never to them places where sacred vessels are kept not had come to pass so miserable schism.	Onc aux sacristes n'avint si piteux scisme.

Note: Originally listed as quatrain number 40 in Centurie IV. This quatrain's use of "dust with fire" (*poudre à feu*) matches it to quatrain IX-99, and others in the series about the last stand of Israel.

On sea them red will be undertaken with the pirates,	Par mer le rouge sera prins des pyrates,
There accord will be by reason of its path disturbed:	La paix sera par son moyen troublee:
The anger & the unreasonable desire will commit through devised act	L'ire & l'avare commettra par fainct acte
At the great Pontiff will be the army largely increased.	Au grand Pontife sera l'armee doublee.

Note: Originally listed as quatrain number 44 in Centurie V. The "sea" is probably the Mediterranean Sea, absorbing the importance of a capitalized preposition. Still, it could also include a path along a lesser sea, like the Black, Aegean, or Adriatic seas. The word pirate is a reference to the pirates of the Barbary Coast of North Africa; although in today's usage, the Somalians could be included in this overview. The red is always an indication of people without religious beliefs, which would be those of Eastern Europe.

Chapter 37 - When the Going Gets Tough, Use a Nuke

At the port for ships of POLAND & to saint Nicolas,	Au port de PVOLA & de saint Nicolas,
To perish Northman in the gulf this Zealot,	Perir Normande au goufre Phanaticque,
Cape from Byzantium wandered ones to cry alas,	Cap. de Bisance raves crier helas,
Escorts with to Cadiz & from the great Philip-like.	Secors de Gaddes & du grand Philipique.

Note: Originally listed as quatrain number 30 in Centurie IX. To see a *port of Poland* makes one remember that was where Lech Waleska became popular as the leader of the dockworker's strikes, at Gdansk. His actions led to an agreement for unions in 1980. The Polish leader feared armed intervention by the Soviets and arrested Waleska (along with others). Here in the Christian West, we easily recognize *Saint Nicholas* as Santa Clause, who obviously bears gifts. The Randle Cotgrave dictionary lists "*Nicolas*", and specifically states it to be a proper name, that of the patron *saint* of Russia. The word *wellaway* is archaic English, which was used to express woe and distress, as a lamentation, like "alas." *Gaddes* can be split into *Gad – des*, where *Gad* was a Biblical prophet of King David, and "*des*" means *de le* (of the) or *from*. The Spanish port city of Cadiz was known as *Gades* in Latin, such that *d'Gades* is the translation used above.

Folk gathered to observe unheard of before public sight,	Peuple assemblé, voir nouveau expectacle,
Princes & Kings by reason of a large number assisting ones:	Princes & Roys par plusieurs assistans:
The Pillars to fail, walls more much like unto monstrous thing,	Pilliers faillir, murs mais comme miracle,
A King delivered from danger & thirty from the moments.	Le Roy sauvé & trente des instans.

Note: Originally listed as quatrain number 51 in Centurie VI. The Latin word "*exspecto*", which is the root for the English word, "expect", should be read into the word written, "*expectacle*," as a "public sight" that comes with much expectation. Prince William was born in 1985. He will thus turn thirty in mid-2015. The secondary theme indicates both *Princes* will become *Kings*, as having joint or co-rulership responsibilities.

Firmi them fields with them Rodanes entrances	Frymy les champs des Rodanes entrees,
Where them ones undertaken to fight against Infidels being well near equal ones,	Ou les croysez seront presque unys,
The two branches of a river in fishes hit upon ones	Les deux brassieres en pisces rencontrees

The Epic Poem Prophesied by Nostradamus

As well a mighty regiment of soldiers by reason of deluge punished ones.	Et un grand nombre par deluge punis.

Note: Originally listed as quatrain number 91 in Centurie VIII. The area known as *les Rodanes* is in the province of Valencia, in Spain. It is a preserved natural park and is on the east-central coast of Spain. Still, in Old French, the word *rodane* meant, "a type of sweet cherry." Provence is where cherries are grown in France. Competition is Mediterranean mostly. The words *en pisces* would mean "in Pisces" if the "p" was capitalized. If intended to mean this, then the *two arms* would represent two planets.

Mighty chief will come to seize port for ships near to Nice	Gran roy viendra prendre port pres de Nisse
Them great empire of there killed so hell of the heathens	Le grand empire de la mort si en fera
With the Diametrically opposite ones will set down its beginning,	Aux Antipolles posera son genisse,
Through sea the Ravaged everything will suddenly be gone.	Par mer la Pille tout esvanoira.

Note: Originally listed as quatrain number 87 in Centurie X. The 1568 Lyon edition makes it appear that line two could end stating one word, "*enfera*," rather than two words, "*en fera*." The one word, "*enfera*" meant the plural form of, "Hell of the heathen." The 1611 French-English dictionary states this as, "*les Enfers*," but another "pocket dictionary," from 1853, shows this translation possibility. The word *genisse* was used as slang to indicate, "selling virginity, or prostituting a maid." Still, the Bible wrote of the sacrifice of a red heifer in Leviticus 19, as a rite of purification. It could be possible to see "*genisse*" as "*s'genies*," which fits Nostradamus' Preface by representing, "oneself good angels, or oneself bad angels."

With the run-away from the mighty fortress,	Au deserteur de la grande forteresse,
Next unto that will occupy his seat abandoned:	Apres qu'aura son lieu abandonné:
One's adverse party will forge in sort noble valor,	Son adversaire fera si grand prouesse,
An Emperor swiftly killed will be overthrown in law.	L'Empereur tost mort sera condemné.

Note: Originally listed as quatrain number 65 in Centurie IV.

NEXT UNTO combat & battle naval,	APRES combat & bataille navale,
Him mighty god of the sea at his more profound alarm bell	Le grand neptune à son plus haut befroy

Chapter 37 - When the Going Gets Tough, Use a Nuke

Red adversary from fear will grow pale	*Rouge aversaire de peur viendra pasle*
Thrusting into them high ocean upon astonishment.	*Mettant le grand ocean en effroy.*

Note: Originally listed as quatrain number 1 in Centurie III. The word *combat* can also mean, "bickering, debate, conflict, strife, contention." The word *bataille* has more certain military meaning, as it applied to the main battles between two armies, and in particular those led by the princes or royal leadership. The word *befroy* can also mean, "the sound of alarm, a sudden fear and a beacon." The use of *pasle* to translate as "whitish" is to show the color change from red to white. *Pasle* most commonly translates as "pale." The word *effroy* can also mean, "astonishment, amazement, fright."

By fire from the sky there warned to appear well nigh burned,	*Par feu du ciel la cité presque aduste,*
A jar for human ashes brought ones themselves still These ones well hidden,	*L'urne menasse encor Ceucalion,*
Extremely grieved Sardinia by reason of the Warlike stripped of everything by violence,	*Vexée Sardaigne par la Punique fuste,*
Next unto that Balance will relinquish its Fallen star.	*Apres que Libra lairra son Phaëton.*

Note: Originally listed as quatrain number 81 in Centurie II. The astrological sign Aquarius is often called, "*The Urn,*" due to the Latin *Aquarius* meaning, "Water-bearer," and depicted as a god pouring water from an urn onto the earth below, from a cloud. The 1568 Lyon edition clearly shows "*Ceucalion*", and not "Deucalion." Deucalion is the Greek equivalent to Noah, and should be seen as intended to give secondary meaning of inundation by waters, or sailing on waters. The translation below stems from the Greek root words that creates the word "*eucalyptus*." Phaeton was the mortal son of Apollo, who wished to drive his father's chariot, pulling the sun. The zodiac sign of Libra is represented by the scales, thus meaning "*balance*" will leave.

Sardinian Non-faith ones so deep will be overflowing,	*Sardon Nemans si hault desborderont,*
That one will think Deucalion to rise again,	*Qu'on cuidera Deucalion renaistre,*
Within them the statue larger than life there majority will be running fast,	*Dans le collosse la plus par fuyront,*
Vesta tomb fire extinguished to be apparent.	*Vesta sepulchre feu estaint apparoistre.*

Note: Originally listed as quatrain number 6 in Centurie X. The copy viewed, of the 1568 Lyon

The Epic Poem Prophesied by Nostradamus

edition, makes it appear line four ends with a colon. This could be opposite page bleed, but if it is indeed a colon, this quatrain will be found further developed in a sequential quatrain. The goddess Vesta was the goddess of the hearth and domestic life. Her eternal flame was central to the Roman society's piety.

Quite as it were touching to the Crested throng there consequence:	Bien pres du Tymbre presse la lybitine:
One almost nothing being due mighty inundation:	Un peu devant grand inundation:
Him principal commander of the ship seized, thrust into there dregs of the population,	Le chef du nef prins, mis à la sentine,
Castle, palace into general burning by fire.	Chasteau, palais en conflagration.

Note: Originally listed as quatrain number 93 in Centurie II. In a Marseille set of Tarot Cards, the 13th major arcana card, known in English as "The Death card", is names, "*La Lybitine*." The card depicts a skeleton, and represents the consequences of one's soul, through the challenges of life. The symbolism is more towards "change" and "transformation" than the moment of "death."

To the lofty of the hill Aventine, sound listened to,	Du hault du mont Aventin, voix ouye,
Waste ones devoid ones from all them two coasts,	Vuydez vuydez de tous les deux costez,
With the race from red ones will be the anger myself assess,	Du sang des rouges sera l'ire assomye,
From Rimini Prato, Column to boot ones.	D'Arimain Prato, Columna debotez.

Note: Originally listed as quatrain number 2 in Centurie IX. *Prato* is a province in the Tuscany region of Italy (northeast of Rome). Line four is stating the whole of the peninsula of Italy, where it is shaped like a "*Column*", to the "boot" toe and heel.

What infection & sword not in scarce habitation to wear away,	Que peste & glaive n'a peu seu definer,
Death inwardly them moreover height of the sky wounded:	Mort dans le puys sommet du ciel frappé:
An abbot will decay at what time will observe to wreck,	L'abbé mourra quand verra ruiner,
Those from the shipwreck a rocky place wanting for to clutch.	Ceux du naufrage l'escueil volant grapper.

Note: Originally listed as quatrain number 56 in Centurie II. The word *grapper* is correctly

Chapter 37 - When the Going Gets Tough, Use a Nuke

spelled, and means, "to glean after grape-gathers." The word "glean" is defined as, "to collect bit by bit, most commonly to have workers pick up the grain left after the reaper." However, the English word "grapple" is rooted in the Old French word "*graper*," which is stated to mean, "to seize, to pluck, to clutch," as relative to a "grappling" hook on ships.

MUSLIM singular ruler them Italy quiet,	*SELIN monarque l'Italie pacifique,*
Governed ones joined together ones Head man of a business professed messiah to the world:	*Regnes unis Roy chrestien du monde:*
Perishing will propose to plant into soil an association	*Mourant voudra coucher en terre blesique*
Following pirates to hold hunted after to the surge of the sea.	*Apres pyrates avoir chasse de l'onde.*

Note: Originally listed as quatrain number 77 in Centurie IV. In the lower case, the word "*chrestien*" begins to be seen as a lesser meaning that the capitalized "*Christian*". As such, the root of the meaning becomes the answer, as the man named Jesus had no last name, such as Christian. The word "*Christ*" comes from the Greek word for the Hebrew "*messiah*". The word *blesique* is not cleanly found, leading to the anagram, "*l'besique*". Still, the word *blessé* appears to be an intended secondary read, as it means, "wounded", with the word "*blesmi*" meaning, "grown pale, weak, whitish or dead colored." In either case, it is useful to understand an "earth" with little support of green growth. It is important to note that Barbary pirates were largely North African raiders.

Light which will be for queen saluted,	*Jour que sera par royne saluee,*
A day after him greeting, there entreaty,	*Le jour apres se salut, la priere,*
The account makes reason & valley drunk,	*Le compte fait raison & valbuee,*
By reason of before submissive never born had been so disdainful.	*Par avant humble oncques ne feut si fiere.*

Note: Originally listed as quatrain number 19 in Centurie X. The word "*saluë*" is defined as, "a volley of shot given for a welcome to some great person." This means the main theme is about a female leader being acknowledged as "a great person."

From without purpose attempted an honor by sinister means that found fault with	*De vaine emprise l'honneur indue plaincte*
Pirates roaming ones on regions surrounding the Latin lands cold, hunger, wandering ones	*Galiotz errans par latins froit, faim, vagues*
Not far from them my Tiber with blood there land stained	*Non loing du Tymbre de sang la terre taincte*

377

The Epic Poem Prophesied by Nostradamus

As well before humans will be diverse ones scourges.	*Et sur humains seront diverses plagues.*

Note: Originally listed as quatrain number 63 in Centurie V. The word *Galiotz* is translated as *Galliot*, which meant a pirate who sailed on a Galleon ship, raiding other ships. The 1568 Lyon edition shows at the bottom of page 93 the word "*Galliot*" as the printers reminder which word is printed next on page 94. However, the word typeset on page 94 is "*Galiotz.*" This word does have a smudge, such that it could be "*Gallotz.*"

Uncivil most supreme power by reason of a third part usurped,	*Barbare empire par le tiers usurpé,*
There more mighty share with its blood will put to death:	*La plus grand part de son sang mettra à mort:*
Through departed this life senile of the quarter blasted as with lightning,	*Par mort senile par luy le quart frappé,*
Because fear that race, of them stock bred may be murdered.	*Pour peur que sang, par le sang ne soit mort.*

Note: Originally listed as quatrain number 59 in Centurie III.

There trust this one Carthaginian upon East undone,	*La foy Punicque en Orient rompue,*
Great Judiciously & Rhone, Loire & Tagus will be converting:	*Grand Jud. & Rosne, Loyre & Tag changeront:*
At what time from the mule the hunger will be satisfied,	*Quand du mulet la faim sera repue,*
Fleet tossed, blood & bodies will be floating.	*Classe espargie, sang & corps nageront.*

Note: Originally listed as quatrain number 60 in Centurie II. A "*Carthaginian*" can be seen as one from Tunis, specifically, or one from North Africa, generally.

Chapter 38

The Flip Side of Persecution is More Persecution

The Tide Has Turned

Of France through bounds, mountain ones will arrive to pierce:	*Gaulois par saults, monts viendra penetrer:*
Will usurp by force lofty dwelling place of him into to creep up:	*Occupera le grand lieu de l'insubre:*
With the more secret his army will cause to go in,	*Au plus profond son ost fera entrer,*
Tortured ones, Monaco will be thrusting fleet red.	*Gennes, Monech pousseront classe rubre.*

Note: Originally listed as quatrain number 37 in Centurie IV.

From Barcelona, to Tortured ones & Venice,	*De Barsellonne, de Gennes & Venise,*
With there the Time infection Money united ones,	*De la Secille peste Monet unis,*
Against Barbarous fleet will be seizing there power,	*Contre Barbare classe prendront la vise,*
Savage, violently put on quite far off until at Tunis.	*Barbar, poulse bien loing jusqu'à Thunis.*

Note: Originally listed as quatrain number 42 in Centurie IX. The Tunisian city *Ras Jabel* was known as *Thunisa*.

Saturn to the beef played upon the water, War with shaft,	*Saturn. au beuf joue en l'eau, Mars en fleiche,*
Six from February subjection unto death will deliver up,	*Six de Fevrier mortalité donra,*
Those of Bayonne in Landing stage in sort mighty breached	*Ceux de Tardaigne à Burge si grand breche*

The Epic Poem Prophesied by Nostradamus

That has Red-bridged general Barbarian will die.	Qu'à Ponteroso chef Barbarin moura.

Note: Originally listed as quatrain number 49 in Centurie VIII. The period at the end of *Saturn* means the word is abbreviated. The Latin form *Saturnus* would simply translate as Saturn; and the French form is *Saturne*. However, using the Latin word *Saturnalia*, the word implies the planet-god Saturn, but adds the date of festival for that god, being December 17th. The use as that one word would then become a timing element. The use of *arrow* means the sign of Sagittarius, the Archer. There is evidence of a capitalized "*Tardagne*", which is related to Bayonne. The "*T*" is clearly printed, such that it in no way could be meant to be "Sardaigne", or Sardinia.

By reason of an inundation of waters & plague massive,	Par le deluge & pestilence forte,
The city noble from wearisome time beleaguered,	La cité grande de long temps assiegee,
There common soldier ordered to stand watch & guarded with public authority dead,	La sentinelle & garde de main morte,
Unlooked for seized, but to no one outraged.	Subite prinse, mais de nul oultragee.

Note: Originally listed as quatrain number 82 in Centurie IX.

With the populous ungrateful deeds the warnings,	Au peuple ingrat faites les remontrances,
By reason of in that time him furnished with arms themselves will lay hold of To edge,	Par lors l'armee se saisira Damtibe,
Within an arc Monaco will be making them lamentations,	Dans l'arc Monech feront les doleances,
And at Frejus the one the besides will embrace seashore.	Et à Frejus l'un l'autre prendra ribe.

Note: Originally listed as quatrain number 23 in Centurie X. The place named Antibes is in France, on the coast south of Nice. However, the 1568 Lyon edition makes it clear an "*m*" is present, as well as showing a capitalized "*D*" (*Damtibe*), making Antibes (no "s" is present either) an intended secondary reading. The place named *Frejus* is on the Mediterranean coast (Cote d'Azur), south of Antibes. Sounds like it goes with the initial invasion scenario.

Chapter 38 - The Flip Side of Persecution is More Persecution

A year what Hardship & War levels enflamed,	*L'an que Saturne & Mars esgaulx combust,*
The blast of wind powerful wasted away continual state of carrying over from shore to shore:	*L'air fort seiché longue trajection:*
Through fires inward ones, with burning substantial state parched	*Par feux secretz, d'ardeur grand lieu adust*
Scarce rain, vapor them furious, war ones, invasions.	*Peu pluye, vent chault, guerres, incursions.*

Note: Originally listed as quatrain number 67 in Centurie IV. In astrology, the word *combust* has a specific meaning, such as, "Combustion" occurs when the unassisted view of a planet from the earth is obscured by the light of the sun. This deeper level of astrological knowledge is not the main intention, however. The main theme is astrological only in a secondary sense. As such, When Saturn and Mars will both next be in the same fire sign together (equally in fire) occurs between March and September, in the year 2016 (with Mars going retrograde and spending parts of May and June in Scorpio, a water sign).

Them nine diminished in value upon utter destruction,	*Le neuf empire en desolation,*
Will be metamorphosis to the pole one of the north,	*Sera change du pole aquilonaire,*
To there Sicily will grow a violent motion of thoughts	*De la Sicile viendra l'esmotion*
To hinder an undertaking with Philip tributary.	*Troubler lamprinse à Philip tributaire.*

Note: Originally listed as quatrain number 81 in Centurie VIII. The main theme, as stated above, would denote the European nations Spain, Italy, France, Belgium, Germany, Switzerland, England, the Netherlands, and Denmark. When read as, "*The new empire in desolation,*" that becomes the United States of America. The word *Philippine* in Old French meant, "an edict whereby Philip the Fair assumed to himself the absolute bestowing and disposal of regal benefices". The word "benefice" is associated with the Roman Catholic Church, as the practice of land (or pay) given to priests (thus the church) for their service to the community providing spirituality to the people. Queen Elizabeth's husband is Prince *Philip*, of Greece and Denmark. The name *Philip* is connected to a line of Macedonian (partially Greece) kings.

At the great marched that one declared of them liars,	*Au grand marché qu'on dict des mensongiers,*
From top Land flood & field of Athens:	*Du bout Torrent & champ Athenien:*
Will be surprised by them calvary swift ones,	*Seront surprins par les chevaux legiers,*

The Epic Poem Prophesied by Nostradamus

For Albanian War, Lion, Saturnine one who pours out.	*Par Albanoys Mars, Leo, Sat. un versien.*

Note: Originally listed as quatrain number 91 in Centurie V. The city *Torrent* is so close to the Spanish city of Valencia that it is considered within the city limits. Line three's "*horses*" could be referencing the Four Horsemen of the Apocalypse, but the Greek reference in line two could mean the 4-horses that pulled mythological chariots bringing surprising results. In French the word for the astrological sign, Aquarius, is *verseau*, meaning the water bearer who spills water upon the land, from the air, as the one spilling. *Saturn* will not be in the sign of the water bearer again until mid-December 2020, when it will be there for several years.

Hardship & War upon lion Spain captive,	*Saturne & Mars en leo Espagne captifve,*
By chief of north African people in the battle entrapped,	*Par chef lybique au conflict attrapé,*
Adjoining with Maltha-bitumen, with Ivy seized quick,	*Proche de Malthe, Heredde prinse vive,*
Likewise Roman monarchy will be through cock struck.	*Et Romain sceptre sera par coq frappé.*

Note: Originally listed as quatrain number 14 in Centurie V. The word *Maltha* appears in English dictionaries, as Latin, from Greek, spelled with an "*a*" at the end, instead of the "*e*" the French use. Both *Saturn AND Mars* will next be in the sign of *Leo* together around July of 2036. However, with the ampersand making a separate statement about *Mars*, this planet will return to the sign of *Leo* next, between September, October and November, 2011, and again, beginning in late August, 2013. At those times, *Saturn* will be in Libra, then Scorpio.

Cross, agreement, under one performed most holy stomach full,	*Croix, paix, soubz un accomply divin verbe,*
Them Spain & France will be joined together ones one in the company of the other:	*L'Espaigne & Gaule seront unis ensemble:*
Great destruction neighboring, & battle very bitterly,	*Grand clade proche, & combat tresacerbe,*
Mind so confident neither will be who bred trembled.	*Cœur si hardy ne sera qui ne tremble.*

Note: Originally listed as quatrain number 5 in Centurie IV.

Chapter 38 - The Flip Side of Persecution is More Persecution

There mighty city of Tarsus by reason of French,	La grand cité de Tharse par Gaulois,
Will be utterly devastated, taken prisoner by war ones all with Turkish hat:	Sera destruicte, captifz tous à Turban:
Assistance on sea in the great people of Portugal,	Secours par mer du grand Portugalois,
Prime of summer them day to the sacred Urban.	Premier d'esté le jour du sacre Urban.

Note: Originally listed as quatrain number 85 in Centurie VI. The capitalization of the word *Turban* gives the impression of a place. However, since the word is not a known name of a place, it become synonymous with Turkey, in particular because of line one, but also of Iran (Persians) and the Taliban – all of whom see importance in the wearing of a *Turban*. Pope *Urban* IV began the feast of Corpus Christi (Body of Christ), which has a date of recognition connected to Trinity Sunday and the first Holy Eucharist. The only dates that will qualify as *summer* will be in 2011, when it will occur on June 23, and 2014, when it will occur on June 19. The *first* day *of summer* occurs around June 19 and 20. The feast is typically in May and early June.

One almost nothing being bound unto monarch slaughtered?	Un peu devant monarque trucidé ?
Beaver, Polluted ones in ship, fate longhaired:	Castor, Pollux en nef, astre crinite:
The brass apparent to all on land & sea emptied out,	L'erain public par terre & mer vuidé,
Pisa, Cast, Weapon Rare, Turin, country prohibited.	Pise, Ast, Ferrare, Turin, terre interdicte.

Note: Originally listed as quatrain number 15 in Centurie II. The words written, "*astre crinte*," are the French equivalent of the Latin *stella crinita*, which means "a comet." *Ast* is not a clean spelling of Asti, as it meant in French, "weapons to be cast." *Ferrare* is a good French spelling of Ferrara, but can also mean *Iron-rare*, which are *weapons cast*, but not often, like nukes.

Swift rejoicing twelve months unlooked for sorrow	Subite joye an subite tristesse
Will be at my Rome with the reputations embraced ones	Sera à Romme aux graces embrassees,
Mourning, shrieks, lamentations, them provided with weapons surpassing all others in goodness	Dueil, cris, pleurs, larm. sang, excellant liesse
Against ones tied together ones taken napping ones & undone ones.	Contraires bendes surprinses & trossees.

The Epic Poem Prophesied by Nostradamus

Note: Originally listed as quatrain number 78 in Centurie X. The 1568 Lyon edition shows some significant differences that other editions do not show. One is the use of *"an"* in the main theme line. This use of *"year"* means much more than the other publications that state, *"en"*, or "into, upon, at". In the second line, the 1568 Lyon edition clearly spells *"Romme,"* with an extra *"m"*. The others do not. In the third line, there is an abbreviation, such that *"larm."* is not limited to being *"larmes,"* or another way of saying, "tears," it can be the cause of tears, as *"l'armée."* There is also the spelling of *"excellant"* in the 1568 Lyon edition, such that the "-ant" ending (the present participle –*ing*) is changed in other editions, to an "-ent" ending, making "excellent." Line four spells *bendes* with an "e", while others make it "bandes", with the last word shown as *"trossees,"* while others add a "u", making it become "troussees." Those last two words are acceptably changed to those forms, but the others are key to interpreting this quatrain correctly.

This lofty absolute prince who at the death will inherit	*Ce grand monarque qu'au mort succedera*
Will deliver up whole time illicit & lecherous,	*Donnera vie illicite & lubrique,*
By reason of recklessness with all will believe,	*Par nonchalance à tous concedera,*
Who to there in the end will be expedient the law Salic.	*Qu'à la parfin faudra la loy Salique.*

Note: Originally listed as quatrain number 38 in Centurie V. The combination *à la parfin* means, "at length, at last, in the end, when all is done and when all comes to all." However, it literally translates to *"in the by-end."*

A tree that has through continual opportunity deceased dried,	*L'arbre qu'estoit par long temps mort seché,*
Within one night will grow to turn back green:	*Dans une nuict viendra à reverdir:*
No Judgment head man of a party ill at ease, sovereign base fought with	*Cron roy malade, prince pied estaché,*
Crying from enemies will cause veil to rebound.	*Criant d'ennemis fera voile bondir.*

Note: Originally listed as quatrain number 91 in Centurie III. The 1568 Lyon edition does not show the first word of line three to be abbreviated (by ending with a period mark). Some editions show it as such. Without that mark, the letters have to be arranged as an anagram to solve its meaning. As *"n'Cor,"* from Latin, the *"malady"* is shown to be a "mental disease," where one is "not of right mind," or "not of emotional stability."

Chapter 38 - The Flip Side of Persecution is More Persecution

Of Mite, Lascivious, there city to the sacred Temple	Cydron, Raguse, la cité au sainct Hieron
Will again flourish them considering deeply support,	Reverdira le meditant secours,
Death sons to chief by reason of murdered with both risen hero,	Mort filz de roy par mort de deux heron,
Him Arabian not Cruel will be making one same course.	L'Arabe Ongrie feront un mesme cours.

Note: Originally listed as quatrain number 63 in Centurie X. The city of *Ragusa* is on the southern tip of the Italian island, Sicily. In French, the city is spelled *Raguse* The name *Hieron* is related to Greek rulers of Syracuse and Sicily.

The under-age son of the great & hated prince,	Le mineur filz du grand & hay prince,
From leprosy will have at twenty years great blemished:	De lepre aura à vingt ans grande tache:
Of sorrow his mother will die very discontented & thin.	De dueil sa mere mourra bien triste & mince,
Likewise he will die there where tomb well-beloved delivered.	Et il mourra la ou tombe cher lache.

Note: Originally listed as quatrain number 7 in Centurie IV.

At what time will be close unto ones a defection from the lunar ones,	Quand seront proches le defaut des lunaires,
To him one with them another neither far removed mightily,	De l'un à l'autre ne distant grandement,
Cold, drought, hazard against them boundaries of a country,	Froid, siccité, danger vers les frontieres,
Very same ones in what place the sentence delivered by God in received entrance into.	Mesmes ou l'oracle à prins commencement.

Note: Originally listed as quatrain number 4 in Centurie III.

The Epic Poem Prophesied by Nostradamus

Into there frontier of Caussade & these Exile ones.	*En la frontiere de Caussade & Charlus.*
Not but little far off to the depth of the valley	*Non guieres loing du fons de la vallee*
To town at Liberty mosque in this place with sound of lutes,	*De ville Franche mosicque à son de luths,*
Encompassed ones dove bones & great public humiliation in pillory with paper miter on the head.	*Environnez comboulz & grand mytree.*

Note: Originally listed as quatrain number 41 in Centurie X. There is a commune named *Carlus* is in the department of Tarn, in the Midi-Pyrenees region of southern France. For that meaning to be seen, one would have to accept the "*Ch*" represents "*C*." *Caussade* is a larger commune, north of Toulouse, whereas *Carlus* is a small commune close to Albi, northeast of Toulouse.

In the fields of Northern Iran, from Arabia & to Armenia,	*Aux champs de Mede, d'Arabe & d'Armenie,*
Two mighty ones troops three course themselves will be drawing together:	*Deux grans copie trois fois s'assembleront:*
As it were touching to the bank of Araxes there household servants,	*Pres du rivaige d'Araxes la mesgnie,*
With the noble Suleiman in country will be tumbling down.	*Du grand Soliman en terre tomberont.*

Note: Originally listed as quatrain number 31 in Centurie III. The *Araxes* is a river in Turkey and the southern border with *Armenia* and Azerbaijan, emptying into the Caspian Sea. The ancient land called *Medes* was north, western and northwestern portions of modern Iran, and parts of Kurdistan and Azerbaijan. The Greek name for *Medes* was Media. The Ottoman ruler *Suleiman* the Magnificent was the Sultan who ruled during the days of Nostradamus.

From Axis THE SPREADS within cavern like a goat	*De Pol MANSOL dans caverne caprine*
Hiding hole & apprehended taken from by force out of by the beard,	*Cache & prins extrait hors par la barbe,*
Captives led like beast mongrel	*Captif mené comme beste mastine*
By reason of people of Bigorre led near to Tarbes.	*Par Begourdans amenee pres de Tarbe.*

Note: Originally listed as quatrain number 29 in Centurie X. *Mansol* appears spelled the same (without capitalization) in quatrain V-57, and IV-27. *Tarbes* is in southwest France, in the Midi-Pyrenees district; and, its Occitan name is *Tarba*. The plains surrounding *Tarbes* represents the

Chapter 38 - The Flip Side of Persecution is More Persecution

northern part of ancient *Bigorre*, with the region known as Gascony.

At the harbor for ships Islam him tyrant laid with dead,	*Au port Selin le tyran mis à mort*
There freedom not yet for all that rescued:	*La liberté non pourtant recouvrée:*
Them fresh War for vengeance & conscious-stricken,	*Le nouveau Mars par vindicte & remort,*
Lady through violence from terror praised.	*Dame par force de frayeur honorée.*

Note: Originally listed as quatrain number 94 in Centurie I.

Chapter 39

Post-War Punishments and Lost Lessons

American Justice

At that time that one Chamber mighty honest,	*Alors qu'un Bour fort bon,*
Bearing on himself them seizures of body to justice,	*Portant en soy les marques de justice,*
From his lineage then yet for all that its title	*De son sang lors pourtant long nom*
By reason of excuse wrongful will admit of one's punishment.	*Par fuite injuste recevra son supplice.*

Note: Originally listed as quatrain number 44 in Centurie VII. : Source is the 1627 Lyon edition. The translation of the word *Bour* is debatable. The word is cleanly found in an English dictionary (online), defined as, "A chamber or a cottage." This would relate to the creation of the word *bourgeois*, which was a term to describe a townsman, or the social middle-class, with the word closely linked to *borg* (or *burc*), meaning "town." As such, when capitalized as *Chamber*, the word becomes representative of the *Chambers* of Parliament, where *Chambers* also means *Houses*. In the English Parliament, there are two *Chambers*, the *House* of Commons, and the *House* of Lords. Both can be read (individually) in the main theme statement.

One lofty of Auxerre will perish quite distressfully,	*Un grand d'Auxerre mourra bien miserable,*
Hunted after from those who under him have subsisted:	*Chassé de ceux qui soubz luy ont esté:*
Restrained with chains, next unto of barbarous big rope,	*Serré de chaisnes, apres d'un rude cable,*
Upon a year that War, Arrived ones, & Land laid into summer	*En l'an que Mars, Venus, & Sol mis en esté*

Note: Originally listed as quatrain number 84 in Centurie IV. Neither of the 1557 and 1568 Lyon editions show any punctuation at the end of line four. This would indicate a the main theme of another quatrain links to the astrological elements in line four. The commune of *Auxerre* is in central France, between Paris and Dijon. As an astrological timing element in line four, the inclusion of the Sun means that only the signs Cancer, Leo and Virgo are to be considered, because

Chapter 39 - Post-War Punishmnents & Lost Lessons

these ore the signs of *summer*. *Mars* is then the planet that would most specifically set the timing, as it would have to enter one of these signs during the time that Venus would next move into and then followed by the *Sun*. That order of presentation will determine the year of this quatrain. A year that may be similar to what line four states will come in 2017. However, when *summer* ends then (*Sun* moves from Virgo into Libra) *Venus* and *Mars* will still be in the sign Virgo, with *Venus* going into Libra before *Mars*, but both going into Libra by October 22nd, before the *Sun* leaves Libra.

To them condemned by judgment ones will be made one high reckoning,	*Des condemnés sera fait un grand nombre,*
At what time the monarchs will be atoned ones:	*Quand les monarques seront conciliés:*
More him one from them will arrive in sort grief encumbered	*Mais l'un deux viendra si malencombre,*
Who debates one with another neither being again allayed ones.	*Que guerres ensemble ne seront raliés.*

Note: Originally listed as quatrain number 38 in Centurie II.

Whole sum them lovers who will be possessing reserved estate,	*Tous les amys qu'auront tenu party,*
In defense of ungentle into letters laid dead & his enclosed,	*Pour rude en lettres mys mort & sacaigé,*
Pleasures divulged ones by trusted with ones noble nothing in them,	*Biens publiez par fize grand neanty,*
Never of Rome people not had been in such manner abused.	*Onc Romain peuple ne feut tant outragé.*

Note: Originally listed as quatrain number 20 in Centurie X.

Them aged in years division of Roman people to anoint in the moment of to the hot baths	*Le vieil tribung au point de larthemide*
Will be thrust close together servile unto not again to purpose for,	*Sera pressee captif ne destinrer,*
Him desires no vow he a harmful reasoning cowardly	*Le veuil non veuil le mal parlant timide*
For legitimate with their paramours to give.	*Par legitime à ses amys livrer.*

Note: Originally listed as quatrain number 85 in Centurie X. It is very possible that *"larthemide"* (minus the "h") is a variation of *artimis*, the twin sister of Apollo, and thus the Moon goddess Leto.

The Epic Poem Prophesied by Nostradamus

Them only ones pledges to them not right delivery,	*Les soulz signez d' n digne délivrance,*
As well to there penalty of forfeiture will be occupying against judgment,	*Et de la multe auront contre advis,*
Transformation monarch placed in peril them deemed,	*Change monarque mis en perille pense,*
Restrained ones in cage him will be seeing vice with visage.	*Serrez en caige le verront vis à vis.*

Note: Originally listed as quatrain number 47 in Centurie IX. The 1568 Lyon edition shows what appears to be a superscript "*9*" following the "*d*", as an indication of a mark meaning more than an apostrophe. This has occurred before, indicating "*d*" as abbreviated from "*des*." There is then no letter following the superscript, leading to an "*n*" that is followed by a space, before "*digne*" follows that. The 1566 Lyon edition shows this as "*d'indigné*", but it clearly is not that. Still, "*n digne*" bears the same meaning as "*indigne*". The word *multe* can also translate as "amerciment" or "amercement", meaning "*Law* to punish by a fine imposed arbitrarily at the discretion of the court." Also, the French words together, *vis à vis*, means in conversation, "face to face." However, as Nostradamus does not tend to repeat the same translation of the same repeated word, *vis* has separate meanings as *visage (face)* and *vice*.

Confessor military leader aged from years, & from desire to drink burdened,	*Pere duc vieux d'ans, & de soif chargé,*
In the light furthest from good sons disavowing them inquired after	*Au jour extreme filz desniant les guiere*
Within a pit alive death will approach over head and ears in,	*Dedans le puis vif mort viendra plongé,*
Senate with the rank there dead long & unsteady.	*Senat au fil la mol longue & legiere.*

Note: Originally listed as quatrain number 15 in Centurie X. Line one could be a statement about Lord Louis Mountbatten, the great uncle to Prince Charles, who was known to have been the confidant to Charles in his youth. Mountbatten was an Admiral, as well as the Earl of Burma, and Viceroy of India. Thus, he was a provincial governor and military leader (a *duc*).

Before them father a child will be killed,	*Devant le pere l'enfant sera tue,*
Him confessor following together bound with cords with bulrush,	*Le pere apres entre cordes de jonc,*
Genevan people populous will be themselves done their utmost,	*Genevoys peuple sera esvertue,*

Chapter 39 - Post-War Punishmnents & Lost Lessons

Lying the chief to the middle much as one headless body.	Gisant le chief au milieu comme un tronc.

Note: Originally listed as quatrain number 92 in Centurie X. The word *jonc* means "rush, bulrush", both words which are referencing the flora of swampy land, particularly plants like cattails. The word *tronc* is referring specifically to the trunk of a tree, but also specifically means the "headless body of man or beast."

With sorrow will depart this life him unfruitful debased,	*De dueil mourra l'infelix profligé,*
Will solemnize in large assemblies of people his stepfather these the sacrifice:	*Celebrera son vitrix l'heccatombe:*
Ancient authority liberal edict brought back,	*Pristine loy franc edict redigé,*
Them protection & Monarch in the seventh day fallen.	*Le mur & Prince au septiesme jour tombe.*

Note: Originally listed as quatrain number 18 in Centurie V. The word "*dueil*" also meant, "mourning attire, and mourning weeds."

The Lost Continents

The places ones inhabited with people will be ones which cannot be dwelt on:	*Les lieux peuples seront inhabitables:*
In defense of lands to use substantial disposing of parcels:	*Pour champs avoir grande division:*
Governments distributed unto ones in circumspect ones unable to conceive ones,	*Regnes livrés à prudents incapables,*
In that time them noble ones priests killed & controversy.	*Lors les grands freres mort & dissension.*

Note: Originally listed as quatrain number 95 in Centurie II.

The Epic Poem Prophesied by Nostradamus

Wearisome times will be without to remain lodged,	*Long temps sera sans estre habitée,*
In what place Seine & Marne round about comes to water gently:	*Ou Seine & Marne autour vient arrouser:*
To there Thames & warlike ones tested by attack,	*De la Tamise & martiaulx temptée,*
Deceived ones them guardians into presuming to slowly accustom.	*Deceuz les gardes en cuidant repouser.*

Note: Originally listed as quatrain number 43 in Centurie VI. The capitalized words – *Seine, Marne & Tamise* – are seen as the names of three rivers – the Seine, the Marne & the Thames. The *Seine* River flows through northwest France, originating just north of Dijon, going through Paris on its way to the English Channel. The *Marne* River is a right tributary of the *Seine*, in the area east and southeast of Paris, thus northwest France. The River *Thames* in England flows from east of the village Kimbal, eastward, through London, into the English Channel.

In Campania him This assaulted one will be so many,	*En Campanie le Cassilin sera tant,*
Which one not will perceive what of to them the fields veiled ones:	*Qu'on ne verra que d'aux les champs couverts:*
Being bound unto following there rain from long time,	*Devant apres la pluye de long temps,*
Out of laid them trees something the one will regard with green.	*Hors mis les arbres rien l'on verra de vert.*

Note: Originally listed as quatrain number 31 in Centurie II. There is an ancient town in Campania Italy, named *Casilinum*, which was the site of a Roman victory over the Franks. This quatrain gives the impression of dead bodies ("*so many*") that cannot be detected at first, due to "*green*" vegetation using their decayed bodies as fertilizer to grow.

And If That Wasn't Enough

To waste away from extreme desire for something, to desire to drink, lineage of Geneva,	*Seicher de faim, de soif, gent Genevoise,*
Confidence next will grow in one to make a default:	*Espoir prochain viendra au defaillir:*
South moment shaking will be course of justice Genoan opening in the wall.	*Sur point tremblant sera loy Gebenoise.*

Chapter 39 - Post-War Punishmnents & Lost Lessons

Armed forces to the great harbor for ships not themselves has power them to strike.	*Classe au grand port ne se peut acuillir.*

Note: Originally listed as quatrain number 64 in Centurie II. The words *Gebenoise, peult* and *acuilir* are open for different translation. The word *Genevoise* was the name for a Genevan currency for a short period of time in the 18th Century, and is the feminine singular spelling for one of Geneva, or "*Genevan.*"

From chamber ones city to lady there Garland	*De Bourze ville à dame Guyrlande*
Many will place on by reason of the treason done,	*Lon mettra sus par la trahison faite,*
The lofty prelates to Leon through Common place to plead for open basket,	*Le grand prelatz de Leon par Formande,*
False them fanatical ones & violent takers overthrown.	*Faulx pellerins & ravisseurs deffaite.*

Note: Originally listed as quatrain number 47 in Centurie X. A prelate is a bishop or abbot (an ecclesiastic) of superior rank.

Migrated ones departed with Geneva ones not one spared,	*Migres migre de Genesve trestous,*
Patience of gold into iron themselves will transform,	*Saturne d'or en fer se changera,*
Them against KING NO WAY POSSIBLE ONES will ruin by banishment all,	*Le contre RAYPOZ exterminera tous,*
Time of the arrival him coming the sky signs will make.	*Avant l'advent le ciel signes fera.*

Note: Originally listed as quatrain number 44 in Centurie IX. In alchemy *Saturne* represented the element (metal) lead. The alchemist is known for having sought to "turn *lead into gold*", but instead of this being an attempt at physical alteration of metals, it represents an esoteric change. The Sun, alchemically, represented *gold*, and astrologically represents "self". This points to a relationship between *Saturn* (the Father) and the Sun (the Self, or Son). It is then a quest to spiritual reward, to seek a heavenly plane. By seeing *RAYPOZ* as *ROY PAZ* (pl. for *PAS*), where the all-caps *KING* is Jesus, and the all-caps *NO WAY POSSIBLE ONES* is any and all who did not believe in the Christ (this includes Jews who forsook Him). In line four, the two words – *avant* and *advent* – have clear ties as religious words, meaning the coming of the Savior, or *Advent*.

The Epic Poem Prophesied by Nostradamus

Him heaven (to this Charlatan there alleged) we presage,	Le ciel (de Plancus la cité) nous presaige,
By reason of easy to discern ones famous ones & by stars settled ones.	Par clers insignes & par estoilles fixes.
Who from his transformation unlooked for oneself drawing near unto the age,	Que de son change subit s'aproche l'aage.
Born for one's benefit not in defense of its offences.	Ne pour son bien ne pour ses malefices.

Note: Originally listed as quatrain number 46 in Centurie III. In the parenthesis of the main theme, Nostradamus alludes to his future reputation as a *Charlatan*.

Will swell the reckoning so high of them astronomers	Croistra le nombre si grand des astronomes
Expelled out of ones, banished ones & books admonished ones,	Chassez, bannis & livres censurez,
Him year millennium six estimate & September for sacred assembled ones	L'an mil six cens & sept par sacre glomes
Who of no value to the sacred ones not being confirmed ones.	Que nul aux sacres ne seront asseurez.

Note: Originally listed as quatrain number 71 in Centurie VIII. The word *astronome* also meant, "teacher of the stars." The censorship would be the 16th Century Catholic Church position, which followed Nostradamus' death. The Church's Index of Prohibited Reading began as part of their plan of further Inquisition. Bruno was burned at the stake in Rome in 1600 for supporting Copernican astronomy. Kepler publishes important work on astronomy in 1607, as well as Galileo. The name *Gomer* was given to the grandson of Noah, with the name meaning, "to complete, to finish."

Them javelin to the sky will cause his disbursed mightily,	Le dard du ciel fera son extendue,
Death upon reasoning: great carrying out of a judgment.	Mors en parlant: grande execution:
The stone into the tree there proud nation given unto,	La pierre en larbre la fiere gent rendue,
Reputation humane thing made contrary to nature justified satisfaction.	Bruit humain monstre purge expiation.

Note: Originally listed as quatrain number 70 in Centurie II. The word *execution* carries the

Chapter 39 - Post-War Punishmnents & Lost Lessons

meaning of a state of action upon a declaration. The word *fiere* fully means, "proud, insolent, scornful, high-minded, bloody, cruel, savage, unmerciful, inhumane, bold, confident and audacious." Line three yields the essence of George Washington, using a stone ax to chop down a cherry tree, and thus the national pride of honesty and truthfulness. Line four makes one think of how nuclear weapons have been justified as a peaceful way to create energy, when in reality it is nothing more than a *monster* for show.

In the state which CONSECRATED PLACE you trusted his body of a church to fabricate,	*Au lieu que HIERON feit sa nef fabriquer,*
So lofty great flood will be & even as swift,	*Si grand deluge sera & si subite,*
That one not will enjoy credit born world anew will pull out hastily	*Qu'on n'aura lieu ne terre saracquer*
A wave to raise Fire them years Olympic.	*L'onde monter Fesulan Olympique.*

Note: Originally listed as quatrain number 16 in Centurie VIII. The word *sacquer* was used to denote someone prepared to quickly draw out his sword. The name *Fesula* is clean Spanish for *Faesulae* (Fiesole, Italy). The use of *Olympic* can be a reference to one from the Greek town of Olympia, which is on the Adriatic coast.

At forty eight way to a thing climaterical-like,	*A quarante huict degré climaterique,*
Has conclusion from Cancer in sort substantial barrenness:	*A fin de Cancer si grande seicheresse:*
Fish upon the sea, stream, lake baked dried up,	*Poisson en mer, fleuve, lac cuit hectique,*
Bearn, Bigorre by reason of death sky in distress.	*Bearn, Bigorre par feu ciel en destresse.*

Note: Originally listed as quatrain number 98 in Centurie V. The word *climatere* (leads to *climactere*) translates as, "the *climaterical* year." This is then defined as, "every 7th or 9th year of a man's 63 years of life, all very dangerous, but the last the most dangerous." Nicholas Devore explains this best in his *Encyclopedia of Astrology*. The years of a man's life that are considered *climaterical* (in the number beginning with 40) are "42, 45, and 49." The word *hectique* also means "feverish" and "consumption." *Bearn* is a former province in southwest France, in the Pyrenees-Atlantic department, with *Bigorre* being a town there. *Bearn* and *Bigorre* are are roughly 43 *degrees* of latitude, around 0 degree longitude. The span between 40 and 48 degrees covers half of Spain (northern), and two-thirds of France (southern).

The Epic Poem Prophesied by Nostradamus

In regard of there hotness belonging to the sun over the sea,	*Pour la chaleur solaire sus la mer,*
To Moor-bridge them fish ones half ones fit to be eaten ones:	*De Negrepont les poissons demis cuits:*
The inhabitants them will be coming to taste of.	*Les habitants les viendront entamer.*
At what time Consuming & Tortured ones theirs will be expedient a biscuit.	*Quand Rod. & Gennes leur faudra le biscuit.*

Note: Originally listed as quatrain number 3 in Centurie II. The literal Greek for *Negrepont* means Black Sea; but, the bridge to the Moor (Muslim) world is the point that separates the Black Sea from the Aegean Sea.

On forty years a Rainbow not to will present itself,	*Par quarante ans l'Iris n'aparoistra,*
For forty years whole sum them lustrous shadows will be prayer:	*Par quarante ans tous les jours sera veu:*
The world withered into want of moisture will rise higher,	*La terre aride en siccité croistra,*
As well great ones vast inundations of water at what time will be in gathered.	*Et grans deluges quand sera aperceu.*

Note: Originally listed as quatrain number 17 in Centurie I. *Iris* is the Greek goddess of the rainbow.

The Return of Christ

Second & third part who make first this harmony	*Second & tiers qui font prime musicque*
Will be through Chief upon renown advanced into dignity,	*Sera par Roy en honneur sublimee,*
By reason of much yielding & meager in a manner half that languishing	*Par grasse & maigre presque demy eticque*
Agreement with Islam lying will render depressed.	*Raport de Venus faulx randra deprimee.*

Note: Originally listed as quatrain number 28 in Centurie X. The use of *third* is a reference to what we have called for years, "the *third* world." This will be the *Second* to the *Muslims*, or their assistants. When *musicque* it seen as *c'musique*, and *musique* is translated as "*harmony*," it means an alignment that there is an, "agreement in feeling or opinion; accord," between the two.

Chapter 39 - Post-War Punishmnents & Lost Lessons

In such manner expected not will come again never	*Tant attendu ne reviendra jamais*
Within them Europe, upon Asia will show himself suddenly	*Dedans l'europe, en Asie apparoistra*
One from there mutual intercourse of kindness the proof of the matter to the lofty Solitary ones,	*Un de la ligue yssu du grand Hermes,*
Likewise above everything chiefs to them east part of the world ones will rise in height.	*Et sur tous roys des orientz croistra.*

Note: Originally listed as quatrain number 75 in Centurie X. The word *jamais* typically means "never," but also has usage (as *"jamais un jamais,"*) that represents *a very long time*, "a mighty while and an everlasting age." *Hermes* was the Greek name for the god of healing. The Romans called this god Mercury. However, Old French had a word *"Herme,"* which makes this become an important state of human being, rather than a Greek god.

From five rent assist years more reckoning many will uphold,	*De cinq cens ans plus compte lon tiendra,*
The one who has been an adornment to one's times:	*Celuy qu'estoit l'aornement de son temps:*
Able with one pruning of trees noble clarity will deliver up,	*Puis a un coup. grande clarté donra,*
Which by reason of it age them will bring to pass most satisfied ones.	*Que par se siecle les rendra trescontens.*

Note: Originally listed as quatrain number 94 in Centurie III.

Ship beneath them covert ones & the battle itself in the night time	*Nay soubz les umbres & journee nocturne*
Will be upon kingdom & virtue one that acknowledges no superior:	*Sera en regne & bonté souveraine:*
Will act to be born anew its lineage from the ancient crematory vase,	*Fera renaistre son sang de l'antique urne,*
Renewing age with gold considering a military decoration.	*Renouvelant siecle d'or pour l'ærain.*

Note: Originally listed as quatrain number 41 in Centurie V. The statement, *"Will make to be reborn his blood from the ancient urn"* is saying that the Holy Grail was the Bloodline of Jesus Christ, which begat the Kings of Europe. This is the return of Christ to restore the bloodline.

The Epic Poem Prophesied by Nostradamus

Him noble younger will make success of the warfare,	*Le grand puisné fera fin de la guerre,*
With them gods assembled the tolerably answered ones:	*Aux dieux assemble les excusés:*
Cahors, Moissac will be marching wearisome to there thrust up together,	*Cahors, Moissac iront loing de la serre,*
Repulse Him edified, them not people of Agen ruined ones.	*Reffus Lestore les Agennois razés.*

Note: Originally listed as quatrain number 12 in Centurie VII. *Cahors* is a commune in southwest France, which is the capital of the Lot department. *Moissac* is another commune in southwest France, in the Tarn-et-Garonne department. The two communes are on opposite sides of the Tarn River. The commune of *Agen* is 84 kilometers south of Bordeaux, on the Garonne River, in the department of Lot-et-Garonne.

There sacred pomp will come humbling them flying ones,	*La sacree pompe viendra baisser les aisles,*
For the arrival of the high lawmaker:	*Par la venue du grand legislateur:*
Submissive will set aloft will extremely grieve them revolted from ones,	*Humble haulsera vexera les rebelles,*
Will take beginning on world someone an emulator.	*Naistra sur terre aucun æmulateur.*

Note: Originally listed as quatrain number 79 in Centurie V.

Accord, league will be & converting,	*Paix, union sera & changement,*
Properties, public charges humble of importance, & haughty thoroughly abject,	*Estatz, offices bas hault, & hault bien bas,*
To govern travels through a product of time and labor foremost hellish anguish,	*Dresser voiage le fruict premier torment,*
Warfare to hold back for a time, secular cases of law debate ones.	*Guerre cesser, civil proces debatz.*

Note: Originally listed as quatrain number 66 in Centurie IX. The French name for the "United States" is (with Old French spelling) "*Estats-Uni.*" This shows that the capitalized word, "*Estat*", can also means a "*State,*" or an independent entity, as a "*Nation.*" This is a quatrain stating the blueprint for the Soviet Union's dominance over Eastern Europe's countries, but it is to be pulled out to model the punishment Western Europeans will face, for not having done anything to free their eastern brothers.

Chapter 39 - Post-War Punishmnents & Lost Lessons

At what time them divided will be supported with two poles,	*Quand le fourchu sera soustenu de deux paux,*
With six half body, & half dozen scissors broad ones:	*Avec six demy corps, & six sizeaux ouvers:*
Him most powerful Lord heir to them toads,	*Le trespuissant Seigneur, heritier des crapaux,*
At that time will subdue, beneath himself everything the universal world.	*Alors subjuguera, sous soy tout l'Univers.*

Note: Originally listed as quatrain number 101 in Centurie X. The 101st quatrain in Century X is found in the 1605, 1627, 1630, 1650 and 1698 Lyon editions (with various differences in spelling, punctuation, and capitalization), following the word "FIN" at the conclusion of quatrain numbered "C" (Roman numeral for 100). Some editions (the later ones) show this as quatrain "101", but the earliest do not number it, instead leading it with a disclaimer, which states, "*Adjusté depuis limpression 1568.*" This translates to say that it is an addition (*adjusted*), presented after (*since*) the publication (*the impression in print*) of *1568*. It is important to also note that these post-1600 editions also present a Century XI, and a Century XII (not a full 100), with some presages (written in 1555 for after 1567), and some "*sixtain*" predictions for the 17th century. This 101st addition to Centurie X, and the 6 additions attributed to Centurie VII, will be all I will be approaching.

The Epic Poem Prophesied by Nostradamus

www.ingramcontent.com/pod-product-compliance
Lightning Source LLC
Chambersburg PA
CBHW031229290426
44109CB00012B/214